THE MORMON CONFLICT 1850–1859

Brigham Young

THE

MORMON

CONFLICT

1850-1859

by Norman F. Furniss

New Haven and London, Yale University Press

© 1960 by Yale University Press, Inc.
Third printing, January 1966.
Set in Baskerville type and printed in
the United States of America by
The Carl Purington Rollins Printing-Office
of the Yale University Press,
New Haven, Connecticut.
Library of Congress catalog card number: 60–7824

Originally published as Yale Historical
Publications, Miscellany 72.

To Susan

Preface

THE year 1857 was a busy one for Americans. The Supreme Court was deciding what to do with Dred Scott; events in Kansas revealed that the argument over slavery had reached an intensity almost beyond solution; a financial panic shook the nation's economy; and William Walker's filibustering expedition against Nicaragua came to an ignominious end. In 1857 also the Mormon War began.

The origins of the war may be traced as far back as the late 1840's, when the Mormons first arrived in the basin of the Great Salt Lake and began to build their New Zion in that unlikely region. At first free of close association with Gentiles, they soon found themselves an organized territory of the United States under the control of the national government. Wayfarers, nonmembers of their Church, began to pass in ever-increasing numbers through their settlements. The Mormons, who had had their fill of trouble with nonbelievers in Missouri and Illinois, treated Gentiles in their midst with severity and were reluctant to obey officials and laws they deemed inequitable. For their part the federal officers, frequently men possessing few qualifications for their posts, stirred the people to anger by their intervention. By 1857 the Church had become so defiant that to President James Buchanan's thinking only a display of force could bring order in Utah. The Mormon War resulted.

Not much blood was spilled during this war, and to Capt. Jesse Gove and other men of Johnston's army the whole affair was a farce from beginning' to end. Certainly it was not a military engagement of glorious report, and perhaps for this reason has not received serious attention in the historical studies of the period.

Yet the dramatic steps leading up to the Civil War should not be allowed to overshadow other occurrences of the 1850's, and the

Government's altercations with the Mormons during the decade merit a closer look than they have received. An institution of considerable importance politically, economically, and socially, the Church of Jesus Christ of Latter-day Saints is a strange phenomenon to many Americans, especially those who have misapprehensions about the Mormon practice of polygamy; most people are, in fact, thoroughly uninformed about the denomination. An investigation of one critical phase of the Mormons' early history will, it is hoped, reveal something of their beliefs, their manner of behavior, their virtues, and their shortcomings.

From the John Simon Guggenheim Memorial Foundation I received a generous fellowship that permitted me to complete my research for this monograph, and both the Guggenheim Foundation and the Yale University Fund for Young Scholars helped to make publication of the book possible. David M. Potter of Yale originally suggested the topic to me and Archibald Hanna, Curator of the Yale Collection of Western Americana, gave me much bibliographic assistance. S. George Ellsworth of Utah State College and Leroy Hafen of Brigham Young University offered valuable suggestions during my research. To my father I acknowledge my greatest debt for his valiant effort to correct the organizational and stylistic deficiencies of the manuscript; if he was not entirely successful in that labor, it is only the fault of the material with which he had to work.

N.F.F.

Colorado State University
Fort Collins, Colorado
January 1959

Contents

Preface   vii

Illustrations   xi

1. Beginnings   1

2. Early Troubles   21

3. The Shadows Lengthen   45

4. Causes of the War   62

5. An Unheroic Anabasis   95

6. The Mormons Organize   119

7. Winter Quarters   148

8. End of Hostilities   168

9. But No Peace   204

10. Afterward   228

Bibliographical Essay   235

Abbreviations   250

Notes   251

Index   303

Illustrations

BRIGHAM YOUNG. *Engraving, Henry E. Huntington Library*
frontispiece

1. THOMAS L. KANE. *Photograph, Henry E. Huntington Library*   8

2. ALFRED CUMMING. *Photograph, Utah State Historical Society*   98

3. MAP OF THE ARMY ROUTE OF MARCH   103

4. ALBERT S. JOHNSTON. *Photograph, Henry E. Huntington Library* 112

5. A TYPICAL MORMON COMMUNITY OF THE PERIOD: EPHRAIM, UTAH. *Original drawing, Yale Collection of Western Americana*   206

1. Beginnings

IN THE SUMMER of 1838 many Missourians found the presence of a large Mormon community in the northwestern corner of their state no longer tolerable. Wholeheartedly sympathetic with this opinion, Governor Lilburn Boggs had informed his militia commander that "the Mormons must be treated as enemies and must be exterminated or driven from the state, if necessary, for the public good." Already the two parties had fought a number of brief skirmishes, among them the Battle of Crooked River, and the outnumbered Latter-day Saints had hastily assembled in their city of Far West to prepare measures of self-defense.

Jacob Haun, an industrious Church member proud of his new flour mill a few miles from the town, refused to retreat, and enough of his brethren joined him to make his position appear secure. Yet on the evening of October 30 two hundred militiamen descended upon Haun's mill, drove the Mormons into a nearby blacksmith shop, and there enthusiastically shot many of them through the unchinked walls of the makeshift fortress. When the attackers finally stormed into the building, they spared no one who showed a sign of life. Even nine-year-old Sardius Smith was dispatched with a bullet through the head because one trooper feared that "nits will make lice." At daybreak, of the thirty-eight men and boys who had sought refuge on Jacob Haun's property, seventeen were dead and fifteen wounded.

Although the massacre at Haun's mill was the bloodiest engagement between Mormon and Gentile in the eight years following the establishment of the Church in 1830, it was not the first evidence that the sect would continue to have trouble with hostile neighbors. A few months earlier the young founder of the new faith, Joseph Smith, had led many of his followers to Missouri

1

from Kirtland, Ohio, where the doctrines of his Church and the failure of his "Kirtland Safety Society Bank" had enraged non-believers. But if he had expected to erect a New Zion in this frontier state without molestation, he was disappointed. From the days of the earliest Mormon colony in Missouri in 1831 the Gentiles had resented the Saints' claim to a superior religion, feared the political power of their united communities, suspected them of tampering with the Indians, and anticipated their free-soil sympathies. To escape this animosity the Mormons had moved from county to county, seeking freedom in isolation, but the inevitable approach of Gentile settlers had always reawakened hostilities. In retaliation some of the Saints had formed a group to protect the Church against attack both from without and from within. Although the actions, and even the existence, of this fellowship— the mysterious Sons of Dan, or Danites—were concealed in secrecy, Gentiles were sure that it was a terroristic band of murderers dedicated to the destruction of any person who incurred the wrath of the Hierarchy. As the opposition of the Missourians to the Mormons rose in intensity, Joseph Smith finally permitted his people to use their weapons in defense of their homes; but the episode at Haun's mill revealed their hopeless military inferiority.

As overpowering numbers of the militia surrounded Far West, the Prophet, Smith, saw that further resistance would surely destroy many of his followers and might even endanger the very existence of his Church. With other Mormon dignitaries he accordingly surrendered himself to his enemies and promised that his people would leave the state. While the prisoners awaited an uncertain future in jail, the Mormons straggled across the Mississippi River to Illinois, sustained only by their faith and the organizational abilities of Brigham Young, the one important member of the Hierarchy to escape the dragnet in Missouri.

For a few years after their grim experiences with Lilburn Boggs' men, the Latter-day Saints enjoyed a period of peace rare in their early history. Joseph Smith and his fellow prisoners were permitted to escape after the officials of Missouri failed to devise a practicable punishment for them. On a bend in the Mississippi the Church began construction of a new city, Nauvoo, which soon outshone Kirtland, Far West, and the other way stations on the road to denominational permanence. Both Whigs and Democrats wooed their votes with political favors, principally a city charter granting Nauvoo an impressive measure of self-government in Illinois. With a bodyguard of hardy fighters, among them William Hickman, Porter Rockwell, Hosea Stout, and John D. Lee, Smith feared neither the wrath of unreconciled Missourians nor the depredations of nearer opponents.

Yet by 1844 opinion in Illinois had hardened into the anti-Mormon sentiments so familiar in the past. Rumors that members of the priesthood were indulging in polygamous marriages offended some Gentile sensibilities. Of more importance, neither political party in the state found that it could depend upon Mormon promises of support, a situation which became dramatically apparent in 1844, when Smith announced his own candidacy in the presidential campaign. Furthermore, the occupants of Nauvoo, no longer satisfied with their position of autonomy, had established courts that recognized no superior review, an army of formidable size called the Nauvoo Legion, a powder factory, and other trappings of an independent community. People in nearby Carthage and Warsaw began to frown upon their neighbors and restlessly awaited an excuse to strike at them.

A plausible pretext for attack at last arrived. Early in June 1844 a few apostates established the Nauvoo *Expositor* to broadcast their dissatisfaction with Church leaders, and published an issue condemning the Hierarchy for despotic control and the introduction of polygamy. Believing that his people no longer were compelled to accept criticism meekly, as they had in past crises, Joseph Smith moved with haste to crush this adversary. On the advice of the city officials and such counselors as Almon W. Babbitt and George P. Stiles, he ordered the *Expositor* destroyed as a public nuisance, a judgment his followers promptly executed. Irate Gentiles needed no further incentive to action. On the threat of reducing Nauvoo to ashes they forced Joseph and his brother Hyrum to surrender themselves for imprisonment and trial. Three days later, on June 27, a mob assaulted the Carthage jail where the captives were held. When it disbanded, the body of Joseph, riddled with bullets, lay beneath the window from which he had jumped; Hyrum was dead on the floor of his cell.

Although the lynching of the two men quieted the anger of many rancorous Gentiles, the Mormons' further residence in Illi-

nois was now patently impossible. An uneasy peace prevailed during the next year, but by September 1845 the Church could forestall an onslaught upon Nauvoo only by a public promise to leave
the state within a reasonable time. During February 1846 the first
Mormons crossed the frozen Mississippi to camp on the Iowa
shore in subzero temperatures. Later in the year more than twelve
thousand Church members followed them across the river and on
over the Iowa hills to temporary settlements near the Missouri.
Throughout the exodus, inflamed Gentiles, impatient with the
slowness of the evacuation, clashed with remaining Mormons embittered by this new enforced emigration. The final days of the
Saints' occupation of Nauvoo were marked by organized warfare,
during which the Mormons discovered an effective commander in
Daniel Hanmer Wells, a recent convert to the faith. Wells would
recall these scenes when, eleven years later, he led the Mormons'
resistance to a federal army approaching Utah.

The Church was not blameless in the difficulties that brought
about its removal from Ohio, Missouri, and Illinois. Although
Governor Boggs had had no valid occasion for his "extermination
order," as the Mormons called it, a few months before the issuance of that unfortunate command Sidney Rigdon, close to Joseph
Smith in the councils of the sect, had also spoken publicly of a
war of annihilation against the Missourians. If Smith received no
justice from the Carthage mob, his "trial" of the Nauvoo *Expositor* had likewise been conducted without a jury and in the absence of the defendant. But the Mormons had experienced shame-
ful persecution in their long search for a home, and as they huddled in their quarters on the banks of the Missouri they realized
that they would find peace only in an area remote from Gentile
neighbors. Texas, California, and Oregon, all sparsely settled in
1846, were nevertheless attractive enough to invite the migration
of many American pioneers in this period of Manifest Destiny;
but between the Rockies and the Sierra Nevadas, the Mormon
leaders knew, lay the basin of the Great Salt Lake, which trappers
and explorers had reported inhabitable. If the Zion of the Church
could not be built on the green plains of Missouri or the fertile
banks of the Mississippi River, the empty reaches of the Far West
might provide sanctuary.

Having resolved upon the region of the Great Salt Lake for its next effort at colonization, the Church early in 1847 sent an advance party to make the initial explorations and settlements there. In this trek from the Missouri River the carefully selected vanguard encountered fewer difficulties than the Mormons had faced as they crossed the roadless, rolling hills of Iowa in cold and mud during their flight from the turbulent scenes surrounding Nauvoo. Fur trappers and Oregon-bound farmers had made the route along the shallow Platte River and across the South Pass of the Continental Divide a much-traveled one. It remained for the Mormons only to find their way from Jim Bridger's Fort in what is now southwestern Wyoming to the Salt Lake Valley, and even here they had the benefit of the hapless Donner Party's experiences the year before. The pioneer band, numbering 148 men, women, and children under the capable leadership of Brigham Young, accomplished the journey in a little over three months. During the latter part of July they reached the shores of the Great Salt Lake, where they were joined in subsequent months by the remainder of their brethren.

In addition to the use of a familiar overland road at a favorable season, the Mormons had assistance in their undertaking from the federal government, never quick in other emergencies of the Church to extend comfort. The Polk Administration, then at war with Mexico, saw that in its plan to acquire California it could make use of a people already determined upon a migration to the West. An agent of the sect in Washington had indeed pressed this consideration upon the President. Accordingly the Mormons received a call for volunteers during their march across Iowa in 1846, and Brigham Young hastily accepted. In this way the Church obtained two fortuitous blessings from the Mexican War: some 300 members were transported to the West Coast at public expense, and the pay these men earned for their services helped to stabilize the group's shaky finances at a critical time. Only in later years, when the Church endeavored to increase the devotion of its members by reminding them of their past martyrdoms, did Young and his colleagues refer to the raising of the Mormon Battalion as another attempt by evil men to dragoon the Saints.

Safely arrived in Salt Lake Valley, the Mormons had no difficulty establishing a framework of government. The organization of the Church provided for authoritarian leadership from the

First Presidency, composed of Young as president and his two counselors, the flamboyant Heber Chase Kimball and the quiet, erudite physician Willard Richards, who had miraculously escaped death in Carthage jail. Only a little inferior to this body was the Council or Quorum of the Twelve Apostles. During the early months of the colony's existence, these officers functioned as executive, legislature, and judiciary. When the system was altered at the end of 1847, the identification of church and state persisted, the Hierarchy retaining general supervision of all affairs but delegating the direct government of the people to officials of the "stake," a name given large territorial units of the Church. Soon the stake was subdivided into wards, each presided over by a bishop, who now exercised secular as well as religious jurisdiction. In this manner the Mormons quietly and effectively constructed a political arrangement from the materials of their own denominational system.[1]

Although the Church had deliberately built its new home in a region far removed from other settlements, its leaders in 1849 realized that Salt Lake Valley would need a more temporal government, in form at least, than the one they had first devised. Already a few Gentiles had passed through the community on their way to California, and more would arrive when news of the West Coast's opportunities became widely known. In early March, therefore, a convention of Church members drew up a constitution for the proposed State of Deseret, and immediately upon ratification of this document the people elected men to fill the offices. But the change in governmental organization did not in the least bring about a relaxation of ecclesiastical supervision; the new officials were for the most part the same members of the Hierarchy who had previously held political power. Brigham Young became governor and his two counselors assumed the next most important positions, secretary and chief justice. In like fashion trusted Mormons filled the other subordinate posts.[2]

Accustomed as they were to complete dependence upon their denominational directors in their previous travails, the Saints would naturally place these same dignitaries of the Church in the provisional state regime. But to make certain that no doctrinally unreliable figure slipped into political office, Young and his closest advisors composed a ticket only eight days before the election and made sure the voters approved it.[3] This authoritarian disposition was to produce strife when individualistic Gentiles moved in among the regimented members of the Church.

When the United States acquired possession of the Salt Lake Basin as a result of its war with Mexico, the Mormons found themselves once more encamped upon American territory. Now under the jurisdiction of the federal Congress, they needed its acknowledgment of their new state if it was to have any pretense to legality. Accordingly, the General Assembly in July 1849 delegated Almon W. Babbitt to secure this recognition from the Government. The choice of emissary was an unhappy one, for Babbitt, whose eccentric conduct later earned him the perilous disfavor of Young, succeeded only in drawing upon himself the dislike and ridicule of Whigs and Democrats in the Capital.[4] As a counterweight to this agent the Mormons had two other advocates, men of greater ability than Babbitt. Dr. John Bernhisel, who had in May brought the formal petition for statehood to Washington, soon proved that his quiet lobbying was more effective than Babbitt's brash conviviality. The other spokesman for the Mormons was young Thomas Leiper Kane, a self-chosen champion of the oppressed who, though not a member of the Church, used his considerable political influence throughout the 1850's to advance its interests.

To the extent that his frail health would permit, Kane had devoted much of his early life to supporting humanitarian causes with missionary earnestness. When the struggle over slavery burst out after the Mexican War, he joined the Free Soil party in 1848 and later took part in the Underground Railroad. In the Civil War he was wounded and captured but later fought at Gettysburg, despite a debilitating attack of pneumonia; his heroism on this occasion earned him the rank of brevet major general. Except in Utah his modest accomplishments were overshadowed by the greater reputations of his father, John K. Kane, judge of the United States district court in Pennsylvania, and his brother, Elisha Kent Kane, whose arctic explorations had made him a national hero in the 1850's. Yet this short, dark-complexioned man, only thirty-five years old when the Mormon War occupied the attention of the country, was a valuable ally to those whom he championed, for he had many friends in Washington, even though he had opposed his acquaintance Lewis Cass in the campaign of 1848.

Kane first became aware of the Latter-day Saints in the spring of 1846, when he heard Jesse A. Little describe the piteous fall of Nauvoo to a sectarian meeting in Philadelphia. He invited Little to his home, where he learned that the elder was bound for Washington to seek help for his brethren. After giving him an introduction to Vice President George M. Dallas, Kane sped to the Mormons' temporary settlements in Iowa, hoping to ease their distress. Instead of helping them, he became deathly ill and almost died on their hands. Later, his health partially restored and now more devoted to the Mormons than ever because of their solicitous nursing, he began his long career as public defender of the faith. In a short pamphlet entitled *Account of the Inhuman Behavior of the Anti-Mormons in Illinois* he described the experiences of a Baptist who, having joined the Church, was driven by angry Gentiles to Nauvoo and later, a bed-ridden invalid, was carried across the Mississippi River to die on the Iowa shore. To Horace Greeley he wrote of the Mormons' encounters with persecutions and of their courageous endurance of hardships. Upon his return to the East he persuaded the Government to let the Mormons occupy the lands of the Omaha Indians until they found a new home; at the same time he advised Secretary of War William Marcy that the Church merited other forms of federal assistance in its desperate struggle for survival. This restless young man also organized public meetings in Philadelphia, New York, and other cities to raise money for the relief of the Saints as they straggled from Illinois to the uncharted region of the Great Salt Lake.

In the summer of 1850 Kane, given to hypochondria, felt that he was dying and wrote a letter to the leaders of the sect. He had fought for them, he said, because "the personal assaults upon myself made your cause become so identified with my own that your vindication became my own defense. . . . We stand or fall together." He had altered his will, he said, in order to leave his estate "to some who need it at home" rather than to the Church, but he would assign his heart to the Mormons, "to be deposited in the Temple of your Salt Lake City, that, after death, it may repose, where in metaphor at least, it oftener was when living."

1. Thomas L. Kane

The clumsily expressed sentiment was sincere, but Kane's premo-
nition of his own demise proved unfounded on this occasion, as
on many others until 1883, and he was soon strong enough to resume his role as the Mormons' champion in the East. To reduce
the popular prejudice against the Saints he delivered a number
of lectures, one of which he printed at his own expense and presented to newspapers, the Library of Congress, the Smithsonian
Institution, and many congressmen.[5]

Despite Kane's and Bernhisel's enterprising work, the Saints
failed to secure the desired position of statehood, receiving only
territorial status. Their request encountered several obstacles. In
the first place the congressmen, now deeply embroiled in debate
over the extension of slavery into the area won from Mexico, were
not in a mood to view the Mormons' arguments with dispassion.
Indeed, the irrelevant issue of slavery was to have deleterious effects upon the Church's relations with the Government during
the entire decade. Furthermore, a number of congressional leaders in 1850 revealed the same uncritical animus toward the Church
that had generated dispute in Missouri and Illinois.

Shortly after the Mormons' memorial reached Washington,
Representative Warner Underwood of Kentucky read to the
House a long indictment of the sect written by William Smith, the
erratic, unprincipled younger brother of the Prophet Joseph and
now among the Church's most dedicated enemies. Several years
earlier Smith had accused the Mormon priesthood of plotting to
establish an independent nation in the West and of oppressing its
followers with a "sacerdotal tryanny." Now, to the great excitement of the legislators, he and his thirteen supporters presented
the sensational charge that the Mormons practiced polygamy,
maintaining also that during the last days of Nauvoo the Saints
had sworn a dreadful oath to avenge the lynching of their mar-
tyred leaders and to "carry out hostility against this nation."
Other animadversions further shocked the congressmen. In March
the unfriendly Underwood presented a second accusatory memorial, this time from Gentiles in Council Bluffs; and later Representative John Wentworth of Illinois introduced a petition from
his constituents requesting for travelers in the Far West federal
protection against the murderous designs of the Mormons.[6]

William Smith's philippic was characteristic of attacks upon the

Church. In this as in many similar cases the indictment came from an embittered apostate. These attacks played upon a fear uppermost in Gentiles' minds when they meditated upon the "Mormon problem," namely that the Saints were leagued together in an infamous conspiracy to destroy or dismember the nation. Furthermore, the sect's peculiar system of plural marriage served to antagonize congressmen as well as the general public.

Bernhisel labored industriously to overcome these unfavorable opinions of his brethren. Senator Truman Smith of Connecticut introduced him to Millard Fillmore, newly elevated to the Presidency by Zachary Taylor's death, and he found the chief executive most sympathetic toward his people, in great contrast to Taylor's antagonism. The quiet doctor's conversation with Secretary of State Daniel Webster and Secretary of the Treasury Thomas Corwin helped to win from these men some expression of support for the Mormons. In the course of his perambulations through Washington he had interviews with Clay, Benton, Calhoun, Cass, Seward, Foote, Chase, Cobb, Douglas, Wilmot, and other influential men. Senator Thomas J. Rusk of Texas offered to help him in any way possible, and Mrs. John McLean, wife of an associate justice of the Supreme Court, even asked him to preach to her. With Truman Smith's permission, Bernhisel had inserted in the *Congressional Globe* a letter to the senator from a recent visitor to Salt Lake Valley enthusiastically praising the Mormons' accomplishments there.[7]

These activities failed to secure legislative acceptance of the State of Deseret. Instead, Congress voted early in September 1850 to establish the Territory of Utah, and Fillmore signed the bill on September 9. Too late, the Church leaders tried to forestall this event by instructing Bernhisel to withdraw their petition, since they realized that they would suffer less from Gentile interference as an unsupervised provisional state than as a territory under congressional regulation, an opinion shared by Senator Stephen A. Douglas. The law, however, had already been enacted. Bernhisel watched this development unhappily: "I feel entirely unwilling," he wrote, "to run the risk of having a set of whippersnappers or brokendown politicians to tyrannize over us . . . for I have every reason to apprehend that we should be constantly brought into collision with the Central Government."[8]

Upon learning of the President's territorial appointees, however, the Mormons in Salt Lake Valley felt no great concern for the future. Of primary satisfaction to them was Brigham Young's continuance as governor under the new dispensation. In this selection Fillmore had depended upon the counsel of Thomas L. Kane, a member of the opposition Democratic party, and Kane had convinced the President that Young possessed two eminent qualifications for the position, an upright character and the undivided allegiance of his people.[9] The Mormons, as one contemporary Gentile observer noted, would have received the appointment of any other man "as in some sort a renewal, on the part of the General Government, of that series of persecutions to which they have already been subjected." [10] Three other churchmen also found places in the territorial offices. True, the secretary and two of the three federal judges were now Gentiles, but there was at first no reason to believe that they would use their powers in inimical fashion. This estimate proved far from accurate.

Even at this point in the chronicle of the Mormons' early history, when the Saints were enjoying an amicable relation with the Government, it is possible to observe causes of future difficulties. True enough, in 1850 there seemed to be little reason to anticipate a recurrence of the old troubles left behind in Missouri and Illinois. A thousand miles of prairie to the east and five hundred miles of sand and mountains to the west separated the Church from that close association with Gentiles that had previously been so unharmonious. With little dispute the Mormons had been accepted into the American nation and a friendly president had selected their ecclesiastical ruler as their governor. Yet within fifteen months this benign situation had disappeared, replaced by a period of stormy accusation and bombast, with many eastern Gentiles speaking loudly of settling the Mormon question by force. A number of factors, both new and old, combined to produce this and subsequent crises.

One basic cause of the difficulties throughout this decade, and indeed in later years, was the existence of a public opinion extremely hostile to the Mormons and prepared to seize upon any pretext, whether valid or not, to renew the attack upon the Church. Many of the reasons for the eviction of the Saints from

the eastern states were still operative in the 1850's, and the dis-
tances temporarily separating Mormon from Gentile did not
greatly obscure them. Polygamy, an open secret at best until it
was officially announced as a doctrine of the Church in 1852, was
not compatible with the "domestic manners of the Americans"
(as Mrs. Trollope called them). And the conviction that the Saints,
despite their denials, were only awaiting an opportune moment
to announce the political independence of their settlement
aroused the anger of patriots. In a land priding itself on its democratic customs, the hierarchical religious and political practices
of the Mormons appeared tyrannous. Furthermore, a large portion of the Gentiles took at face value the charges of William
Smith and others that the Mormons had formed a secret, armed
band, known as Danites (above, p. 2), sworn to shed the blood
of nonbelievers. Finally, a great many Americans found unbearable the Saints' serene assumption that their sect, the only one on
earth possessing God's endorsement, would speedily spread until
all peoples and denominations had acknowledged Joseph Smith
as Prophet, Seer, and Revelator. Holding these beliefs, Easterners
were disposed to believe any unfavorable report concerning the
Latter-day Saints.

Hostile American opinion not only accounted the Mormons
guilty of murderous plotting, subversive desire, and other criminal inclinations; it also considered the Church in great part composed of recent immigrants drawn from the lowest classes of other
lands. In the 1850's the United States was experiencing in the
Know Nothing movement a wave of nativism later to find expression in the American Protective Association, the Ku Klux Klan,
and periodic immigration acts. As the people watched a host of
new Mormon converts from abroad arrive on their shores, many
were easily convinced that the Church was as dangerous to their
institutions as they supposed the Roman Catholics, the swollen
Irish minority, or any other alien group to be.

At the present time it is difficult to estimate the number of aliens
in Utah during the late 1850's, or even to fix with certainty the
actual population of the Territory.[11] Yet in 1857 Stephen A.
Douglas, his early friendliness toward the Church now grown
cold, stated that possibly seven out of ten Mormons in Utah had
emigrated there from other countries, and many commentators of

his day agreed in general with his conclusions. The popular view further held these newcomers to be for the most part indigent, illiterate men and women menacing the economic and social standards of the United States. Reports to the contrary did not greatly weaken the judgment that the Mormons were undesirable candidates for American citizenship, since it was based less on dispassionate investigation than on prejudice drawn from the spirit of the decade.[12] In the words of one historian, "These individuals, so long as they remained members of orthodox denominations of the day, were regarded as worthy members of society. Only when they affiliated with the despised sect, known as Mormons, did they become objects of execration." [13]

A second cause of trouble between the Mormons in Utah and the Government was the selection of inferior men to fill the Territory's offices. Although good appointees did on occasion make their toilsome way to Utah, Bernhisel's prediction of an infestation of "whippersnappers and brokendown politicians" frequently came true. To Easterners, Utah was a remote and desolate region; political jobs there brought a remuneration inadequate to pay expenses; and the problem of living with the Mormons and governing them was known to be exacting. It was accordingly not strange that few men of ability regarded appointment to office in the Territory politically or financially rewarding. As a result, administrations in Washington could often find only inept or, on occasion, morally reprehensible men to fill the positions. The common practice of using the Territory's posts as payment for political debts reduced even further the possibility of selecting suitable men for public service. The wisdom of Solon would have been severely taxed to keep peace in the relations between Utah and the rest of the Union, given the many factors productive of friction, but the presence of men like Perry Brocchus and W. W. Drummond, too often typical of federal place-seekers, could only exacerbate the difficulties.

Another irritant, of lesser importance than some mentioned here, was the question of landownership. When Brigham Young embarked upon the trek to the Salt Lake Basin in early 1847, his pioneer band journeyed to a region that was part of Mexico; but by the time the Church had built its permanent settlements, the place had come into the possession of the United States. Before the Saints could claim the land as their own, therefore, certain procedures established by Congress had to be followed, among them disposal of Indian rights and a survey of the area. Only after they had met these requirements could the Mormons acquire the land lawfully, and even then they were compelled to obtain legal title by purchase or other means. The Government was slow in negotiating treaties with the Indians. In addition, the process of surveying Utah, tentatively begun in 1855, was suspended for ten years after 1857. Thus when anger toward the Mormons increased, opponents of the sect could threaten it with another expulsion by warning: "Not an individual in all Utah now holds a foot of land the title of which is derived from the United States, and it follows . . . that all parts of the Territory are at the present time open to pre-emption." [14] As their speeches and writings revealed, the Church's leaders were acutely aware of their tenuous possession of the New Zion and apprehensive lest the Government move to evict them.[15]

For their part, the Mormons' characteristics and activities were as conducive to strife as the temper and policies of their opponents. Some of these elements were of minor significance yet increased the accumulation of irritations during the decade. After their experiences with inflamed Gentile mobs, the Mormons were quick to look for new attacks in Utah, an attitude that at times became unjustified truculence. Furthermore, their continual insistence upon the superiority of their faith under divine sanction proved most objectionable to other Christians in Utah, as it had in Missouri and Illinois. When Heber Kimball announced, "We are the people of God . . . the foundation of which in these last days was begun by the Almighty sending an holy angel to Joseph Smith," [16] he left no place in the divine scheme for non-Mormon denominations. With exasperating regularity the Church's spokesmen contrasted the purity of their own people, the self-styled Saints, to the wayward conditions existing elsewhere in the nation, and their references to the Mormons as "this people," in other words the Lord's anointed, failed to win any measure of good will from nonbelievers.[17]

The political and ecclesiastical government evolved by the Mormons at the start of the 1850's inevitably became a major cause of strained relations between them and the Gentiles in later years.

The Saints, believing their Church divinely instituted, yielded to their leaders an authority beyond that of merely elected officials. Their early travails had strengthened this tendency toward willing acceptance of monolithic control. While suffering persecution at the hands of tumultuous crowds in the East, traversing the Plains to a little-known country, and struggling for sustenance in a desert climate, they learned that survival depended more on obedience than on the privileges of discussion and dissent. In Utah the Mormons erected a theocracy and sustained it with unanimity. It operated without friction so long as only Church members made up the area's population, but when Gentiles came to the Territory in significant numbers the system drew bitter protest. It was the same difficulty that had prevented the Mormons' permanent residence in Missouri and Illinois; the cohesive unity of the Church and the docility of its members in religious and political matters had at best an uneasy place in the disparateness of American individuality. Enemies of the denomination soon came to view it as an undemocratic institution that had to be reformed or destroyed.[18]

Gentiles in Utah during the 1850's could discover no effort on the part of the Hierarchy to relax its strict and all-permeating control over its followers once territorial status had been attained. On the contrary, the leaders of the faith, believing theocracy "the most perfect government," held before their people as essential virtues the twin characteristics of submission and obedience. At times Heber Chase Kimball, a member of the First Presidency, was not always coherent as a public speaker: "I am almost a good mind to talk a little; that is, if you want I should, but I certainly do not want to without you want I should, and then again if I felt really like it, I should talk whether you wanted I should or not."[19] But on the subject of obedience he was clear; drawing from his experiences in former professions, he instructed the Saints to be as pliant as clay in the hands of the potter or iron under the blacksmith's hammer. "If it is necessary for me to be subject to my file leaders," he once asked, "I wish to know whether it is not equally for you, and for every high priest, elder, seventy, apostle, and all the others, to be obedient to the priesthood of those who are appointed to direct them?" On another occasion he summed up his advice to his listeners: "Our Father and our God has sent Brigham and his brethren; if you rebel against them, you rebel against the authority that sent them." [20]

Brigham Young and his colleagues heartily joined Kimball in urging dutiful obedience upon the Mormons. In elections to territorial offices they occasionally published a ticket of approved candidates to guide those who wished to cast their ballots "understandingly." To forestall any possibility that Church members might disregard the wishes of their leaders and place in political office a man unacceptable to the priesthood, the territorial legislature in 1853 established electoral procedures designed to prevent this eventuality. In the selection of denominational officials and establishment of policy there was a similar absence of democratic practice, for the Church members could do no more than approve or reject the choice of the Hierarchy. During this period the dictum of Brigham Young prevailed: "It is the right of the Twelve [Apostles] to nominate the officers and the people to sustain them." [21]

The great majority of Mormons in Utah needed no lectures or regulations, for they were prepared to support willingly in secular matters the men upon whom they relied for spiritual salvation. In his first three elections as delegate to Congress, Bernhisel received unanimous support twice and only one negative vote on the third occasion. In other canvasses the Mormons endorsed the nominees with similar uniformity. The balloting for three territorial legislators in Utah County in 1852, for instance, gave Edson Whipple 245 votes, Leonard Harrington 245 votes, William Pace 243 votes, and Benjamin F. Johnson one vote. Hosea Stout, commenting on the general election in 1857, noted that "There was no opposing candidates but all went off peaceably and harmoniously as usual." [22] This tendency of the people to accept wholeheartedly the men who were officially endorsed for public office produced an interlocking of church and state that was usually complete except for the positions filled by presidential appointment. As a result, the Gentile in Utah felt that he was living in an atmosphere stifling to his liberties.

It was in the judicial rather than the political field, however, that non-Mormons felt most keenly the dictatorial authority of the Church. Lacking sufficient numbers to overcome the united vote of the Saints in the election of territorial officers, the Gentiles turned to the courts as instruments of protection from discrimination in this theocracy. The effort failed. At first the Mormons, believing that Gentile courts did not dispense justice, followed the advice of their leaders to use their own ecclesiastical tribunals in settlement of their mutual difficulties.[23] When the influx of Gentiles brought the Saints into legal entanglements that could be resolved only in territorial courts, other devices were employed to guard the interests of Church members. The legislature, for instance, by enactment in 1852 permitted anyone, with or without legal training, to serve as attorney in court; two years later a more extensive act declared that only territorial laws, and those of Congress "when applicable," could be "read, argued, cited or adopted as precedent in any trial." [24] Thus the Mormons tried to escape all laws, including English common law, that might serve to prejudice their search for autonomy.

After the federal courts were organized and upon occasion presided over by judges unsympathetic toward the Church, the Mormon priesthood attempted to control them or to reduce their effectiveness, an effort resulting in a storm of protest from Gentiles in Utah, the eastern states, and Washington. Since the juries were in most cases drawn from the predominant Mormon community, one simple expedient was for denominational officers to advise jury members concerning the decisions they should reach. Jedediah M. Grant, whose untimely death in 1856 deprived his people of a fearless, brawling, and loose-tongued fighter, described the operation of this device in a sermon: "Last Sunday the President chastized some of the apostles and bishops on the grand jury. Did he succeed in clearing away the fog which surrounded them, and in removing the blindness from their eyes? No, for they could go back into their room and again disagree, though to their credit it must be admitted that a brief explanation made them unanimous in their action." [25] The case to which Grant referred was an exceptional one; in most trials the Mormon jurymen were not usually so unresponsive to their instructions. In another move to protect their customs from outside interference through the judiciary, the legislature appointed a territorial marshal whose authority infringed upon that of the United States marshal.[26]

Of all the judicial defenses raised by the Church to protect itself, none caused so much trouble as the probate courts. In February 1852 the legislature gave to these tribunals such exceptional powers that they came to have jurisdiction in criminal and civil cases. In explanation of this action, the Mormons maintained that the frequent and prolonged absences of the federal judges from the Territory had rendered the administration of justice almost impossible; the probate courts thus of necessity provided the only tribunals available to the people. In reply, many Gentiles insisted that the extravagant augmentation of the probate courts' authority was obvious proof of the Mormons' ultimate intention to establish a community effectively independent of all federal control. W. W. Drummond, a federal judge who more than any other man brought about the Mormon War of 1857–58 (see below, pp. 54 ff.), used this strange legal situation as one of his arguments for the need of an expedition against the Latter-day Saints. Only when Congress in 1874 passed the Poland Act, curtailing the expanded powers of these courts, did the controversy over them subside.[27]

As early as 1851, consequently, there were a number of factors capable of disrupting the relations of the Mormons' new territory with the central government. Some were trifling, others were of primary significance; but behind them all, and as a cause of many of them, stood the major irritant to the Gentiles, Brigham Young. The Saints called him President, Lion of the Lord, Prophet, Seer, and Revelator, and bowed to his authority. To many Gentiles he was the model of an oriental tyrant, a seducer of women, Anti-Christ with a Vermont accent. Only a man of his outstanding abilities could have guided the Mormons to a new home, given his people in that distant place a period of religious and temporal security, and laid the foundation for their future growth. Only a figure of his unquestionable stature could have become so intolerable to Americans of the 1850's that they demanded a military campaign to oust him from his position of political power.

Young's influence over the Mormons was nearly supreme, and he knew it. They listened with delight to his long sermons and worried about his frequent periods of bad health. Since they came to him with their problems, he could often divine their very thoughts; it was fitting that one of the sect's cherished symbols was the all-seeing eye, for Young was Big Brother to the Latter-day Saints. When in 1857, at the outbreak of the Mormon War, he

called the settlers in the Church's outlying colonies back to Salt
Lake, only a handful in San Bernardino and Carson Valley hesi-
tated to leave the property they had accumulated over a number
of hard years. If on rare occasions some muttered against him, he
could say, "I ask no odds of them," knowing his position to be un-
assailable. He struck down sternly any theological innovation that
might have reduced his powers, and he showed his superiority to
his advisors by heaping public criticism and even biting ridicule
upon such Mormon dignitaries as Orson Hyde and Orson Pratt.[28]
A man of limited formal education who had no books in his home
and who frequently in formal addresses gave evidence of illiteracy,
even incoherence, he possessed a hard common sense and prac-
ticality that won for him the position of benevolent autocrat in
his Church.[29] He could live amicably with anyone, Mormon or
Gentile, who accepted his dominion, but he was quick to loose
his fury upon those who opposed him.

Some Gentiles considered this Moses of the Mormons pleasant
and agreeable,[30] but a great many more found him unbearable, as
a man and especially as Governor of Utah, and were not hard
pressed to find arguments to advance their plea for his dismissal.
He had been the prime mover in the establishment of a political
system that provided no place for a dissenting Gentile minority.
He had urged his people to avoid non-Mormon courts, had continually instructed Mormon juries on the proper decisions to
render, and had helped to establish the other devices used by the
Saints to circumvent the federal courts. When he ordered the
meetings of an apostate faction, the "Gladdenites," to be forceably
broken up in 1853, and threatened to "unsheath my Bowie knife"
against them, Young revealed that constitutional guarantees did
not always protect unfavored residents of Utah.[31] His fondness for
incendiary speech, disclosed in frequent references to the cutting
of throats and the "shearing down" of refractory people,[32] kept
the excitable Mormons in a mood prejudicial to the safety of Gentiles in the Valley.

Finally his despotism antagonized a multitude of Americans in
Utah and throughout the nation. "Though I may not be Governor here," he announced in a celebrated speech in 1855, "my
power will not be diminished. No man they can send here will
have much influence in this community unless he is a man of their

[the Mormons'] choice. Let them send whom they will, and it does not diminish my influence one particle." [33] This statement offended the Gentiles, who believed that the United States had no place for a man of such unbounded authority.

The assertion may have been un-American, but it was nothing more than plain truth. Unfortunately, few non-Mormons recognized the fact.

2. Early Troubles

DESPITE these foreboding conditions, the decade of the 1850's began harmoniously enough. Brigham Young, with remarkable charity, asked his people to treat Gentile wayfarers with kindness and to "let no man go hungry from your doors." [1] Although his primary purpose was to speed the travelers' departure, the policy if pursued would have prevented some later crises. The Church's lower courts, presided over by the bishops, dispensed stern but usually impartial justice to non-Mormons, and excessively punitive decisions could occasionally be appealed to Young, who did not hold all his subordinate priests in high regard. Some Gentiles newly arrived in California complained bitterly of oppressive fines and similar harassments; others spoke of their good treatment in Utah, and at least one, stopping in the Territory to learn more of the new faith, was baptized into the Church. [2]

The earliest federal representatives to arrive in the Valley also expressed pleasure with their reception. Gen. John Wilson, an Indian agent who soon decided that California held better opportunities for him than Utah, wrote flatteringly of the Mormons in the letter to Senator Smith which Bernhisel had used in 1850. Capt. Howard Stansbury, in charge of a surveying party of Topographical Engineers, was similarly impressed. Although he warned that the Church would resist by arms any officious interference, he was so moved by the "kindness and warmhearted hospitality" of the Saints during the winter of 1849–50 that he later tried to reduce the animus toward them in the East. At the same time Lt. John W. Gunnison, whose murder by Indians three years later was charged to the Mormons, also enjoyed his visit to Utah. [3]

This cordial atmosphere continued briefly after the arrival of Fillmore's appointees in 1851. Lemuel G. Brandebury, chief justice and the first officer to reach the Territory, was entertained by

a banquet and several dances. Secretary Broughton D. Harris and
his wife, having been comforted on their arduous trip across the
Plains by their companions Almon Babbitt and John Bernhisel,
were greeted on their entrance into the Valley on July 19 by a
party carrying champagne and fruit. Fifty years later Mrs. Harris
still remembered her welcoming present from Brigham Young,
four delicious peaches grown in the governor's garden. This enthusiastic reception was not a hypocritical pose, for Young and his
colleagues were prepared to think well of their first Gentile officials.[4] But for all that, the concord was soon broken. The Mormons themselves, with apprehensions uneasily suppressed beneath
this benign exterior, helped to provoke the sudden upheaval of
the summer and fall. Of equal importance was the fact that Fillmore, despite his sympathy toward the Church, had selected men
remarkably unfit for important territorial positions.

Two of the new officers who took little part in the succeeding
disturbances may be dismissed with brief comment. Although
Federal Judge Zerubbabel Snow was a Mormon, his peaceable nature kept him from coming vigorously to the defense of his
Church in this controversy. Lemuel Brandebury was colorless, a
vacillating individual apparently of no strong convictions. In after
years Young referred to him as "a tolerably good man, after all";
other Mormons remembered only that he bathed with noticeable
infrequency and guessed that he habitually carried an umbrella
to keep rain water from his noisome shirt.[5] Broughton Harris, the
secretary, soon became far more obnoxious to the Saints. A young
man of twenty-seven having custody of considerable sums for
territorial expenses, he developed a willfulness that incensed
Young. The governor later complained that Harris had boasted
to him of secret instructions from Fillmore directing him to watch
carefully all actions of the Mormons. Although the secretary
denied this accusation, he tactlessly demonstrated to the obdurate
Young a firm resolution to act in complete independence of his
superior.[6]

Harris and his bride brought with them to Utah much the same
posture of condescension that the nation later exhibited toward
Latin Americans—viewing the natives as objects of curiosity, with
whom imperative business but little social intercourse was required. Intrigued, perhaps titillated, by the idea of living in a

polygamous community, the young couple were prepared to treat the Mormons as they would a tribe of Arapahoe Indians—not as animals, exactly, but certainly not as civilized people. Mrs. Harris later expressed this aloof attitude in an account of her adventures in Mormondom: "Sunday was a peculiarly long and trying day for us. Of course we did not join in the Temple services, and after we had watched the Saints file by, each with a long train of wives trailing on behind him, there was nothing to do." Her reaction to polygamy made the secretary more than usually unbending in his relations with the Church leaders. At one time Mrs. Harris unexpectedly found herself at tea with six of Heber Kimball's wives: "On my return home, my pent-up feelings of disgust, indignation and horror found vent in a severe attack of hysterics, quite frightening my young husband, who at once decided not to subject me to such a trying ordeal again." Her occasional baiting of Young when they met did not endear either herself or the secretary to the Lion of the Lord.[7]

Nor did the character of Associate Justice Perry E. Brocchus promote harmony in Utah. One congressman, describing Brocchus' later service as federal judge in the Territory of New Mexico, spoke of him as "one of the very best, most faithful and efficient federal officers," but a businessman called him a "great humbug" and accused him of running away from a debt to his firm. Albert Carrington and other prominent Mormons considered him a cheap politician of limited endowments. Their charge that he accepted the Utah appointment solely to secure the more attractive post of delegate to Congress has only the statements of Mormons for substantiation, and it must always be remembered that the Church consistently used as one method of rebutting a critic the blackening of his character with accusations of dishonesty, duplicity, and debauchery. Yet Perry Brocchus was unquestionably pompous and somewhat foolish. His infatuation with the sound of his own voice, his delight in rolling periods and classical references, almost lifted him off the ground before a Mormon audience on the occasion (see below) which brought the first major rift between Utah and the United States in the 1850's.[8]

Almost from the first day the Saints had trouble with the new officers. The Government had given Babbitt $20,000 to deliver to Governor Young for the construction of a statehouse, but this

wayward Mormon doled out the sum in exasperatingly small
amounts. Secretary Harris was equally unmanageable, his possession of another $24,000 in gold making him the more uncoopera-
tive. Upon his arrival he learned that Young had conducted a
census of the Territory's population without his supervision, the
use of official blanks, or other paraphernalia of bureaucracy. He
therefore refused to accept as valid both the census and the subsequent election to the legislature. Arguments that neither he nor
the forms had arrived in Utah in due season failed to sway him;
he demanded instead, in precise observance of the law, the com-
pletion of another census and a new apportionment of territorial
representatives.[9]

If the sniping of Babbitt and Harris was irritating to a man of
Young's nature, the actions of the bumbling Brocchus enraged
him and his people. On July 24, 1851, the Mormons had celebrated Pioneers' Day, commemorative of their arrival in the Valley in 1847, and as usual on such occasions their thoughts had
turned to their sufferings in Missouri and Illinois. Daniel H.
Wells, who had fought the Gentiles in Nauvoo, spoke bitterly of
these wrongs. He also introduced the martyr-mongering myth,
later to be frequently heard in Utah, that the requisition of the
Mormon Battalion in 1846 had been intended as a blow at the
weakened and homeless Saints. Brigham Young, perhaps remembering Zachary Taylor's opposition to the Mormons' request for
statehood, asserted that Taylor was undoubtedly suffering the
torments of Hell for his wickedness. Brocchus arrived in Utah too
late to attend the Pioneers' Day festivities. He did, however, read
Wells' speech in the *Deseret News,* and the other Gentile officials
assured him that disloyal sentiments were part of the Mormons'
everyday conversation. The judge accordingly felt a patriotic
sermon, delivered with suitable rhetorical flourishes and a nice
wit, was necessary to remind the people of their duty as citizens.
Since the board of managers of the Washington Monument had
commissioned him to invite the contribution of a block of marble
from the people of Utah, he decided to fit the request neatly into
a lecture on conduct delivered before a general conference of the
Church.[10]

Brocchus began his speech with urbanity and for a time held
the good will of his audience. He referred to the Mormons' recent

troubles in sympathetic words, but advised that certain states, not
the officials of the central government, should receive the blame
for those misfortunes. He also found time in the early passages of
his windy, two-hour address to praise the industry and behavior
of the people in their new home. The preliminaries over and
warming to his subject, Brocchus next introduced the invitation
of the Washington Monument committee. Such a contribution,
he warned, should come only from citizens inspired by a lofty
devotion to the Union and its Constitution; "If the people of
Utah cannot offer a block [of marble] in full fellowship with the
United States, it were better to leave it unquarried in the bosom
of its native mountain." The inference that the Mormons' patriotism was questionable caused restlessness among the members
of the audience, but Brocchus, engrossed in his subject, was unaware of it. Now near the end of his speech, he turned from patriotism to morality. In a transparent reference to polygamy and
with possibly an attempt at facetiousness he lectured the women
at some length on the importance of virtue. His duty to elevate
the Saints fulfilled, the judge at last resumed his seat on the platform.

Instead of receiving exuberant applause for his efforts, Brocchus
found himself in imminent peril of an unpleasant death at the
hands of an incensed throng of Mormons. In later security he remembered his fear that the people would "spring upon me like
hyenas and destroy me." Although Brigham Young, rising to answer him, spoke of hair-pulling and throat-cutting, he managed to
prevent bloodshed, but he also permitted himself to dilate with
great heat upon several topics. The Government of the United
States, he said, was guilty of the Saints' past troubles in that it had
done nothing to protect or to recompense the Church during its
dark hours. He dealt even more severely with Brocchus. He commented on his overweening political ambitions, accused him of
profligate debauchery, and summed him up as one of those "corrupt fellows" whom the governor could buy, with a thousand of
his kind, and put in a bandbox. Afterward Young said that he
could have loosed the congregation upon Brocchus with a gesture
of his little finger, but he satisfied himself with a tongue-lashing.
The ashen-faced Brocchus, with Brandebury and Indian Agent
Henry R. Day, who shared the platform on that unhappy occa-

sion, was thankful to escape with his life. Only the first act of the drama had ended, however; recriminations and explanations were to follow until the entire country, not merely the Mormon community, was in an uproar.[11]

The excitement attendant upon the speech convinced Brocchus, Harris, and Brandebury they could no longer fulfill their duties in Utah, and within a week they were making preparations for departure. During his last days in the Territory the judge found time to conduct a correspondence with the Governor which began with Young's suggestion on September 19 that Brocchus address the Mormons again and explain his earlier remarks. Brocchus promptly excused himself on two grounds: his discourse, a carefully prepared one, needed no further elaboration, and also he understandably wished to avoid assassination.[12] Young sent two more lengthy communications to Brocchus; this epistolary activity was in all probability prompted by the Governor's intention to publish the letters in the East as a reply to the versions of the incident which Brocchus, Brandebury, and Harris were sure to broadcast upon their arrival there. Certainly Young's third letter reads like a campaign document; moreover, it was written two days after the officials had left Salt Lake, and made the implausible assertion that the judge had apologized for his behavior in hopes of re-establishing friendly relations with the Mormons.[13]

Brocchus was to the Mormons an odious person, to be denounced and perhaps intimidated; his only importance to the Church was the possible effect he might have upon public opinion in the States. Harris presented a more immediate problem, for he had in his charge a large amount of federal money badly needed in Utah. On September 17, therefore, Young tried to persuade him to abandon his plan for departure, and failing in that endeavor took energetic steps to secure the funds entrusted to him. On September 18 he issued a proclamation declaring the results of the August election, and hastily convened the legislature. Upon opening its session, that body, noting the secretary's intention to "absent himself or abscond" from Utah, ordered Harris to disburse $500 for territorial expenses, with the added resolution that if he should fail to comply, the territorial marshal should seize all official goods in his possession, including the seal, documents, and the $24,000. Harris' reply to this declaration revealed

his character as a meticulous, overbearing, but basically honest
young man. He rejected the command on the ground that the
legislature was sitting illegally, since its election had violated
many provisions of the Territory's Organic Act.[14] Certainly Harris was guilty of unnecessary quibbling, for the overwhelmingly
Mormon population would have voted as it had under any electoral system. But the secretary showed an interest in fair play not
always characteristic of federal appointees, or of the Latter-day
Saints for that matter, when he coupled his rejection of the legislature's order with the suggestion that the Mormons appeal to the
Treasury Department, or even to the President, for a review of
his decision.[15]

Litigation marked the Mormons' last contact with the "Runaways." Since the Supreme Court of the Territory was dominated
by the two Gentile judges, with Snow an ineffective minority of
one, the outcome of this final clash was disappointing to the
Church. An injunction prevented the marshal from carrying out
his order, and when on September 26 Young appealed to Chief
Justice Brandebury for a ruling on the legality of Harris' deser-
tion of his post with public moneys in his possession, the court
gave as its informal opinion the statement that no branch of the
territorial administration could interfere with Harris, a representative of the federal government. At the end of the month
Harris, Brandebury, and Brocchus, alarmed for their personal
safety, set out for Fort Bridger in eastern Utah.[16]

With the departure of these officers the controversy was transferred to the larger arenas of Washington and the Gentile press.
Young, aware that an unfriendly Government and public opinion
could embarrass his people—controlled politically as they were
from the East—opened the debate while Brocchus and his companions were still traveling across the Plains. On the day following their flight he gave the Mormons' side of the controversy in a
strongly worded, at times even defiant, letter to President Fillmore. He defended the legality of his official actions from the
charges he anticipated would be made by the Runaways, and,
using a favored Mormon technique in such debates attempted to
weaken the influence of his enemies by attacking their characters.
Contrary to Brocchus' slanders, Young continued, the Mormon
people were as attached to the United States as any citizens, but

their patriotism did not blind them to previous betrayals of their
constitutional rights. The long letter, whose polished style was
probably the result of Willard Richards' careful editorial labors,
flowed on in defense of the Mormons. Toward the end Young
offered suggestions concerning the future choice of officers, advice
which was presumptuous but nonetheless valid if difficulties were
to be avoided in the future. The Government, he demanded,
should appoint territorial residents, not pettifogging time-servers,
to public positions in Utah.[17]

Brocchus, Brandebury, and Harris, still traveling east, could
not take up the debate at once. Unhappily for them, they failed
to use this time to prepare their own appeal to the President. As
a result, several versions of their report, contradictory and containing portions capable of drawing ridicule upon the officers, appeared in the New York *Herald* and other newspapers.[18] The men
charged that agents of the Church, probably guided by Bernhisel,
had planted the different versions to discredit them. They worked
diligently to produce a document calculated to arouse the American people against the Mormons and at the same time clear themselves of possible blame for having abandoned their posts. They
sent the result of their labors to the President on December 19.

The report of the Runaways included all but one of the general accusations that caused Americans in 1857 to demand the use
of force against the Mormons, neglecting only the Church's supposed efforts to turn the Indians upon the United States (and
Brocchus corrected this omission in a later communication).[19]
The three men attributed their flight from the Territory to the
"lawless acts and the hostile and insidious feelings and sentiments
of Brigham Young," all of which had made their service as federal
representatives in Utah impossible. The documented arraignment
left little doubt that its writers considered the Mormons ready
to throw over their hypocritical pose of allegiance to the Union:
it mentioned Young's recent reference to President Taylor's unenviable status in the next world, Wells' subversive remarks on
July 24, and the seditious behavior of other Church dignitaries.
The Hierarchy, they declared further, exercised an autocratic
domination over its followers, Young presuming to rule as God's
chosen spokesman on earth. A portion of the report, probably
Harris' work, brought up the charges against the Governor of

fraudulent actions in the census and election, and insisted that
he had several times tried illegally to get his greedy hands on the
money guarded by a courageous, dedicated secretary. In highly
colored language Brocchus' near encounter with death after his
speech on patriotism and morality was described; other passages
told how Brandebury and Babbitt had suffered indignities from
the Mormon leaders. The polygamous marriages of the people
received attention, although the lurid emphasis of later years
and the customary attempt to estimate the number of wives in
Young's household were missing.

No respectable anti-Mormon declamation of this period was
complete without startling revelations of the Saints' criminal
activities. The Runaways' letter to Fillmore included accounts
of the murders of two Gentiles, James Munroe and Dr. John R.
Vaughn. No mention was made of the fact that Munroe had
met his death at the hands of a man whose wife he had seduced;
rather it was described merely as a "cool and deliberate murder"
of an innocent man.[20] The report of Brocchus and Harris, with
the ineffective Brandebury carried along with them, left unclear
whether the people habitually kicked their dogs; otherwise their
calendar of infamy in Utah was complete.

It is of no value to weigh the truthfulness of Brigham Young's
assertions and the Runaways' counterattack. The Church, whether
understandably or not, was in a mood incompatible with submis-
sive acceptance of territorial status. For their part, Brocchus
and the others had shown a remarkable indifference to the feelings of their temporary constituents, had without due cause deserted their offices, and had explained their behavior with statements of at best partial accuracy. In this argument neither side
was capable of narrating the events of the summer with fine im-
partiality. But both Mormons and Gentiles had at least outlined
the positions they would assume in subsequent struggles.

Having received the two reports of the summer's activities in
Utah, the Government had now to decide what to do with the
Mormons. Both parties to the controversy lobbied industriously
to influence the decision. Territorial delegate John Bernhisel
was on hand earlier than the Runaways, since he had left Salt
Lake City before the final explosion. This strikingly handsome

honor graduate of the University of Pennsylvania was frequently embarrassed in his defense of his people, for the Church, as in the case of its official announcement of polygamy in 1852, often took actions that jeopardized his delicate negotiations in the Capital. The serene confidence of Brigham Young and his associates that the Almighty would advance the interests of the Saints, Bernhisel must at times have felt, overlooked the importance of congressional and public opinion. In this crisis, however, he was ubiquitous—counseling President Fillmore and his cabinet, championing his people's rights in the House of Representatives, and arranging publication of appropriate literature.[21]

With Bernhisel in Washington was Jedediah M. Grant, one of Young's counselors, but the delegate, possibly distrusting Grant's excitable nature, severely restricted his association with governmental officials and the press. Of far greater assistance to him was Thomas L. Kane, classmate of Bernhisel and the perennial foul-weather friend of the Mormons, whom the Church kept supplied with arguments favorable to it.[22] Kane's pamphlet answering the charges of the Runaways won for the Mormons some supporters, among them Senator Hannibal Hamlin of Maine, who told Bernhisel that it had convinced him of the departed officers' worthlessness.[23] To counteract these pressures Brocchus and Harris, with the help of Indian agents Henry Day and Jacob Holeman, defended their accusations in a number of letters to the Administration.

Bernhisel's persuasive powers were sorely taxed, for opinion in Washington during the winter of 1851–52 flowed strongly against the Mormons. In great excitement men talked of replacing Governor Young with a Gentile, perhaps to be supplied and protected by a military expedition. This sentiment was most vociferously expressed in the House of Representatives, which on December 15, in a resolution indicating its acceptance of the Runaways' report as credible, requested the President to submit to it information on conditions in Utah. Upon receiving this intelligence the House debated a motion to deny Bernhisel his seat on the grounds of the possible fraudulence of his election. The delegate's statements that he had received every vote cast and had not even been in the Territory when the election took place were ignored. David Cartter of Ohio proved to be the most

persistent critic of the Saints. With the support of William A.
Richardson of Illinois he suggested that only force could compel
proper behavior and acceptance of constitutional rights from the
people of Utah. In the early part of these debates there were only
a few representatives, among them Alexander Stephens of Georgia
and Joshua Giddings of Ohio, who did not share these anti-Mormon sentiments.[24]

Two tendencies worked to prevent Congress from reaching a
sane effective policy in its debates on the Mormons in 1852, and
they were to muddle the issue even more disastrously later in the
decade. In the first place, members of the opposition, at this time
the Democrats, tried to make political capital of the episode in
order to embarrass the Whigs. Undoubtedly Cartter was sincere
in his dislike, almost loathing, of the Mormons, whom he described as led by Brigham Young "with his fifteen harlots around
him, polluting the very atmosphere in which he lives," a "ruf-
fian" and an "inspired prophet of Hell." Cartter's language, however, would have been less extravagant if he had not also wished
to make the Administration seem "pusillanimous" to the nation.
In the second place, the slavery question, entering this debate as
it did all others at this time, helped to obstruct the formulation
of a workable policy. Giddings based his appeal for charity toward
the Saints upon the assertion that the abuse of the female slave in
the South was a more suitable cause of reproach than Utah's
polygamous practices. In such an atmosphere Bernhisel's suggestion that the Government send an investigating commission
to the Territory received little attention.[25] The action, if taken,
might have settled the dispute, but in 1852, as in 1857, it was
cavalierly dismissed.

While Congress was deliberating, Harris, Brocchus, and Indian
agents Day and Holeman assailed the Administration with their
correspondence. At first the Government seemed as prepared as
Cartter to give the Runaways thoughtful attention, for Comptrol-
ler Elisha Whittlesey informed Young in November that the
Department of the Treasury would not honor his drafts, past or
future, until the serious charges against his official conduct had
been satisfactorily answered. President Fillmore, according to
Harris' assertion, even considered appointing the former secretary
as governor in place of Young, a position Harris reportedly re-

jected when his demand for a regiment as an escort was refused. During the winter Bernhisel made his calls upon Washington's influential politicians with anxiety in his heart.[26]

In spite of its initially unsympathetic reception of the Mormons' explanations, the Government eventually took the side of the Church in this dispute. A number of factors seem to have brought about this reaction: the different versions of the Runaways' report cast doubt on the value of any of them; slavery and other more pressing problems drove the issue of Mormonism from men's minds; and it became clear that interference in Utah would be more productive of strife than a policy of watchful waiting. The answer of Congress to the Runaways' report at last came in a law of June 15, 1852, prescribing forfeiture of pay if any territorial official should absent himself from his post without cause. The Administration accepted the Church's arguments to a greater extent than Congress. Daniel Webster advised Brocchus either to return to Utah or to resign his commission. The President, who had previously conferred with Bernhisel, even considered for a time the appointment of three prominent Mormons —Kimball, Orson Hyde, and Willard Richards—to the vacant positions in Utah. With good reason the Saints named their territorial capital Fillmore, located in Millard County.[27]

Public opinion toward the Mormons as expressed in the newspapers was divided in this first clash with the Church since the days of Nauvoo. Some editors agreed with Horace Greeley's New York *Tribune,* usually during the decade an advocate of fairness toward the Latter-day Saints, and urged upon their readers an impartial examination of the Runaways' charges.[28] Others, such as the editor of the *Missouri Republican,* had more difficulty making up their minds. At first highly censorious of Brigham Young's "abusive and seditious language" and his indulgence in polygamy, this frontier publication early in 1852 became so critical of the former federal officers that thirty-five Mormons in Utah sent in their subscriptions.[29] In general, however, eastern opinion was antagonistic to the Mormons, and for a time the Church leaders feared that it might result in a military expedition against them. Apprehensive of this possibility, Lt. John Gunnison inserted a warning in his book about his recent experiences in Utah: "To enforce rulers over [the Mormons] from abroad, by the power of the bayonet, will entail perpetual war." As excitement in Washington subsided, the people eventually ceased demanding the dispatch of troops to Utah. Yet the furor provoked by the Runaways revealed the existence of a strong anti-Mormon disposition in American thought; if it became dormant in the summer of 1852, it was ready to reappear when new alarms came from Utah.[30]

In addition to such matters as the Mormons' alleged disloyalty, the episode brought up another issue that aroused Gentile suspicions, namely the Church's relations with the Indians. In a letter to Daniel Webster dated April 30, 1852, Perry Brocchus charged the Mormons with pursuing a policy toward the Indians of their Territory detrimental to the interests of the United States.[31] The assertion that the Church was in league with native tribes for some insidious reason was not a new one, for as early as the 1830's the Gentiles in Missouri had based a desire to expel the Saints from that state partly on the ground that they had incited the savages to attack white men. Although people in the East did not seize upon Brocchus' indictment as worthy of great interest in 1852, the accusation grew more familiar in a few years and ultimately became one of the causes of the Mormon War.

It is understandable that Mormons and Gentiles should have disagreed radically concerning the Indian. To most pioneers of the West, the Indian was an obstacle to exploration and settlement, a cruel, wild thing to be destroyed if he opposed the advance of civilization. The Church's widely divergent attitude was drawn from the Book of Mormon. In the Mormons' theology second in importance only to the Bible, this holy writ purports to be a history of the Western Hemisphere before the arrival of the white man. According to Church dogma, in 1823 young Joseph Smith, guided by a heavenly spirit, had found golden plates bearing hieroglyphic characters in "Hill Cumorah," near Palmyra, New York. For four years Smith's heart was not clean enough of human impurities for him to receive the plates, but in 1827 the Almighty at last found him ready for a task of cosmic importance. The young man uncovered the tablets and with the aid of two "seer stones," called Urim and Thummim and fortunately included among Hill Cumorah's treasures, he proceeded to translate the strange characters.

He read that 600 years before the birth of Christ the family of Lehi had left Jerusalem and after a series of adventures had reached the New World. In the course of time the six sons of Lehi had quarreled among themselves. A thousand-years' war had resulted. The descendants of Nephi, representing Good in this engagement, had eventually all perished, but not before they had recorded their history on the golden plates now before Joseph's eyes. Although the evil Lamanites, the followers of one of Nephi's elder brothers, had triumphed, God had cursed them with dark skin for their wickedness. The Book of Mormon went on to indicate that these people were the ancestors of the American Indian. Thus the Red Man was indeed a brother of the White; missionary work might save him from his fallen state, and the Mormon looked upon the Indian with hope of redemption. Gentiles in Missouri and Utah who were unenlightened by the Book of Mormon viewed their activities with the greatest distrust.

After the creation of Utah Territory, the Government had experienced some difficulty organizing the administration of its Indian affairs.[32] By the summer of 1851, however, three officers had arrived at their posts and were ready to perform their duties. The two Gentiles, Agent Jacob Holeman and Sub-Agent Henry R. Day, as well as their Mormon colleague, Stephen B. Rose, found the Indian relations of the Territory serene. Young, who was both Governor and superintendent of Indian affairs under the Organic Act, had already inaugurated a policy toward the neighboring tribes designed to pacify them. Perhaps he, like other Saints, thought of them as the fallen people of the Book of Mormon; more likely this eminently practical man knew that some action other than attempted extermination was necessary if his followers were to have peace in Salt Lake Valley during their critical early years there. At any rate he urged the Mormons to treat the Indians with absolute justice, and at the same time he suggested to the Government that the Indians might become peaceful neighbors if taught domestic arts under the guidance of white farmers, blacksmiths, and similar tutors.[33]

Although Day revealed considerable talent for his work, he soon destroyed his usefulness by joining Harris and the federal judges in their controversy with the Church. Holeman had better luck at first in avoiding disputes that might have affected his job, and as a result won the praise of Governor Young.[34] But the harmony lasted only through the summer of 1851. In September of that year Holeman attended a conference of several tribes at Fort Laramie and there found cause to criticize certain of the Mormons' activities. He heard and believed that the Church was evicting the Indians from their land, and he received other complaints from the mountain men in the region, a group of hardy trappers and pioneers who had difficulties with the Saints throughout the 1850's.

When the Mormons arrived in the Salt Lake Basin, their plans for their New Zion envisaged the creation of a vast empire in the West, with a number of far-flung settlements radiating from the central hub of Salt Lake City. Thus their Provisional State of Deseret encompassed in its boundaries all of present-day Utah and most of New Mexico, Nevada, and California, with some of Wyoming and the Pacific Northwest included. Although Congress severely reduced this domain when it delineated the Territory of Utah, the Church established colonies at San Bernardino, Carson Valley, and Limhi, on the Salmon River. These missions were placed at strategic locations on the western and northern approaches to the Valley, but the eastern route of travel, through what is now southern Wyoming, still lay open. Mormon country contained that portion of the region where Jim Bridger, the indestructible mountain man, had built a fort, but it did not extend to other trappers' settlements and ferries scattered along the Green River. These men, and especially Bridger, were an undisciplined lot who had adopted an anti-Mormon posture on first contact with the Saints. What was more, their marriages with the Indians had given them influence over the tribes in the region. Their trade on the Overland Trail was lucrative; their location at the eastern entrance to the Mormons' settlements was most objectionable. Therefore the Church had early tried to penetrate this area, and in so doing ran into the opposition of the powerful tribes that Holeman visited.

After his conference at Fort Laramie, Agent Holeman adopted

a more critical view of Young's activities than he had formed upon his arrival in Great Salt Lake City. In November he was prepared to draw up a broad indictment of the Saints, touching upon a number of general causes of Gentile-Mormon friction. With the Runaways, he believed that the Church was defiant of the Government's authority and was planning resistance to it. The mails, he further stated, were no longer safe for the communication of important messages, since the Mormons opened and read everything. In its most important passage Holeman's dispatch accused Young of using the powers of his office as superintendent and the judicious distribution of gifts to insinuate his Church into the sympathies of the Indians, to the detriment of the Government's interest. Because of this correspondence Holeman's position in Utah ultimately became as untenable as that of Brocchus, but unlike this official he stuck it out there until 1853. Never a man to deal circumspectly with an antagonistic personality, Young sought to place as many impediments as possible in the way of the Indian agent's labors when he learned of his attitude. For his part, Holeman throughout 1852 bombarded the Indian Office in Washington with a number of letters pressing his accusations that the Mormons had sent unprincipled men among the Indians for sinister purposes and were planning to seize the Green River region by force. Young denied as many of these complaints as he could anticipate or discover. Since the Commissioner of Indian Affairs praised the Governor's work as superintendent and wrote no word of encouragement to Holeman, the Mormons apparently won the Government's approval in this argument, just as they had in their controversy with the Runaways.[35] The question of the Saints' relations with the tribes in Utah, however, was not dead.

When Edward A. Bedell replaced Holeman, the Mormons temporarily had in their Territory an agent sympathetic toward them, but his death in 1854 cut his term short after one year. At the same time the new Commissioner in Washington, George Manypenny, far less amiably disposed toward the people of Utah than his predecessor Luke Lea, began both to scrutinize Young's drafts with slow, suspicious thoroughness and to recommend that the Governor be relieved of his duties as territorial superintendent of Indian affairs.[36] Coincidentally the uneasy situation in the

Green River region worsened. Pursuing the Church's effort to extend its jurisdiction over the area, and at the same time following its established practice of bestowing valuable concessions upon members of the Hierarchy, the Utah legislature granted to the Mormon Daniel Wells a monopoly of ferry transportation on the river. The action so aroused the mountain men and their Snake Indian friends that the commanding officer at Fort Laramie feared "bloodshed and disturbance" as a result.[37]

The focus of excitement in the Green River Basin during the middle part of the decade was old Jim Bridger, trapper, scout, and storyteller now become merchant to the overland pioneers. In the 1840's, with Louis Vasquez, he had opened a post on Black's Fork. Because of its strategic location and Bridger's considerable influence with the neighboring Indian tribes, the fort thwarted the Mormons' plans to control the whole region. As a step preliminary to his removal, in 1853 the Saints established a settlement, Fort Supply, about twelve miles southwest of Bridger's post, under the leadership of Orson Hyde. The Church then moved to eject the mountain man. Details of the ensuing struggle are unclear, for in this incident, as in so many Mormon-Gentile encounters, each side gave a contradictory account of the events. The Mormons maintained that Bridger, or at least his partner, had sold them the fort and its possessions for $8,000 in gold. To the day of his death Bridger insisted that he had never sold the place but instead had been forced to abandon it to avoid being murdered. Many believed his story. At least a portion of Bridger's statement was true; far from peacefully yielding his fort, he fled from it during the night to avoid a Mormon posse of 150 men authorized to arrest him for selling weapons to the Indians.[38] Wherever the truth lay, the Church had for the moment achieved its purpose of securing the eastern approach to Salt Lake Valley.

After the disturbance over Brocchus, Harris, Brandebury, and the Indian agents, the three years following 1852 brought better relations between Mormon and Gentile. Unaware that the period was only prefatory to events culminating in the Utah War, the Saints could enjoy the fact that for once in their turbulent history no powerful voice cried for their chastisement or obliteration, or even for the removal of Governor Young. Fillmore, con-

tinuing to treat the people of Utah with benevolence, appointed
as replacements for the Runaways men with tact and restraint.
Pleased with the calm after the high adventures of 1851 and
1852, Young stated in one official message: "The full complement of the federal officers for this territory, except for an Indian agent, are now resident with us; and so far as I am informed,
a good degree of cordiality and reciprocal kindness exists between
them and the people of the territory." [39] For the only time in
the decade the Mormons had on the Supreme Court bench men
favorably disposed to them. Zerubbabel Snow, the one important
federal representative to remain in Utah after 1851, was a member of their Church. The new justices, Lazarus Reed [40] and Leonidas Shaver, were peaceable individuals who had no intention
of interfering with the customs of the people. Accordingly they
received praise from the Territory's ecclesiastical rulers as cour-
teous, dignified, and upright, capable of giving an honest interpretation of the law; and their deaths in 1855 brought unanimous
expressions of regret from the leaders of the Church.[41]

To be sure, during this brief respite from serious altercation
there were a few discordant incidents foreshadowing future trouble. Shaver's demise ultimately brought twofold grief to the Saints.
For some months in ill health, the judge in 1855 developed an
inflammation of the middle ear which soon became fatal. Dr.
Garland Hurt, later an outspoken opponent of Brigham Young,
testified to these facts at the inquest, and there seemed no doubt
that Shaver's death was from natural causes, although the end
had perhaps been hastened by his habit of taking opium. Unfortunately the jury at the inquest attributed Shaver's death to
a "disease of the head," an ambiguous phrase at best. When in
later months Gentiles were searching for atrocities to charge
against the Church, the story began to circulate that Shaver had
been done in by Mormon assassins. He had been in excellent
health, this report stated, until he quarreled with Brigham
Young; after that incident he was suddenly found dead of some
incredible malady.[42] If Reed had not died in Bath, New York,
it is probable that he, too, would have been added to the growing
list of Mormon "victims." Another and more important result
came from Shaver's death: President Pierce filled his vacancy by
appointing W. W. Drummond, who proved much more successful

than Brocchus in raising an expedition against the people of Utah.

The new secretary of the Territory, Benjamin G. Ferris, had as little trouble as Shaver and Reed during his brief residence in Utah, and Young twice referred to him as a cooperative individual. Later Ferris wrote of his kind reception among the Mormons; on his departure in the spring of 1853 he even offered to urge as his replacement anyone whom the Church might favor. Yet once away from Utah, Ferris altered his opinion of his recent hosts, and the book he published in 1854 became grist for the mill of anti-Mormonism. The government of the Territory, he then declared, was an intolerable theocracy "calculated to concentrate despotic power in the hands of a few." With the Runaways he attributed to the Church many crimes, including murder by the Danites, and was appropriately scandalized at polygamy. When in 1857 the Government was preparing to enforce obedience in Utah, Ferris wrote to the New York *Times* that the action was indeed necessary to punish this "unscrupulous set of villains." The appointment of the man may therefore be taken as another evidence that the selection of officers unsuited for their responsible positions was a potent cause of friction between the Mormons and the country. Certainly the behavior of Brocchus and Harris revealed the need for a careful selection of federal representatives. In a book on Utah, Ferris confessed that his principal motive in accepting the post of secretary had been a "curiosity, long cherished, to visit a portion of the world about which marvelous accounts had been given"—in other words to observe the exotic Mormons in their native habitat, not to perform duties of a delicate and important nature.[43]

The attitude of Mrs. Ferris may well have reduced the effectiveness of the secretary. Like Broughton Harris' wife, she went to Utah prepared to be shocked, and she was not disappointed. In her letters she summed up her experiences: "We are unquestionably in the midst of fanatics, who are controlled by a gang of licentious villains." She complained that all Gentiles in Utah were spied upon and at the same time told how, on one of her walks, she gratified her curiosity about the people "by peeping into doors and windows." Together with Mrs. Harris and a host of eastern Gentiles, she was outraged at polygamy. The system as she saw it brought evil to all who engaged in it. The

women's chalky faces, sunken eyes, and tearful natures were
indications of their inner agony of spirit; the men bore the outward signs of sinners' dissipation.[44] Few non-Mormons in the
1850's, and even much later, could accept the fact that while
some women were unhappy in polygamous households, there
were others who did not experience unbearable spiritual and
moral distress. To most Gentiles plural marriage, forced upon
defenseless women by debauched priests, could result only in
red-rimmed eyes and pinched faces.

The peaceful interlude of 1852–55 therefore held portents
of future difficulties for the Latter-day Saints. The appointment
of unsuitable federal officers, occasional anti-Mormon diatribes,
and trouble in the Green River region indicated that the serenity
following the episode of the Runaways was only on the surface.
In Washington the Congress, it is true, approved Utah's statutes,
praised its criminal code, and passed appropriations for necessary territorial purposes. But it also ignored the Mormons' petition for statehood. Furthermore, several congressmen continued
to link the Mormon problem with the irrepressible controversy
over slavery.[45] Another aggravating development of the period
was the arrival of Lt. Col. Edward Jenner Steptoe with a party
of 300 soldiers and civilians in 1854. This was no military
expedition to occupy a recalcitrant people, for Steptoe had orders to examine the possibility of constructing a road from Salt
Lake City to California.[46] He and his men found it necessary
to pass the winter in Utah, during which time his troops were
thrown into intimate contact with the Saints, with unpleasant
results for the peace of Gentile-Mormon relations.

Steptoe himself became embroiled in the political affairs of
the Territory. His orders included instructions to investigate a
particularly unpleasant murder in Utah the year before. Lt.
John W. Gunnison's second visit to the Basin had been more
unfortunate than his first in 1849, when he had received a cordial
welcome from Indians and white men. Ordered to survey a route
between the 38th and 39th parallels for the proposed Central
Pacific Railroad, Gunnison had reached Utah with about a dozen
men on October 26, 1853. Like the ill-fated Fancher Party, victims
of the Mountain Meadows Massacre four years later, he had arrived at a bad time, when the Indians had become infuriated by

unnecessary acts of cruelty on the part of recent travelers. Although Mormons in Fillmore warned Gunnison of the Indians' hostility, he trusted his previous friendship to protect him and his men. At the Sevier River on October 28, however, Indians ambushed the detachment, killing Gunnison and seven of his command.[47]

To defend the prestige of the Government and the security of other troops in the West, the War Department demanded the punishment of this crime. Furthermore, ugly rumors had begun to circulate that the Mormons had had a hand in the affair, the principal evidence being their slowness in bringing the murderers to justice. The charge, like many heard in the decade, was unreasonable, for the Church had enjoyed warm relations with Gunnison. Informed persons also knew that the territorial government could not punish the murderers summarily without provoking a costly war with the Indians. The rumor nevertheless persisted and in time, under the influence of anti-Mormon propagandists, took on the nature of a war cry.[48] It was Steptoe's task to investigate the incident.

Through his inquiry into the massacre Steptoe became involved in the thorny issue of the Mormons' relations with the Indians. Like Holeman, he concluded that the Church was tampering with the local tribes in a most reprehensible fashion. To his thinking the Mormons' eventual trial of the three Indians held for the crime had been nothing more than a farce, a transparent artifice by the Church to beguile Gentile opinion rather than dispense stern justice. No other conclusion, he felt, was possible in the light of the jury's incomprehensible verdict of manslaughter, which ignored both the nature of the crime and Judge John F. Kinney's instructions to find the prisoners guilty of murder or acquit them. On April 5, 1855, Steptoe wrote an angry letter to Secretary of the Interior Robert McClelland. The trial of the Gunnison murderers, he warned, revealed a dangerous attempt on the part of the Church to win the allegiance of the Indians away from the United States: "the General Government would act wisely in taking *immediate* steps to neutralize any pernicious influence that has been, or may be, attempted." Lest the one letter fail to sound the alarm effectively in Washington, Steptoe, on the same day, also wrote the Commissioner of Indian Affairs that he

and the present Indian agent, Garland Hurt, were apparently
the first men in Utah to inform the Territory's tribes of their
true relation to the Government.[49]

Other Gentiles were also indignant at the outcome of the trial.
Judge Kinney, who had presided, later became such a favorite of
the Mormons that they conferred upon him the important post
of territorial delegate to Congress. At this time, however, his
experience in court had made him a bitter if secret critic of the
Church and an advocate of Governor Young's removal. On April
1 he wrote the Attorney General that the verdict in the Gunnison case "can only be accounted for on the ground that the *authority* of the *Priesthood* is paramount to the law of the land." [50]
A member of Steptoe's command, Capt. Rufus Ingalls, did not
limit his report to the charge that the Church's Hierarchy had
for dark reasons influenced the jury's decision; he further accused
the Mormons of ignoring common law and the Constitution, the
Church of ruling its ignorant followers despotically, and the
priests of wallowing in "sensuality and corruption." With words
reminiscent of the Brocchus affair and prophetic of the 1857
crisis, Ingalls concluded: *"The* [Territorial] *government, then,
should be changed without delay,* if for no other reason, to sepa-
rate Church and State there." [51]

To the Mormons in 1854 and 1855 Edward Jenner Steptoe was
more than an army officer whose orders had injected him into
their Indian affairs. Before his arrival in the Territory, Bernhisel
had written Willard Richards that President Pierce had resolved
to appoint Steptoe governor upon the expiration of Young's first
four-year term. During the remainder of 1854 and on into the
the next year the Salt Lake community buzzed with excitement
over this possibility. Steptoe was not objectionable to the Mormons, Young himself having said publicly that if the officer had
been given the appointment he would accept this "gallant gentleman," but the selection of any Gentile for this position of authority was cause for alarm among the Saints, who wished to be
ruled only by members of their Church. Although leading Mormons earnestly petitioned Pierce to reappoint Young, some feared
that Steptoe had the President's commission in his pocket when
he arrived in the Territory.[52]

The maneuvers surrounding the final disposition of the gov-

ernorship are as confused as those concerning Jim Bridger and
his fort. For many weeks after his arrival in Great Salt Lake City,
Steptoe gave no indication whether he had the commission or
was even interested in the matter. Chief Justice Kinney was one
man who felt that Pierce had not made his selection, since in
October he wrote the President advising a change in the executive
office and recommending Steptoe as a man eminently suited and
available for the post. Later Steptoe joined Kinney in counseling
the Mormons to favor the appointment of a Gentile as governor,
in order to end eastern criticism of Brigham Young's power in
both church and state.[53] Yet on the same day they made this suggestion, indicative of the desire to remove Young from his position, they also affixed their signatures to a petition requesting
the President to renew the Governor's commission because Young
had the approval of the entire settlement, was a "firm supporter
of the Constitution and the laws of the United States," had diligently defended the interests of the nation, and in sum "would
better subserve the territorial interests than the appointment of
any other man." Steptoe and Kinney were not alone in these
sentiments, for forty-three prominent persons, among them District Attorney Hollman, United States Marshal Joseph L. Heywood, and Judge George P. Stiles, endorsed the memorial.[54]

In spite of this petition the Mormons continued to fear that
Steptoe, or possibly even Kinney, would get Pierce's appointment.
Their anxiety was well founded, for the lieutenant colonel's attitude toward the Saints began to harden into hostility during the
first months of 1855 as a result of the trial of Gunnison's alleged
murderers and perhaps also because of bitter public tirades by
Kimball and Grant accusing his soldiers of "wickedness and abom-
inable corruptions." By the first of April he was no longer ready
to concede Young's acceptability as governor. When he and Kinney and Garland Hurt advised President Pierce to remove Secretary Almon Babbitt because of his role in the recent trial and
also his "intimate and confidential" relations with the sect's Hierarchy, the letter assumed that a Gentile would replace Young.[55]

Yet when the agitation had quieted and all the letters and
petitions had been filed, Steptoe was on his way to California,
Kinney was still only a federal judge in Utah, and Young still
occupied the executive seat. It is impossible now to understand

all the factors contributing to this resolution of the problem. Perhaps Pierce felt that the unavailability of Steptoe left Young as the only suitable appointee. It is less clear why the lieutenant colonel did not take the governorship, in view of the bitterness of his remarks about the Church in 1855. One contemporary observer implied that the Administration had refused to accept certain stipulations he had presented as prerequisite to his acceptance; another stated that he had chosen a promotion in rank in preference to the civil office.[56] In any event the Church had again, as in the case of the Runaways, received a satisfactory decision from the Government. The victory, however, was ephemeral.

One other aspect of Steptoe's visit to Utah, the relations of his men with the Mormon population, was as important as were the machinations behind the selection of the governor. After the arrival of the party in late August, Steptoe had first established a camp in Rush Valley, south of Salt Lake City. Within two weeks, however, he had moved his command to the city in order to be more conveniently situated for the punishment of Gunnison's murderers. These troops gave the Saints their first contact with a number of armed Gentiles since the days of Nauvoo. For a time, relations between the two groups were free of incident and even pleasant to both; but the situation soon deteriorated. Street brawls between the soldiers and Mormons became almost a common occurrence. The Church's leaders also began to charge that the troops had seduced a number of women and had generally brought depravity into the community for the first time since its establishment.[57] After their experiences with this small detachment of soldiers, the Mormons dreaded any new visitation from the army to their Valley, an emotion in part explaining their resistance to the more formidable expedition in 1857.

3. The Shadows Lengthen

THE short period between 1852 and 1855 was in general a peaceful interlude in the relations between the Mormons and the nation. Although Steptoe, Ferris, and Holeman had raised brief disturbances, the years were as free of painful incident as any before 1896, when Utah gained statehood. But the harmony, such as it was, soon faded. Within a few months voices more powerful and strident than those heard in the past were demanding federal intervention in the Mormons' country; and a stormy petrel reached Salt Lake City in the person of David H. Burr, the newly appointed surveyor general of the Territory.

Almost at once Burr ran into trouble with the inhabitants of the Valley. Their title to the land they occupied was tenuous at best, in the absence of an Indian treaty or congressional enactment. Knowing this, they looked upon a survey of their region as a move preliminary to their eviction by the Government. Their fears had some justification, for Burr soon wrote to his superiors that the Church had illegally appropriated areas of the public domain, a reference to the recent introduction of an experiment, tried without success in earlier communities, to persuade the Mormons to deed their property to the Church.[1]

In alarm, the Saints sought to impede the surveyor general's labors in every way possible, using intimidation, violence, and their influence over the Indians. A chief of a neighboring tribe, Arapeen, informed one of Burr's employees that the Mormons had warned his people against the surveying parties, calling them a part of a larger scheme to seize the Indians' land. Garland Hurt, whose position as agent brought him into greater difficulties than Holeman had encountered, was even more explicit. In a letter to Brigham Young he charged that a bishop had stirred up the Indians in southern Utah by circulating the lie that the surveyors were really a posse sent in disguise to arrest Gunnison's murderers. Other Mormons in Fillmore, Hurt added, had stoned a house where Burr and his men had stopped for the night. The surveyor general himself reported the Mormons' removal of corner posts, the theft of his animals, and other obstructive acts, none of which could be prosecuted in the Church-controlled courts.[2]

In the spring of 1857 Burr gave up his work in Utah, offering a number of explanations for this decision. His life was in danger, for the priesthood was denouncing him from the pulpit. One of his associates, Joseph Troskolawsski, had been beaten nearly to death, perhaps permanently crippled, by a group of the infamous Danites. Neither the law of 1830, designed to protect surveying parties, nor any other act shielded him, he maintained, for the "[federal] courts have been broken up and driven from the Territory," and Brigham Young had ominously declared in public that his, Burr's, work was at an end. In this lawless atmosphere three apostates had been murdered; Burr's friends predicted the same fate for him if he remained. This was rebellion against the country, Burr cried.[3]

After his departure in April 1857 the lives of his assistants, at least according to their reports, became even more precarious, for the community was now in a state of hysteria. The wife of one surveyor, Charles Mogo, later testified in court that her husband had barely eluded a band of Mormons sent by Brigham Young to kill him, and in his absence prominent members of the Church had rifled his office. Two clerks did not escape so easily. The Danites seized one of them, William W. Wilson, and, putting a rope around his neck and a pistol to his head, forced him to answer their questions. During this same night of terror C. G. Landon, the other clerk, leaping from his window half-dressed as midnight assassins broke down his front door, started on the long journey to Placerville, California, on foot. Surveying had become a hazardous occupation in Utah.[4]

As was frequently the case in more significant episodes, the truth about Burr's clash with the Mormons is not easily found. The Gentiles involved in the controversy described the Saints as a pack of villains whose deeds ran from petty crime to treason; the Church, denying the charges, portrayed its accusers as corrupt, degraded, and completely untrustworthy. So it had been with Brocchus, and so with Burr. The Mormon leaders collected and published a number of affidavits to show that the surveyor general had really been engaged in defrauding the Government by means of vouchers for work never even begun, had falsified maps, and had formed a conspiracy with Mogo to cheat the public of $30,-000. Burr had advocates ready to defend his character, and one man who had sworn to his malfeasance later repudiated his testimony, saying that it was extorted from him by Young and other Mormons. Subsequent official investigations did reveal inaccuracy and fraudulence in Burr's survey work, but this discovery had little bearing upon the question of the extent of the Mormons' obedience to the authority of the United States. From the statements of Burr, Hurt, Craig, Mogo, Wilson, and Landon it appeared that the people of the Territory were, if not actually rebellious, at least ready to impede the work of duly appointed federal representatives.[5]

More important than Burr's encounters with the Saints in Utah was the concurrent reappearance of the quarrel over the Church's policy toward the Indians. Previous agents, especially Jacob Holeman, had collided with Young on this matter and had helped to broadcast the conviction that the people of Utah were seeking to subvert the Indians. Garland Hurt, the new agent, now brought the situation to a head. He and the Mormons inevitably became bitter enemies. His opposition to their Indian policy was more determined than that of any other man in this period, and he further antagonized the Church by winning a wide influence among the tribes under his jurisdiction. In addition, unlike many federal officers, he did not react in panic to the anathemas of the Saints' leaders; instead he continued his work after his Gentile colleagues had fled from the Territory in 1857 and left only when the emotions of the excited populace seemed to threaten his life. The Mormons found in him a man whose character could not easily be assailed, for Hurt, a doctor from Kentucky, was educated and respectable.[6] It is a measure of his importance that his letters to Washington influenced the Government's decision to impose military occupation upon Utah.

Hurt's career in the Territory pursued the pattern by now familiar to other Gentile officeholders: an introductory phase of amicable relations with the Church, during which each gauged the other, and then a period of acrimonious dispute. The Mormons at first considered the new agent acceptable and even placed his name upon its official ticket in an election. For his part, Hurt was so pleased with the Saints that he urged the appointment of Porter Rockwell, Brigham Young's strong right arm, as sub-agent. Hurt and Young might have worked well together, for they agreed on the proper way to pacify the Indians, namely teaching them the arts of civilization in order to make them more as-similable in a region of growing white settlement. Under Hurt's energetic supervision three Indian farms were created, where the tribes could be won over from their nomadic practices to a more settled economy.[7]

Until June 1857 Hurt experienced no great difficulty in the Territory and remained after the departure of Drummond, Burr, and the other officials. The Indians were peaceful; and since Governor Young was away, Hurt's relations with the Church were uneventful. But when they learned that President Buchanan had ordered an expedition to Utah, the Mormons resolved that Gentiles in their settlements should not be allowed to remain in a position to weaken them at a time when they faced an invasion. Preparatory to moving against Hurt, the denominational leaders investigated the situation at Spanish Fork, the central Indian farm. They were not pleased with what they found. In mid-August Aaron Johnson wrote Daniel Wells that the Indians under Hurt's supervision were hostile to the Church and that their chief, Peteetneet, had expressed fondness for Hurt, sympathy for Americans, and dislike for the Saints. "It raised the query in my mind," Johnson wrote, "if an influence for evil has not been used by some *one* in that quarter."[8]

There is confusion surrounding Hurt's hasty departure from Utah late in September 1857. According to the agent's version he fled for his life to the protection of the army when 300 armed Mormons marched up the road toward his house, obviously with the intention of doing him physical harm. Brigham Young denied this. In a letter to James W. Denver, Commissioner of Indian Affairs, Young said that Hurt "saw fit to leave the field of his official duty on the 26th day of September last . . . without having made any report to me of his wishes and designs, or of the disposition he made of the affairs of his agency," an "occasionless and unwise movement on his part." [9] It was the former governor's position that he had written to Hurt offering an escort and a carriage to take him safely to the expedition, but Hurt had ignored this generous gesture as well as an order to deliver the property under his care to Aaron Johnson.[10]

Indisputably, after the Mormons discovered the true feelings of Hurt's Indians, they placed his farm under close observation, and on September 26 Johnson learned that the Indian agent was planning to leave Spanish Fork with some of the farm's stock, accompanied by many of Peteetneet's followers. Urging the local bishop, Charles B. Hancock, to "keep all *still* and *watch*, not only at the Farm, but that no such one leave as contemplated, without our knowing it," Johnson set out for Salt Lake City to get instructions directly from Young. On the way, he was informed by an express that Hurt and his Indians seemed to be preparing for flight; and returning, he worked out with Hancock a plan to seize Hurt without the risk of a clash with his guards: the Mormons would go to the farm with a force large enough to cow the Indians, who usually fought only when sure of victory, and take the agent into custody. When Johnson wrote to Young of this scheme, the Mormon leader replied, as he sometimes did, with an equivocal pronouncement which could be taken as expressing approval of the project, yet which, if the undertaking should fail, might be read as leaving the entire matter in the hands of the local officer. By this time, however, Hurt had made his escape.[11]

According to Hurt's story, September 27 was an exciting day down on the farm. Believing his life to be in danger from the Mormons, he had decided to quit the Territory but was reluctant to submit to the "humiliating ceremony of applying to Brigham Young for a passport." He therefore went to the farm near Spanish Fork in order to assemble an escort for the trip to the army. On this critical day an Indian rushed into his office with the news that a large body of Mormon dragoons was a mile away. Calmly Hurt began to gather up his papers and make leisurely preparations for departure. A second Indian sprinted in with another urgent report of the approach of an armed and hostile detachment. If Hurt's story was correct, a total of four Indians crowded into his office on that Sunday with various hair-raising accounts of the Saints' menacing gestures. At this point

he took fright and left the farm with three young braves, riding west in order to escape the Mormons. At first detected and
followed, he later eluded his pursuers; when night came he returned to the Spanish Fork station under cover of darkness. The
next day he was off again, this time going eastward with a large
band of Indians. With some difficulty he reached the expedition
near South Pass late in October.[12]

After his flight to the army's winter quarters near Bridger's
Fort in late 1857, the Indian agent had leisure to think back over
his experiences in Utah. It had been a trying time, he concluded,
and he wrote the recently appointed governor, Alfred Cumming,
of his ordeal. His communication was in reality a list of offenses
supposedly committed by the Saints, reports of which were at that
time inflaming Gentile opinion in the East. Heading Hurt's
catalogue was the Church's defiance of the nation, its "heartfelt
hatred for the people of the United States." The un-American
nature of the Territory's "theocratic autocracy" was also noted in
Hurt's letter. He ended with mention of the atrocities committed
during his residence in Utah: The Saints' burning of the homes
of apostates or other offensive persons, usually helpless women
with young babes, and the Parrish-Potter murders, which with
the Mountain Meadows Massacre was on every Gentile tongue at
the moment. These victims of the Church, Hurt declared, could
obtain no justice, for the Hierarchy had inspired the assaults, and
the probate courts, the only tribunals available, were the tools of
Brigham Young.[13]

Although it was otherwise thorough in its accusation of Mormon wickedness, Hurt's letter curiously ignored the greatest source
of conflict between himself and the Church after 1855, the matter of Indian relations. Perhaps he felt that his reports to Washington from Salt Lake City after the first harmonious weeks had
provided adequate information on this subject. According to this
earlier correspondence the Mormons, in violation of an act of
1834, had sent out a number of missionaries to cultivate the Indians, selecting for this task "rude and lawless young men, such
as might be regarded as a curse in any civilized community." The
purpose of this and other movements, the agent insisted, was to
ingratiate the Church with the tribes, to make a "distinction between *Mormons* and *Americans,* which was calculated to operate

to the prejudice of the interests and policy of the government toward them." [14] Having heard this sort of warning before from Brocchus and Holeman, the Government took the charges seriously. The Commissioner of Indian Affairs protested against the expense of Hurt's Indian farms, designed by the agent to counteract the Mormons' strategems; but when Buchanan's Administration finally resolved to send an expedition to Utah, the reports of Garland Hurt, like those of Surveyor General Burr, apparently influenced its decision.[15]

Unfortunately a significant passage in one of Hurt's letters was disregarded or overlooked: "[The Mormons] always have, and ever will thrive by persecution. They know well the effect it has upon them, and consequently crave to be persecuted." [16] Although the Church had not deliberately courted oppression in the past, it had nevertheless emerged from each encounter stronger than before. Gentiles who in 1857 and 1858 cried for a reduction of the sect's power would have been well advised to remember, as perhaps Hurt did, that the lynching at Carthage jail had only given the Mormons a valuable martyr and a new, more formidable leader.

Another significant prelude to hostilities concerned the carrying of the mails between Utah and the States, a vital matter to a people situated far from the frontier. In accordance with the procedure then followed, the Government awarded a contract for this service to the individual or company submitting the lowest bid. The Mormons had been displeased with the operation of the system, for the mails had often arrived late or had even been lost during the journey. Efficiency had not improved after 1854, when W. M. F. Magraw received the new four-year contract, and so unsatisfactory was his work that the Government after two years canceled his contract. This event gave the Mormons a chance to remedy the situation: if they could obtain the new contract, they might assure themselves of better service. Mass meetings were held to arouse public interest in the plan, and as a result one Hiram Kimball submitted a bid, ostensibly on behalf of himself alone; but when the Church learned that Kimball's estimate, approximately half that paid to Magraw, had won governmental approval, it proceeded enthusiastically to support the new project.[17]

Although Kimball had once been affluent in Nauvoo, his
finances in 1857 were not adequate to meet his new obligations,
and he accordingly sought help from William Hickman and Porter Rockwell. Brigham Young's ambitions, however, had by now
outgrown such a modest venture. He dreamed instead of a great,
Church-controlled company carrying not only the mail but all
goods between Utah and the States. Such an arrangement would
assure the Mormons prompt delivery as well as the opportunity
to inspect all official correspondence concerning the Territory; it
is possible that Young even hoped to use the company as an instrument to control the economic life of much of the West.
Whatever his objective, he took over Kimball's contract and
soon had created the "Brigham Young Express and Carrying Company," to accomplish his purposes.[18]

With some of the expenses defrayed by Church funds and the
rest borne by private subscription, the great undertaking began.
Hardy Mormons established way stations on the Plains and in the
mountains. At one depot a fort 320 feet square enclosing forty-two
buildings rose from the once barren ground; an irrigation ditch
was constructed and fifteen acres of land planted; sixty tons of
flour, supplies of grain, and some 200 head of cattle were assembled.[19] It was much the same story of frenetic activity at the
other stations. Then, before the "Y. X. Carrying Company," as it
was called, could start its operations, Hiram Kimball received a
letter from the Second Assistant Postmaster in Washington, dated
June 10, 1857, announcing the cancellation of his contract.[20] The
great transportation scheme had crashed to the ground.

This episode has a significant place among the events leading
to the Mormon War. It caused two Gentiles, Magraw and Thomas
Twiss (Indian agent for the Upper Platte River region) to write
letters highly critical of the Church which, added to the communications already received from Hurt, Burr, and Drummond, helped
to bring on the clash. On their side, the frustration of cherished
plans further embittered the Mormons, already hostile toward the
Government. What most aroused them was the excuse offered for
terminating Kimball's contract: that he had waited six months
to fulfill it. The mails bringing the official announcement of the
award had been delayed during the winter by impassable roads,

and the Y. X. Carrying Company had accordingly been unable to begin its full-scale operations until the following spring. This quibbling policy seemed to the Mormons only a cloak screening the Government's real purpose—to strike one more blow at them. As another result of the affair, the loss of the money poured into the enterprise, at least $125,000, perhaps much more, added to the Church's financial embarrassment when war finally came. And the whole incident revealed something about the Mormons and their leader. Here was a people, already taxed by the struggle to plant a settlement in an inhospitable region, who nevertheless willingly responded to an additional demand upon its energies from the Church; here also was a man whose dreams were spacious and whose authority was complete. Together they would be difficult to bring to terms.

Coincident with the failure of the Y. X. Carrying Company, the Mormons experienced difficulties with their federal officeholders. Burr and Hurt had become their outspoken enemies. In the case of other appointees the situation was often confused, so rapid was the succession of men. Almon W. Babbitt, who had replaced Ferris as secretary, was killed on the Plains in 1856 by marauding Indians.[21] His death was no great loss to the Latter-day Saints, for this bon vivant who had a taste for oysters, good liquor, and intrigue had always been too unmanageable for Brigham Young's autocratic policy. Rabid anti-Mormons, however, ascribed his murder, with those of Gunnison and Shaver, to the Danites, and thus heightened feeling in the East against the Saints. The next secretary, William H. Hooper, was more amenable to the dictates of the Church, which used him first as an intermediary with the Gentiles and then as Utah's delegate to Congress in 1859. But the Government, after sending Hooper his commission in 1856, refused six months later to recognize his appointment as legal. It was the same story with the marshal, Joseph L. Heywood. A polygamous Mormon, he was acceptable to the Hierarchy; the Administration, however, removed him after a very brief tenure in 1856 and subjected his accounts to close scrutiny.[22] With reason, Brigham Young complained of the absence of territorial officials to Thomas L. Kane, the Mormons' unofficial ambassador in the East.[23]

Although after 1854 the Mormons reckoned on the hostility of
two of their federal judges, they accepted the third, John F.
Kinney, as decidedly favorable to them. In Iowa, where he had
served as a member of the supreme court, he had come to be
known as a "Jack Mormon," a Gentile friendly to the Church.[24]
Since he appeared to carry these sympathies to Utah, he was castigated by anti-Mormons as a besotted, pompous, slow-witted tool
of Brigham Young, and was rewarded by the Saints with several
honors.[25] Both the Mormons and their critics, however, erred
greatly in their evaluation of Kinney: his outward behavior in
Utah, as well as his offer in 1858 to "render essential service" to
the Church during its crisis with the nation, were acts of duplicity. Like Hurt and Burr, he sent angry dispatches to the Government. He condemned Utah's probate courts as devices to deny
justice to the Gentile, and he spoke of his fear of "personal violence at the hands of some of these assassins." In the critical
months before Buchanan's ultimate decision to send an army to
the Territory, he informed Attorney General Jeremiah Black:
"The Mormons are inimical to the Government of the U.S. and
to all its officers who are not of their peculiar faith." They had
beaten up Joseph Troskolawsski (see above, p. 46), he said, had
tried to arrange the murder of Hurt and Burr, and were guilty
of other crimes.[26]

The Mormons had no cause to misunderstand the nature of
Judge W. W. Drummond, who became to them as much an object
of execration as Col. Robert Ingersoll to the Fundamentalists. In
the first thirty lines of an editorial in the *Millennial Star*, the
Church's publication in England, Drummond was branded an
"infamous scoundrel and dastardly wretch," a "beastly criminal,"
"horrible monster," "black-hearted judge," "poor wretch," "lying, adulterous, murderous fiend," "loathsome specimen of humanity," and a number of additional names falling into various
categories of iniquity.[27] As was their practice with their enemies,
they investigated his past for evidences of turpitude, even sending
one red-faced Saint to a house "of known bad character" in Washington for painful interviews with "the woman who kept it" and
with its boarders.[28] Until 1885 they followed his downward career,
carefully noting in their records his conviction for fraud, indictment for perjury, and at last his sentence in New York to a house

of correction for stealing stamps from a mail box in order to get enough money for a drink.[29]

Although the Mormons' research into Drummond's former conduct occasionally took them into unfamiliar byways of society, it was not difficult for them to establish the facts of his unrighteousness, since the judge was as unsavory as any man appointed to office in Utah by a thoughtless Administration. Only in 1857, when anti-Mormons belabored the Saints with any weapon available, were a few voices raised to speak well of the man; otherwise all who knew him or who later wrote of the Territory's early history agreed in general with the *Millennial Star's* evaluation.[30] On going to Utah he deserted his wife and children and took with him a prostitute from Washington, whom he occasionally seated beside him during court sessions. It seems equally certain that he bragged of his great desire for money and highly probable that he used his position to make it by unscrupulous methods.[31] Judge Kinney, despite his secret antagonism to the Church, urged the removal of Drummond, "who, although an anti-Mormon, is in consequence of his immoral conduct . . . entirely unworthy of a place upon the bench." [32] Years later an Illinois judge remembered that the state's lawyers who were acquainted with him before his elevation to Utah's supreme court considered his appointment "an imposition" upon the Mormons and did not blame them for treating him severely.[33]

Once in the Territory Drummond outraged the community with his behavior. The Mormons under any circumstance were sensitive to criticism of their polygamous practices, but they reacted with especial heat when condemnation came from an open libertine. His squabble with a Mormonized Jew, resulting in a suit against the judge for assault, heightened the general contempt felt for him. But it was his official actions rather than his extracurricular conduct that most infuriated the Mormons. He began to strike boldly at the heart of the Church's authority by attacking the jurisdiction of the probate courts, which by a territorial law of 1852 had come to include civil and criminal cases. Shortly after his arrival he advised a grand jury to investigate the records of these courts and, if it found evidence of illegal activity, to indict both the judges and the juries involved. Drummond was the first federal official publicly to challenge the Mormons' peculiar

judiciary system, and the Church recognized in the attack a
serious peril to one of its front-line defenses against Gentile interference.[34]

It was, however, as a writer of letters that Drummond seriously
endangered the Saints; while still in the Territory he joined Kinney, Hurt, and other officers in warning Pierce and his cabinet
against the wickedness of the Church.[35] And the composition of
these communications served only as a preparatory exercise to a
more significant appeal by the judge once he had returned to the
East early in 1857. A new Administration was now in office and
Drummond was prepared to give it the benefit of his advice in its
formulation of a policy toward the Mormons. His letter of resignation of March 30, 1857, to Attorney General Jeremiah S. Black,
enclosed with a letter of April 2 that named substantiating witnesses to his charges, was a major factor in the precipitation of
the war.

Drummond's accusations moved from the general to the specific. His first two paragraphs repeated what many Gentiles had
said before, that Brigham Young ruled his Territory with a despotism the more intolerable for its pretense to divine sanction,
and that his Church, secretly sworn to "resist the laws of the country," was a "blind and treasonable organization." A third paragraph spoke of a secret group in Utah, presumably the Danites,
instructed "to take the lives and property of persons who may
question the authority of the Church." In the fourth and fifth
sections of his arraignment Drummond charged the Mormons
with inflicting cruel indignities upon representatives of the
United States and with destroying the records of the courts upon
the orders of Young. This broad summary of Mormon wrongdoing closed with a paragraph worthy of quotation, since its violent language and its denunciations, both reminiscent of Perry
Brocchus, were characteristic of the Gentiles' polemic writings at
this time: "the Federal officers are daily compelled to hear the
form of the American government traduced, the chief executives
of the nation, both dead and living, slandered and abused from
the masses, as well as from the leading members of the Church,
in the most vulgar, loathsome, and wicked manner that the evil
passions of men can possibly conceive."

His general indictment concluded, Drummond proceeded to

list definite crimes committed by the Mormons: they had imprisoned a number of innocent men without trial, and, worse, were directly implicated in the murders of Gunnison, Shaver, and Babbitt. At the end of his long letter to Black, Drummond submitted his suggestion for the solution of the crisis in Utah: "I do believe that, if there was a man put in office as governor of that Territory, who is not a member of the church, (Mormon), and he supported with a *sufficient* military aid, much good would result from such a course." Although Buchanan's Administration failed to choose the judge for that role, as he evidently hoped it would, it did take cognizance of his letter and ultimately followed his suggested plan.[36]

The third member of the supreme court, with Kinney and Drummond, was George P. Stiles. In earlier days he had been prominent in the Church, as a city councillor in Nauvoo and, with Babbitt, one of the men who advised Joseph Smith in his ill-starred decision to destroy the *Expositor* in 1844.[37] More recently, however, he had turned away from the faith and had been excommunicated. Like the appointment of a profligate to high office in Utah, the selection of an apostate as United States judge could only increase political strife in Utah. Furthermore, Stiles, like Drummond, was determined to defend the federal courts against the attacks of the Mormons. His stay in the Territory was to be a short and a stormy one.

While Drummond labored to reduce the powers of the probate courts, Stiles sought in another fashion to check the Mormons' autonomous inclinations. Since the United States marshal was usually a Gentile, the legislature had created the post of territorial marshal and had given to it jurisdiction in all matters pertaining to the domestic affairs of Utah, which comprised the vast majority of legal business. In this way the Hierarchy hoped to have a reliable churchman empowered to serve writs, make arrests, and perform other important functions, and thus to weaken the authority of the district courts. Stiles found this improvisation objectionable and accordingly issued a ruling from the bench that the United States marshal should be the executive officer in the district courts during territorial as well as federal cases.[38]

The decision brought the Mormons, already heated by the actions of other officials, to an ugly emotional pitch, and scenes of violence resulted. Several lawyers, with the usually even-tempered James Ferguson as their leader, entered Stiles' court and threatened him with physical harm if he should continue his offensive behavior. When he appealed to Brigham Young for protection, the Governor told him to close his court if he could not enforce the law.[39] Further defiance was soon to follow. On the night of December 29, 1856, a mob broke into Stiles' office, in which were kept the records of his court as well as his books and those of Thomas S. Williams, a colorful merchant and lawyer recently excommunicated from the Church. The raiders removed everything. When Stiles, Hurt, and others arrived on the scene they found what seemed to be the entire contents of the office burning in the backyard privy. Williams merely bemoaned the loss of his valuable law library, but Stiles was enraged at the destruction of his books and records, for they were the property of the Government.[40] He promptly left for Washington, where with Drummond he offered these occurrences as proof that the people of Utah were in open rebellion against the United States.

There is considerable doubt as to what was burned in the privy that night. Governor Alfred Cumming and Indian Agent Jacob Forney, when they were trying desperately to establish good relations with the Mormons after the end of the war, stated in 1858 that they had accounted for the records, books, and all other articles once in Stiles' possession.[41] So far as the law books were concerned, these men were in error: Tom Williams and Judge Charles Sinclair, who replaced Stiles, later reported the disappearance of many of them, a declaration substantiated by a number of correspondents for eastern newspapers. Garland Hurt, an eye witness to the affair, saw the conflagration and later examined some of the partly burned volumes.[42] There remained the more serious matter of the court records. Stiles assumed that they, too, had been consumed in the unusual incinerator, and Drummond affirmed this in his letter to Black. Apparently feeling that if the one accusation by Drummond could be proved false his entire indictment would collapse, the Church produced many affidavits from men who had inspected the papers and had found none missing.[43]

The evidence is overwhelming that the Mormons, in the course of their backyard antics, did not burn the court records, but rather

placed them in safekeeping. All of their protestations of innocence in this matter, however, befog the central point: they had
violently disrupted the functioning of a court of the United States
by driving a federal judge from his bench, closing his court, and
destroying books owned by the federal government. Although
they had not simultaneously destroyed official papers, they had
certainly stolen them and had secreted them so thoroughly that
their whereabouts remained a mystery for over a year. During
this episode the governor of the Territory, offering neither protection nor comfort to the judge, mocked his impotency in the
face of a hostile community. The appointment of Stiles, the
apostate, to a high position in Utah had been unwise, and his attempt to tamper with the people's judicial arrangements, if le-
gally justified, was foolhardy. Yet these circumstances did not
easily excuse the Mormons, and the Church as an accessory, of
lawless behavior. For years Gentiles in Utah had charged the
Saints with subversive desires, and eastern public opinion tended
to support the Gentiles, despite their flimsy and often fabricated
evidence. Now the people of Utah had engaged in an activity
close to rebellion. In so doing they had given their enemies in the
East, and the Administration as well, a suitable pretext for armed
intervention in Utah.[44]

By the early part of 1857 all the important Gentile officers of
the Territory with the exception of Garland Hurt were back in
the States circulating their complaints against the Mormons. Some
went to Washington, where they urged the Government to curb
the insurrection in Utah; some concentrated on winning public
support for their position. The Church had always attributed
much of its trouble with the nation to the work of "scribblers,"
men who sought to turn the country against it. In Drummond it
had the perfect example. Over his own name he wrote many vitriolic letters to the press, repeating the charges contained in his
letter of resignation and adding new ones, such as the presence in
Utah of many illegally naturalized aliens. In addition to these
communications, the newspapers of the day carried a number of
letters signed "Verastus" which in content and style bore evidence
of Drummond's hand.[45]

These activities produced the desired result on public opinion.
Except in a few scattered cases [46] the nation's editors were pre-

pared to accept without question the truth of the late officeholders' reports. Since Drummond had made the most sensational charges, the press paid him the greatest attention. Some printed his letter of resignation in its entirety; others expanded upon certain portions of it: the Mormons' implication in the murder of Gunnison, their hatred for the country, and the rest.[47] But the experiences of the other officials also received consideration in the newspapers. Editors expressed a sense of shock at the treatment given David H. Burr and his surveyors by the people of Utah. They were even more incensed at the destruction of Stiles' court, for they interpreted this act as open defiance of the federal government.[48] In general, they agreed with a California editor's grandiloquent reflection upon the significance of these events, that the behavior of the Mormons was "enough to rouse the ire of every honest American heart, and thrill us with horror to think that such a foul stain blots the fair land which we rejoice to call our birthright." [49]

On July 24, 1857, the Saints held their annual celebration of Pioneers' Day at the head of Big Cottonwood Canyon, some twenty-five miles southeast of Salt Lake City and 10,000 feet above sea level. For weeks before the event those whom the Hierarchy had designated worthy of invitation had made their arrangements and had readied their wagons for the long trip. It was a gala occasion. Five bands played for the 2,500 merrymakers. Elements of the Utah militia added color to the crowd. There were speeches on the glory of the Church, and evening dancing. Suddenly four travel-worn men, one of whom had ridden the long road from Eastern Kansas, rushed upon the scene with the information that a new governor, with a large military escort, was on his way to establish Gentile rule over Utah.

It is a part of the Mormons' folklore that the people participated in their Pioneers' Day revelry innocently unaware of the Government's plan to accomplish their destruction. The grimy couriers, it would seem, had played the part of Pheidippides before the battle of Marathon. In reality the leaders of the Church could not have been greatly surprised at the ominous news. They had known of the hostile attitude toward them in the East, and Brigham Young, always remarkably astute, surely must have anticipated an explosion when Drummond and Stiles reached the

States. In the early months of 1857, it is true, their speeches and writings carried little apprehension for the future, and Young even expected Buchanan to become as great a friend of his people as Fillmore had been. But by the end of June at the latest Young was cognizant of impending trouble, for at that time he wrote Kane of the possibility of armed intervention in Utah. Throughout July spokesmen for the Church referred—at times plaintively, on other occasions resolutely—to a possible clash with the forces of the United States.[50]

Whatever warning the Saints may have had, the fact remains that after seven turbulent years relations between the Territory and the nation seemed about to dissolve in civil war.

4. Causes of the War

ON JANUARY 27, 1858, the House of Representatives requested President Buchanan to furnish it with information concerning the war in Utah. At the moment the expedition which had been sent to the Territory six months earlier was huddled in tents and other makeshift shelters near Fort Bridger, with the snows and cold of a mountain winter cutting it off from entrance into the Salt Lake Basin or even from reinforcements across the Plains. There was considerable anxiety in the East whether the army could survive until the spring thaws, for during the fall campaign the Mormons had burned three provision trains. Public opinion, once highly favorable to the plan of imposing military occupation on Utah, was now sharply divided, and some editors had begun to criticize the Administration for involving the country in an expensive, foolhardy, and ill-planned adventure. Congressmen accordingly wanted to know not only what course the "war" had followed but also why Buchanan had felt it necessary to send any military escort with the new governor to the Territory of Utah.

In obedience to the congressional mandate cabinet members searched their files, and in due time the President was able to submit a bulky dossier of official correspondence and private communications accusing the Mormons of objectionable activities over a period of many months.[1] The collection was a hodge-podge of both significant and irrelevant material. It included some letters the Administration must have received after it had already commanded troops to march upon Salt Lake City. It also contained documents that initially had been given little attention in Washington. And it omitted important dispatches from recent officials describing their unhappy experiences in Utah. The compilation therefore did not include all the information "which gave rise to the military expedition ordered to Utah Territory," as the House had requested; it merely showed that the President and his cabinet, placed under the necessity of explaining an embarrassing situation, had been able to uncover quite a few communications critical of the Mormons' uncooperative behavior in the past.

To exclude extraneous elements from the causes of the Administration's warlike policy toward Utah, one must first discover when its decision was reached. It is a difficult task, for Buchanan kept his purposes secret as long as he could.[2] Since in his inaugural address of March 4, 1857, he made no reference to difficulties in Utah, he apparently entered office unaware of a situation in that Territory which, almost four years before the firing on Fort Sumter, challenged the authority of the federal government. Yet during the next two weeks he began to consider the desirability of removing Brigham Young from office; by the end of April the press, having accepted a change in Utah's executive office as inevitable, was speculating upon the name of the appointee.[3]

As he pondered the selection of a new governor, Buchanan was compelled to consider the necessity of supplying that man with effective military support, in view of the treatment recently accorded federal judges in the Territory. Although on April 4 General Harney was ordered to move from Florida to Fort Leavenworth—the logical mobilization point for any expedition to Utah—it is likely that affairs in Bleeding Kansas rather than Salt Lake City dictated the transfer. Through the rest of April the Administration made no final decision about a possible escort for the new governor, but on May 8 the New York *Herald* announced that the President had determined to send an army to Utah in order to preserve peace. Although the story revealed the trend of Buchanan's thought, it was premature, for the army's official correspondence did not contain orders for such a campaign until the last week in the month. Since it is unlikely that the President would have delayed the issuance of these orders once his mind had been made up, it is probable that his decision came on or about May 20.[4]

When Buchanan requested his cabinet officers to gather correspondence justifying his policy toward Utah, the Secretary of State, old Lewis Cass, could locate only one document in his files, but it was a dandy. It came from W. M. F. Magraw, whose hatred

of the Mormons had been heightened by loss of his mail contract
to Hiram Kimball.[5] At considerable length Magraw charged the
Saints with crimes against the laws of the nation and humanity.
According to his letter the Church had destroyed all non-Mormon
courts in the Territory, thus leaving the Gentiles to the mercy of
"a so-styled ecclesiastical organization, as despotic and damnable,
as any ever known to exist in any country." The result was violence and murder by "an organized band of bravos and assassins";
"indiscriminate bloodshed, robbery and rapine" at midnight or in
full daylight. Along with other anti-Mormons, Magraw insisted
that the members of this sect were dangerously unlike the gener-
ality of mankind: "Many of the inhabitants of the Territory possess passions and elements of character calculated to drive them
to extremes." [6] Such was the letter that Cass transmitted to Buchanan. But there is doubt that Magraw's vitriolic dispatch influenced the Administration's decision to send the army against the
Saints. Written in October 1856 and addressed merely "Mr. President," it appears to have been directed to Pierce, who then occupied the office. It was an excellent document to offer in explanation of the display of force against Utah, but the Secretary of State
may have seen it for the first time six months after hostilities had
begun.

Like Cass, Jeremiah S. Black could not find many papers in his
files to defend the Administration's policy, but he did have Drummond's two communications, which had caused a greater public
sensation than any other attack upon the Mormons. Although
Buchanan and his advisors may not have read all the documents
later transmitted to Congress, it is patent that they had studied
this judge's report with attentive care, for Buchanan's annual
message of December 8, 1857, described the situation in the Territory in words closely approximating those used by Drummond,[7]
whose communications accordingly deserved a place in the President's reply to Congress.

The Secretary of the Interior, Jacob Thompson, could supply
Buchanan with a bulkier dossier than could Cass or Black, for his
department included the General Land Office, which had heard
frequently and at length from the outraged surveyor general,
David H. Burr. Commissioner Thomas A. Hendricks gathered together nine letters pertaining to Burr's troubles in Utah, the ex-

periences of his assistants, and other aspects of the strife over public land in Utah. A few of the dispatches had reached Washington much later than the end of May, but Hendricks included these items with the earlier ones as if the Administration had considered them, too, before it decided to use force against the Mormons. The Commissioner also neglected to note, when he submitted the letters to Thompson, that he had received many charges of malfeasance against Burr and had summarily removed him from his position. Yet some of Burr's reports furnished the cabinet with timely reasons for chastizing the Mormons.[8]

Charles E. Mix, Commissioner of Indian Affairs, contributed much to the defense of the Administration's policy by drawing upon the letters and reports of agents who had clashed with Brigham Young. From Henry R. Day's dispatches of 1852 he produced evidence that the Mormons not only mistreated the Indians but also were abusive toward the Government and its representatives. Holeman's correspondence was another rich mine of anti-Mormonism, and in his letter to the Secretary of the Interior, Mix called Thompson's attention to many choice passages. But Garland Hurt had provided the office of the Commissioner with the best reasons for intervening in Utah, for he had most vigorously attacked the Church's authoritarian government and had introduced the suspicion that it was diligently stirring up local tribes against the United States.

Mix's assortment of documents formed an impressive indictment of the Saints for subversion, near rebellion, and similar crimes. They may not, however, have received appropriate consideration when Buchanan's cabinet was weighing the choice of alternative policies toward Utah. Mix learned from Thompson on January 30, 1858, that the President wished to be given a collection of all important materials relative to the Mormon problem in order to answer the request of Congress. The Commissioner did not submit his discoveries until February 22.[9] If the Administration had studied these documents during its deliberations on affairs in Utah, they should have been more readily assembled. Since it took Mix three weeks to locate and read the documents, apparently he and his superiors were unfamiliar with them.[10] Another weakness of Mix's collection of letters as evidence of Buchanan's reasons for making war is its inclusion of four letters from Thomas S. Twiss, Indian agent in the Upper Platte region. These dispatches, which maintained that the Mormons had expelled Indians from their lands while establishing way stations for their overland mail system, seemed at the time, and even later, to have played a significant part in the formulation of the Administration's policy. Yet Twiss did not write them until the advance detachment of the army was preparing to leave Fort Leavenworth.[11]

The correspondence sent to Congress in February 1858 is therefore not a completely reliable guide to the information which persuaded Buchanan and his advisors to assume a belligerent posture toward Utah. While some of the documents had undoubtedly been given close scrutiny in the spring of 1857, others had been overlooked, and a few had not reached Washington in time to exert any influence whatever upon the Government. It is also puzzling that the President's cabinet did not consult, or present for congressional examination, a number of dispatches pertinent to the need for a display of military power in Utah. In 1855 Steptoe had written two letters accusing the Mormons of tampering with the Indians, but Mix had not sent them to Thompson with the reports of Day, Holeman, and Hurt. The office of the Attorney General had at least five anti-Mormon communications from Judge John F. Kinney, but none appeared in Black's small collection—an especially surprising omission, since Kinney had written two of the letters in early 1857 at the request of Black himself.[12]

In another way Buchanan's report to Congress is an incomplete statement of the causes of the expedition. Including as it does only the written messages of territorial officials, it makes no reference to personal interviews the Administration had held with some of these men. Drummond arrived in Washington during May 1857 and talked with several governmental officers. The nature of his earlier letters is proof that he would use whatever influence he could muster to brand the Mormons traitorous villains, and his desire for the governorship undoubtedly increased his energetic lobbying. With Drummond in Washington were Stiles, Burr, and many other erstwhile officeholders in Utah, possibly including Kinney, all eager to reinforce their written complaints with personal accounts of the Mormons' perfidy. Stiles later took much of the credit for having precipitated the Mormon War. When he wrote Black in 1859 requesting a political appointment in Carson Valley, he said: "And it does appear to me that I have a righteous claim to an official position there, seeing that I was one of the Fathers of the Military Expedition." [13]

Whatever the explanation given after the event, the Administration had unquestionably come to the conclusion in May 1857 that Utah's defiance of the United States demanded stern measures. The conviction was often repeated in important official communications. The War Department's orders to Gen. William S. Harney and Cass' instructions to the new governor, Alfred Cumming, both accused the Saints of unruliness. After the army had started across the Plains, Jeremiah Black, summarizing the problems Buchanan had faced upon assuming office, reflected that Utah, with Kansas, had been "in a state of organized and open rebellion against the laws."

Further evidence of the Administration's attitude on the eve of the war came in subsequent papers. The statements in Buchanan's first annual message concerning the ecclesiastical despotism, fanaticism, and illegal Indian policy of the Mormons all carried against the people of Utah the charge of rebellion. Secretary of War John B. Floyd, the Government's most vigorous exponent of the forceful suppression of the Saints, agreed with the President in his own annual report. Finally, when Buchanan issued his proclamation of pardon to the Saints in 1858, he referred to the expulsion of federal officers, disruption of the courts, and other forms of misbehavior as evidence of "insubordination" in the Territory.[14]

In assessing the factors that led to the ordering of armed forces to Utah, one is well advised to observe the part played by ignorance and misinformation. In the spring of 1858, after the expedition had suffered through a severe winter at Fort Bridger with insufficient provisions, the Washington *Union* felt called upon to defend the Administration from charges of incompetence imperiling the lives of the soldiers. The *Union* stated that the preparation for the campaign had been thorough, that everything had been done to anticipate the crises of the fall and winter. "The common error of despising one's enemy has not been committed in a single particular with reference to the Mormons," the pro-Buchanan editor wrote. "The story of the enemy's weakness and indisposition to fight has been properly disregarded." [15] Thus it was inferred that the lateness of the troops' departure in the summer of 1857, the Mormons' destruction of three supply trains, and the other misfortunes of the army during the campaign should not be charged to negligence on the part of the Government. Like portions of Buchanan's report to Congress in 1858, the *Union's* estimate was an inaccurate *ex post facto* justification.

In reality the President and his cabinet evidently hoped that Brigham Young did not intend to resist their demonstration and could not do so if he wished. The view of Utah's population in the East during 1857 was of a people oppressed by a religious tyranny and kept in submission only by some terroristic arm of the Church. Since Gentiles would not have accepted the rule of Brigham Young, they assumed that the Mormons themselves were discontented with the militant theocracy erected in a democratic nation. The Saints, these non-Mormons falsely reasoned, would not oppose the entrance of the army into their Territory; rather they would welcome it with open arms as a savior come to redeem them from a living hell. The introduction of polygamy, it was further assumed, must have fatally cracked the unity of the sect. Simply offer protection to all people who want to leave, one editor said. "This will cause a stampede among the women, and at once blow the Mormon Church to atoms or bring the Saints to terms." [16] There seemed to be a considerable amount of evidence to support these misconceptions. Hurt, Burr, and Drummond had all spoken of the Mormons' dissatisfaction with Brigham Young's satrapy and had declared that many Saints would welcome rescue. A number of editors took up the refrain. Only an occasional newspaper warned that the Mormons, by calling home their far-flung missions in San Bernardino and elsewhere, gave evidence of determined preparation for war.[17]

The Administration evidently foresaw scant possibility that the Mormons would offer resistance to the army. In his annual report at the end of 1857 Floyd apologetically said that he had considered the expedition completely equipped for its task. "It was hardly within the line of reasonable probability that these people would put themselves beyond the pale of reconciliation with the government by acts of unprovoked, open, and wanton rebellion." [18] Since Cass instructed the new governor to offer federal

protection to all in Utah who wished it, the President and the
Secretary obviously believed a large portion of the Territory's
population wished nothing more than to escape from the cruelties
of Mormondom. The idea died hard. As late as June 1858, when
the hostilities had been peacefully resolved, two representatives
of Buchanan's Administration reported that many Mormons were
unhappy and would flee Utah except for their fear of assassination
at the hands of the Danites.[19]

Misjudging the temper of the Mormons, the Administration
also ignored the difficulties confronting any armed demonstration
against them. Although the Rockies were known for their early
and severe winters, the Government delayed sending the first detachment of men so long that these troops had need of good luck
and a speedy trip in order to reach Salt Lake City before snow
blocked the mountain passes. They were not that lucky. Furthermore, the War Department expected the soldiers to find ample
provisions and forage once they had reached Utah, an incredible
misreading of the Mormons' intentions.[20] Only in the fall of 1857
did the Administration learn from Capt. Stewart Van Vliet,
who had been sent to Utah ahead of the army to arrange with the
Mormons for supplies, that the people, aggressively hostile to the
expedition, would give it nothing if it ever reached them.[21] Thus,
although the primary cause of the decision to use force in Utah
was the desire to punish the Mormons for their rebellious behavior, the President reached this decision the more readily because of his failure to discern any serious obstacle on the road to
Salt Lake City.

The Government's ignorance, like that of the majority of Gentiles, was inexcusable. True, the winter of 1856–57 had held up
the mails between Salt Lake City and the East, thus limiting
Washington's intelligence to the reports of such dubious authorities as Drummond. It was also true that some discontent did exist
in Utah, for the Church Historian noted the departure of a number
of apostates in April 1857.[22] But the Gentile view of the Mormons
as a mass of restless, ill-suppressed people was wishful thinking.
No Danite band could have restrained the flight of freedom-loving
men from a Territory possessed of many exits; yet a flood of emigrants poured *into* Utah each year, with only a trickle of renegades ebbing back. The devotion of the Mormons to their Church

was best disclosed not in the scattered letters of Drummond and Hurt but in the Saints' wholehearted sacrifices for the Brigham Young Express and Carrying Company.

It would not have been difficult for Buchanan to inform himself of the situation in Utah. During the affair of the Runaways five years earlier Bernhisel had wisely urged that an investigating commission be sent before an anti-Mormon policy was adopted, and the suggestion was equally valid in 1857. But in this latter crisis the Government was disposed to accept "rumors and reports" as true. By rushing into the adventure of an armed demonstration in the West, Buchanan laid himself open to the legitimate accusation that he had not even inquired into the facts before angrily seeking to punish the people of Utah. As a result he later found himself in the embarrassing position of sending the army in 1857 and a peace commission in 1858, instead of performing these actions in a reverse order. In the far graver crisis of 1860 and 1861 the President became vascillating and distraught. His resolution of 1857, if carried over into the emergency three years later, might not have prevented secession, but it is certain that a little hesitancy before the start of the Utah War would have spared him a good deal of discomfiture.

It is difficult one hundred years after the war to evaluate some of the other factors which were said to have shared in its origin. Partisan controversy had become so bitter that reckless charges against men in political life were made with irresponsible frequency. In this atmosphere members of both political parties and editors of the nation's newspapers sought to indict Buchanan's Administration for colossal misbehavior, and they often found in the conflict materials useful to this purpose. The President and his cabinet, they insisted, had plunged the country into an adventure with the Mormons for ulterior purposes, not merely to bring rebellious citizens to an observance of the law. Thus in 1858 two newspapers accused Buchanan of being less concerned with the Saints than with the dream of seizing Sonora and other parts of Mexico.[23] It is true that the President had expressed an interest in western America; Secretary of War Floyd, a prime mover behind the Utah expedition, may also have acquired the spirit of manifest destiny from his father, who as early as 1821 had advocated in Congress the settlement and territorial organization of Oregon.[24]

Yet idle speculation rather than knowledge was responsible for the insistence that secret, expansionist motives lay behind Buchanan's policy toward Utah, since by no statement or action did the President at any time display designs upon land lying southwest of the nation. In 1857 the Mormons, not the Mexicans, occupied his attention.

Another explanation of the Mormon War—advanced with vigor for many years—centered upon John B. Floyd and concerned the growing rift between the North and the South. According to this interpretation, Floyd and his Southern sympathizers in Washington, traitors first and last, saw in an involvement of the United States with the Mormons an opportunity to advance their treasonable purposes. Fearing a Republican victory in the 1860 election, they were determined, it would seem, to bankrupt the treasury by a costly expedition to Utah and thus leave the North financially incapable of opposing secession.[25] Other investigators accused the Secretary of scattering the nation's military forces, again with the objective of rendering the North powerless to preserve the Union if its partisans should gain control of the Government.[26] Taking a different approach but still assuming Floyd's perfidy, a Mormon publication accused him of trying to distract the attention of patriots from various of his nefarious schemes.[27]

During the secession crisis Northern congressmen came to have a low opinion of Floyd. After he had relinquished his cabinet position late in December 1860, a number of representatives accused him of having recently transferred arms from Northern to Southern arsenals in order to strengthen the South's military power, a charge soon repeated by implication in an investigating committee's report. In calmer days, however, men noted that Floyd had transferred obsolete weapons and had taken the action only after failing to dispose of them through public sale.[28]

Similarly, the accusation that Floyd, and indirectly Buchanan himself, had provoked the Mormon War as a means of destroying the nation is a product of heated or cloudy thinking. It appears to draw its strength from two coincidental circumstances, Floyd's enthusiastic advocacy of the Utah expedition and his later support of the South in the Civil War. Such reasoning uses guilt by chronological association. Furthermore, it ignores certain facts.

When the Government ordered an army to Utah in 1857 Buchanan and Floyd had little reason to fear the imminence of the
Civil War. The Democratic party seemed powerful in the nation,
and the Administration contained a majority of Southern sympathizers. Not until the congressional election of 1858 did the
party suffer a defeat serious enough to raise the fear of a Black
Republican victory in the next presidential campaign. If Floyd
and Buchanan had indeed been motivated by a desire to weaken
the North when they sent 2,500 troops to Utah, they should in
1858 have sent even more men to the remote Salt Lake Basin. It
could have been easily done, for early in that year the Government had already mobilized and dispatched another large detachment to Utah. It is significant that, rather than scatter these additional troops in the Rocky Mountain West, the Administration
arranged a peaceful settlement of the Mormon question, recalled
the reinforcements, and later reduced the size of the garrison in
Utah. Finally, Floyd was not a hot-headed Southerner. Like other
Virginians he was greatly troubled by the crisis before the Civil
War, and he opposed secession until December of 1860.[29] It is
therefore unlikely that he was working clandestinely to destroy
the Union as early as 1857.

To some observers, Gentile and Mormon, the Utah War was
less a secessionists' plot than a vast boondoggling scheme on the
part of John B. Floyd and certain businessmen. Even before the
hostilities in Utah had been pacifically settled, the incident became known as the "Contractors' War." When the expedition
bogged down in the snows near Fort Bridger—and later, when
the whole military maneuver changed in appearance from a gallant march against rebellious fanatics to the uninteresting occupation of a remote Territory—some editors began to wonder aloud
why the Government had sent troops to Utah in the first place.
Conveniently forgetting their earlier wrath at the Mormons, they
now studied the great costs of the campaign and persuaded themselves that they had been incurred merely to enrich the company
supplying the army with provisions and transportation. Since the
Mormons refused to admit their own actions as a cause of the conflict, they also seized upon this convenient explanation of the
episode. "Who has this enormous expenditure of public funds
benefited," the Deseret News demanded, "except it be army con-

tractors, speculators and depraved politicians?" So great was the
public clamor over possible corruption that the House of Representatives in April 1858 asked the Secretary of War to transmit all
contracts arising from the expedition.[30]

Instead of disappearing after 1858, the charges of fraud continued to be pressed as the basic cause of the Mormon War. Historians of the Latter-day Saints have made much of this interpretation.[31] They could draw encouragement from Lt. Gen.
Winfield Scott, the commander in chief, who later wrote: "The
expedition set on foot by Mr. Secretary Floyd, in 1857, against the
Mormons and the Indians about Salt Lake was, beyond a doubt,
to give occasion for large contracts and expenditures, that is, to
open a wide field for fraud and peculation." [32] Much more recently an eminent student of this period reinforced Scott's verdict
by noting that "army contracts, made during recent Indian difficulties in Florida, were running out and the contractors wanted
to switch their profits to Utah." [33]

At this distance it seems to have been true that the Mormon
War was accompanied by a considerable degree of fraud. The Administration awarded contracts without competitive bidding and
occasionally with an astonishing indifference to price; perhaps, as
one contemporary newspaper maintained, it also endeavored to
recruit support for its Kansas policy by permitting congressmen
to make lucrative profits from the sale of mules to the army.[34]
These facts, however, do not prove that greedy contractors, with
Floyd as their tool, engineered the war; rather they indicate only
that certain individuals were quick to take advantage of the situation once it had come about. None of the men, Mormon or Gentile, who accused the Administration of malfeasance offered substantiation for their charges. Even Scott apparently reached his
conclusion about Floyd's motives from "observing the desperate
characters who frequented the Secretary, some of whom had desks
near him," not from more serious evidence.[35]

One development would seem definitely to clear the principal
contractor involved in the struggle of any implication in its origin. In February 1857 the firm of Russell, Majors, and Waddell
had signed a contract with the Government to supply the military
posts in the western part of the country. With this monopoly already established, it might well have lobbied diligently to pro-

duce the Mormon War, if it had been in a position to profit from it. But in fact William Russell was quite surprised when the War Department suddenly required his company to move three million pounds of materials to Utah. Since he objected to the order as bankrupting to his firm, it is apparent that neither he nor his associates had brought pressure upon Floyd to send an expedition against the Mormons.[36]

Unfortunately for the stability of his firm, Russell was correct in his initial reaction to the Government's requisition. Undertaking to transport too many supplies and meeting with great losses on the Plains, his company experienced a disaster from which it failed to recover. Its efforts to save itself subsequently brought embarrassment to Floyd, Jacob Thompson, and others. In serious financial difficulties as a result of its part in the war, the firm turned to Floyd for rescue. During the period between 1857 and 1860 the Secretary of War provided it with drafts amounting to $870,000, all of which were in the nature of a loan to Russell, Majors, and Waddell against the firm's future earnings. When the banks finally refused to honor these drafts, Russell persuaded a clerk in the Indian Bureau to take them and to give in exchange an equal amount in bonds held in trust for certain tribes. Commenting on this highly irregular transaction, a committee of the House of Representatives in a unanimous report of February 1861 declared Floyd's behavior "deceptive and fraudulent in character." Much later, in 1876, the Government sued Jacob Thompson for the money lost, alleging that as Secretary of the Interior in the Buchanan Administration he was responsible for the misconduct of a clerk in his department. Long before that date, however, the company of Russell, Majors, and Waddell had collapsed, for Floyd's acceptances had not saved it after all. Thus the Utah War was no bonanza to contractors and unscrupulous cabinet members; instead, it brought ruin to some and trouble to others who had been connected with it.[37]

Another consideration, irrelevant to the formulation of a sound policy toward Utah, may be mentioned as a possible factor in the origins of the Mormon War. When his cabinet was debating the use of force against the Saints, Buchanan received a communication from a Southern leader proposing a way to divert the American people from their perilous absorption with slavery. On April

27, 1857, Robert Taylor wrote the President: "I believe that we can supersede the Negro-Mania with the almost universal excitements of an Anti-Mormon Crusade . . . Should you, with your accustomed grip, seize this question with a strong, fearless and resolute hand, the Country I am sure will rally to you with an earnest enthusiasm and the pipings of Abolitionism will hardly be heard amidst the thunders of the storm we shall raise." [38]

Buchanan may not have had Taylor's suggestion in mind when he approved the use of force against the Mormons. It is certain, however, that the slavery controversy, by precluding dispassionate meditation upon the state of affairs in Utah, helped to bring about the war. It has already been shown that early in the decade congressional opponents of slavery interjected that perplexing question into the debates of Mormonism. As the doctrine of popular sovereignty advanced by Douglas became a national focus of partisan argument, there were many who conjoined the Mormon question with it, thus further obstructing any real understanding of the situation in Utah. When Lincoln struck at Douglas' proposed solution to the issue of slavery, he advanced as one of his telling arguments the proposition: "If the people of Utah shall peacefully form a State Constitution tolerating polygamy, will the Democracy admit them into the union?" The Administration's Washington *Union,* instead of informing its readers about the Utah problem and Buchanan's attitude toward it, used the controversy as an instrument with which to belabor popular sovereignty, and also sought to link the Republicans' disregard of the fugitive slave law with Brigham Young's defiance of federal authority.[39]

The intrusion of these irrelevant elements should not becloud the fact that one major cause of the war was the Administration's conviction of the Mormons' rebelliousness. The Church's expulsion of such officers as Burr, Drummond, and Stiles, its efforts to overthrow the federal judicial system, and its Indian policy all seemed evidences of a riotous disposition which could not be tolerated without weakening the fabric of the Union. In one petition of their territorial legislature the Saints had declared that they would judge for themselves whether their federal officers merited obedience, and had added the significant statement that they would observe the enactments of Congress "so far as

they are applicable to our condition in our territorial capacity." [40]
The authority of the national government would have been seriously shaken if territorial peoples had appropriated the power to
decide for themselves what officials and laws were to be respected.

The mistreatment of non-Mormons in Utah seemed an ugly
part of this rebellious pattern. Not only did the Church occasionally try to interdict all commercial relations with them—it
openly warned Gentiles that to marry a Mormon was to invite
trouble.[41] Other events, such as the unpunished Parrish-Potter
murders and the experience of the Gladdenite apostates, further
revealed indifference to constitutional guarantees in Utah.

If the Latter-day Saints were frequently defiant of the Government and its representatives, they could advance arguments in
justification for their behavior. After their persecution by mobs
in Missouri and Illinois, they were apprehensive of any new assault. It appeared to them that the Government was continuing to
pursue a stony-hearted desire to injure them; like American colonists of the mid-eighteenth century, they considered themselves
the subjects of a remote and unfriendly power. Appropriations
from Congress were niggardly, when indeed they were made at
all. The Mormons' title to the land they occupied remained un-
clarified, a device, it seemed to them, designed to deprive them of
their very homes. Their petitions to Washington for statehood,
or at least for redress of crying evils, were received with contempt
or treated as political footballs by the defenders and opponents
of slavery.

But the Mormons' greatest complaint against the federal government, and their justification for their seemingly insubordinate
acts, was the quality of the officials sent to their Territory from
Washington. In the preceding pages we have seen the unwisdom
of some of these selections: the men were pompous, profligate,
prejudiced, or in other ways unworthy. Before the student accepts
this fact as an adequate explanation of the Church's behavior, he
must observe that the Government's representatives, while undesirable at times, were probably not so odious as they may at first
have seemed. Much of our information concerning these men
comes from the Mormons, who spared no effort to destroy the
reputations of their enemies. As an apostate later revealed, the
Saints used this method, together with bribery and blackmail, to

control intractable federal officers.[42] They accused Burr, Drummond, and Bridger of criminal activities. Possibly because their doctrines imposed upon them—although ineffectively, it must be noted—the avoidance of spirituous liquors, they suggested drunkenness more often than corruption as their enemies' moral flaw. In their writings Drummond, Hartnett, Stiles, Craig, Cradlebaugh, and other federal officers appear as besotted incompetents; if these reports are true, Judge Charles Sinclair's drunken body became a hazard to the pedestrians of Salt Lake City.[43] Had the Mormons divined John F. Kinney's secret opposition to them, it is likely that he, too, would have assumed a spongelike quality in their histories. Undoubtedly far too many of the federal officers were unsuited to their posts; it is conceivable, however, that the chief offense of some of those whom the Church denigrated was their outspoken criticism, not their disreputable character.

It is also proper to inquire whether the Mormons' mistreatment of federal representatives was justified even if those men were as depraved as the Church so painstakingly endeavored to prove. The disruption of Stiles' court and the theft of his records and books were acts of desperate violence. Garland Hurt believed, and there is evidence substantiating his fear, that his life would have been in danger if he had remained in the vicinity of Salt Lake City after the fall of 1857. The Mormons in these and other episodes revealed a fanatic determination to expel, or even to injure, men who held federal positions. Buchanan declared by his choice of documents to transmit to Congress in early 1858 that the Mormons' abuse of federal officials had caused him to send the army to Utah. It is not adequate to reply merely that these men were of inferior quality.

If some causes of the Mormon War are only dimly visible today, the part played by eastern public opinion is not. Throughout the 1850's, hostility toward the Latter-day Saints had increased until it approached unreasoning frenzy by mid-1857. The emotions of the decade provided fertile soil for such an outburst against the Church, for it was the period of the Know Nothing party's rise to temporary political importance by battening upon Americans' deep-rooted fears of aliens and Catholicism. Although this party did not turn its attention to the Mormons, its campaign against other fancied enemies prepared many people to abhor

that sect. When its spokesmen dwelt upon the peril of the immi-
grant to the American way of life, many listeners remembered
that a significant segment of Utah's population was composed of
recent recruits from abroad. The murderous, subversive plottings
charged to the Danites appeared similar to the Catholics' fancied
determination to prepare the United States for the arrival of the
Pope. The Gentiles' books depicting details of life in the Mormons' "harems" are remarkably akin to the "revelations" of spu-
rious monks and nuns that were a hallmark of the Protestant
Crusade during the early 1850's.

Hostility toward the Saints was all but universal in the eastern
states. One author called Mormonism "the most daring and dangerous conspiracy ever formed against the liberties of man"; after
describing the early sweep of Mohammedanism, "with the irresistible argument of the 'Koran or the sword,'" another asked
"whether the known aims of the successor of Joseph Smith may
not point to a similar destiny for this continent." [44] The Louisiana
Courier called Brigham Young "this horrid Mormon"; the New
York *Times* dilated upon his oppressive tyranny; and Greeley's
Tribune spoke of his followers as "ecstatico-religious, tyrannico-
politic, and poly-uxorial loafers." [45] If Buchanan had reason to
feel that the rebelliousness of the Saints demanded forceful correction, the inflamed public opinion made such a policy almost
mandatory in 1857. The editor of the New York *Times* summed
up the situation: "The general feeling of the people in the Union
in all sections, and of all sects and parties, is so decidedly adverse
to the Mormons that the government is not likely to be held to a
very strict account for its acts towards them, even though they
should be utterly exterminated." [46]

Through ignorance, Gentiles have frequently misunderstood
the Mormons. At different times this situation provoked friction
and occasionally persecution; in 1857 it produced war. Non-
Mormons were mystified by the Church's terminology and accordingly misinterpreted some of its nomenclature. Stakes (see above,
p. 6) were thought by some Gentiles to be the cells of spies, and
Seventies (one of the divisions of the priesthood) were regarded
as "secret religious societies" whose purpose was to murder apostates.[47] It is even possible that Brigham Young's title of President
was taken as evidence of the Mormons' intention to capture po-

litical domination of the country and place their leader in the highest executive office.[48] Motivated by wishful thinking, many editors also believed, as we have seen (p. 68), that discontent was spreading in the sect, that Brigham Young had fled for his life to California, and that the Church of Jesus Christ of Latter-day Saints was disintegrating.

One prominent Mormon, Jedediah M. Grant, remonstrated with Gentiles over their misconceptions of his brethren: "It is an error, the prevalent opinion that we all cleanse the nasal orifice with the big toe, and make tea with holy water." [49] It was a lost cause. So great was this popular, almost purposeful misunderstanding of the Saints that one newspaper editor led himself into a blind alley of reasoning. The Mormons, he said, must be unhappy in their Church, and yet here they were, in 1858, docilely following Brigham Young in an exodus from Utah, when the army was at the Territory's very portal, ready to deliver them from their ecclesiastical bondage.[50] Investigation would have convinced many that the Mormon men were overwhelmingly loyal to their faith, that their wives were not in all cases driven to madness by polygamy, and that the Church was not a mammoth conspiracy against American liberty. But Gentiles believed these things, and accordingly their support of an expedition against Utah gained strength.

Considering the available sources of information about Utah and Mormonism, one is not surprised that ignorance of the Church was widespread in the States during the 1850's. Quite frequently these sources were prejudiced to the point of worthlessness. A number of books had appeared, but the authors often seemed motivated more by a desire to exploit a popular issue than shed light.[51] Gentiles frequently obtained their knowledge from former federal officers who for one reason or another had carried away with them a deep animus against the Mormons. Although Benjamin Ferris' volume, for instance, contained some accurate statements, it was on the whole an unreliable portrayal of conditions in Utah. Two years later his wife produced a book strengthening the conviction that Mormon women *universally* suffered torments under the barbaric practice of polygamy.[52] Brocchus, Drummond, Magraw, and other enemies of the Church did not let any scrupulous concern for facts deter them from formulating a

sweeping indictment of the Mormons for countless crimes. Newspaper editors, to feed the demands of the American people for anti-
Mormon literature, also acted with a reprehensible disregard for
the truth. The New York *Herald,* the only influential paper to
sympathize with the Church in this period, noted in 1857 that
many of its competitors carried dispatches under a Salt Lake City
dateline at a time when none had a correspondent in Utah. All
these communications, it concluded, had been written East of the
Mississippi and were therefore wholly unreliable.[53]

Their information thus limited, Gentiles relied upon apostates
to instruct them concerning the mysteries of Mormonism, a group
not likely to promote understanding. Throughout their early history the Saints had found wayward brethren among their most
persistent enemies. As early as 1833 an excommunicated member
with the improbable name of Dr. Philastus Hurlbut had vented
his wrath upon his former fellows by collecting affidavits to document the follies of Joseph Smith's young manhood.[54] Disaffected
individuals later launched the short-lived Nauvoo *Expositor.*
When in 1850 Congress was debating the proposal to organize the
Salt Lake Basin as a state or a territory, it was a letter from William Smith, Joseph's younger brother, and Isaac Sheen which convinced many congressmen that the Church was a subversive organization pledged to destroy the nation.

In 1857 apostates continued their efforts to turn Gentile against
Mormon. Smith and Sheen were still describing the sect's leaders
as murderous, iniquitous villains when John Hyde's book, *Mormonism: Its Leaders and Designs,* appeared; it gained wide attention and reinforced the popular conviction that something had to
be done about the Territory. Many people considered it a fair
description of the Church. Lewis Cass had read it and President
Buchanan thought that is "contains much valuable information."
Hyde's lectures to crowded audiences in California further served
to increase hostility toward the Saints.[55] Frederick Margetson, another renegade, joined Hyde on the lecture circuit.[56] In their
time, these renegades were regarded by their Gentile audiences
as trustworthy authorities on Mormonism.

The Saints could therefore properly complain that animosity
toward them was in part the product of prejudice built upon
wildly inaccurate statements. Yet the leaders of the sect them-

selves contributed to the belief of non-Mormons that they were
indifferent to constitutional rights and callous toward the property and even the lives of Gentiles in Utah. The violent language
they frequently employed in public seemed to bear out these
convictions. When the editor of the *Deseret News* printed the
addresses of the Church's high priests, he tried to revise or elim-
inate passages that might have brought criticism upon his people.
He was not always thorough in this work: quite often, sentences
denouncing the Government and its representatives or threatening Gentiles with summary vengeance escaped his attention, and
in the sermons published in the *News* Brigham Young sometimes
spoke as a traitor to his nation and an inciter to crimes, Kimball
as a coarse-mouthed minion of his superior, and Grant as a reckless religious enthusiast. Undoubtedly the printed word was not
an accurate guide to the true character of these men. Sometimes
they chose their words primarily with regard to the immediate
effect upon their audiences; on occasion they, like Perry Brocchus,
may have been carried away by their eloquence. It made no difference to anti-Mormons; newspapers used the remarks to document
the need for a campaign against them, and the antipathy of at
least one congressman toward the Church was aroused by the
extravagant words of Young as reported in the *News*.[57]

There is no doubt that the Saints' practice of polygamy was
another potent force inflaming the Gentiles against Mormonism.
While there is some evidence that Joseph Smith embarked upon
this peculiar, one might say hazardous, marital program before
1843, he did not produce his revelation from God establishing it
as a doctrine of the Church until that year. For a time the leaders
of the faith kept their plural marriages secret, but in 1852 Brigham Young permitted Orson Pratt, the Mormons' scientist-
theologian, to announce them to the world. The Church's explanation of "The Principle," as plural marriage came to be
called, was an intricate one, postulating the existence of innumerable spirits that were awaiting human bodies to occupy on
this earth during their progression to the worlds of eternal bliss.
Thus it became the duty of men and women to procreate taber-
nacles of flesh for these spirits to use. It was also maintained that
a woman could be saved only through marriage, and further that

a man's reward in the afterlife would be the more glorious if
he had many children to rule, concepts which encouraged celestial
as well as terrestrial marriage.

After Pratt's exegesis, the polygamy of the Saints became a subject of heated condemnation, sometimes morbid fascination,
among non-Mormons. President Wilford Woodruff in 1890 pruned
it from the essential dogma of the Church, but this did not remove
polygamy as an obstacle to the acceptance of the Mormons by
America. Even today many Gentiles—ignoring the Church's
remarkable growth over the past century, its missionary work at
home and abroad, its effective programs for the young, its care for
the needy or aged, its financial interests in banking, mining,
merchandizing, and countless other business enterprises—merely
wonder whether Brigham Young had sixty wives, or perhaps even
more, and whether plural marriage is secretly practiced today.
Such emotional thinking was perhaps inevitable, as Kimball Young
has said,[58] in a society that insisted upon repression of sexual
desire, maintainance of purity in the home, and cherishing of
children—in a society, furthermore, that was also encouraging
improvement in the status of women.

To many Americans of 1857 the real purpose of the Government's expedition to Utah was to root out polygamy as an affront to Christian morality. They did not know that many Mormon
men accepted it reluctantly as a doctrinal requirement, or that the
women in Utah were not universally revolted at the system—that
many polygamous households were, in fact, happy, and that, indeed, only some 5 per cent of the Territory's population were involved in plural marriage. Rather, they pondered on Young's relations with his "concubines" and fancied that he had the devil
of a time keeping Mormon men out of his many beds. They referred to Daniel H. Wells' "seraglio," comparing it with the harems
of the Mohammedan world. Polygamy, they were convinced, must
have produced not only sensuality but bestial behavior, with men
marrying women and their daughters at the same time, sleeping
with several wives in the same bed, and committing other dark
acts akin to "oriental" degeneracy.[59] Mormonism, as interpreted
by Mrs. Ferris and many other Gentiles, was a repulsive ex-
crescence on American culture.

Newspapers during 1857 branded polygamy "the enslavement

of women," referred to Salt Lake City as "that sink of iniquity," and to the Church as a "giant of licentiousness, lawlessness, and all evil." [60] A spate of novels, and some works posing as fact but in reality deserving to be classified as fiction, were rushed from the presses to answer the Gentiles' palpitating desire to be shocked by the hideous aspects of Mormondom. The authors strove to be frank. One book, *The Prophets: or, Mormonism Unveiled,* began in the proper manner with a frontispiece bearing the caption "Lizzie Monroe in Her Prison—Brigham Young Making Insulting Proposals." Others revealed the purpose of their authors in their suggestive titles, for example *Female Life among the Mormons* and the inevitable follow-up, *Male Life among the Mormons.*[61] Some dealt with the Church's endowment ceremonies, which Gentiles felt must be utterly depraved since they were secret.[62]

The Saints understandably took great offense at this condemnation of their morals. Their system of relations between men and women, they insisted, was openly proclaimed and honorable, not the practice of casual midnight assignations so customary in eastern cities. If a Mormon chose to live with several women, he married and supported them and acknowledged his obligation to them; he did not imitate one judge who deserted his wife to form a brief liaison with the resident of a "bad house" in Washington. They felt that theirs was the chaste society; the "civilization" of the Gentiles was a shabby cloak unable to conceal moral and spiritual rottenness.

In this argument the Mormons had plenty of evidence to strike telling blows. One issue of the San Joaquin *Republican* called Mormonism "that monstrous combination of superstition, ignorance and debauchery," and Brigham Young "the arch imposter, tyrant and debauchee." In the same issue it also advertised "Dr. Pareiras's Great Italian Remedy, for the certain and speedy Cure of Diseases of a private nature, no matter how long standing." [63] The New York *Times,* which in 1857 joined other newspapers in criticizing the Mormons for license, devoted much of its space to news of corruption in Congress, evidences of graft in New York City's police force, the antics of Mayor Fernando Wood, and the full court transcripts of two sensational murder trials. Even so, there was room in the paper for notices of "Dr.

Ward's Unfortunate's Friend, the *ne plus ultra* of venereal medicines." Noting these indications of Gentile misconduct, the Mormons recalled a certain parable on the casting of stones.

This rebuttal received little attention from non-Mormons. The newspapers and publishing houses of the East and the West Coast poured out their literature unabated. Congressmen, too, showed that their conception of polygamy as the unashamed flaunting of degenerate desires influenced their attitude toward Utah. In 1852 Representative Cartter urged this consideration in his struggle to deny Delegate Bernhisel a seat on the floor of the House. Two years later another representative tried to attach to the bill creating the office of surveyor general of the Territory an amendment aimed at punishing polygamists. In 1854 Smith, Millson, Kerr, Walbridge, and Lyon, from states both Northern and Southern, spoke of the enormity of the Mormons' marital system. Later, Schuyler Colfax had much to say concerning the immoral practices of Utah's inhabitants. [64] Like other Gentiles of the decade, these members of Congress were outraged by the Saints' practice of plural marriage and believed that the situation demanded corrective treatment.

To eastern minds the Mormons were guilty of more than immoral conduct; they also formed a society of conspirators against the national government. There was some difference of opinion among Gentiles over the exact nature of this menace. A few enemies of the Church believed that it intended to acquire political domination of the United States and to replace its democratic institutions with those of a despotic theocracy. Thus apostate John Hyde warned his readers to be on their guard: "Brigham Young has one design, and only one. However wild in theory and impossible in execution, he entertains it seriously; and that is, to make the Mormon Church by-and-by control the whole continent." [65] According to this thesis, the Saints were bringing hordes of converts to Utah, not for their religious salvation alone but to increase the sect's voting power in an effort to win secular domination. The missionaries scattered throughout the East thus became more than proselyters; they were political actionists.

There was even greater concern among anti-Mormon Gentiles that Young might seek the more treasonable goal of complete separation from the Union. According to this view the Saints had made the long journey to Salt Lake Basin to build an independent empire in the far West, not to escape persecution in the States. This interpretation, it was felt, explained many of the Mormons offensive actions. Why would Brigham Young harry every strong-willed governmental representative from his Territory, unless he planned to sever all political ties with the country? Was not his policy of wooing the Indians to his Church evidence of his preparation for a war of independence? Had he not said, on reaching the Valley in 1847, that given ten years of peace he would ask no odds of the United States, and later, unintentionally or perhaps defiantly, had he not revealed his true intentions with the celebrated remark: "I am and will be governor, and no power can hinder it"? What other explanation than treason was there for the Saints' methodical efforts to aggrandize their ter-ritorial hegemony by establishing outposts at Fort Bridger, Car-son Valley, San Bernardino, and other strategic sites? Easterners did not relish the creation of a Mormon empire athwart the over-land trail, and they saw in Brigham Young's actions the flowering of that evil.[66]

No doubt the thought of freedom from Gentile political con-trol was an attractive one to Brigham Young and his followers, for it would have relieved them of the irritating antics of federal officeholders. Yet the evidence is overwhelming that the Saints never seriously contemplated separation from the rest of the coun-try, but on the contrary wished to regain and even strengthen their ties with it. When they left Nauvoo under the attacks of anti-Mormons, they publicly proclaimed their unshaken attach-ment to the nation, promised to support it in its foreign wars, and affirmed their desire to remain under its authority wherever they should settle. They repeated the same declaration later in the year and again in 1847.[67]

Once in the Salt Lake Valley, they disclosed no interest in the creation of an independent nation. The committee that had drafted the constitution for the proposed State of Deseret in 1849 urged its adoption "until the Congress of the United States shall otherwise provide for the government of the territory," words that carried no separatist connotations.[68] During the decade their constant appeals for statehood, for the construction of a Pacific railroad through their region, and for the establishment of weekly mails indicated a desire to tie Utah ever more firmly to the country rather than to preserve an independent remoteness from the States. During the crisis of the Mormon War, when the Government's expedition lay at Utah's border, an act of the legislature required all civil officers to declare under oath their support of the Constitution of the United States, and the Deseret Currency Association, organized to produce the scrip needed in this emergency, printed a five-dollar note illuminated by a bust of George Washington and a picture of the American eagle.[69]

If at times the Mormons' speeches seemed to give substance to the charge of sedition, more frequently they rang with patriotic fervor. The Fourth of July celebrations, always festive occasions in Utah, included salutes, toasts, orations on the Founding Fathers and the Declaration of Independence, and other demonstrations of loyalty so typical of every American community in this period.[70] It was the Saints' standard reply to Gentile charges of treasonable intentions that they loved the Constitution and laws of the land, and only fought the men who ignored these legal restraints in their efforts to persecute the Church. Even during the war, when the Church might well have contemplated striking for independence, Young asked in one sermon: "Do we wish to be free of the United States Constitution? No, there is not a word in it but what we can ascribe to with all our hearts. Do we wish to be free from the laws of the United States? No, they are as good laws as we can ask for." [71]

True, during the 1850's the Mormons interrupted the courts and in other ways were riotous citizens. On these occasions they had displayed a disposition to accept federal laws and representatives only under the inadmissible condition that their Church determine which acts were applicable to Utah, which appointees were suitable to hold office there. This situation was a potent cause of the war. But such behavior, after all, was insubordination, not treason. It arose from a desire to prevent Gentile interference in their personal affairs, not from a longing for independence. Eastern opinion, however, did not observe the distinction; rather, it accepted as a working maxim the conviction that the Mormons were awaiting an opportune moment to strike off their ties with the rest of the country. The editor of the New York *Times* expressed the evaluation clearly. In the spring of 1857, when rumors of war were afloat, he wrote that the Government had a clear choice whether to subdue the Saints then, while they were still relatively weak, or wait till they could support their inevitable demand for political sovereignty with a perilously swollen population.[72]

Agents Holeman and Hurt, supported by other federal officials, accused the Mormons of tampering with the tribes in their region, seeking to entice them from their dutiful allegiance to the country. The charge received wide popular credence and took its place as another Gentile conception of the Saints' perfidy. Convinced of the Church's implication in the Gunnison massacre, one Cleveland editor used that tragedy as proof of the Mormons' plan to enlist the Indians' help in any clash with the United States.[73] In a speech Senator Douglas warned Americans that the Mormons were making treaties with the Indians, and the New York *Times* accused Brigham Young of teaching these savages both the techniques of farming and the arts of war.[74] Alarm at this possibility approached hysteria in 1857, when the nation came to the brink of war with the sect. A West Coast newspaper announced that Young had recently gone on an exploring expedition the real purpose of which was "to prepare his Indian allies throughout the Territory, and among the adjacent tribes, for a desperate and sanguinary struggle with the 'Gentiles.' " There was cause for anxiety, the editor felt, since the Church could mobilize the assistance of some 200,000 savages. Less conservative newspapers increased the figure by another 100,000.[75] The Americans of this period, to whom the Indian was a mortal enemy, trembled for the safety of the frontier settlements. During the fall of 1857 editors feared that the Mormons would first annihilate the Government's little expedition in the broken terrain of the Rockies and then with their fierce allies would ravage the entire border to recoup the costs of the campaign.[76]

The conceptions of the eastern Gentiles, then, pictured the Saints as libidinous villains, eager to terminate their relation with the country and prepared to transgress every standard of moral behavior by forming alliances with the hated Indian. On the other side of the anti-Mormon stereotype the leaders of the Church were held guilty of innumerable murders, indeed had a powerful secret society of assassins to commit their infamous deeds. During their troubles with their Gentile neighbors in

Missouri the Saints, as mentioned above, had formed the organization known as the Sons of Dan, to defend themselves against the
assaults of their adversaries. According to eastern opinion, the
society had been carried over to Utah, to become Brigham
Young's secret police. Removed as they were from a narrow
observance of law, the Danites, at least according to the reports
of the Church's opponents, became a counterpart of the later
rurales of Porfirio Diaz' Mexico, an instrument to carry out
Star Chamber decrees with murder by day or night. Newspapers
of 1857 reported that the band had been used to harass apostates
in the Territory, had chased Stiles, Dotson, and other officials
from Utah by threatening to kill them, had murdered many innocent people, and had even placed its "wily emissaries" in
important eastern towns, where they were "watching with lynx
eyes" the movements of all Gentiles. Capitalizing on this great
excitement, Senator Douglas referred to the society when he
advocated the use of force against Utah, and Governor James
Denver of Kansas blamed some of his state's troubles upon it.[77]
To Americans of the 1850's the Sons of Dan were a sort of nine-
teenth-century Communist party, a conspiracy for treason and a
covenant with death.

According to the statements of irate Gentiles, the Mormons
did not delegate to the Danites the entire task of tormenting
their opponents. Saints who were not members of the society,
the charge maintained, also turned their hands to these deeds
of violence. In actual fact the Church's treatment of nonbelievers
was often fair and just—occasionally severe, to be sure, but only
at rare times marked by atrocities. The shocking Mountain
Meadows Massacre of 1857, in which the sect's authorities were
at least accessories after the fact, involved the cold-blooded
murder of some 120 Gentile emigrants in southern Utah by
Indians and white men.[78] But that terrible affair, coming in
September of the year, did not affect Buchanan's decision to send
an expedition against Utah, and is pertinent to this study only
insofar as it casts light upon the Mormons' emotionalism. There
were, however, gruesome incidents of an earlier date that eastern
Gentiles accepted as proof of the Church's criminality—for one,
the Parrish-Potter murders.

In March of 1857 William Parrish, whose faith had grown cold, decided to leave the Territory and planned to accomplish this defection by stealth in order to escape the priesthood's usual condemnation of apostates. Before he could escape, he and one of his sons were lured into an ambush and killed, together with one Potter, the hapless decoy in this scheme. Possibly the Hierarchy of Springville plotted and executed these murders; at the very least, the Church took no effective steps to investigate them.[79] News of the crime, reaching the states in May 1857, received great attention in the press. Editors reported additional acts of violence in Utah during the spring: the murder of several Gentiles, the destruction of apostates' homes, and the mistreatment of Burr's assistants.[80] Whether fact or fancy it is impossible now to judge, but these accounts convinced eastern Gentiles that the Mormons' character included murderous inclinations as well as other traits of moral anarchy.

With such an opinion of the Saints firmly lodged in their minds, the Gentiles of 1857 were almost unanimous in their hostility toward the Church. They treated its missionaries with a roughness that frequently endangered their lives.[81] One episode, the murder of Parley Parker Pratt, revealed this animosity most dramatically. Pratt was honored in the Saints' community as one of its most beloved members. Although like most of the Mormon leaders he had had only a limited formal education, he had shown some talent for writing and had become the poet laureate of the sect as well as one of its most effective propagandists. He was called the Church's Isaiah and had been given the name "The Archer of Paradise." An early convert to Mormonism, he had risen to the position of apostle in 1835 and had served the sect well with tongue and pen until 1857.[82] In that year his choice of a plural wife resulted in his death.

Early in the decade he had met the wife of Hector McLean, a San Francisco customs house official, and had so impressed her that she embraced Mormonism and fell in love with its missionary. The enraged McLean, failing to persuade her to abandon her new religion, sent their children to her parents in New Orleans; later he permitted her to join them there. After a trip to Salt Lake City, where she apparently became Pratt's twelfth wife, Mrs. McLean returned to New Orleans, spirited the children away, and joined Pratt in an effort to return to Utah. When

he learned of this development, McLean searched frantically
for the eloping couple and in May 1857 found them in Arkansas.
Acting on McLean's wild charge that Pratt had stolen some clothing, the United States marshal arrested the Mormon missionary,
but later released him. McLean's anger was too hot to let the
Mormon escape so easily; he pursued Pratt on horseback and near
Van Buren shot him to death.[83]

To those Gentiles who had taken the Stiles affair and other
events in Utah as proof of Mormon lawlessness, the murder of
Parley Pratt in the scrubby brush country of Arkansas was a
merited punishment. The man was transparently a "poor curse,"
a "hoary-headed seducer," a "lecherous old villain" who had not
deserved to live. His death was but "another painful narrative
of Mormon iniquity, seduction and villainy." [84] To the editor of
the Van Buren newspaper the real victim was not Pratt: "Deeply
do we sympathize with McLean in the unfortunate condition
in which Mormon villainy and fanaticism has placed him." [85]
Mrs. McLean's version of the tragedy received little serious
consideration. When she wrote that she had voluntarily left her
husband, an evil-tempered, drunken wretch, to live openly
with Parley Pratt, "a fountain of light," and his other companion-
able wives, her statements were greeted with incredulity. The
woman was obviously insane, one paper commented, to accept
"the coarse, sensual imposter, as a canonized saint." [86] Since prevailing opinion regarded polygamy as a degrading institution
forced upon terrorized women, few Gentiles would believe that
one woman at least had found happiness in it. The disposition
to view the Pratt murder as justifiable homicide revealed the
extent of anti-Mormon antipathy in the East. As will be seen
later, it also stiffened the Saints' resistance in the war, increased
their fears of close contact with Gentiles, and strengthened their
martyr complex.

The widespread condemnation of Mormons continued to find
expression in newspapers. The editor of the New York Times,
after attributing the recent "six years of treason" to Fillmore's
vacillating policy on Utah, forcefully advanced his solution to
the Mormon problem: "A new Governor should be sent at once
to Great Salt Lake City—backed by an imposing military force
—to render the Constitution with one hand while a drawn sword

is held in the other." The Baltimore *Sun* was in agreement with the proposal: "The man who is sent to govern them *must carry the sword with its edge turned towards the leaders of the Mormons.*" Others repeated the same refrain, intimating by certain overtones that they trusted the contest would not end pacifically. In this warlike chorus the few dissenting voices who urged an unprejudiced investigation were lost. Buchanan and the Congress accordingly knew, as the New York *Times* indicated, that "the Government is not likely to be held to a very strict account for its acts toward [the Mormons] even though they should be utterly exterminated." [87] With this clamor in his ears, the President could the more easily read into the dispatches of former Utah officers the need for an expedition in 1857.

If Gentiles in the 1850's found abundant reasons for antagonism toward the Church, the Mormons also had strong motivation for unruly activities. In their early history they had been treated with a cruel intolerance, the memories of which they carried with them to Utah. After struggling against famine in their new home, and at times reduced to eating the animal skins used as shelter, they had at last built the basis for economic survival. Then had come new trouble with their opponents, indicating that their patient suffering had not after all taken them beyond persecution. Federal officials had meddled in their affairs, apparently with the intention of overthrowing their carefully devised political system. The uncertainty of their title to the land, the cancellation of their mail contract—these and other important events seemed to them proof of the Government's intention to oppress them even in the remoteness of the Salt Lake Basin. They could interpret these signs as a return to the days of Nauvoo, or they could see in them a larger significance, the desperate effort of Satan to destroy this true church of God, the New Dispensation in the Last Days.[88] In either case they determined to resist further assaults upon their political autonomy and their faith.

The leaders of the Church never let their people forget their past misfortunes. Holidays, such as Pioneers' Day on July 24, provided the best opportunities for a recapitulation of former travails, but any other public celebration sufficed to remind the Saints that they were, both as individuals and as a sect, martyrs to diabolical oppression. The "extermination order" of Governor

Boggs, the murder of Joseph and Hyrum, the sufferings on the
banks of the Mississippi and at Far West—these and other incidents along the road to Utah received due attention in speeches,
sermons, and the columns of the *Deseret News*.[89] The constant
reference to their past mistreatment was understandable, but it
served to keep the Mormons in a state of emotional excitement
inimical to peaceful relations with the rest of the nation. During
the crucial period immediately prior to the outbreak of the war
the people had their memories jogged again by reading in the
Deseret News the serial biography of the murdered prophet.[90]
The painful scenes of the past came to life again. It was not surprising that in early 1857 John McAllister was frequently requested to sing a song of his own composition entitled "The
Mormons and Their Enemies." [91]

The leaders of the Church endeavored also to show that intolerance of them by the middle of the 1850's was as determined
as ever. In their speeches they envisaged the faithful in Utah as
surrounded by a host of enemies, in public office and out, who
ceaselessly plotted their ruin. Indeed, Heber Kimball warned, they
were already within the very gates: "There are men and women
in our midst, and some who profess 'Mormonism,' who would take
my life in a moment, if they dared, and the life of President
Young." [92] Possibly because of this atmosphere Steptoe refused
the position of governor. It was in this spirit that the office of
a federal judge was rifled.

The tendency toward emotionalism on the part of the Mormons,
so unsettling to the relations between Utah and the nation, was
heightened by a religious revival during 1856. Apostasy had become a problem within the Church at this time, and a number of
once-devoted members had left for California. Many no longer
kept a devout observance of the Sabbath. Instead of piety, greed
had become so noticeable that people often sold grain to Gentiles
when their own brethren were hungry. There were still other
evidences of backsliding.[93] Reacting against it, Jedediah M. Grant
warned in July 1855: "The Church needs trimming up, and if
you will search you will find in your wards certain branches which
had better be cut off." During the next months both Grant and
Young continued to bemoan the spiritual condition of their fol-

lowers, accusing them of "evil ways," of "blindness and stupidity, fog and darkness." [94]

After this preparatory period of criticism and accusation from the pulpit, a reformation—launched in September 1856 by Grant's exhortations—began to sweep the Territory. Like similar waves of revivalism in the "burned-over" region of New York, where Mormonism was born, it became an all-engrossing movement that compelled the people to listen, pray, and search their souls. In a two-day conference at Kaysville the local Saints heard twenty-one speeches and sermons by Grant and other preachers, an exhausting schedule duplicated in most of Utah's towns.[95]

The leaders of the Church, however, did not limit the work of the reformation to large public gatherings; they also inaugurated a more personal type of campaign, which brought the searing fire of purification into every Mormon home. The Church appointed at least two trusted men to act as "home missionaries" in all wards of Salt Lake City. Further, they selected men to act as confessors in every block, to visit each house and ask its members a long list of questions—a catechism designed to reveal past offenses against the Ten Commandments, the tenets of the Church, and the laws of men. Excitement reached a fever pitch during 1856. "Bishops are deposed and their counsellors, when slothful at the duties, or *when ruled by their wives,*" Franklin D. Richards wrote. "Misdeeds are not only publicly denounced, but the doers and their deeds are named before the public congregations. The arrows of the Almighty are with the Presidency. The terrors of the Lord are upon them, and are coming upon the people." Preachers on occasion "had to refrain from speaking, for the people have shrunk before them." [96]

Violence of language had been characteristic of the Saints in the past. During the reformation, when the leaders of the Church shared the excitement of their congregations, speech from the pulpit became even more frenetic. Grant, whose fiery anger often seemed less restrained than that of Brigham Young himself, showered denunciations and threats upon non-Mormons in Utah. "I want the Gentiles to understand that we know all about their whoredoms and other abominations. If we have not invariably killed such corrupt scoundrels, those who will seek to

corrupt and pollute our community, I swear to you that we mean
to, and to accomplish more in a few hours, towards clearing the
atmosphere, than all your grand and traverse juries can in a
year." [97] In their enthusiasm for a moral and spiritual regenera-
tion of Utah, Grant and Young brought the dark concept of blood
atonement into their sermons. At times these men spoke of a
voluntary sacrifice by the transgressor; more ominously they
occasionally referred to the killing of unrepentant evil-doers who
objected to purchasing eternal salvation in this fashion. [98]

It was inevitable that the reformation, as its emotional frenzy
increased, should affect not only the lives of the people but their
relations with the United States, for it made the Saints more in-
tolerant of Gentiles in Utah and more unresponsive to the Government's authority during 1856 and 1857. Some writers have
blamed the Mountain Meadows Massacre upon the hysteria let
loose by the revival. [99] Certainly the experiences of Stiles, Burr,
Hurt, and other federal officers in Utah during this time were
in part the result of turbulent feelings. Furthermore, the people
now became prepared to work, sacrifice, and die in defense of
their desert Zion. In a sermon Grant said: "We are lawful and
loyal citizens of the government of the United States, and a few
poor, miserable, pusillanimous, rotten stinking rebels, come here
and threaten us with the armies of the United States. We wish all
such characters to understand that if the generals and armies
and those who wish to send them, are as corrupt as those who
threaten us, and as vile as most of those heretofore sent, we defy
them, and the sooner we come in contact with them the better." [100]

One sobering result of the reformation was the untimely death
of Grant, who had taken a "mortal chill" during one of his frequent services of baptism in the cold of winter. Had he lived to
continue his exhortations, the Mormons might have been driven
during the war to acts of resistance precluding an easy arrangement of peace between them and the country. At any rate there can
be no doubt that the revival, by increasing the hostility of the
Saints toward the Gentiles and their Government, helped to precipitate the Mormon War of 1857. [101]

5. An Unheroic Anabasis

IN THIS FUMBLING FASHION—swayed by public opinion, the correspondence of territorial officials, and other pressures—the Administration in 1857 finally groped its way to the conclusion that the Mormon people were in revolt against the United States. Although it was no later than May when the President decided to send an armed force to Utah, the season was already dangerously advanced for such an undertaking, since the Saints' country was far removed from the frontier outposts, the army was scattered from Florida to Minnesota, and the Rocky Mountain winters were known to set in early. If the campaign were to succeed, it now had to be prosecuted quickly and efficiently.

Yet the Administration allowed crucial weeks to slip past without organizing the expedition, its early enthusiasm for belligerent action having been somewhat dampened by the opposition of important military officers. Winfield Scott, the able commander in chief, refused to let the frenzied public outcry against the Mormons influence his evaluation of the President's policy; he was interested primarily in the problems of terrain and logistics confronting a demonstration against Utah, so that when in late May John B. Floyd, on Buchanan's direction, solicited the General's comments, Scott replied that it was already too late to send any troops west that year. The Mormons could field 4,000 men, he said; in order to meet so formidable an adversary and to protect the supply lines at this season, the Government would need to send an impossibly large force. Better to wait until 1858.[1] It also became apparent from the actions and letters of Gen. William S. Harney, to whom had fallen command of the expedition, that he was reluctant to accept the honor and would prefer to wait another year, or, better still, to escape the assignment altogether.[2]

Another impediment to the departure of the troops in a propi-
tious season was the Administration's difficulty in finding a suitable
replacement for Brigham Young. The Government's strategy was
to put a Gentile in Utah's executive office and to support him
against a possible Mormon insurrection by a strong detachment
of men, acting as a *posse comitatus*. But this plan required that
the governor accompany the soldiers into Utah. If the army should
arrive first, without civil officers, the Mormons could with some
reason claim that they were being invaded by a hostile force
sent solely to destroy them, and war, not a pleasant possibility
to Buchanan, might ensue. Therefore, final preparations for
the campaign could not be made until the new governor had
been appointed. The search for a candidate consumed precious
weeks, since the job was not especially attractive. The Government was looking for a capable, tactful, and courageous individual to fill a position two thousand miles from Washington in a
community composed of people who had treated federal officers
with rough hands in the past. And the compensation to be paid
a man of such endowments would probably not meet his expenses.

It took the Administration a month to realize that its first choice
for governor, Ben McCulloch, would not take the job. Although
he rejected the offer once, he was urged to reconsider, and only
in late May did Cass finally understand that McCulloch's duties
in Texas, and perhaps his opinion of the office as a political
death-trap, definitely precluded his acceptance. During the rest of
the month and part of June the search went on, the press reporting variously that a prominent politician in Indiana, an influential former member of Congress, or the recent governor of Mary-
land had been selected. At last, in the second week of June, the
Government found a suitable candidate in Alfred Cumming.
Even he had refused the appointment at one time, but after a
change of heart had come to Washington armed with the effective sponsorship of the omnipresent Thomas L. Kane. Yet
Cumming's initial acceptance was apparently conditional, for he
journeyed to Fort Leavenworth, Kansas, presumably to inspect
the preparations for the campaign, before finally agreeing to take
the position. Secretary of State Cass did not send him his commis-

sion until July 13, when the days were growing shorter and the
nights a bit cooler in the country beyond South Pass.[3]

The Government had equal difficulty filling the other posts
in Utah. The whole process again revealed that the designation of
territorial officeholders was frequently made under a pressure for
patronage heavy enough to militate against the nomination of
worthy men. Almost three months passed before the names of the
new federal judges, Delana R. Eckels, Charles E. Sinclair, and John
Cradlebaugh, were reported in the press, and during that time
supporters and enemies of various supplicants squabbled over these
somewhat seedy political plums.[4] It was much the same story
with the office of superintendent of Indian affairs. John C. O'Neill
had first received the position, but he had immediately used a
letter of credit in such a way as to arouse strong doubts concerning
his integrity. After that, the labors of his friends could not save
him. Forced to resign, he entered the safer and more profitable
profession of supplying the thirsty residents of the Capital with
liquors, brandies, and wines.[5] When the news spread that O'Neill
was no longer superintendent, the partisans of Jacob Forney
began to beat the drums for their man. He was almost illiterate
and had never been to Utah, but he was a staunch Democrat,
knew Jeremiah Black personally, and had worked harder for
Buchanan in the town of Kittanning, Pennsylvania, during the
1856 election than anyone else. In due time he was offered the job
and in August wrote Black: "I am pleased to inform you, that my
wife is willing that I shall go to Utah." [6]

It is desirable to pause here in the account of the early preparations for the campaign to note the instructions that the principal civil and military officers carried with them to Utah, for they
revealed the Government's attitude toward the Mormons and
inadvertently produced another crisis in the Territory. From
the Secretary of State, Cumming learned that his task was to up-
hold "the supremacy of the law." Although the President, Cass
stated, foresaw no opposition from the Mormons in this regard,
Cumming was nevertheless authorized to employ a civil posse
to enforce obedience and, if that action should fail, to call upon
the army as a *posse comitatus*. On the subject of polygamy the new
governor's orders were more confused. Although they clearly

advised Cumming to observe the constitutional guarantee of freedom of worship, they worded the admonition in a fashion indicative of the Administration's attitude toward the Latter-day Saints:
the Government, Cass wrote, did not intend to interfere "with
any peculiar opinions of the inhabitants, however deplorable in
themselves or revolting to the public sentiment of the country." [7]

Harney's instructions differed at several points from those given
to Cumming, perhaps because the bitterly anti-Mormon John
B. Floyd had composed the former, while the latter had come
from the more phlegmatic Cass. Where the Governor had been
merely cautioned indirectly about the Saints' insubordinate
tendencies, Harney was definitely told: "The community and,
in part, civil government of Utah Territory are in a state of sub-
stantial rebellion against the laws and authority of the United
States." Cumming's orders expressed the Administration's expectation of a peaceful outcome of the Utah trouble, but the General
was warned: "The prudence expected of you requires that you
should anticipate resistance, general, organized, and formidable,
at the threshold, and shape your movements as if it were certain."
The contrast foreshadowed later developments in Utah; Cumming
ultimately worked for a peace based upon charity and understanding, while Albert Sidney Johnston, Harney's replacement, always
thought of the Mormons as traitorous rogues whose actions
merited the closest and most suspicious scrutiny. In these circumstances the War Department's admonition that the commander
was "responsible for a zealous, harmonious, and thorough co-
operation with [Cumming], on frequent and full consultations"
was forgotten. There was another cause of future disagreement.
Cumming had been authorized to summon the troops as a posse
comitatus, and accordingly assumed that he alone held this power.
Harney's orders, however, contained the provision that the federal
judges also possessed this authority, if they should feel the need
of assistance in the performance of their duties. This confusion
was to precipitate serious trouble between the executive and the
military in Utah during 1859.[8]

In Harney's instructions was the significant admission by the
War Department that "The lateness of the season, the dispersed
condition of the troops and the smallness of the numbers avail-

2. Alfred Cumming

able, have seemed to present elements of difficulty, if not hazard, in this expedition." Having deliberated carefully upon a policy toward Utah and then wasted valuable time culling acceptable officers from the political chaff, the Administration by the end of May suddenly awoke to the perils facing its campaign against the Mormons and began at last to act promptly. The General Orders providing for the assembly of troops at Fort Leavenworth demanded the fulfillment of this charge "with the least possible delay." Later in June the quartermaster for the expedition informed an officer of the Fourth Artillery Regiment that the Government in its haste to accumulate necessary provisions had told him to "annihilate space and time by money." As the month dragged by without a single soldier starting on the long road to Utah, the War Department repeatedly prodded the commanders of elements in the expedition to leave Fort Leavenworth as soon as possible.[9] The obstacles to the success of the operation grew with each passing day. Even after the advance detachments had started late in July, the Administration was still concerned about their safe arrival in Utah and according to one newspaper for a time debated whether to recall them.[10] These fears proved well founded.

Seven weeks of frantic preparation separated the Government's final formulation of its Utah policy and the departure of the vanguard from Fort Leavenworth. According to General Order No. 8, May 28, the force was to be composed of the Fifth Infantry and eight companies of the Tenth, with the Second Dragoons serving as the cavalry; later in June the command received further strength from the addition of two artillery batteries under Capt. John W. Phelps and Lt. Jesse Reno. It was difficult to assemble these troops quickly. The Dragoons, it is true, were already near at hand, having been used in Kansas during the recent political convulsion there. But the Tenth Regiment was in Minnesota and the Fifth, under Harney, had been engaged in tracking Billy Bowlegs' elusive Seminoles through the Florida swamps.[11] These men had to be moved by train and boat to eastern Kansas, and in the case of the Fifth the soldiers needed a period of rest at Jefferson Barracks, St. Louis, to take care of their wounds and cure their fevers. In the meantime the quartermaster scurried about

trying to purchase tons of provisions, hire two hundred teamsters
for the supply trains, and buy horses, wagons, and other necessary
materiel.[12]

The troops straggling into Fort Leavenworth in June and July
did not have the appearance of a well-drilled, patriotic band of
men ready for an arduous march to the West. From New York
came raw recruits whom the War Department foolishly believed
could easily be instructed to serve in either the artillery or the
infantry.[13] The Tenth Infantry, a vital element in the campaign,
arrived with its companies at half strength and, more ominously,
its colonel highly unpopular with some of its younger officers.
Edmund Alexander, who was later to assume temporary command of the expedition, had served well in the Mexican War,
having at that time been breveted major and then lieutenant
colonel for "gallant and meritorious conduct." But to Capt. Jesse
Gove of the Tenth he was the "old granny," the "old woman,"
interested only in the health of his wife and "entirely neglect-
ful of his command." [14]

In the oppressive heat that settled over this camp on a bend
of the Missouri River the morale of the troops sagged. A number
of men had previously deserted on learning the nature of their
new duties, and many who did arrive at the fort were rebellious.
This condition prevailed especially in the Fifth Infantry. In the
Big Cyprus Swamp of the Everglades it had battled mud and
insects as well as Indians, had suffered from scurvy and disease,
and had come to think itself entitled to a respite from disagreeable
assignments. When ordered upon the fatiguing tramp to Utah,
at least 200 men deserted and several officers submitted their res-
ignations in protest. So poor was the unit's condition that General Harney felt compelled to delay its final departure. When the
time to march had at last come, Captain Phelps studied the men
who were about to take part in a demanding military maneuver
and wrote in his diary: "We are none of us prepared for such
a move and my battery less than any other command." [15]

Other complications interfered with a smooth and timely departure of the troops. In the first place there was great confusion
over the availability of the Second Dragoons. This regiment had
arrived at Fort Leavenworth during June, but because of desertions and the debilitation of scurvy it was patently unfit for im-

mediate service in the West. When it had regained its fitness, the
governor of Kansas, Robert J. Walker, suddenly requested that
the Dragoons act as a posse to preserve peace at Lawrence and
other trouble spots, and General Harney accordingly detached
seven companies under Lt. Col. Philip St. George Cooke.[16] Since
Cooke and his men did not follow the other elements of the expedition until mid-September, the advance column had to conduct its operations beyond South Pass without cavalry support.

The political crisis in Kansas placed another obstacle in the
way of the campaign. Governor Walker felt that he needed more
than the Dragoons to maintain peace in his state: he had to have
the services of General Harney himself.[17] Thus while the vanguard pressed on farther and farther across the Plains, its commander remained behind in Kansas. At last the War Department,
realizing the foolishness and even the peril of this arrangement,
in late August acknowledged that Harney was assigned to duty in
Kansas and appointed Col. Albert Sidney Johnston to lead the
Utah army.[18] When Johnston finally assumed command on September 11, he warned his men to expect "toil, privation, and
hardships incident to frontier service." [19] To the troops by then
in the vicinity of Fort Laramie, about 700 miles from Fort Leavenworth, the admonition was unnecessary.

Despite interference from the troubles in Bleeding Kansas,
the Mormon War began formally on the 18th of July with the
departure of the Tenth Infantry Regiment from Fort Leavenworth. A day later Phelps' battery of four six-pounders and two
twelve-pound howitzers followed from a camp nearby, and shortly
thereafter the weary Fifth Infantry started for Utah. For the 1200
men in these units the first weeks of the journey were unexcit-
ing. Arising at sunup, they had two hours to prepare breakfast
and break camp before receiving the order to march. They then
tramped until the early part of the afternoon, by which time they
had traversed some fifteen or twenty miles and had arrived at
a camp site with accessible forage and water. In general they
followed the trail familiar to overland pioneers: west from Fort
Leavenworth to the Big Blue, north on this river, and then northwest on the Little Blue, its tributary. The troops finally came
to the wide, shallow, and lethargic Platte, the vital highway to
the Rocky Mountain country.

Occasionally the boredom of the daily routine or the unpleasant anticipation of a winter campaign in the mountains against the strange Mormons caused a few men to desert, each risking if caught fifty lashes "well laid, on his bare back, with a raw hide." John Phelps continued to complain in his diary that his command, badly trained and equipped, was not withstanding the labors of the march well, for some of his men suffered from lack of adequate clothing and the horses were lame or badly galled. Among the officers of the Tenth, Capt. Jesse Gove wrote to his wife, there was still much dislike for Alexander, a "mere cypher" who kept to his ambulance and avoided walking. Yet these were the normal and temporary vicissitudes of such a campaign. Alexander could inform the Adjutant General's Office after the first nineteen days of the march that his men were developing a fine endurance and were "now fit for any kind of service." [20]

As a forlorn oasis on the road along the Platte stood Fort Kearney, a shabby military post garrisoned by one company of the Sixth Infantry. When the troops reached it in early August, they did not find many opportunities for amusement; the scattered collection of wooden, adobe, or stone houses, erected on the barren plain some distance from timber and water, offered nothing more than the facilities needed to repair wagons and other damaged equipment.[21] But at least it was an outpost of civilization. Once beyond it, the soldiers found nothing but the level monotony of the Platte, with its quicksand and its horse flies that drove the animals mad, and finally the first prominent swellings of the ground near Fort Laramie. During this segment of the trip there were a few more desertions, and Alexander's popularity in his regiment sank even lower. In a letter asserting that "not one officer in the line but what perfectly hates him," Captain Gove criticized Alexander's solicitude for his private possessions at a time when the column had to work its wagons over difficult country. It is probable, however, that the dislike of the men of the Tenth for their colonel was due less to contempt for his personal behavior than to irritation at his meticulous order of march, with its prescribed ninety-six to one hundred steps a minute, and his equally thorough system for guarding the camp at night.[22]

The army plodded along the Platte to its fork, turned up the South branch for a few days, and finally, still following the usual

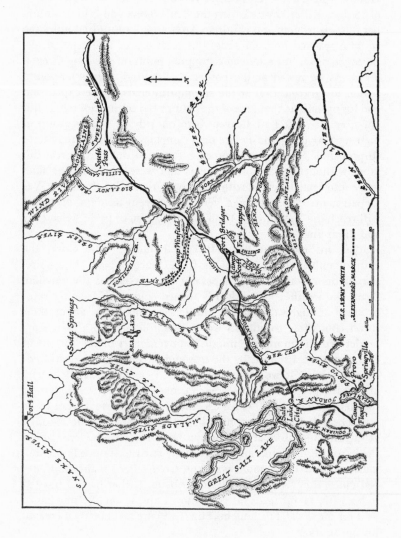

route, jumped the height of land to join the North Fork near Ash Hollow, where a few years earlier William Harney had won his title of "Squaw Killer" by defeating the Brulé Sioux and killing a number of their women and children. After another hundred miles the column reached Fort Laramie, like Kearney an understaffed, decayed garrison, but a welcome stopping point on the long Oregon Trail. As he rested at the post, Col. Edmund Alexander found reason for gratification at the accomplishments of the expedition and for optimistic thoughts of the future. His command, the Tenth Infantry, had left Fort Leavenworth on July 18, a raw group of men starting dangerously late on a campaign for which they were ill prepared. Now, by September 3, they had traveled a great distance without any untoward events and were ready for the final drive into Utah. Pleased with this work, Alexander wrote the War Department: "Unless some very unforeseen accident occurs, I will reach the Territory of Utah in a condition of perfect efficiency and discipline." [23]

After his regiment had left Fort Laramie, Jesse Gove, the earnest, ambitious young captain from Concord, New Hampshire, shared his colonel's high hopes for the success of the mission. True, the weather had suddenly turned cold, with freezing rains or snow at night that forced the officers to huddle about their stoves. But these conditions were not intolerable to a New Englander. Furthermore, the minor inconveniences of the inclement evenings were assuaged by the uncommon rations Gove enjoyed: antelope, beef, stewed tomatoes, boiled rice, and other delicacies artistically prepared by his French cook. "When I get into winter quarters won't I live!" Gove exclaimed, in words that were to be a mockery before two months had passed. Nor was he alarmed at the growing number of Mormon horsemen who hovered about the expedition's flanks and occasionally tried to stampede the animals at night. They would not fight, Gove felt, or if they did offer resistance, they would present no problem. Earlier he had boasted to his wife: "I am ready, as you know. I always am. No one has to wait for the 'I's'." The long hike up the Platte had merely increased his optimism.[24]

Colonel Alexander may not have been worried about the morale of Gove's company after the army had left Fort Laramie, but his evaluation of the entire campaign had undergone a drastic change

three weeks after he wrote his confident letter to the War Department. The weather gave him more cause for alarm than it did
Gove, perhaps because he was more alive to the numbing sudden-
ness of winter's descent in the high elevation. Furthermore he was
concerned for the column's supply trains, which were at this point
spread across the Plains west of the fort, some of them beyond his
protection. Toward the end of September he sent an order to the
train farthest advanced to retrace its steps, but lack of water
compelled it to ignore these instructions and to press on to the
Green River. Apprehensive for the safety of his men in a region
of increasing coldness, inadequate forage, and hostile Mormons,
Alexander advised Captain Phelps, commanding one of the batteries of artillery, that his expectation of an early entrance into
Utah was now gone. "If we winter near Bridger's Fort or Fort
Supply, I think we can get wood, stone and sod for building and
at least enough grass to keep animals alive," he announced rather
dejectedly. "It is almost certain that nothing but self-protection
can be attempted this season." Three days later he warned Phelps
to guard his animals with sleepless vigilance against possible surprise raids by the enemy.[25]

The senior officers of the expedition soon found further cause
for concern over their position. Toward the end of September they
received an informed explanation of the Saints' plans from Capt.
Stewart Van Vliet, who had made a hurried trip to Salt Lake
City and on his return had met them west of South Pass. He
brought Alexander the grim news that the Mormons were sure
to refuse the army any supplies and that they might very well
defend their homes by force.

The Government's decision to send Van Vliet ahead of the main
army was a result of its previous mishandling of the whole Mormon problem. Having impatiently declined to investigate conditions in Utah before sending troops there, and then having delayed the departure of these men beyond the point of safety, the
Administration at last awoke to the fact that the obstacles facing
the soldiers jeopardized the success of the campaign. It therefore
moved with some resolution to forestall a catastrophic conclusion
to its blunders. After the first elements of the expedition had
left Fort Leavenworth in July the Adjutant General's Office ordered Harney to send "a discreet staff officer" to the Territory on

a special mission. By July 28 Van Vliet, an assistant quartermaster in the army, had received his instructions. With a small detail he was to hurry past the column already on the road to Utah and to go "with utmost dispatch" to Salt Lake City, where he was to make arrangements with the Mormons for the arrival and provisioning of the army. If the great importance attached to this mission by the War Department did not appear clearly in Van Vliet's formal orders, it was soon made evident. When Harney discovered that the Captain had spent ten days in traveling the short distance from Fort Leavenworth to Fort Kearney, he reminded him of his "most important and delicate mission" and warned that he would be held responsible for "any disasters which might befall the troops, for want of proper information from you." [26]

Van Vliet now pressed ahead with more determination and reached Utah in early September. His initial reception in Salt Lake City betrayed the fact that the Mormon leaders had not yet resolved upon their strategy toward the approaching federal army. As shall be seen later, they had for some time considered three alternatives: to stand and fight; to submit peacefully; or to resort to guerrilla warfare, using their mountain fastnesses as redouts against a numerically superior enemy. When Van Vliet arrived in the Valley on September 8, the Church appeared at first to have chosen peace as the wisest policy, so pleasantly did it welcome him. [27] But the Mormons' cordiality quickly disappeared. After their first friendly conversations with Van Vliet, the spokesmen of the Church labored with considerable bluster to assure him that their people, cruelly treated in the past, considered the present expedition merely another wave of persecution and were prepared this time to defend themselves. The Saints, said Young, Taylor, and other dignitaries, had enough supplies for the army but would sell nothing to it. Instead, they were determined to defy the troops. Brigham Young, a penetrating student of his fellows, had known well how to impress such a buffoon as Perry Brocchus, and he knew also the proper techniques to use upon Van Vliet.

Whether or not the victim of a bluff, the Captain left Utah a sober man, greatly concerned for the safety of the army. His report to General Harney from a camp on the Oregon Trail disclosed his dark surmisings. The Mormons, he wrote, would resist the entrance of the army into Utah to the death, although they would probably confine their campaign as long as possible to the burning of grass and other bloodless harassments. If confronted with superior forces, they would destroy everything, and using three years' supplies of food already cached would hide in the mountains, where they could annihilate any force sent against them. In the light of this ominous situation, and because of the lateness of the season and the nature of the terrain, Van Vliet urged Harney to consider the possibility of ordering the troops to winter near Fort Bridger.[28]

Thus Van Vliet entered the camp of the Tenth Infantry in September in a pessimistic frame of mind. If the army stopped at Bridger, he counseled Alexander, it would be left at peace, but if it should advance beyond that point the Mormons, by burning the grass, stampeding stock, and committing similar depredations, could cause it serious embarrassment. The prospect of spending the winter in the mountains appalled the bellicose Jesse Gove, but he took heart from the belief that the expedition had enough provisions to avoid starvation.[29] Alexander, as we have seen, was more alarmed. His supply trains were scattered across the desert, and one large contractor's train of more than 100 wagons and 1,100 head of cattle had stopped for several weeks on Ham's Fork of the Green River, presenting an especially inviting target for Mormon raiders. He accordingly advised Phelps to guard his stock and at once took his regiment by forced marches through blinding clouds of potash dust to Ham's Fork. For the moment these emergency measures prevented serious losses. By the end of September, the Tenth Infantry Regiment, Phelps' battery, and their supply trains had all reached Ham's Fork safely. The Fifth Infantry and a recently arrived battery of artillery commanded by Jesse Reno were on the Green River, only two days' march to the east.[30]

During these last frantic days of September and throughout the whole of October, Alexander, as senior officer in an army without a commander, undertook another chore in addition to the grim task of preserving his men's security. He entered into a lengthy duel by correspondence with Brigham Young and, like Perry Brocchus before him, found it an unrewarding occupation. He learned little from the exercise that he had not discovered a few

days earlier from a proclamation issued by Young as governor of
the Territory. Young had begun with the fervid statement: "Citizens of Utah—We are invaded by a hostile force, who are evidently assailing us to accomplish our overthrow and destruction."
After rehearsing the history of the Church's previous mistreatment at the hands of the Gentiles and complaining of the Government's decision to send an "armed, mercenary mob" rather
than an investigating committee on the "instigation of anonymous
letter-writers," "corrupt officials," "hireling priests and howling
editors," he declared that his people must "resort to the great first
law of self-preservation and stand in our own defenses." He accordingly prohibited any army from entering Utah, ordered the
people to ready themselves for action, and imposed martial law
upon the Territory.[31]

Alexander saw in this document verification of Van Vliet's
warning. From Young's first communication he perceived that
the Saints would justify their resistance to the expedition by a
legalistic quibble: since the President had neglected to notify
Young of his removal, of his successor's appointment, and of the
purpose of the present demonstration, the governor was pretend-
ing that the column of troops was an unauthorized, irregular mob
of private citizens. This letter also commanded the colonel to
withdraw from Utah, or, if he chose to remain within its borders,
to turn over all the weapons of his command to the Mormons.[32]

If Alexander had been conversant with the nature of the Saints,
he would have known that little profit lay in an exchange of letters. Instead, with great incaution, he assayed a lengthy explanation of the army's mission. After announcing that its primary
purpose was the innocuous one of creating a military post in Utah,
he criticized the bellicose tones of the governor's proclamation,
condemned the Mormons' guerrilla tactics as "far beneath the
usages of civilized warfare," and declared the strength of his
force "ample to overcome any obstacle." [33] His effort to score
points against his opponent was merely a stick thrust into a hornets'
nest, for it evoked only a storm of scornful and occasionally confused messages from Salt Lake City. In a long, involved letter
Young charged that the expedition's real purpose was to destroy
his people and urged Alexander to avoid the responsibility of
precipitating civil war.[34] Two days later Young was at his desk

again, warning the Colonel that the Mormons would treat his
men as "open enemies," alluding to the Government's "infernal
requisition" of the Mormon Battalion, and asking with effective
sarcasm why Alexander, if his forces were adequate for any emergency, "dallied so long on Ham's Fork, at this late season of
the year?" [35] So it went through October, the Lion of the Lord
finding many opportunities to express his people's grievances.[36]

On October 2 Alexander again gave thought to his position and
was distressed. His Tenth Regiment, with Phelps' battery close
by, was protecting a large supply train on Ham's Fork. The Fifth
Infantry, under Col. Carlos A. Waite and recently strengthened
by Reno's battery, was camped on the Green River some twenty
or thirty miles to the east. Between these two units straggled a
number of the trains belonging to contractors Russell, Majors,
and Waddell. The winter was coming on, and the Mormons, with
Fort Bridger as the base of their operations, were hovering in the
hills above the troops. Also conducive to Alexander's misgivings
was the absence of the expedition's commander, which left the
army without a senior officer and without orders. A conservative
gentleman, Alexander did not seek the dubious glory of leading
this bastardized expedition through the defenses of the Mormons
into the Valley of the Great Salt Lake. On October 2 he informed
his still nebulous commanding officer of his troops' position and
requested rather plaintively that this commander come as fast
as he could.[37]

While Alexander scrutinized the problems facing his disor-
ganized and leaderless army, the Mormons struck. On October
4 a small band of mounted Mormons led by Major Lot Smith
bypassed the Tenth Infantry and fell upon two of the contractors'
trains camped along the Green River, a very few miles from Colonel Waite's command. Secure in the knowledge that the army's
cavalry, the Dragoons, was some 700 miles to the east, Smith
burned these trains and the next day surprised and destroyed a
third nearby on the Big Sandy. All told the flames lit by Smith
and his few dozen men consumed seventy-two wagons containing
300,000 pounds of food, principally flour and bacon—enough
provisions to feed the troops for several months. The officers of
the army could take only meager comfort in the thought that if
the Mormons had wiped out other trains in the vicinity, as they

might well have done, the expedition would have lost boots and other articles of clothing essential for survival in a Rocky Mountain winter.[38]

When in 1860 members of the firm of Russell, Majors, and Waddell came to meditate on their experiences in the Mormon War, they were to consider themselves victims of their own generosity and of the army's eminent folly. In that year they presented a claim to the United States Congress for certain sums which they felt the Government in all fairness owed them. When they had been required by the War Department in 1857 to transport an unexpectedly large amount of supplies to Utah on very short notice, they had not demanded a new contract. Instead, they had accepted the promise of the Assistant Quartermaster at Fort Leavenworth that Congress would reward the contractors with a fair profit, or at the very least would protect them from financial loss. Subsequent events proved the worthlessness of this guarantee. Furthermore, the contractors complained that their trains could have reached Utah unharmed by the Mormons if the army had not interfered with their normally rapid rate of travel by forcing them to move with elements of the expedition. Even worse, Van Vliet had ordered the trains in advance of the main army to halt at the Green River, where they were compelled to sit in idleness until the Mormons pounced upon them.[39]

What most enraged the managers of the company, however, was the fact that three of their trains had been destroyed almost within sight of the army and after its two senior officers had received ample warning of impending trouble. Colonel Waite's command had passed the trains only the day before Smith's raid and was still no more than fifteen miles west of them when the attack came. Furthermore a civilian, B. F. Ficklin, advised both Alexander and Waite that numerous Mormons had expressed to him their determination to destroy any wagon trains in the region, but neither officer had moved to forestall this disaster. Only a few days before Ficklin's report had been received, Waite had refused the wagon master of one train a military escort on the ground that the Mormons presented no real danger; now he again failed to use the resources of his regiment to protect the possessions of the contractors when they were but a few miles from his camp. Russell, Majors, and Waddell felt that they had suffered unbearable indignities and asked Congress for the soothing compensation of money.⁴⁰

The contractors' charge of negligence against Colonel Waite had some justification. Although, according to Alexander's later assertion, Waite had been preparing to send a detachment of men to the wagons at the very moment of the attack, it remained clear nevertheless that the Colonel as well as Alexander had failed to provide adequate guards for essential supples in a region alive with unfriendly Mormons.⁴¹

Regardless of where the blame for the loss of the supply trains lay, it had now become apparent to the officers of the expedition that a time for decision had arrived. The various parts of the little army—Alexander's Tenth Regiment, Waite's Fifth Regiment, the artillery batteries of Reno and Phelps, and a great number of supply trains—were at this time, early October, located at a temporary post, Camp Winfield, sixteen miles up Ham's Fork. The men were well protected from the elements, they had enough rations for at least six months, and their position was secure from surprise attack. But they could not remain there indefinitely. Forage in the vicinity of the camp would be adequate for only another two weeks; after that the animals, already weakened by the cold weather, would soon be unable to move the wagons and the other impedimenta of the expedition. Alexander and Waite were also mindful that they had been ordered to establish a military post in Utah. Already ten days of beautiful weather had been lost while the army waited irresolutely for some word from its commander. Unless it began to move, the arrival of winter might well lock it in Camp Winfield until the following spring.

Alexander had permitted this precious time to slip by in the belief that his commanding officer with a number of reinforcements was only a few days to the east. He erred in his estimate of its nearness. In August two companies of the Tenth Infantry, which had remained in Minnesota after the rest of the unit had proceeded to Fort Leavenworth, set out to join their regiment under Lt. Col. Charles F. Smith. At the moment when Alexander was anxiously considering his next move, this detachment had almost reached South Pass. Another body of soldiers, some 200 men, including Dragoons and elements of the Tenth Infantry under First Lt. W. D. Smith, was only a few days to the east. Alexander

would have been heartened to learn that still more important assistance was on its way. On September 11 Albert Sidney Johnston
had taken over command from the reluctant Harney and within
a week had set out to reach his men. Leaving Fort Leavenworth
with him, but traveling more slowly, were six companies of the
Second Dragoons, at last reassigned to the expedition after having been used to quell troubles in Kansas.[42] Thus it seemed that
the army would finally have two things the lack of which had
seriously impeded its progress—an energetic commander and
cavalry to send against the well-mounted Mormons.

Johnston was an alert officer, the type of man greatly needed
to vitalize a campaign hesitatingly launched and ineptly prosecuted. Immediately on assuming command, he characteristically
began to cope with the problems facing him: the difficulty of moving the mail between Fort Leavenworth and Utah during the
winter months, the need for congressional appropriations to meet
the cost of erecting barracks once the troops had reached the Territory, and other details both petty and major.[43] He was aware,
however, that his chief problem was the shortness of time, and so
he sped across the Plains toward his army, guided by that astute
mountain man Jim Bridger. He hurried past the Second Dragoons
under the colorful Philip St. George Cooke, past Lieutenant
Smith's detachment and the two companies of the Tenth Infantry
led by Lieutenant Colonel Smith, and by October 13 had reached
the Sweetwater near South Pass, where he paused to wait for the
other elements to assemble. Soon all parties except Cooke's force
had joined him, and he had also received increased strength by
the enlistment of some 100 men employed in building a wagon
road from Fort Kearney to the eastern boundary of California
under the supervision of W. M. F. Magraw.[44] Johnston was now
ready to join his command. But it was too late. Alexander, having
at last shaken off his indecision, had started lumbering again toward Salt Lake City.

On October 6, while Colonel Johnston was still at Fort Laramie,
Alexander had called a council of war and requested the presence
of Waite, Marcy, Reno, Phelps, and other officers. After a general
denunciation of the Government and William S. Harney for
placing them in their present predicament, the men debated the
best strategy to pursue. They could retreat to the Wind River

4. Albert S. Johnston

Mountains, about ninety miles to the northeast, an excellent site for winter quarters; they could remain at Camp Winfield; or they could struggle on into Utah. The majority opinion favored the aggressive policy of the third alternative, the more so because Colonel Smith and a large body of reinforcements were expected to arrive soon. But this decision in turn raised other questions. From Van Vliet, Alexander had learned that the Mormons had fortified Echo Canyon, the shortest avenue into Salt Lake Valley, with formidable defenses. Furthermore, since all the forage on this road had been burned, the lives of the animals might be endangered if the army should proceed along it.

After discussing various aspects of the situation, the conference finally hit upon a plan so fantastic it astonished Johnston and other military men when they learned of it. The army would move northwest up Ham's Fork, jump across to join Bear River, and follow this route until it reached the northern border of Utah, where several gentle and unfortified valleys led directly into the settlements of the Mormons.[45] Thus, with winter near, Alexander and his advisors decided to turn from the most direct entrance into Utah in favor of a road one hundred miles longer that had few if any real advantages. Brigham Young's sabre-rattling before Van Vliet seemed to have served the Mormons well.

On October 7, the day after the conference in his tent, Alexander assumed command of the expedition and ordered his men to make ready to march. He entertained the hope that somewhere along the Bear River road the Mormons would stand and fight, thus giving his men an opportunity to inflict a crushing defeat upon them and compel them to sue for peace.[46] After completing its final preparations, the army began to leave Camp Winfield on October 11. For three days the column, seven miles long from the Tenth Infantry in the van to the Fifth Infantry at the rear, made fair progress along Ham's Fork, and the morale of the troops was high, despite the presence of Mormons in the nearby hills. Although the weather was cold and the road rough, the men were healthy and delighted to be moving again, after so many stagnant days.[47]

This pleasant situation was short-lived. By October 13 the road had become nearly impassable and the army's animals, reduced to a sage-brush diet, became incapable of more than short marches.

The skies filled with clouds, an ominous sign at this late season. Mormon cavalry hovered incessantly around the column, and, although a detachment of soldiers under Capt. Randolph B. Marcy almost succeeded in ambushing one party, the Saints' superior mounts usually kept them out of rifle range. On October 17 the threatened snowstorm arrived and halted the army after it had traveled a scant thirty-five miles from Camp Winfield. At this point Alexander began to question the soundness of his decision to follow the Bear River route into Utah. It was now apparent that the reinforcements under Lieutenant Colonel Smith were not near at hand after all. Furthermore, orders from the Mormon commander Gen. Daniel Wells, recently found on a prisoner, revealed to Alexander that the enemy was prepared to harass the expedition in all possible ways except by an open attack: burning grass, destroying fords, stampeding cattle, and committing other obstructive acts. The arrival of bad weather was but one more factor causing Alexander alarm.[48]

In the light of these unfortuitous developments the Colonel called another council of war to discuss strategy. Again the officers were divided in their proposals, some urging continuation of the march into Utah by the Bear River route; others suggesting that the column turn east and winter in the Wind River Mountains; and a few, in the folly of desperation, proposing that the army burn its cumbersome supply trains and with two months' provisions make a dash into Utah. At length Alexander decided to plod back to Camp Winfield, which he had left more than a week before. Once again, however, lethargy settled upon him; he permitted his men to remain at their present camp on the upper banks of Ham's Fork for another eight days.[49]

At this point, with the Colonel paralyzed by irresolution, Johnston finally established contact, and for the first time since the expedition had left Fort Leavenworth it received an authoritative message from its commanding officer. Johnston realized that Alexander, if he tried to continue his present line of march, might so entangle himself "in the midst of the deep snow of the valley of Bear River . . . as to place him beyond the means of extraction." Accordingly he ordered the troops to return to their former camp on Ham's Fork, where he would meet them.[50] The Mormons had achieved one of their primary goals, avoidance of open hostilities in 1857; now there would be an opportunity for peaceful negotiation of their difficulties with the Government before the spring thaws permitted the army to reach their community.

But the threat of civil war had not passed. There were many in the army, as in the nation, who hoped for a showdown with the Saints. When Alexander abandoned his advance, he wrote: "Nothing causes me such poignant regret as to be obliged to give up my designs of penetrating to Salt Lake City." [51] The more forceful Johnston, already a dedicated opponent of the Mormons, told Winfield Scott that Brigham Young's proclamation of September 15 proved "the necessity of a conquest of these traitorous people." [52]

Painfully the soldiers and their 4,000 animals struggled down Ham's Fork to the place of rendezvous chosen by their commander. Badly worn, they arrived there on November 2. Having gained nothing by their exertions of the past weeks, they had returned to a camp with pitifully inadequate forage and dangerously low temperatures. But worse was to come. When Johnston at last joined the army, he saw immediately that its present location would not suffice for winter quarters. Its only hope, he realized, was Fort Bridger, thirty-five miles away.[53]

On November 6 began the desperate race for that sheltered valley before the animals failed completely. Intense cold froze the feet of the Dragoons on patrol and congealed the grease on the caissons' axles. Captain Gove wrote his wife that in the subzero weather outpost duty had become almost unbearable, that he himself had almost perished from the cold one night. Savage snowstorms at times forced the men to huddle under any natural protection available. The animals, already weakened by the cold, had little to eat beside cottonwood bark and sage; the eighty horses in Phelps' battery received only twelve bushels of corn during the first eleven days of November. The stock accordingly died in such great numbers along the road that a soldier who followed the trail of the army in the summer of 1858 found carcasses of mules and oxen at every hundred steps. As the cattle staggered and fell, the time came when there were no longer enough animals to move the trains; the oxen remaining on their feet therefore had to drag some wagons a few miles and then return for others. With Johnston occasionally leading his men on foot, the troops

bore the ordeal in good spirits, and their hardness, the result of
several months' labors, stood them in good stead. Yet Johnston was
not melodramatically enlarging upon the facts when he later wrote:
"The army under my command took the last possible step for-
ward at Bridger, in the condition of the animals then alive." [54]

As Johnston suffered through this last stage of the 1857 campaign, his methodical nature caused him to investigate the army's
recent losses in order to ascertain its position. Three trains with
300,000 pounds of food, he knew, had been burned by the Mormons a month earlier. He learned also that the daring Porter
Rockwell had stolen some 800 head of cattle belonging to Russell,
Majors, and Waddell in the third week of October, and that another 300 animals had been run off by the Mormons just before
the army left Ham's Fork. Weather and the lack of forage had
further depleted the stock: during Alexander's futile advance up
Ham's Fork and the final march to Bridger, at least 3,000 head of
cattle perished of starvation and cold. The military effectiveness
of his force was badly impaired, too, for both batteries had only
half their requisite number of horses and almost two-thirds of
the Dragoons had no mounts at all.[55]

Unenviably situated, Johnston looked upon the Mormons in
their homes beyond the Wasatch Mountains with a baleful eye.
"They have with meditation," he concluded, "placed themselves
in rebellion against the Union, and entertain the insane design of
establishing a form of government thoroughly despotic, and utterly
repugnant to our institutions . . . I have ordered that wherever
they are met in arms, they be treated as enemies." [56] In the
Civil War Albert Sidney Johnston and Jesse A. Gove were to
disagree on the matter of secession, and in 1862 each gave his life
as a warranty of his conviction. In 1857, however, they agreed
that the Mormons had engineered a reprehensible attack upon
the nation and must be severely punished.

Although the expedition's desperate march to Black's Fork had
brought it to a satisfactory haven for the winter, Johnston's command was still not safely united. One detachment of cavalry under
Lt. Col. Philip St. George Cooke remained on the snowy road
east of the new camp. After their tour of duty in Kansas, during
which time Governor Walker had called upon them only once,
the Second Dragoons had hastily assembled at Leavenworth in

mid-September preparatory to joining the rest of the Utah army. This force was needed not only to protect the expedition from the raids of the Mormons but also to provide an escort for the corpulent person of the Territory's new governor, Alfred Cumming, and his charming if loquacious wife. To the valorous Cooke the whole episode became a nightmare. After several months' service in the field, the six companies of his regiment had been allowed less than a week to reorganize, transfer men, obtain animals, and make the other urgent preparations for a thousand-mile journey. On September 16 the inspector general reviewed the troops in a rain that prohibited any careful investigation of their fitness. After Cooke had received 100 footsore mules and a few inexperienced teamsters, he was declared ready for the trip. Johnston had confidently expected him to reach Salt Lake City by November 20; when on that day he reported to his colonel at Fort Bridger he felt himself fortunate to have come as far as he had.[57]

From the first, Cooke's party had experienced difficulty on its trek to Mormon country. At the end of the first four days it had traveled only twenty-two miles, the condition of the animals and the poorness of the road impeding its progress. By the time the Dragoons had reached Fort Kearney, seventy-seven soldiers had deserted. West of Kearney the command first met rain, then eleven days of snow and sleet, which decimated its horses, already weakened by the absence of sufficient forage. At Fort Laramie, where Indian agent Jacob Forney, Attorney General John Hartnett, and Marshal Peter K. Dotson joined them, the Dragoons rested for their encounter with the dreary wastes separating them from the expedition. Cooke's orders would have permitted him to winter at Fort Laramie, but the conscientious officer had learned of the army's need for cavalry and so pressed on.

This final march was an ordeal for everyone. Early in November a savage snowstorm scattered the troops and their stock near Devil's Gate. On November 8, when the temperature reached 44 degrees below zero, Cooke abandoned five of his wagons, hoping that thus unimpeded he could make more rapid progress, and struggled on through two feet of snow. On November 15 the severe cold inflicted serious damage when thirty-six soldiers and teamsters were frostbitten. Maddened by the cold and lack of food, the mules destroyed the wagon-tongues to which they were tied, ate away their ropes, and attacked the camp's tents, dying in great numbers. Mrs. Cumming was annoyed at being unable to wash for many days, but Cooke feared that if their animals should all die, they, too, would perish in this howling desert. Like Johnston before him, he was aware when he finally stumbled into Fort Bridger that his party could not have gone many miles farther.

Because of Cooke's ability as a leader only one man died during the arduous march, and he had been a victim of lockjaw. When General Scott praised the expedition for its courageous march to winter quarters, with justification he chose Cooke for special commendation. But of the 144 horses in his original command, 130 lay dead on the thousand miles of Plains behind him. Furthermore, the morale of his men had been shaken by their travail. Johnston's army was now united on the banks of Black's Fork, but it was not an impressive fighting machine.[58]

6. The Mormons Organize

I N UTAH the summer and fall was a feverish period, for the Church faced a number of urgent problems. It needed first to estimate the peril facing it, and then to formulate an appropriate defensive strategy. Furthermore, it had to arrange its propaganda, in order to prepare its people for coming sacrifices. If the future should bring war, or at least a lengthy period of tension with the United States, the Church had to mobilize its financial resources and assemble food, clothing, weapons, and other necessary supplies. Although in early 1857 Brigham Young and some of his counselors might well have anticipated a military demonstration against them, they had made no preparations to meet it when Rockwell and his begrimed comrades broke into the Pioneers' Day celebration in Big Cottonwood Canyon. With troops already on the march toward Utah from Fort Leavenworth, the Mormons had need to act quickly.

In his correspondence with Colonel Alexander, Young had justified his hostile attitude toward the troops on Ham's Fork by certain legalistic quibbles. The Organic Act of the Territory, he maintained, gave the governor a term of four years unless he was replaced by a person duly qualified and appointed. Since Young had not been notified of his dismissal, a serious oversight indicative of the carelessness with which Buchanan had framed his policy toward Utah, he now insisted that he still held the executive office. Because he had not been formally apprised of the expedition, Young as noted (above, p. 108), could contend that it was a mob, not an army of the United States. On this pretext he used his power as commander in chief of the territorial militia to protect his people from invasion by a gang of irregulars.[1] Obviously delighted with these arguments carelessly provided by the President, the Mormons frequently drew upon them; even after the crisis

had passed, Young still spoke of having averted "the progress
into our settlements of certain armed forces (subsequently ascertained to be a detachment of the U.S. Army)." [2]

Although such questionable reasoning was useful to the Mormons in the war of words accompanying the military aspects of
the campaign, its comparison of the army to a mob also revealed
their actual fears of the soldiers. Possibly Young realized that the
Government had not ordered a force to Utah in order to hang the
leaders of the Church and drive the Saints from their homes.
Yet the days of anguish in Missouri and Illinois and the more recent experiences with Steptoe's soldiers had made him apprehensive of any collection of armed Gentiles. Buchanan might have
sent the men merely to compel obedience in the Territory to the
laws of the United States, but would they remember the true purpose of the expedition once they had reached Utah? Young thought
not. To his mind the troops, be their orders ever so pacific, would
become a pack of incensed Mormon-haters like those who had
besieged Far West and stormed through the streets of Nauvoo.[3]

The Mormons' unflattering estimate of the troops was accurate
to a certain extent. In an effort to strengthen its military establishment, the Government in 1855 had increased the pay of officers
and men, so that by April 1857 an unmarried person entering the
army received between eleven and twenty-two dollars a month,
with such additional benefits as food, clothing, and medical supervision; but these inducements failed to stimulate enlistment.
Civilians of the 1850's clung to their opinion that the service was
a particularly unattractive career. As the editor of the New York
Times observed, the common soldier was rarely billeted in comfortable towns but instead "passes from swamp to swamp and forest
to forest." Because of its unpopularity, the army frequently drew
its recruits from the less stable elements of society, men who were
persuaded to enlist because of desperate poverty or some similarly
compelling reason. When in 1858 General Smith ordered that
none of the troops be paid until the column had reached Fort Laramie, the editor of the *Missouri Republican* protested the ruling
as unfair to the soldiers, for "it is to get money for present necessities that induces them to adopt *this kind of life*." [4]

John W. Phelps found the men in his battery "exceedingly
stupid," "naturally defective in intellect," so depraved that "they

would sell their last article of clothing for liquor." [5] With reason, therefore, the Mormons became alarmed as the army approached their borders, fearful lest it precipitate "scenes of bloodshed and cruel oppression" when it reached their settlements. The editor of the *Times* agreed with the Saints in this matter, for in 1858 he wrote of the campaign: "Was it right to send troops composed of the wildest and most rebellious men of the country . . . to deal out fire and sword upon people whose faults ever were the result of honest religious convictions?" [6]

Believing the common soldiers of the expedition to be individuals of dangerous passions, the Saints were also convinced that they were commanded by men whose anti-Mormon antipathies were deep-rooted. Despite Captain Marcy's statement that he knew of no officer who wished to interfere with the Church, this dread of the army officers' hostile attitude was well founded. According to his biographer, General Harney "had fully determined, on arriving at Salt Lake City, to capture Brigham Young and the twelve apostles, and execute them in a summary fashion, and winter in the Temple of the Latter-day Saints." Perhaps Harney's plans were not so bloodthirsty as this authority indicated; at any rate he had no opportunity to act upon them. But the temper of other officers who made the long march to Utah was equally violent. When Phelps reported for duty at Fort Leavenworth in June 1857, he declared in his diary: "Their [the Mormons'] opposition to our Government cannot be overcome without the destruction of its cause, which involves the complete destruction of their life as a public body." From his camp on the Sweetwater Colonel Smith of the Tenth Infantry wrote in October 1857: "I shall regard [the Mormons] as enemies and fire upon the scoundrels if they give me the least opportunity." At the same time Captain Gove was ardently hoping for a chance to meet the Saints in battle.[7]

The Mormons had not only the expedition's soldiers to fear. During the summer and early fall contractors Russell, Majors, and Waddell had sent 328 ox wagons to Utah; the sutlers and other merchants traveling with the column had another 160 wagons in their trains. When the army reached the Territory, it would therefore bring a great horde of drivers and wagon masters with it, men who had been recruited by advertisements in the barrooms and on the

streets of Leavenworth City. A lieutenant of the Fifth Infantry
reported that the teamsters under his charge were an unruly
bunch, careless with government property and obedient only to
a regimen of the strictest discipline. One of the drivers in the
employ of the contractors complained that most of his fellows were
hot-headed Southerners who had come west to fight Free Soilers
in Kansas; a worthless lot, constantly wrangling among themselves
when no one else was available. There were even more outspoken
condemnations: "scum of the great Western Cities—a class more
dangerous, because more intelligent and reckless, than the same
class of population in New York." If the Saints managed to live
in peace with Johnston's army, they would still run the risk of
collision with the civilians who accompanied it.[8]

Another fear of the Mormons in 1857 centered upon the newly
appointed territorial officers. With a reprehensible indifference
the Government had not told the people of Utah who their officials were to be; the Saints knew only that they were Gentiles.
Aware of the enmity toward them in the East, they presumed that
these men were antagonistic to the Church and had been selected
because of the strength of their animosity. Learning that the new
governor was a man named Cumming, they confused this bumbling
Georgian with a well-known Mormon-baiter of Missouri. A memorial of the Legislative Assembly bitterly complained: "You
have appointed . . . a full set of officers for Utah from among entire strangers, and to do so were obliged to hawk about the offices
from State to State . . . until at length you succeeded in finding
the requisite number among the reckless, the drunken, the unprincipled, the dissolute, the houseless, the penniless." [9]

For these reasons the Mormons entertained little doubt that
the Government's expedition, if permitted to enter their Territory,
would certainly shatter the peace of the Valley and might even
destroy the Church. What, then, was their strategy in the face
of the peril? It is evident that this devout folk relied upon the
power of God to preserve them from the assaults of their enemies,
for often in the anxious days following the summer of 1857 the
Hierarchy predicted that the Lord would not permit His people
to be destroyed. At times Young, Kimball, and others even read a
cosmic meaning into the events of the period, seeing in the campaign against them Satan's last mighty effort to crush the Chil-

dren of Light, with Buchanan, Floyd, Drummond and the rest acting as instruments of the Prince of Darkness.[10]

Although Young was a pious man, he was also a practical Yankee who believed that the Lord helped those who helped themselves. He was therefore not disposed to limit his defense merely to prayer. His specific plans for meeting the emergency, however, are difficult to ascertain today, either because they were recorded in volumes not now available to the Gentile historian or, more probably because of his own indecision. Study of the Mormons' speeches and writings reveals that the Church did not pursue a single policy in the critical months of 1857 and 1858. Its strategy passed through two distinct phases.

The Church's first course, followed from July to early October 1857, seems to have been one of determined resistance to Buchanan's expedition. When Daniel H. Wells sent orders to the district commanders of the Nauvoo Legion on August 1, he warned: "In such times when anarchy takes the place of orderly Government, and mobocratic tyranny usurps the power to rule, [the Mormons] are left to their inalienable right to defend themselves." In early September, Young wrote to the Saints in Honolulu that the people of Utah would resist aggression "by making an appeal to God and our own right arms," and later in the month S. W. Richards repeated the same belligerent sentiments to Kane. As if preparing for a long war, the Church recalled its missionaries from abroad, closed its outposts in California and Carson Valley, and made other arrangements of a military nature.[11]

For all this bold talk, however, it was not the purpose of the Mormon Hierarchy to plunge its people into a sanguinary struggle with the forces of the United States. The resistance envisaged by Brigham Young and Wells was confined to the burning of grass, stampeding of stock, and other acts designed to slow the advance of the army. Behind this policy lay the belief of the Mormon leaders that if an engagement could be avoided until the arrival of winter, negotiations between the Church and the Government might settle the difficulties existing between them.[12]

But in case the harassments of the Nauvoo Legion and the toll taken by the weather should fail to halt the army's entrance into the Valley of the Salt Lake, the Mormon leaders in these early months were prepared as a last resort to fight behind the natural

fortifications of the Territory, first in Echo Canyon and then in
other strongholds. For a number of years Brigham Young had
convinced himself that there were many regions in the mountains where his people could hide, retreats capable of concealing
the entire Church from its adversaries.[13] In mid-September he expressed this consideration to Col. William H. Dame, a military
district commander in southern Utah: "The plan of operation is
supposed to be about these [sic]. In case the U.S. Government
should send out on overpowering force, we intend to desolate the
Territory and conceal our families, stock, and all our effects in
the fastnesses of the mountains, where they will be safe while the
men, waylaying our enemies, attack them from ambush, and stampede their animals." [14]

Despite these sober preparations for war, the Mormon strategists
in their first deliberations were hopeful of gaining their preferred objective, a non-military settlement of the crisis. They felt
that several factors in addition to their own raids might stop the
expedition before it had reached them. Learning of grumblings
in the army, they hoped that the low morale of the soldiers might
prevent their arrival in an opportune season, and they scattered
circulars among the troops, offering inducements to deserters.
This unwarranted expectation received encouragement when
Wells wrote in mid-October that many soldiers in the expedition
were eager to go over to the Saints. The Mormons also thought
that eastern opposition to Buchanan's Utah policy, the troubles
in Kansas, the rebelliousness of the Plains Indians, or other disturbances might compel the Administration to recall the army,
if only peace, however uneasy, could be temporarily preserved.
Occasionally this confidence had a rude shock from reports of
the expedition's size and of its rapid advance across the prairie,
yet in general the Mormon leaders did not at first doubt that all
would be well. Although at times they cautioned their people to
prepare for evacuation and the destruction of their property, they
also fostered the comforting belief that in all probability such ex-
treme measures would not be required. "Our enemies are in the
pit," the Church Historian wrote, "and [there is] a fair prospect
of their being destroyed without our shedding their blood." [15]

The Mormons' strategy entered another phase in November

1857, when the mood of the Hierarchy began to shift from assurance to concern for the future. At this time the raids of Lot
Smith, the army's tardy departure from Fort Leavenworth, and
the arrival of winter finally created the situation the Mormons had
desired—avoidance of an early engagement with the troops. "The
enemy baffled, crippled, and dispirited were compelled to seek for
Winter Quarters," Adjutant General James Ferguson grandilo-
quently reported in early January. "Without the firing of a single
gun on our part, they were most effectively defeated; and all their
loud bravado epilogued into a cold seat around the ashes of Forts
Bridger and Supply." [16] Having gained their objective, the Mormons might have been expected to regain their earlier attitude of
confident crusaders. Instead, the gloom of the Church's spokesmen deepened during the winter months. Their speeches dwelt
upon the misfortunes of the Saints, hounded in the past by angry
mobs and now set upon by a government openly seeking their
destruction.[17] This plaintive reference to persecution rather than
victory indicates a new stage in their strategy-making, akin to the
pessimistic period of late 1857.

There were a number of causes for their depression at a seemingly auspicious time. News of the Government's activities was
far from encouraging. Instead of re-examining its policy, now
that its expedition had become winterbound at Fort Bridger, the
Administration by January was making preparations to reinforce
the army and also to launch an attack from California upon
Utah's indefensible western border. Other hopes of the Church
had also failed to materialize. Although a few newspapers in the
East had become critical of the Government, there was no significant Gentile demand for negotiations with the Mormons.
Among the troops, furthermore, no enervating collapse of morale
occurred. Finally, the Hierarchy came to realize early in 1858 that
for all their euphoric talk of the previous summer they were woe-
fully unprepared for any encounter with an organized and well-
equipped army. Supplies of clothing were low, production of
powder completely inadequate, and the territorial arsenal "dilap-
idated." The desperation of the position was dramatically revealed when Ferguson recommended the manufacture of bows
and arrows for his troops. It was becoming apparent to Young,

Wells, Kimball, and their associates that it would be folly to resist the expedition either in an open battle or by a scorched-earth campaign.[18]

With these ominous considerations in mind the high priests began to place their hope of safety in flight from still another country made inhospitable by Gentiles. In the past Young had referred to this possibility, and early in 1858 a number of towns had approved resolutions supporting it if it should prove mandatory. A formal council of war of March 18, attended by the First Presidency, eight Apostles, and a number of military officers, heard Young advise the Saints to "go into the desert and not war with the people [of the United States], but let them destroy themselves." [19] On March 21 at a special conference in the Tabernacle, Young delivered a lengthy exposition of this new strategy in words lacking his former bravado.

If he had been Joseph Smith in the last days of Nauvoo, Young announced, he would have left the people and escaped into the wilderness, instead of submitting meekly to imprisonment in Carthage. Having in this fashion posited the wisdom of flight, he then described the Church's position in grave terms. The anti-Mormons were plotting "to blot us out of existence if they can." Resistance was futile, he warned. "If we open the ball upon them by slaying the United States soldiery, just so sure they would be fired up with anger to lavishly spend their means to compass our destruction, and thousands and millions if necessary would furnish means, if the Government was not able." Retreat into the uninhabited areas near by was the only alternative left to the Saints. At this point Young introduced his favorite, and mistaken, conviction that in the desert expanses of the Territory there were regions sufficiently supplied with water to support a population of 500,000. To these mythical oases, then, the Mormons would go, first a band of 500 pioneers and then the emigration of the entire Church to a New Zion.[20]

Thus the strategy had traveled the full distance from defiance of the federal army to retreat from Utah. Soon the leaders would be preparing for the "Move South," packing away the papers of their archives and making their other arrangements. The martial tones of their earlier speeches had now faded. With only an echo of his former boldness, Young announced that if the soldiers tried to enter the Valley before the Saints had left, "we will send them to their long home." But, he added quickly, prudent retreat rather than bloody warfare was the better policy. To an audience which had once heard him speak of smiting the adversary he explained: "Some may marvel why the Lord says, 'rather than fight your enemies, go away'; it is because many of the people are so grossly wicked, that were we to go out to fight, thousands of the Elders would go into eternity, and women and children would perish." [21]

The propaganda of the Church, reflecting the shift in tactics during the course of the war, also fell into distinct phases. In the first period it was apparently designed to instill in the Mormons a firm hostility toward the Government's expedition and confidence that victory, like virtue, lay upon their weapons. Having decided to oppose Johnston's army, at least by bloodless means, the leaders of the faith sought the support of an aroused populace willing to bear the burdens of an exacting campaign. Then at the end of the year, when the Hierarchy was beginning to experience grave fears for the future, the appeals changed in tone, now becoming less aggressive and even at times plaintive.

In other years Young and his assistants had not let their people forget past misfortunes. They recognized the elementary fact, apparent to religious figures through the ages, that persecution heightens faith, that men love to think of their sect as God's remnant, loyal to His truth in spite of the ravings of the wicked. During the crisis with the central government in 1857 the Church's need for this devotion increased. Accordingly the sermons and other public addresses of the Mormon oracles harked back with even more frequency to the earlier persecutions visited upon this people: the sufferings in Missouri and Illinois, the requisition of the Mormon Battalion, and the difficulties with the United States during the 1850's.[22] At the same time the Saints' leaders also undertook to see to it that their followers entertained no illusions concerning the purpose of the present expedition. Wilford Woodruff, the plain-spoken, earnest workhorse of the faith, put it clearly: "An army has been sent by the United States to make war upon us for the sole purpose of destroying the Church of Jesus Christ of Latter-day Saints." Kimball envisaged wholesale executions if the troops should arrive: "when they come here, the first dab will be to take brother Brigham Young, and Heber C. Kim-

ball, and others, and they will slay us. That is their design; and if
we will not yield to their meanness, they will say we have muti-
nized against the President of the United States, and they will put
us under martial law and massacre the people." [23]

Having thus darkly defined the crisis in order to strengthen the
will of their people, the Mormon priests in these first optimistic
weeks declared their sect to be a church militant, prepared to resist the assaults of the Gentiles by all means, including force.
Young's sermons at times skirted an open declaration of war; the
words of other speakers became increasingly violent. As though
to fill the place left by the death of the uncontrollable Jedediah
Grant, the beloved Kimball frequently became bombastic: "Send
2500 troops here, my brethren, to make a desolation of this people! God Almighty helping us, I will fight until there is not a drop
of blood in my veins. Good God! I have enough wives to whip
out the United States, for they will whip themselves: Amen." In
their efforts to arouse a sentiment favorable to their policy of resistance, Young and Kimball even spoke of possible independence
from the United States, thus at last revealing a secessionist spirit
which the Gentiles thought they had detected earlier. These
harangues aroused the people to a defiant mood. "What say you,
brethren, will we go it?" asked Kimball. "If so, raise your right
hands and say aye. (One loud 'AYE' rang through the congregation.)" [24] The Hierarchy could rest confident that the Mormons
supported its initial plan to prevent the army from reaching Salt
Lake City.

During the summer and fall of 1857 the Saints listened excit-
edly to these belligerent exhortations. In November a change entered the sermons. Although on rare occasions Young still said
that he "carried a long Bowie knife and swore by the eternal Gods
that if they come to take him he would send them to Hell across
lots," [25] more frequently his words, reflecting the new strategy of
the Church, did not have their former combativeness. Instead of
demanding the destruction of the army, he told his people why
they should not mete out swift punishment to the troops. The
soldiers, he once announced, were only the innocent tools of evil
men. At other times Young offered different excuses for his refusal to annihilate the army, despite his maledictions of the early
campaign, among them the curious reasoning that "if we spilt

their blood there was an atonement but if we let them kill themselves they would go to Hell and stay there." [26] Whatever the public explanation, by the end of 1857 Young and his advisors had
resolved upon flight, and accordingly ceased trying to arouse in
their followers a belligerent attitude. Young's vague predictions
of eventual victory now dwelt upon the long reach of the future,
not the immediate emergency.[27]

In their mobilization for war the Mormon chiefs were not compelled to shift their policies, as they had their defensive plans and
their appeals to the people. From the hostility of eastern opinion
and the size of the Government's forces they could judge the grav-
ity of the crisis facing them and prepare for the worst. One of
Young's early acts, after his conversations with Van Vliet, was the
proclamation of September 15 declaring martial law and restricting civilian movement within the Territory. By this order the
Church was empowered to halt any unfriendly conduct by Gentiles or backsliders behind the lines. In the course of the war the
Church's control became so complete that men needed the permission of the militia's officers to travel within Utah.[28]

Under this strict supervision the Saints treated the few Gentiles
who strayed into their country with much the same mixture of
severity and honesty as during earlier years. Newspapers occasionally carried accounts of the Saints' atrocities, such as Hickman's murder of a young man on the command of Young, the
long imprisonment and attempted slaying of one F. E. McNeil
and several other men once attached to the expedition, and the
murder of the six men in the Aikens Party by Mormon assassins.[29]
But these reports seem to have had little basis in fact. The story
of two teamsters who spoke of good treatment during a trip
through Utah in the winter of 1857–58 more accurately revealed
the Mormons' wartime behavior toward Gentiles in their midst.[30]

Along with Young's proclamation came another act which indicated the Saints' anxiety, namely the recall of missionaries and
colonists who were scattered about the country and abroad. The
Church stopped its two principal periodicals, the *Western Standard* in San Francisco and the *Mormon* in New York. Apostles
Orson Pratt and Ezra T. Benson, who were in England, and some
thirty elders in other European countries were ordered home at
the same time. Of greater significance was the closing of two mis-

130   THE MORMON CONFLICT

sions in the West, Carson Valley in present-day Nevada and San
Bernardino on the Coast. Begun by private individuals in 1849,
the former attained importance when the Church sent Orson
Hyde with a number of Mormons to that desert region in an effort
to make it a "subsidiary gathering place." By 1857 450 people
had settled there. Despite this early labor and auspicious start,
Young did not hesitate to break up the colony in August 1857. A
similar policy was carried out in San Bernardino. Filling the vital
position as the Mormons' only access to the sea, it had grown rapidly in population and wealth after its founding in 1851, until
it had become a town of at least 1,500 people, perhaps even twice
that figure. At the end of the summer of 1857 Young instructed
the residents to sell their property and return to Salt Lake City.[31]

There is some disagreement over the real purpose of this disruption of settlements established at much expense and labor.
According to one interpretation, Young had always opposed the
work of colonization, especially in San Bernardino, for he feared
that Mormons located far from the central offices of the Church
would lose the earnestness of their faith. According to this view
he used the war as an excuse to end an undesirable diaspora of his
people.[32] A more plausible explanation lies in the Mormons' need
for supplies, primarily ammunition and weapons. Badly equipped
for a long contest with a determined and well-organized army,
the Church could acquire desperately needed stores if its people
in Carson Valley and San Bernardino sold their property and
with the revenue purchased powder and arms on the West Coast.
Peter Conover, who took to Carson Valley the order to disband
the colony, collected at least $12,000 from the settlers, with which
he bought supplies in California. Before they left San Bernardino,
the Saints there accumulated such a large stock of weapons that
nearby Gentiles debated for a time whether to blockade Cajon
Pass in order to prevent this material from passing into the hands
of the rebels in Utah.[33]

Recognizing the campaign against them to be no ephemeral
storm, soon to disappear with the heat of the summer, the Mormons became aware that one of their most pressing problems was
finance. Even in quiet years the people of Utah had been embarrassed by lack of specie, for they exported nothing to the States
and thus had an unfavorable balance of trade. Until 1857 their

primary source of money had been the California emigrants, who had frequently purchased cattle and provisions in Utah. When the outbreak of the war halted travel on the overland roads, this lucrative traffic disappeared. Young's interdiction of all mining activity in Utah, based on his conviction that the greedy search for gold destroyed men's faith, denied the Mormons a possible source of wealth. In its system of tithing the Church had an effective taxation device, but the people soon had no currency with which to pay this levy and were forced to make their contributions in stock or goods. The failure of the Y. X. Carrying Company further impoverished the sect. In addition to pouring its own funds into this abortive enterprise, the Church had become indebted to Livingstone and Kincead, a Gentile firm in Utah, which by October 1857 had begun to press for payment.[34] In January, Adjutant General James Ferguson finally wrote Young that the Ordnance department of the militia was completely without money. The territorial legislature, he said, must act to meet the costs of the campaign.[35]

By this time Young had come to see that his Church could meet its increased obligations only by the issue of paper, in view of the shortage of specie and absence of revenue. During their first years in the Salt Lake Basin the Saints had manufactured their own money, first gold coins minted from the dust brought by the members of the Mormon Battalion from California, and then three issues of scrip.[36] In the financial crisis of 1858 Young resorted to the latter expedient. At a general convocation in the Tabernacle on January 19 he proposed the creation of the Deseret Currency Association, a banking venture with capital composed of livestock, authorized to issue and redeem notes of various denominations. Within two days the people had approved the plan by pledging at their ward meetings to sustain the paper. As was the case with the Y. X. Carrying Company and indeed all important activities of the Church, the officers of the new bank were members of the Hierarchy, with Young serving as president, Daniel Wells as treasurer, and Hiram B. Clawson as secretary.

Since the shortage of money in Utah was acute, the Currency Association hastily printed its first notes on the presses of the *Deseret News* until David McKenzie, later convicted of forgery under a Gentile judge, had finished the engraving of plates.

Throughout the war and the "Move South" the Association continued to produce the paper, until it had put some $100,000 into
circulation. At first the people kept their promise to honor it, but
in May, Young began to hear reports of a growing opposition,
and by July a large portion of the Territory's population would
not accept the Currency Association's notes in business transac-
tions. By this time, however, the undertaking had accomplished
its purpose, for the active phase of the Mormon War had ended.[37]

The Church employed other means than the issuance of paper
money to meet the financial demands upon it. Of great importance were voluntary contributions of brethren who offered
money and, more often, supplies to support the militia. In response to a request from Young, the Saints in every ward raised
popular subscriptions to equip units of the Nauvoo Legion. Residents of the Seventh Ward gave wheat, corn, horses, steers, cows,
hats, shoes, and a variety of other items including personal service
to the army, a generosity duplicated in many other divisions of the
Church. Before the legislature adjourned in December, each
member was asked to state how many soldiers he could outfit.
Since the soldiers of each military unit were obliged to pay all
the debts of their command, their families and friends had the
duty of helping them shoulder this burden as well.[38]

When voluntary donations proved inadequate, the officers of
the sect resorted to requisition. Thus one person complained that
men had taken his cattle to feed the Mormon troops, and Pace, a
commander of one of the Territory's military districts, reported
to Wells that he had seized two horses from an individual who had
been unwilling to part with them. Faced with a shortage of clothing in the fall of 1857, Brig. Gen. Aaron Johnson revealed the
Church's determination to secure supplies by force if necessary
when he wrote a colonel in Springville that if he knew "where
[clothes] might be spared, please help yourself, for *now* is the time
it is needed by our brethren." [39]

In spite of these measures, Mormon soldiers suffered from lack
of certain essentials, especially protection against the penetrating
cold of winter. In early November, when the Saints were still fearful lest Johnston's army attempt to force its way into their Valley,
1,300 militiamen were sent to reinforce the troops already in the
mountains. Many of these recruits left Salt Lake City with poor

shoes, straw hats, and no tents, to battle eight-foot drifts on Big
Mountain. A teamster captured by the Mormons during the
winter wrote that the soldiers he saw in Echo Canyon were a
ragged collection of men: "And such clothing! It was impossible
to tell what the original goods were. Remnants of old bed quilts
and blankets served as overcoats." One member of a company
from Lehi had no shoes at all for a time, and James Nelson,
covered only by a suit made of flax, remembered: "I had to mend
my pants about every other day." The shortage of clothing eventually became so serious that by May 1858 the Mormons had difficulty outfitting men for service in the mountains. Since there
was little the Church could do to remedy the situation, its people
were compelled to bear the privations throughout the course of
the war.[40]

Inadequate food supplies brought as much concern in Utah as
lack of clothing. The War Department's bland assumption in 1857
that Harney would find ample provisions once his column had
reached Utah was ill-founded, for severe weather had badly damaged harvests in recent years. The low reserves and the dim pros-
pects for their replenishment made the Saints careful husbandmen.
Young and Kimball, who had urged a tight-fisted frugality upon
their people even in years of plenty, cautioned Mormons to save
every particle of food and every drop of milk. Officers of the militia
used their authority to conserve rations. Wells ordered Pace to
thresh the grain as his first duty, and Aaron Johnson requested his
subordinates to report "the names of persons who waste or needlessly feed grain to animals." In a number of localities men in companies of tens, equipped with wagons and teams, harvested crops
belonging to men absent in the militia, lest these provisions be
lost. Where there were not enough men for these tasks, women
and children worked in the fields, at times to the detriment of
their health.[41]

But for Young and the other Mormon leaders, who in the early
weeks of the campaign had determined to resist the expedition
pacifically if possible but resolutely in any case, the most alarming deficiency continued to be of weapons and ammunition. In
July 1857 muster rolls of nineteen companies numbering 807
officers and men listed only 198 muskets and 242 rifles.[42] Ferguson's formal report of January 1858 revealed this problem more

clearly. In July, he announced, there had been 6,100 militiamen in the Territory's military districts, with perhaps another 1,000 "efficient men" also available, for whom there were 2,364 rifles, 1,159 muskets, 99 pistols, and 295 revolvers. In other words fully a third of the soldiers were unarmed and many of the rest were badly equipped. According to Ferguson's letter, affairs had not brightened in the intervening months. With a show of confidence he announced that many guns, previously cast aside because of "trifling damages," had been fixed and were now in use.[43] Since it was unlikely that the Mormons, or any frontier people, would have possessed enough weapons to allow a careless discard of impaired items, the arms reclaimed by Ferguson must have been of dubious value in a war with the United States army.

Lack of guns and ammunition impaired the Church's early defensive maneuvers. Peter Conover wrote in his diary that Young had instructed him "to take a company of men and go out to meet the Army" but had later countermanded the order because of the command's unpreparedness. From Warren Snow in Manti, Wells received a report of a "poor situation for arms very much so . . . Ammunition we must have in order to use what fiewe arms we have got." Johnson in Springville and other officers also wrote of their needs. If the Church was determined to prevent the expedition from entering Utah, it would have to find adequate equipment.[44]

There were several places to which the Mormons could turn for relief. New converts arriving in Utah often came well armed for the crossing of the Plains: when 800 Mormons reached Boston from the British Isles early in 1857, most of the men had at least two pistols and some had as many as four.[45] Furthermore, Gentiles traveling through the Territory were often forced to exchange their guns for provisions. But the Mormons needed more effective weapons than pistols and a more dependable source than overland travelers, whose way to Utah was blocked in the early part of the war. Another technique the Church used was to buy materiel in the East and on the West Coast. Its attempts to bring in 8,000 pounds of gunpowder concealed in boxes marked "dry goods" and carried in the trains of Russell, Majors, and Waddell failed when Colonel Alexander, informed of the stratagem, detained the entire shipment. But the residents of San Bernardino,

Carson Valley, and other Mormon outposts had more success in bringing a quantity of military supplies to Salt Lake City with them.[46]

With all other sources unreliable or inadequate, the Mormons came to realize that if they were to have enough weapons, they would have to produce them in the Territory. In March 1857, before the Saints had any reason to fear an invasion, several men had begun the manufacture of revolving pistols, and within two months had made a serviceable product. In early 1858 an employee of Livingstone and Kincead told eastern Gentiles that the Saints were turning out twenty Colt holster revolvers a week.[47] But although pistols were of some use at this critical time, the primary need was for rifles, and here the shortage remained acute. Driven to desperation, Ferguson described to Young the comparative merits of the long and the cross bow and urged adoption of the former by the militia. It was the same problem with respect to cannon. Ferguson knew that the Mormons would need heavy ordnance if they intended to resist the army, and he was disheartened to see that no one had tried to produce it, although, he said, cannon could be constructed in the Territory.[48]

Equal failure attended upon the Mormons' efforts to make the other tools of war. In letters to Young, Ferguson bitterly complained that no gunpowder had been manufactured in Utah, despite the Territory's resources. Although the Mormons had discovered lead in their country, only insignificant amounts were extracted to meet the need for munitions during the war. And despite heroic sacrifices and the investment of $150,000 over a period of seven years, the Church was unable to exploit iron deposits discovered by Parley Pratt.[49] The mineral resources of Utah are today known to be extensive; in the earliest years of the Territory, however, farming, not mining and industry, supported the population, a fact which created great problems when the people tried to mobilize. In all probability the shortages of critical materials influenced the decision of the Mormons' leaders to retreat rather than to oppose the entrance of the army into the Salt Lake Valley.

In the preceding paragraphs we traced the changing mood of the Mormon leaders and called attention to the resulting shifts in military strategy and in propaganda designed for home consumption. We also appraised the morale of the Mormon people during this tense period and summarized the steps taken by their government to obtain the resources required to support a military campaign. In the following pages it will be necessary to describe in some detail the actual military operations of the Church's armed forces.

When planning the defense of their Territory against the Government's expedition, the Mormons could draw upon considerable experience gained over past years. In Missouri, before Joseph Smith had decided that resistance to the Gentiles would only result in massacre of his people, the Saints had formed an irregular army and had fought a few small engagements with their enemies. Once established in Nauvoo, Smith created a more potent militia, in part perhaps to satisfy his desire to parade in the dashing accouterments of a lieutenant general, but also to protect the Church from further attack. Chartered by the Illinois legislature at a time when the state's political parties sought the votes of the Mormons, the Nauvoo Legion soon became an impressive force of some 5,000 men. Indeed, it grew so formidable that the legislature repealed the charter in 1845, the Gentiles of both parties now fearing that the Saints had more aggressive intentions than mere self-protection.

After this enforced dissolution, the Church for a time had no military branch, although former members of the Legion retained much of their discipline. The Mormons' flight across Iowa after their expulsion from their Zion on the Mississippi River, their desperate struggles to survive in their makeshift winter quarters, and their trek to the Salt Lake gave them no opportunity to organize an army. But in their new home they soon created a militia to protect their weak settlements from the Indians. By April 1849 the new Nauvoo Legion had been officially constituted, and provision was made for it in the constitution when later the Mormons established their state of Deseret. By law the Legion included all able-bodied men between the ages of eighteen and forty-five, with a unit called the Juvenile Rifles for the youth and the Silver Greys for those beyond the maximum age. For a time Brigham Young, who became military as well as religious leader of the Church after Smith's murder, acted as lieutenant

general, with the quiet but capable Daniel H. Wells serving as
major general under him. When Young relinquished his position
early in the 1850's, Wells became commander of the Legion and
was re-elected to this office by the people just prior to the outbreak of the Mormon War. Under his guidance the Saints conducted regular musters and drills, and fought well in the Indian
wars of the period.[50]

To increase the effectiveness of the Nauvoo Legion, Wells took
action in April 1857 to divide Utah into military districts, each
under a commandant, and at the same time ordered a new election of officers. These actions gave the militia an efficient organization on the eve of its contest with the United States.[51] In selecting the higher echelon of its armed force the Church departed
from its customary practice of placing prominent ecclesiastical
officials in positions of importance. Except for Daniel Wells and a
very few other individuals, the men who were to play significant
military roles in the war were not members of the Hierarchy.
James Ferguson, the lawyer who had baited Stiles and had been
instrumental in driving that distraught judge from his court,
served as adjutant general during the campaign, as he had during
most of the 1850's. Colonel Robert T. Burton and Major Smith led
the cavalry raids upon the expedition. None of these men had
achieved a position of authority in the counsels of the Church.
On the other hand the names of the great figures in Mormondom
—Hyde, Pratt, Kimball, Taylor, Woodruff, and the rest—did not
appear in the lists of the Legion's senior officers. For a time the
portly George A. Smith, a cousin of the Prophet and the "Father
of the Southern Settlements," served as an aide to Wells, but
when war came Brigham Young replaced him with Charles C.
Rich, one of the founders of San Bernardino. The Apostles and
other high priests of the sect continued to have great influence
in forming strategy, but they did not assume a military rank cor-
responding to their station in the Church.

Within a few days after learning of the Government's expedition the Mormons had made their defensive arrangements. In an
order to the commanders of Utah's military districts dated August
1, Wells reminded his officers of the outrages previously inflicted
upon the Latter-day Saints and, saying that the time had come to
fight back, ordered them to place their troops in readiness for a

winter campaign. George A. Smith, who carried these instructions to the districts south of Salt Lake City, found time in the localities along the way to deliver the same kind of exhortative sermon he had given in 1856, when his fire-eating preachments had so aroused the people there that they had carried out, condoned, or at least concealed the Mountain Meadows Massacre. Upon receipt of these orders William Pace, Aaron Johnson, and the other commanders mobilized their men. Within less than a month Wells could place some 800 men in the mountains east of the settlements as the first line of defense against invasion. Soon thereafter 1,400 militiamen from Utah, Tooele, and San Pete counties arrived in Salt Lake City and camped upon the city's public square, prepared to protect their people from attack. In the course of these hasty preparations the headquarters of the Nauvoo Legion even called upon the commanding officer of the Silver Greys for thirty of his "youngest, strongest and in every way ablest" men, and advised him to be prepared for future requisitions.[52]

During the early part of August, Wells sent reconnaissance forces to inspect all overland roads near Utah, since he had no knowledge of the army's progress or of the route it would follow. Some of these detachments scurried about the countryside with great energy but little accomplishment. Capt. James S. Brown, commanding a small unit from the Weber military district, was sent out to circle Bear Lake to the north of Salt Lake City, lest the federal army take this path in order to bypass Echo Canyon. After a long march, on which his men with some justification charged Brown with having lost his way in the rough terrain, the group came across signs of a cavalry party and, skillfully avoiding an ambush, captured it, only to find that it was composed of Mormons on a similar mission. After this adventure, in which all escaped injury, Brown returned to Ogden, but he soon was in the mountains again. Like many other Saints a firm believer in the prophetic power of dreams, he this time became alarmed when he learned through a vision of the approach of 250 mounted men. The danger was not real, however, for once again he encountered a portion of the Nauvoo Legion, not the United States army.[53]

Maneuvers by other units of the militia were not so inept as those of the imaginative Captain Brown. The first important demonstration by Mormon troops began when Wells dispatched cavalry under Col. Robert T. Burton eastward along the main roads to help Mormon immigrants, observe the approach of the army, and harry it west of South Pass. The campaign started inauspiciously, for Burton left Salt Lake City on August 15 with only seventy-five men, half the number originally assigned him. The colonel's command unexpectedly made contact with the expedition's vanguard just as the latter was increasing its rate of travel by forced marches. Aware that his detachment was too puny for any engagement, he was happy to escape without a fight; he was even unable to burn the grass along the road, so rapidly was Alexander moving. But Burton was a hardy individual, as he showed a few years later when, ordered to break up a group of schismatics called Morrisites, he overcame their defenses, shot Joseph Morris to death, and killed some of Morris' followers.[54] Having avoided the initial danger of a battle with the army, he followed on its flank, and on September 24 finally launched a raid near South Pass in an effort to stampede its cattle. This was the first action of the Mormon War. Shortly thereafter he retired to Fort Bridger, where Wells and other officers of the militia and the Church had gathered to discuss tactics.[55]

While Burton's small party was charging about the barren wastes east of Utah, Gen. Daniel H. Wells deployed his available troops for a battle at the entrance to the Valley, in case the cavalry raids failed to halt the expedition. Since Alexander at this time apparently planned to take the most direct route to Salt Lake City, Wells and the other Mormon strategists resolved to make their stand at Echo Canyon, the eastern portal to their settlements. Accordingly they set units to work erecting fortifications at one of the narrow points in the ravine. These men built stone walls on the upper slopes and excavated trenches into the sides of the canyon to protect the snipers who were to pour a hail of bullets upon the soldiers as they marched below them. Boulders were balanced so that a push would send them hurtling down. Some parties dug deep ditches in the valley floor and constructed dams which, when opened, would send water through the conduits into the army's path.[56]

There is a difference of opinion over the value of Echo as a defensive stronghold and the impregnability of the redoubts the Mormons built there. Some writers have described the canyon as a narrow defile overhung by towering cliffs on either side, a gorge so deep that one would expect its floor to be in eternal shadow.[57] A few determined men crouching behind fortifications, it would seem, could withstand any number of enemy troops. This estimate is inaccurate; the place was not a fissure-like cleft carved into the mountains but rather a small valley of questionable usefulness to beleaguered defenders.

The strength of the Saints' defenses in the canyon is also disputed. Mormons of the day, as well as a century later, believed Echo Canyon "impassable," an "impenetrable mountain defile" so skillfully fortified that the Saints would have been able to "defeat an army a thousand times their force." [58] On the other hand, Jesse Gove thought that a battery of mountain howitzers could have easily destroyed the walls and forced the Saints to retreat. Another army officer, agreeing that the breastworks were flimsy, wrote: "A singular idea seems to possess these people, that being regulars we were necessarily to move in solid and compact bodies to whatever point was most convenient to them to resist us." [59]

In all probability the troops, with their superior weapons, could have forced the canyon, but the many Mormons who garrisoned it would certainly have inflicted serious damage. It is fortunate for the sake of peaceful relations between Mormons and Gentiles that the army made no such assault in the wintry weather of 1857. The memory of Carthage, the Mountain Meadows Massacre, and other unhappy events had created enough animosity without the addition of a Battle of Echo Canyon. And it must also be noted that the Mormons' defenses in the canyon did indeed serve a purpose. Whether or not the expedition could have destroyed them, as its officers later thought, in the fall of 1857 Alexander and his advisors convinced themselves that the canyon was a death trap. When in consequence they decided to approach Salt Lake City by the Bear River route, they lost precious time and energy on pathless Ham's Fork and thus gave the Mormons their desired respite.

During September and October many militiamen, both infantry and cavalry, were ordered into Echo Canyon, and a small detachment of volunteers from Lehi put up walls there before journeying on to join Lot Smith. Brig. Gen. Franklin D. Richards dispatched 400 men from his Second Brigade and later sent several

hundred more troops to reinforce them.[60] When an express arrived in Salt Lake City with information that Harney and a number of Dragoons had joined the army, Brigham Young sent off
letters posthaste to eight of his district commanders instructing
them to raise another 500 men for service in Echo Canyon. On
October 14 the commissary general reported that the Legion had
already placed 1,100 men in the mountains, that 700 more were
awaiting orders in Salt Lake City, and that 3,000 troops could be
thrown into the canyon on fifteen hours' notice. With these forces
blocking the route into the basin the Mormons felt safe for the
time being.

On September 27 Wells and a party of important civil and military officers left Salt Lake City to establish headquarters in Echo.
On the way, however, reports from Mormon parties in the vicinity
of the army caused the lieutenant general to change his plans. According to one message federal troops were rapidly driving to the
very gates of the Basin, having treated with contempt Van Vliet's
urgent advice to establish winter quarters where they were. Also
Wells heard the alarming news that some of his men under Colonel Cummings were preparing for a pitched battle with a portion
of the army, a plan which ran counter to the Mormons' desire to
postpone an engagement as long as possible. Leaving other men
to command the militia in the canyon, Wells hurried on to Fort
Bridger, where he gathered his officers about him for an analysis
of the situation. The military was represented in these discussions
by Robert Burton, Major John McAllister, Lot Smith, and Adjutant General Ferguson. George Smith and the unwarlike John
Taylor spoke for the Hierarchy.[61]

On October 3 Wells and his advisors reached a number of important decisions under the threat of Alexander's rapid advance.
First they resolved to destroy Fort Bridger and Fort Supply, lest
these two settlements prove of service to the expedition. The
scorched-earth policy envisaged by the Mormons as an emergency
measure had begun on a small scale. As more aggressive moves
Wells divided his cavalry into several units, under Smith, Burton,
Rockwell, and McAllister, and sent them to harass the army. Although the imminent peril of the soldiers' entrance into the Valley justified these actions, the Mormon command was still eager
to avoid outright conflict with the enemy. Accordingly the coun-

cil instructed McAllister's men to "use great caution in attacking the trains of the troops. Should they be pursued, let the cattle go and let the brethren take care of themselves." If the army should start to march toward Salt Lake City, Burton with McAllister's help was to "annoy them all that lays in his power without risking men." [62] Having set the policy for the next stage of the war, Wells and his staff then burned Forts Bridger and Supply and started back for the eastern portals of Echo Canyon.

From Wells' temporary headquarters at Fort Bridger the cavalry detachments sped off on their duties with little delay. Colonel Burton, with eighty fresh men recently sent to him by Richards, successfully kept ahead of the soldiers as they toiled up Ham's Fork on their fruitless quest of an easy road into Salt Lake Valley. So long as they followed this circuitous route, Burton merely watched their exertions, but he was ready for more vigorous action if Alexander should strike off on a straighter line toward the Mormon settlements.[63] With a detachment of thirty men McAllister patrolled the country between Fort Bridger and Ham's Fork; the veteran scout Porter Rockwell and forty well-mounted Saints also hovered about the region, awaiting an opportunity to stampede the army's cattle.[64] Since the difficulty of the road and the severity of the weather took a heavy toll of the expedition's stock, these Mormon detachments contented themselves with gloating over the soldiers' struggles and in obedience to their instructions avoided direct contact with the enemy.

Major Joseph Taylor furnished the only excitement during this phase of the campaign. On October 4 Wells had sent him out to join McAllister and Burton, with orders to bother the expedition "in every possible way." "Take no life," Wells advised, "but destroy the trains, and stampede or drive away their animals, at every opportunity." [65] Taylor bungled the assignment. After serving with McAllister's command for a time, he took a detail of four men on patrol near Fort Bridger on October 16. Although his men opposed his choice of route, he pressed on until he saw smoke from a camp near by. Assuming it was McAllister's command, Taylor and his adjutant hurried toward it without investigation and suddenly found themselves surrounded by United States troops. "I drew my pistol and cocked it at them," the major later explained, "when something suggested to me not to shoot." Pos-

sibly the still, small voice pointed out to Taylor that he was outnumbered and alone with his aide, his men having escaped into
the woods.[66] The capture of these two Mormons was of importance to the army, for the careless adjutant, William Stowell, had
failed to destroy his orders from Wells, and Alexander was given
information concerning the Mormons' plan of defense much
more reliable than Young's letters and proclamations.

In his journal Taylor tried to conceal the ignominy of his capture by insisting that he had handled his interrogation by the
expedition's officers with great skill. During one round of questions, Taylor stated, Alexander had asked him the size of the
Mormons' forces; "I replied, 'From 20,000 to 25,000 good war-
riers.' At this broad statement, he stood aghast, while I could
have hung my hat upon his eyes." Although Alexander's cautious
disposition had won him the scornful epithet of "the old woman"
in his regiment, this veteran of the Mexican War was not so gul-
lible as to be fooled by a young prisoner. Even if he had been in
a state of mental anguish, Wells' instructions to "take no life"
would have quieted some of his fears.

Yet Taylor's capture had decisive effect upon the army's march
up Ham's Fork, for Alexander and his fellow senior officers
learned from Wells' orders how determined the Mormons were
to impede their advance. Alexander halted the column and while
debating his next move received Johnston's order to retrace his
steps down the stream. It might be argued that Taylor by stopping the army had served his people well. On the other hand, it
might also be maintained that by so doing he had saved the federal expedition from annihilation. As Johnston observed, if Alexander had pressed much farther into the rough terrain near Bear
Lake, he might have placed himself in a predicament from which
no power could have extricated him without serious loss.[67]

While Joseph Taylor was providing this rather comic relief,
Major Lot Smith and his little squadron of cavalry precipitated
the only real action in this bloodless campaign. With forty-three
men Smith left Fort Bridger on October 3 as one of the groups
sent out to follow the expedition. After he had met and turned
back a supply train of the army, he divided his small forces into
two units, retaining twenty-two men under his command and
sending the others to steal Alexander's mules. In the early morn-

ing hours of October 5 Smith and his weakened company came
upon the camp of two more trains, each with twenty-six wagons,
halted along the Green River. Although the teamsters, had they
known it, could have held the Mormons off until help arrived
from Alexander's forces near by, in the darkness they were uncertain of their enemies' strength; several believed that Smith had
more than 100 men with him. The teamsters, furthermore, were
civilians, not soldiers, and they had no stomach to die in defense
of government property. Thus without a shot the raiders were
able to fire the two trains. Later in the same day the Major met
a third train on the Big Sandy and destroyed it with equal ease.
In this case the wagon master, Lewis Simpson, a son-in-law of Alex
Majors, wanted to fight, but again his men preferred the less
dangerous alternative of surrender.[68]

After this productive day's work, the impact of which the army
was to feel as it rationed its provisions during the long winter,
Smith joined his forces with those of Porter Rockwell. Together
the two men burned the grass ahead of the army on Ham's Fork,
their hearty dislike for each other not diminishing the effectiveness of this strategy. Their most significant accomplishment was
the theft of 1,400 head of cattle, while startled guards watched
without interfering. After Rockwell took these and the other
recently captured animals into Salt Lake City, Smith continued to
patrol the countryside in search of new conquests. But the Major's
successful raids were at an end. Already Wells had sent him a
letter cautioning against overenthusiastic assaults upon the army:
"If we could learn of a surety that they purposed making winter
quarters at Fort Hall, we would cease molesting them." [69]

Smith's aggressive disposition was also sobered by an encounter
with a patrol of the army. On October 16 the Major learned that
a group of soldiers under Capt. Randolph Marcy had left the
main column, and he pursued the party, hoping to run off its
mules. When Smith thought he saw the animals unattended, he
ordered his command to charge, only to discover too late that
Marcy and his men were actually waiting for him astride their
mounts. Smith sent his men into a defensive formation and then
rode up to the Captain. Their conversation was inconclusive,
Smith venting his irritation at his mistake in sarcasm and Marcy
commenting upon the clarity of the Major's eyesight. When Smith

at last returned to his men, he found himself almost surrounded. Although he broke from the still unclosed trap in a hail of bullets, he soon abandoned his headlong flight and proceeded so leisurely that he was almost caught again. The Mormons escaped by splashing across a stream and scrambling up a hill in another precipitate retreat. From this episode Smith learned that his earlier exploits had been successful because the army lacked cavalry. Now that it had organized this branch, even though it was equipped only with mules, the expedition was capable of protecting itself and even of making limited offensive demonstrations.[70]

During the remainder of October several Mormon detachments circulated through the countryside near the army as it marched up and down Ham's Fork. Late in the month Colonel Burton and his command came into the Valley, but after a three-day rest returned to their patrol. Fifty cavalrymen under Major Warren Snow hovered about the soldiers in these last weeks of the campaign.[71]

Back in Salt Lake City the Mormon leaders were delighted at the developments in the war, for every report brought fresh evidence that the army's ineptitude, the weather's severity, or perhaps God's merciful providence had favored their strategy. From his camp on Bear River General Wells sent an encouraging express: "The army is weakening daily. . . . They are in a close place. Their provisions are fast diminishing and there is but little prospect of anything but starvation before them." A great many of the federal troops, he added, wished wholeheartedly to desert and would do so if the Mormons offered them protection.[72] When on October 21 Brigham Young received another message from Wells to the same effect, he announced: "I think it is best for Gen. Wells to call in his forces in Echo and there rest and not ride his horses to death unnecessarily, but let the enemy alone and they will soon use themselves up." [73]

This optimistic view was soon jolted. After Albert Sidney Johnston finally reached his command, as it lay huddled near the conjunction of Ham's Fork and Black's Fork, he ordered his men to march with all possible haste to Fort Bridger. This movement was to Johnston a last, desperate effort to reach the meager protection of that place, but to the Mormons it appeared that the newly arrived commander had breathed life into the expedition, heartening it for a final dash into their settlements. On November 8 a tired expressman reached Young with an urgent request from Wells for reinforcements. Late that night and on into the small hours of the next morning Young sat at his desk signing muster rolls. Within two days 1,300 men had been ordered to Echo Canyon to beat back the army's expected invasion.[74]

The excitement over the news of Johnston's advance lasted only a little more than a week; then the Mormon officers became aware of the army's true objective as it staggered down the road to Fort Bridger. On November 15 Young received word that the danger of attack had passed, for the troops could not in all probability move very much farther toward Utah. Throughout the rest of November the Mormons maintained a close watch on the expedition lest it launch a surprise thrust toward the Valley, and more than 2,000 Saints manned the makeshift fortifications in Echo Canyon. But they knew that the long-awaited winter had come and the soldiers would be unable to leave their camp on Black's Fork for another six months. On the last day of November an order from Wells' headquarters directed most of the Nauvoo Legion left in the mountains to return home. Soon the only militiamen east of Salt Lake City were a band of fifty troops instructed to remain at the defenses in Echo Canyon and to stop all parties passing down the road. As the snow fell during the next two weeks, even the most cautious in the Mormon command realized that Johnston was beleaguered. Accordingly Wells reduced his outposts still further, leaving only two units of ten men each for patrol duty. The first part of the Mormon War was over.[75]

During the months of December and January the Mormons enjoyed a pleasant, social winter, the weather affording them more protection than 10,000 rangers. Except for sending troops periodically to relieve the men in Echo Canyon, they had few military duties. In February, however, the leaders began to bestir themselves. Their mood, as we have seen, had passed from optimism to anxiety, and having subjected their strategy to an agonizing reappraisal they had determined to leave the Territory rather than suffer the human cost of its defense. Yet the army, they thought, might lunge upon them before they had completed their preparations for flight. Accordingly officers began to mobilize a number of brigades of the Nauvoo Legion; by the end of February 1,000 mounted men were ready to guard Salt Lake City. As the weather grew milder during March, the Saints' fears of a sudden attack from Fort Bridger increased, and additional militiamen were called up. By April 9 there were more than 600 troops in Echo Canyon and other strategic points east of it. But by this time the Mormon War, at best never known for its heroic feats on the battlefield, had passed from the phase of aimless marches to negotiation.

7. Winter Quarters

JIM BRIDGER always maintained that his strategically located fort had been stolen from him. The Mormons, he insisted, had never bought him out in 1853, as they had said, but had evicted him by force. Years later he wrote: "I was robbed, and threatened with death, by the Mormons, by the direction of Brigham Young, of all my merchandise, stock—in fact of everything I possessed, amounting to more than $100,000 worth—the buildings in the fort partially destroyed by fire, and I barely escaped with my life." [1]

After he returned with Johnston's expedition to his post—left a smoke-blackened ruin in accordance with Wells' instructions—Bridger had further trouble, this time with the federal government. In November 1857 he leased the property, some 4,000 acres, to Capt. J. H. Dickerson, acting as the army's agent, for $600 a year, with a ten-year option to purchase included. One clause in the contract proved troublesome to Bridger: it stated that no payment would be made on the lease until he had established his title.

When Bridger built his post, the country surrounding Black's Fork had belonged to Mexico. Although that nation had not objected to his presence in a region so remote from its settlements, it had given him no legal evidence of ownership, and he was never able to prove his title to the satisfaction of the United States. Between 1869 and 1878 he appealed five times for a settlement of his claim, always without success. In 1884 Congress authorized the old trapper to sue the Government, but the case dragged on. Finally his attorney wrote to the deputy quartermaster general in 1889 that he was dropping the suit because "Capt. James Bridger and nearly all of his witnesses have died." [2] Old Gabe had survived the ambushes of the murderous Blackfeet Indians; he had seen Jedediah Smith, Bill Williams, and a host of other hardy mountain men go under in the treacherous West; he had outlived Brigham Young, Heber Kimball, George A. Smith, Edmund Alexander, Jesse Gove, and Albert Sidney Johnston. But bureaucratic procrastination defeated him at last.

Regardless of its rightful owner, Bridger's Fort and the country near by was a satisfactory site for the troops' enforced hibernation in the winter of 1857–58. Although the Mormons had tried to destroy the post by burning its buildings, they had been unable to damage the fifteen-foot stone walls Bridger had built to discourage hostile Indians. When Johnston placed cannon in two lunettes at the southwest and northeast corners of this enclosure and added earthworks and a moat, the fort became invulnerable to any surprise attack. Behind these defenses the army stored some of its supplies and guarded them with several companies of infantry. With Fort Bridger as the northeastern anchor, the various units of the command stretched up Black's Fork for a number of miles, the entire settlement assuming the name of Camp Scott in honor of that crusty but able general. Since this high mountain region, 6,600 feet above sea level, lacked forage for the expedition's remaining stock, the mules and other animals were sent with Cooke and six companies of Dragoons to graze on neighboring streams, where they remained until March 1858. Otherwise the environs of Bridger's Fort could sustain the troops, not luxuriously but at least satisfactorily, through the winter months.[3]

Camp Scott was a busy community, for some 1,800 officers and men of the regular army occupied it during seven snow-bound months. In addition, other volunteers were recruited during this period. Although the contracting firm of Russell, Majors, and Waddell had hired its teamsters for the trip to Salt Lake City with the promise of employment on the return journey if they chose, these contracts were broken when the trains halted at Fort Bridger. After the wagon master suddenly left for the States, his agent had no money for the drivers, and the teamsters therefore received drafts payable at Fort Leavenworth, paper which had as much value on Black's Fork as the frosty sage brush around the camp. For many of these men the only alternative to unprofitable idleness was enlistment for nine months in the army, with the promise of the same pay, allotments of clothing, and provisions given the regulars. This situation provided Johnston with another 340 "young, active, and hardy men" for any future collision with the Mormons.[4]

In addition to the regular and volunteer soldiers in Camp Scott, there was a handful of federal officers and their servants who lived in a strange collection of houses called Eckelsville, after the territorial chief justice. The sprawling camp also contained the supply trains that had survived Lot Smith's raids. There were the many ox wagons of Russell, Majors, and Waddell, upon which the expedition would depend for its provisions; the Fifth and Tenth Infantry Regiments each had its sutlers' trains, their wagons drawn into a circle protecting their stock; and the private mercantile firm of Livingstone and Kincead added their wagons to the mélange. Camp Scott may have been hurriedly established as makeshift winter quarters for a desperate army, but for more than half a year it was a bustling, populous settlement.

At the end of November, Johnston took inventory of his available stores and discovered that food, clothing, and other necessities were in short supply for the months ahead. The troops, he learned, were well equipped with metallic scales, insignia of rank, and cap covers; more important articles, such as greatcoats, trousers, flannel shirts, and boots were not so abundant. As spring approached, one officer commented upon the shabby appearance of the soldiers: "The men go about in pantaloons patched with pieces cut off coats . . . For stockings, many have adapted the sleeves of coats, making an elbow, like a stovepipe, and sewing up one end for the toe. The shoes worn are, many of them, as far past description as mending." The situation soon became worse. To meet this emergency Johnston in early March was compelled to order Barnard E. Bee, the senior officer of the volunteer companies, "to employ men on extra duty for the purpose of mending shoes and making mocassins for your command." While the Mormons were considering adopting the Indians' weapons, the United States soldiers had copied in part the Indians' mode of dress.[5]

Food was another problem. On November 28 Capt. H. F. Clarke of the commissary reported that the expedition had 2,000 animals at Scott and Henry's Fork and could draw upon 46,800 pounds of bacon, 5,000 pounds of ham, 405,500 pounds of flour,

122,450 rations of dried vegetables, and other supplies in the contractors' trains. With 2,400 persons to feed, Clarke believed that these stocks would last until the command received supplies from the East. Johnston agreed that his men would not starve, but quite obviously the commanding officer would have to exercise great care if his men were to be ready for a campaign when the snows melted and the road down Echo Canyon became clear. Accordingly he cut the flour ration, normally eighteen ounces a day, to fourteen, then to thirteen, and finally to less than ten ounces. The allotment of meat—two pounds, established by the "Regulations for the Army"—was not reduced for a time.[6] "But such beef," Gove complained; "all bone, driven as it was in ox wagons, hauling supplies from Leavenworth, nearly dead when it got here." [7] Cooke called it "moribund." [8]

Many commodities were impossible to obtain or exorbitantly priced. In December Mrs. Cumming wrote to her sister-in-law that she had no eggs, milk, butter, and lard. The camp's merchants sold sugar and tobacco at high prices, occasionally 400 per cent above those at St. Louis, and offered a poisonous concoction they called whisky for twelve dollars a gallon.

Lack of salt was felt most keenly. In the early weeks of winter quarters some profiteers sold it for six dollars a quart; even at that figure the supply was quickly bought up. Always ready to mock his enemies, Brigham Young sent Johnston bags of salt under the pretense of trying to ease the soldiers' critical predicament. When the stiff-necked Johnston rejected the gift, many of his men applauded his refusal to traffic with the black-hearted Mormons, but some enterprising troops who felt that nonfraternization could be carried too far followed Young's agents out of the camp, obtained the salt, and sold it for five dollars a pound.[9] Soon even this small supply was gone. In March young Capt. Albert Tracy, who tried with indifferent results to keep a witty journel, wrote: "Salt! It is but a few days since, that an inspection of the soup in my company kettles, the odor thereof, made up as it is, from perfectly black and rotting beef of our November slaughter, and with no sign of seasoning—compelled me absolutely to turn aside my head." [10]

In this fashion the men of the expedition struggled through the winter. With the stocks on hand, supplemented by two hun-

dred bushels of turnips and some other vegetables uncovered from
a Mormon cache, the soldiers escaped scurvy and suffered very
little sickness in the salubrious Rockies.[11] But as the weeks
dragged by, the food reserves dwindled in alarming fashion.
When the animals failed because of inadequate forage, the troops,
in addition to their regular chores, had to haul the wagons several
miles a day to bring in firewood. So long as the commissary kept
the rations high, the men could bear the strenuous work; but
when in early May the allotments were again cut, the situation
became serious. "Our provisions are nearly out," Gove wrote.
"The ration of flour to camp followers and citizens is reduced to
8 oz. per day. Our beef is mostly gone." Another officer complained to the New York *Tribune:* "We are still existing, not living." Late in November the prudent Johnston had purchased
several hundred head of cattle from nearby mountain men, but
the army needed more food if it was to reach June as a fighting
force, not as a famine-scourged rabble. Neighboring Indians began to bring in dog meat, which they offered for sale as mountain sheep.[12]

The nearest available stocks lay at Fort Laramie, more than
350 miles to the east, where three months' supplies for the army
had been caught by the snows. Johnston was aware that the deep
drifts and subzero temperatures would prevent any large train
from transporting these provisions to Camp Scott until spring,
and he hoped to survive until that time on his own resources. But
it was close timing, he knew; if his food should not last as long
as his commissary had predicted, or if relief should be delayed,
his men would be in trouble. Therefore in early November he
ordered Lt. Col. William Hoffman, commanding officer at Fort
Laramie, to make all preparations necessary for a flying trip to
the army when the thaws finally came. At the end of the month
the meticulous Johnston repeated these instructions and stressed
the urgency of the expedition's need.[13] In reply he received two
keen disappointments. From Major Lynde, now commanding the
post, he learned that Hoffman had been ordered east to serve on a
court-martial. Lynde also advised Johnston not to depend upon
assistance from him in the spring. His animals, he reported, were
broken down and with scanty forage available would probably
suffer further debilitation; he only hoped he could keep them

alive during the winter. According to Lynde, "it is as much as we can do to supply the post with wood from day to day."[14]

Johnston's reaction to these developments revealed his character. He concentrated upon Lynde as the agent to help forestall an emergency some five months away, telling him he must be prepared to move his supplies in March and ordering him to use "every resource within your reach." At the same time he began a correspondence with his superior officers in Washington. Even under normal conditions Johnston was prone to give the War Department advice; in his critical position at Scott he was even freer with recommendations. To have Hoffman recalled from Fort Laramie so unexpectedly had caused "no little embarrassment," he protested, and he asked that the colonel be sent back to his post "immediately." He further insisted that a mule train be sent from Fort Leavenworth to Laramie in time to carry provisions on to Black's Fork, warned the commander in chief to provide ample guards for the supply trains, and further (after complaining that no orders had reached him for some time), suggested proper techniques for transmitting messages during the winter season.[15] Johnston was often humorless and officious, but his unsolicited admonitions to his superiors were sound enough to merit careful attention.

The War Department acted upon his suggestions. On February 28 it ordered a supply train of 156 wagons and 1,400 animals to leave Fort Leavenworth as soon as possible, with an escort of two cavalry and two infantry companies under Hoffman. By April 21 this column had reached Fort Laramie, where Hoffman combined four contractors' ox trains with his detachment. From this point westward it became a race against time. Fearful of renewed raids by the Mormons, Johnston sent a squadron of Dragoons eastward to keep the road open and commanded Hoffman to "treat as enemies all persons interfering with or molesting your march, and take prisoner all persons known to be Mormons or furnishing them with information on the army, or with supplies."[16] He cautioned him to deliver his supplies at Camp Scott as soon as possible; with his customary attention to detail he also specified a strict ration for Hoffman's men, advised him on the best route to follow, and suggested methods for keeping discipline in camp. While stocks of food at Camp Scott were running dangerously low, Hoffman was halted by a snowstorm on La Bonte's Creek for almost two weeks. When he at last learned of the expedition's straitened circumstances he sent his fastest trains ahead. They all reached Camp Scott by June 10, in time to feed the hungry troops and prepare them for the final drive into Utah.[17]

Another problem plaguing Johnston almost as much as inadequate food was his lack of animals, for only 357 of the army's horses and a few mules had survived the bitter weeks of October and November.[18] Since the forage near Camp Scott was thin, Johnston could expect that his remaining animals would be in poor condition when spring came. The commanding officer was eager to coerce the Mormons into submission as soon as the roads opened; he might even have hoped that the Saints would give him an excuse to attack them. But such a Carthaginian policy required an army prepared for war. If it lacked a cavalry, it might well suffer the same indignities Alexander had received at the hands of Lot Smith, and it might even be unable to mount any offensive against the enemy.

It was therefore apparent to Johnston that he must obtain animals quickly, and this busy officer set about the task the moment his men had all reached Fort Bridger. The nearest accessible source of supply was Fort Union, near Taos, New Mexico, a twenty-five day march from Camp Scott. To this post, then, he would send for help. To lead a party on this hazardous trip across the Rockies he selected Randolph B. Marcy of the Fifth Infantry. The choice was a wise one; Captain Marcy not only had wide experience on the frontier, from service in Wisconsin, Oklahoma, and on the Texas border, but was a mature man of courage and resourcefulness.[19] On November 24 Marcy received his orders; after only three days of preparations he was ready to leave. With forty enlisted men who had volunteered for this duty, twenty-four civilians to serve as guides and assistants, sixty-five mules, and enough rations for thirty days, he set off to the south. Jim Bridger, who knew the climate and topography of the West as well as any man, said that Marcy would never make it.[20]

For once Bridger was wrong, but his prediction very nearly came true. After crossing the Uinta Mountains in the snow, Marcy and his men followed the brawling Green River for a time,

then traversed the high plateau separating it from the Grand
River, today's Colorado. The perilous 1,800-foot descent to this
stream safely accomplished, the party struck out for Cochetopa
Pass over the Continental Divide. This was the most critical part
of the march, as Marcy realized, for the party had to follow the
present-day Gunnison River and then choose among its upper
tributaries the only one that would lead them to the pass. If the
detachment selected the wrong stream, it would in all probability
bury itself forever in the snow-covered, jumbled ranges of the
Rocky Mountains. Marcy pressed on along the Gunnison and
chose the correct tributary. As they labored up the mountain
slopes toward the all-important pass, the men knew their rations
were almost gone. Their jaded mules dying or unable to walk,
they took turns breaking the trail by crawling on their hands
and knees. At this point, as the little detail struggled on frozen
feet through deep snow, Marcy's guide, the veteran mountain
man Jim Baker, admitted that he was lost.

Marcy's command fortunately included Miguel Alona, a Mexican mule-trader who had some knowledge of the region. When
Baker confessed his bewilderment, Alona volunteered his services. He took the party safely, though with back-breaking toil,
almost to the crest of the divide and on December 28, with a
companion, left to obtain help from Fort Massachusetts, the nearest post, some sixty miles away. On January 1 Marcy's men consumed the last of their rations and were thereafter reduced to
eating their bony mules. When they reached the foot of the range
they could go no farther, and here the relief train from Fort
Massachusetts finally found them. Its torment over, the party
reached the post on January 18 and then continued to Taos.
The terrible march across a broken terrain in the cruel cold of
winter had taken only one life, a sergeant who died "from ex-
posure and imprudence in eating" when he at last was given food.

Marcy, leaving Fort Union March 17 on the return journey,
chose a safer road than the Cochetopa route, one that lay along the
eastern foot of the Rockies. With a party of 179 men guarding
160 horses, almost 1,000 mules, and a few sheep, he had traveled
for two weeks when he suddenly received orders to halt and wait
for reinforcements—a detachment, comprising more than 200

mounted riflemen under Col. W. W. Loring, which joined Marcy
near Pike's Peak. The troops proceeded to Camp Scott, arriving
there on June 11.[21]

Johnston was pleased to get this addition to his livestock and
troops, but Marcy came back an embittered man. In spite of his
toilsome journey to Fort Union—during which he had kept his
command alive even though snow-blind and starving—the War
Department had placed the return party under Loring, who out-
ranked him. The appointment, however, was not a studied rebuff.
In May Winfield Scott sent him a commendation for his "uncon-
querable energy" and at the same time advised Floyd that "Captain
Marcy has again richly earned by gallantry and good conduct, the
rank of major by brevet." Three months later, in August, Marcy
and Col. Edmund B. Alexander left Utah and the expedition's adventures with the Mormons, their labors having won them leaves
of absence.[22]

While Johnston was struggling with the problem of supplying
the 2,400 people under his care, his officers and men were faced
with the less crucial but equally trying task of amusing themselves during the seven long months of winter quarters. Certain
military chores—early morning drills and the like—occupied some
of the soldiers' time, and until April 24 the troops hauled their
own fuel, ten to twenty men pulling a large wagon through the
deep snows. But these exercises left much free time during each
day. For entertainment the more talented soldiers erected a thea-
ter and produced a few plays; others formed five tents into a large
ballroom, where dances were held on Christmas, New Year's Eve
and a few other occasions. As a result of these activities Johnston
reported that his troops were in excellent condition, their spirits
high and their health good. Others agreed with the commander's
appraisal of the genial atmosphere at Camp Scott.[23]

These pleasant descriptions of army life were not entirely accurate. Although Colonel Alexander was no longer the target of
complaint among the subalterns of his command, there was bitterness in the hearts of other officers. Philip St. George Cooke,
himself not popular with the Dragoons who were herding the expedition's animals, became so upset at some of Johnston's orders
and actions that he appealed to superior authorities for redress.
At this time Cooke also fell out with Fitz-John Porter, Johnston's

adjutant, a feud that carried over into the Civil War, when Porter asked McClellan to relieve Cooke of his command after the Battle of Gaines Mill.[24]

Violence and other forms of misbehavior were frequent occurrences during this period of the campaign. It is true that some of the trouble came from the teamsters, "scum of the great Western cities," who became unruly as idleness drove them to seek adventure or liquor along the frozen banks of Black's Fork. Some of them opened gambling dens, where soldiers were robbed and at times savagely beaten, until Judge Eckels closed them down in March. But most of the trouble came from the enlisted men. Growing restless and irritable during the interminable weeks, they became drunken, stole government property, attacked one another, twice broke up parties given by Eckels for his friends, and in other ways expressed displeasure with their associates' company.[25]

Evidence of this misconduct appears in the records of courts-martial for drunkenness, acts of violence, and theft of public or private property. At the same time there was some deterioration of morale. A large number of soldiers whose terms of service had expired refused to re-enlist in their own corps. At least ten men deserted, some of whom made their way to the Mormons' lines, where they informed the Saints of conditions at Scott. Although most of the men had a high regard for Johnston, many considered their immediate officers contemptible. Toward the end of November, Private Henry Evans forced his way into the tent of his company commander in search of a drink and, when ordered to leave, announced that "he would be damned if he would go till he got ready and further that he did not care a damn for Lieut. Dudley or any other cursed sergeant in the company." Several months later Bugler John F. Burns, who had met with more success than Evans in his quest for liquor, began to abuse Judge Eckels and his friends. When a lieutenant tried to quiet him, Burns punched him in the face shouting "God damn you, Thompson, I won't obey you, you son of a bitch," or words to that effect—action which a military court decided was "prejudicial to good order and military discipline." [26]

In spite of the unruliness displayed by some enlisted men, Colonel Johnston with his customary vigor made Camp Scott an armed

garrison ready for battle at a moment's notice. To his thinking
the Mormons' defiance of the expedition and their destruction of
the supply trains had branded them as open traitors. In Washington the Buchanan Administration had begun seriously to question
the wisdom of its stern policy toward the wayward followers of
Brigham Young; at the same time the Saints in Salt Lake City had
decided that their military weakness precluded any resistance to
the army. But on Black's Fork there was no peace. Johnston assumed that the war which the others now wished to avoid had
started, with the decisive battle deferred only until the deep
snows had disappeared. "Treat all men as enemies who interfere
with your movements or threaten your charge," he ordered Cooke,
". . . and should you be convinced of the proximity of any
armed parties of men, large or small, become acquainted with their
intentions, and, if necessary, pursue, capture or rout them." [27]
When he warned Marcy against surprise raids, he advised him that
the Mormons were "in open rebellion," and he cautioned Hoffman, bringing supplies from Fort Laramie, on no account "to relax
the vigilance which should be exercised in an enemy's country." [28]

In keeping with his belligerent attitude Johnston put his expedition on a wartime footing. Besides placing details of men as
guards around Scott and upon the bluffs above it, he sent scouting
parties many miles to the west in search of Mormon detachments.
Aware that in the past the Saints had learned of the troops' movements from spies who had visited the army, he appointed a provost
marshal to safeguard the internal security of the camp. From this
officer, of whom Gove said "Life and death is in his hands," every
civilian was to obtain a certificate of employment as a pass to be
used when entering or leaving the post. All guards were instructed
to stop and examine strangers, an order that almost cost Thomas
L. Kane his life when he bounded into the settlement on another
of his missions to assist the Latter-day Saints. With the soldiers thus
prepared to shoot at the Mormons whenever the opportunity
arose, there would have been a number of engagements during the
winter months if the two armies had not been separated by many
snow-covered miles. As it was, only a few brief and bloodless
skirmishes took place on the plains about Camp Scott in early
1858. [29]

For their part the Mormons believed that Johnston and the

other officers of his command were taking more aggressive action
against them than merely dispatching patrol parties. The army,
they felt sure, had sent the Indians on the warpath. In their daily
records the Church scribes reported that the expedition had issued ammunition and other military supplies to the Indians, had
offered rewards for dead Mormons ranging from $150 for a com-
mon soldier to $1,000 for Lot Smith, and had inspired the savages
to think of Brigham Young as a weaker fighter than Joseph Smith,
who had been easily killed.[30] In April, Young wrote a bitter, sarcastic letter to the Commissioner of Indian Affairs concerning this
matter. The Indian depredations in Tooele and Rush valleys and
similar events, he maintained, were clear proof of Johnston's plot
to turn the Indians against his people. Perhaps remembering
Alexander's criticism of the Mormons' irregular mode of warfare,
Young satirically commented upon the army's "civilized" manner of fighting.[31]

There is no evidence to substantiate these accusations. On the
contrary, W. M. F. Magraw and Jim Bridger said they had heard
the colonel urge several chiefs to take no part in the quarrel between the United States and Utah.[32] The reliability of Magraw
and Bridger, two implacable enemies of the Mormons, is of course
dubious, but the accuracy of the Saints' charges is also open to
question, since the Church was eager to show that the legions of
Hell were employing inhuman devices to overwhelm it. Furthermore, other sources substantiated Magraw and Bridger. Jacob
Forney, the new superintendent who in time became a friend of
the Saints, heatedly replying to an article in the *Deseret News* of
April 1858, denied that anyone in Camp Scott had sought to turn
neighboring tribes against the Mormons or had tried to buy their
loyalty with presents.[33] Although for a brief time Johnston contemplated hiring bands of Indians to operate the ferries on the
Green River and Ham's Fork, he gave no indication of a desire
to bring them into a close alliance with his army.[34]

The activities of two parties sent out from Camp Scott strengthened the Mormons' suspicions of the army's Indian policy. On
December 9, 1857, B. F. Ficklin, one of the young men recruited from Magraw's wagon-road company, set off with ten men,
thirty days' rations, and four gallons of whisky to visit the tribes
at the headwaters of the Missouri River. In this same region the

Church in 1855 had established the outpost of Limhi, also known
as the Salmon River Lamanite Mission, as part of its campaign to
convert the Indians, the dark-skinned people whose history the
Book of Mormon had chronicled. While the expedition's company was in the area, some Bannocks and Snakes attacked the
settlement, killing two people and wounding others. The Mormons cried that there was more than coincidence between Ficklin's
presence and the massacre. On his return Ficklin reported that he
had adhered strictly to his orders from Johnston merely to buy
horses and beef, and that he had cautioned all Indians to remain
at peace. He also said in a deposition before Eckels that the Mormons at Limhi had brought the attack upon themselves by furnishing arms and ammunition to the Nez Percés while refusing to give
weapons to the Bannocks and Snakes. Two Gentile traders supported Ficklin's statement, and one of them added that Brigham
Young had earlier tried without success to gain the support of
these two tribes in his war with the United States.[35]

The Mormons were also suspicious of another civilian party
sent to visit the Indians, this time under the leadership of United
States Marshal Peter K. Dotson. In April, Chief Justice Eckels
sent Dotson to the camp of Ben Simonds, chief of the Weber Utes,
for the purpose of buying beef, vegetables, and other supplies.
Eckels' orders bound Dotson to make no "warlike movements"
against the Mormons except in self-defense or in the execution
of his official duties; they also included the admonition: "Should
you be inquired of by the Indians on the subject—you will advise neutrality in our Mormon troubles." [36] On April 24 Dotson
and thirteen men struck out for the Bear River Valley, where
they soon found Simonds' camp. According to the reports of the
marshal and several other Gentiles, however, he was unable to
carry out his orders, for a band of mounted Mormons chased him
back to Scott. He had found no time, he said, even to discuss the
purchase of supplies before making his hasty flight; certainly he
had not negotiated an alliance with the Indians.[37]

Another factor increasing the Mormons' misgivings was the
presence in Camp Scott of their steadfast opponent Dr. Garland
Hurt, the agent whom Brigham Young had found most troublesome. Since he had previously opposed the Church on his Indian
farms and in his letters to Washington, the Saints were sure that

he would continue this activity after he had moved his headquarters to Black's Fork. Knowing the man's popularity among the Utes, the Mormons believed that he would use this power to bring the Indians into close association with the army. This fear gained strength when the agent left Camp Scott in January and crossed the Uinta Mountains to spend the remainder of the winter with the Utes. A number of Gentile correspondents insisted that Hurt made this trip for two legitimate purposes, to discover if the Mormons were planning to ambush Marcy on his return from Fort Union and at the same time to learn if the winters in the Uinta Basin were mild enough to permit the establishment of an Indian farm there. The Saints scouted these explanations. Instead, they recorded in their daily "History of Brigham Young" the belief that the doctor had urged a number of Utes to aid the army in the destruction of the Mormons. As proof they noted that the neighboring tribes, peaceful in past years, had suddenly launched raids in northern and central Utah. In two letters to the new governor, William H. Hooper insisted that Hurt was responsible for these attacks and had even been involved, in some unexplained fashion, in the Salmon River Massacre.[38]

Johnston rejected Hooper's assertions when he learned of them, and Hurt, in defense of his reputation, said: "At the proper time and place I shall be ready to confront my accusers, and expose their malicious chicanery." For two years the agent labored without success to clear himself of the serious charges. On 1858 he demanded of the territorial commissioner of Indian affairs, Jacob Forney, an investigation of Hooper's allegation; during the next year he assembled affidavits from twenty men who praised his "prudence, justice and moderation" as Indian agent; and in 1860 he petitioned Commissioner Charles Mix, saying he "was charged with crimes of a high character" and requesting an investigation. It is impossible now to determine Hurt's innocence or guilt in this matter. It is perhaps worthy of note, however, that he petitioned for a thorough examination of his entire record and that the Mormons never produced evidence substantiating their charges against him.[39]

The Saints' accusations against the army and Garland Hurt evoked a reply from Gentiles denouncing the Mormons for the same crime. The New York *Tribune's* correspondent in Camp

Scott wrote that Ben Simonds had told of being asked by Brigham Young to arouse the Snakes against the expedition; other commentators recorded much the same observations. According to Fitz-John Porter, Johnston's adjutant, the great Shoshone chieftain Washakie reported a similar proposal made to him by Young.[40]

Already suspicious of the Mormons on this score, officials in the Department of the Interior became even more concerned in the fall of 1857 over the Church's relations with the Indians. From Agent Thomas Twiss they received the warning that the Saints had sent men among the Arapahoes for sinister purposes. Commissioner James W. Denver accepted Twiss' reports as accurate and in November ordered him to counteract this subversive work by visiting all tribes along the eastern edge of the Rocky Mountains. In the same month Denver cautioned the superintendent in Santa Fe to watch out for efforts by the Mormons to seduce the Indians in the Territory of New Mexico.[41] In his annual report Secretary of the Interior Jacob Thompson soberly concluded: "it is much to be feared that they [the Indians] have been tampered with, and their feelings towards the United States alienated to such an extent by the Mormons, that in any difficulties with the latter a large portion of them may be found on the side of those enemies of our government and law." [42]

In their earlier dealings with the tribes in or near Utah the Church, perhaps accidentally, had impressed upon the Indians the idea that a difference existed between Mormons and Gentiles and that the former were the true friends of the Red Man. It is difficult to ascertain whether during the war the Saints tried in a more forthright manner to correct the unfavorable odds against them by the acquisition of Indian allies. There is some evidence, however, that such a development took place, despite a brief entry in the "Journal History" of November 2: "Pres. Brigham Young wrote a letter to Washakie, Chief of the Shoshones, requesting him to fight neither for nor against us." The Utah Historical Society has a "Report of a Party of Observation" describing the trip of twelve men into the region of Bear Lake in August 1857. The purpose of this undertaking was ostensibly to search out defensive positions and to investigate the availability of timber, water, and other valuable resources. The report, however, contains cryptic accounts of several conferences with Indian bands.

On one occasion "Br. Jas. Brown 3d gave them the necessary instructions. They recd. it [sic] with a good spirit. They know nothing of importance about the soldiers." At least four different times
Brother Brown gave these "necessary instructions" to the Indians
who camped in the country through which the Oregon Trail
passed.[43]

Possibly these Mormons were merely preaching to their Lamanite cousins. Other documents, however, indicate that, early in
the war at least, the Church's leaders had a deliberate policy
of seeking military assistance from the Indians. In her exhaustive
study of the Mountain Meadows Massacre Mrs. Juanita Brooks
quotes a letter of August 4 from Young to Jacob Hamblin, one
of the Saints' missionaries: "Continue the conciliatory policy towards the Indians, which I have ever recommended, and seek
by works of righteousness to obtain their love and confidence, for
they must learn that they have either got to help us or the United
States will kill us both." [44] In equally plain language Wells ordered William Pace: "Instruct the Indians that our enemies, are
also their enemies and how they are continually fighting against
them somewhere, and that it will come upon them as well as
the Sioux and Cheyennes, in due time; that they must be our
friends and stick to us for if our enemies kill us off, they will be
cut off by the same parties." [45] Secretary Thompson's fears had
some basis in fact.

While the men in Johnston's army fretted about the shortage
of food, held their drills, went out on patrols in sub-zero weather,
and performed the other duties of military life, the civilian officials marooned in Eckelsville, about 100 yards west of Camp
Scott, struggled through the winter as best they could. The person
for whom the temporary settlement was named, Chief Justice
Delana R. Eckels, was a disgruntled man throughout most of
this period. He knew that some of the army officers were well
housed in a new type of tent devised by Capt. Henry H. Sibley
which copied the conical shape of the Indian lodge. It was difficult to put up and to strike, but once up, with its central fire,
stove, or sod-chimneyed fireplace, it provided its fortunate occupants with a comfortable accommodation. Eckels also felt himself ill-favored when he compared his facilities with those of the
other territorial officials. Since Forney could call upon the Indians

in the camp for assistance, he soon had the largest house in the community. Alfred Cumming, however, lived in even grander style, as befitted the new governor. With five tents attached together, he had a diningroom, storeroom, kitchen, combination parlor and bed chamber, and a room for his young servant girl. For his part Eckels had first lived in a hole in the ground and then in a small hut built of frozen sods.[46]

In Eckelsville, with its motley collection of dwellings, most of the territorial officers passed the long weeks of winter quarters. Only two important authorities, associate justices Charles E. Sinclair and John Cradlebaugh, had failed to reach Johnston's army when it established Camp Scott. Otherwise there was a full complement of federal officials: Governor Cumming, Eckels, Territorial Secretary John Hartnett, United States Marshal Peter K. Dotson, Attorney General J. M. Hockaday, Garland Hurt, Jacob Forney, and Postmaster H. F. Morrell. David A. Burr, the son of the controversial first surveyor of Utah, was justice of the peace.[47]

Alfred Cumming, a Georgian born in 1802, appeared well qualified for the governorship of Utah. In the 1830's he had served as mayor of Atlanta and had revealed such courage during a cholera epidemic, when he labored without thought of personal safety to help the stricken, that the citizens paid him high tribute at the end of his term. He had been a sutler with Scott's forces in the Mexican War and later in California and Missouri. During the mid-1850's he was Superintendent of Indian Affairs at St. Louis, his territory including a vast area of the West. These three positions would seem to have fitted him admirably for his new task, since they gave him administrative experience, a familiarity with the army, and an understanding of frontier problems. Furthermore, he had none of those preconceived biases against the Mormons that had rendered former Gentile officers unfit to serve in Utah. Finally, his wife was something of an asset to him. Albert Tracy liked her, and Jesse Gove, although he complained that she was "one of the most intolerable talkers on earth," in reality enjoyed her conversation and her "pleasing anecdotes." [48]

Yet Cumming, well-meaning though he was, failed to promote the cause of peace in Utah. His appearance was unfortunate. Grossly fat, he seemed at times more like a waddling clown than a territorial executive. George A. Smith, whose 230 pounds made him no lightweight, in physique at least, recorded his first impressions of Cumming in the Church's "Journal History": "his head was small around the top; one would think that he had more chops than brains, probable weight about 240 lbs." [49] This drawback was of minor importance, however, and the Mormons' initial accusation that their new governor was a tosspot may also be dismissed as their familiar blackening of Gentiles whom they distrusted. Cumming's greatest weaknesses came from his personality. Like Perry Brocchus, he was convinced of his own importance and greatly concerned for his reputation. During his early negotiations with the Mormons, and later, when he had entered upon his official duties, he revealed a neurotic anxiety lest people in the States disapprove of his actions. He was jealous of his authority, insistent upon his prerogatives, and apprehensive of any assault upon his powers.

Since Cumming soon established cordial relations with the Church, his nature did not provoke its antagonism. But in these trying months it was also necessary for the Governor to reconcile the federal and army officers to a policy of peace. Many of these men, among them Eckels and Cradlebaugh, were dedicated anti-Mormons; Johnston, an inflexible martinet, was also convinced that the Saints were contemptible traitors meriting severe punishment. The tactless, self-important Cumming was not the person to placate these men.

Cumming revealed no intention of taking the side of the Church during the period of winter quarters. One of his first official actions at Camp Scott was to issue a proclamation "To the People of Utah Territory" dated November 21. After announcing his appointment, he warned the Mormons that their defiant behavior was in reality treason and ordered all armed parties to disband. Placed between these two stern admonitions was a short paragraph of slightly less militant tone promising a just administration and freedom of conscience.[50] Although the embittered troops huddled along Black's Fork criticized this proclamation as too lenient, the Latter-day Saints could find in it little hope that their new governor would be well disposed toward them.

With this message Cumming sent a letter to Brigham Young, "Ex-Governor of Utah Territory," in which he forcefully con-

demned his "violent and treasonable acts." [51] Cumming's letters
to Washington also reveal that in this phase of the campaign he
shared the sympathies of the other civil and military officers. To
Cass he wrote that the people of Utah were mutinous; he also
rejected Young's effort "by assertions and the most puerile reasoning to justify his own treasonable acts and those of his associates in rebellion." [52]

Delana R. Eckels, the chief justice with whom Cumming temporarily agreed, became anathema to the Mormon Church. He was
a political appointee, his selection having been dictated by his
loyalty to the Democratic party and his support by powerful men
in public life, particularly by the Indiana delegation in Congress.
In selecting him for a position of responsibility in Utah the Government had been motivated less by a desire to secure a suitable
man for a difficult post than by the necessity of discharging a political debt.[53]

Stout and bald, about fifty years old, Eckels had been an editor,
lawyer, judge, politician, and businessman in Greencastle, Indiana,
before he accepted appointment in Utah. His friends called him
"honest, able, discreet, and prudent"; the editor of the *Kansas
Weekly Herald* described him as "a very pleasant, sociable and
intelligent gentleman." [54] It is certain that he was a far better
choice than Brocchus, Drummond, and many of the other officeholders who had come to Utah before the outbreak of the Mormon
War. It is also apparent that Eckels' intransigent attitude toward
the Saints prolonged the tension between Utah and the nation.
Although Eckels did not receive the office of governor, his first
objective, he had sufficient power to embarrass the Mormons in
his position as head of the Territory's judicial system.

While Cumming remained idle during the winter, having no
people to govern other than a few territorial officers and the brawling teamsters who had not enlisted in the army, Eckels busied himself with a number of legal matters. When the army captured
Joseph Taylor and William Stowell, he ordered his marshal to
arrest and imprison them on the charge of treason, thus indicating
that he interpreted the Mormons' resistance to the United States
army as a serious crime, not as a justifiable act of self-defense.
Through the rest of the month Eckels collected statements from
Lewis Simpson, William Eads, James Rupe, and other civilians

employed by Russell, Majors, and Waddell, in an effort to amass more evidence of the Saints' rebellious behavior for future use in court. For the same purpose he gathered testimony designed to prove earlier mistreatment of Gentiles by the Mormons.[55]

Having taken these preliminary steps, Eckels formally convened his court in December and impaneled a grand jury, a shabby group drawn from the civilians in Camp Scott. Under his direction this jury soon indicted Joseph Taylor, Stowell, Brigham Young, Wells, Lot Smith, and many other Mormons for treason. In the April session of his court Eckels launched a more ambitious attack upon the Church, for at that time he charged the grand jury with the task of investigating the Mormons' practice of polygamy, with a view to establishing what laws, if any, had been broken. Utimately nothing came of these activities: Taylor escaped his captors, Stowell was released when he took an oath of allegiance to the United States, a presidential proclamation removed the charge of treason against Brigham Young and his followers, and the study of polygamy proved inconclusive. But all this litigious industry by the judge proved to the Mormons that Eckels was an opponent as dangerous as Stiles or Drummond had been in their day.

8. End of Hostilities

AS WE HAVE SEEN, the Mormons' military strategy during the fall of 1857 centered upon a delaying but bloodless campaign designed to stop the Government's troops before they entered Salt Lake Valley. Behind this plan lay the hope that the Church might be able to settle its difficulties with the United States during the long winter if it could prevent the outbreak of war while tempers on both sides were hottest. Although the execution of this strategy was not brilliant, the objective was attained. The expedition, launched against Utah with the fervent support of eastern Gentiles, could advance no farther than Black's Fork, its progress halted not so much by the Saints' actions as by its tardy departure from Fort Leavenworth. During the winter important conferences took place in Washington and Salt Lake City; when the army again resumed its march, its officers and men aching to fight the Saints, it found only peace in Utah. Instead of dragooning a traitorous rabble into acceptance of its duties as American citizens, it merely had the task of establishing a military post carefully removed from the Mormons' settlements.

Church historians have without serious strain ascertained the causes of this peaceful dénouement. To their minds the whole war had arisen not because the people of Utah had disregarded laws and persecuted federal officials but because evil-disposed men, playing upon Gentile prejudice and ignorance, had aroused a popular desire in the East to destroy the sect. The stout-hearted resistance of the Saints to this invasion of their rights, this assault upon their very existence, persuaded James Buchanan to abandon the policy as too costly. He therefore agreed to a peace, actually a capitulation in which the Mormons gained all their demands. At the same time congressmen, newspaper editors, and many common people began to demand cessation of hostilities against a weak and innocent people. In their studies these authorities have not wholly neglected the part played by other factors in the pacific settlement of the crisis—the troubles in Kansas, the financial difficulties following the Panic of 1857, and the work of Kane, Bernhisel, and other individuals. Yet in general their conclusions stressed the success of Lot Smith and the other heroic cavaliers of the Church in delaying the actual outbreak of war long enough for Easterners to regain their sense of justice.[1] Unhappily, research cannot end with these simple explanations.

We should first point out that Buchanan and his advisors did not quickly give up their intention of using force in Utah. Instead, they clung for a long time to the conviction that the Saints, by their early behavior and their resistance to Alexander's forces, merited stern treatment rather than sympathetic conciliation. Thus the peaceful arrangements in mid-1858 signified not a surrender but rather the acceptance of a desirable but not mandatory policy alternative to war.

As was to be expected, John B. Floyd, early and late an outspoken critic of the Mormons, had no stomach for an accord. In his annual report of 1857 he vitriolically reviewed the recent relations between the Government and the Territory, playing up many of the prejudices and misconceptions that had initially given rise to the expedition. Having thus drawn the measure of Mormon infamy, he ended with an appeal to Congress for five new regiments.[2] In his report the next year he continued this display of animosity toward the Saints, indicating that among the members of Buchanan's cabinet *he* at least favored no compromise. "These people," he cautioned, "still evince a spirit of insubordination and moody discontent. They keep up strictly their organization, which has for its object and end the complete exclusion of federal authority from all participation in the governmental affairs of the Territory beyond a mere hollow show."[3]

President Buchanan was as slow as his Secretary of War to give up his conviction that the Mormons' recalcitrance demanded stern countermeasures. In his first annual message of December 8, 1857, he criticized their theocratic society and rebelliousness in phrases reminiscent of Floyd's recent report and Drummond's earlier letter of resignation. He spoke of Brigham Young's plotting to preserve his "despotic power" by separation from the United States

and of his "tampering with the Indian tribes." There was no
evidence of peaceful intent in the President's admonition to Congress: "This is the first rebellion which has existed in our Territories; and humanity itself requires that we should put it down
in a manner that it shall be the last." Nor did his request for
four new regiments suggest a disposition to consider the Utah
problem from a more compassionate point of view.[4] Buchanan's
second message a year later was also lacking in conciliatory expressions; and his proclamation in the spring of 1858 was equally
austere, for it charged the people with the crime of treason. In its
final pages this latter document ordered the Mormons within the
Territory to accept their new officials and promised all who did
so "a free pardon for the seditions and treason heretofore by
them committed." But Buchanan also sternly warned those who
continued to oppose the authority of the United States to "expect
no further lenity." [5]

It is possible, of course, that in their public messages the President and his Secretary of War were not wholly candid. They might
have slipped on the mask of righteous determination in order to
conceal an abrupt and embarrassingly inconsistent shift in their
policy toward Brigham Young's followers. Furthermore, under
pressure from congressmen to explain the outlay of great sums during a year of financial reverses for the nation, the two men might
have wished to portray the conditions in Utah before 1857 as
utterly intolerable, thus justifying their campaign. Indeed, Floyd
seemed to protest too much; in his report of 1858 he referred so
often to the Mormons' sinfulness that one suspects him of trying
to convince Congress of the inescapable need for the expensive
demonstration against these wayward people.[6] Yet in fact the Administration's constant belligerent denunciations of the Mormons,
both before and during the war, do not substantiate the finding
of denominational historians that the President and his advisors
were anxious to bring hostilities to a close at any cost.

In his dealings with Thomas L. Kane, Buchanan revealed no
desire to terminate the campaign as an admittedly expensive and
unpopular blunder. In the winter months Kane journeyed back
and forth between Salt Lake City and Camp Scott in an effort to
avert a full-scale war once the roads had become passable. One
authority, seeing in this mission evidence of the President's eager-

ness for peace, insists that the President had made Kane his
personal representative and had given him secret messages for
Cumming and the Mormons that would have established the
basis for compromise.[7] This explanation appears faulty. In his
letter to Kane of December 31, 1857, Buchanan took great
pains to stress that the young man was in no way the official or
unofficial spokesman of his Administration. The repetition of this
warning precludes any thought that the President was merely
protecting himself from future embarrassment should Kane fail
to settle the difficulties satisfactorily. In addition, Buchanan was
not sanguine as to the possibility of any arrangement with the
Mormons: "I would not at this moment, in view of the hostile
attitude which they have assumed against the United States, send
any agent to visit them on behalf of the government." [8]

The President's peace commission to Utah in 1858 has also been
cited as evidence of Buchanan's frantic desire to extricate himself
from a situation politically and militarily unprofitable. Yet the
instructions to these men, Lazarus Powell and Ben McCulloch,
show that far from approaching Brigham Young from a position
of weakness Buchanan was not prepared to make any concession
to the Mormons. The tenor of this document was reflected in
Cass' note to Cumming explaining the purpose of the mission.[9]

Taken by themselves, these communications to Kane and to the
commissioners could be dismissed as unreliable. Public instructions may serve only to hide the private purposes of politicians,
contained in secret orders of a radically different nature. Yet the
Government at this time and later displayed an equally aggressive
disposition in other ways than by mere words. For a time in January 1858 the War Department planned an attack upon Utah
from the West Coast that would crush all resistance there.[10] Its
efforts to increase Johnston's military effectiveness provide even
more convincing evidence of the Administration's continuing anti-
Mormon posture. In his annual message of 1857 the President
requested Congress to authorize four new regiments of soldiers.
While the Senate and the House of Representatives were debating this and other Administration proposals at great length, the
War Department proceeded in January to send Johnston the reinforcements he would need to confront a people in arms: the
First Cavalry Regiment, the Sixth and Seventh Regiments of

infantry, two companies of the Second Artillery, and the two companies of the Second Dragoons that had not taken the weary march
under Cooke across the Plains in the fall of 1857.[11] With the addition of another 850 recruits, these units totaled almost 4,000
men. Obviously Buchanan and Floyd considered a major engagement with the Mormons altogether possible in 1858.

The War Department issued other bellicose orders. It created
a Department of Utah, to be commanded by the gallant Gen.
Persifor F. Smith, and, following his death in May, by William
S. Harney. Finally aware that its army could not obtain adequate
provisions in the Salt Lake Valley, it also prepared to send a year's
supplies for the expedition, enough to support the troops until
the emergency in Utah had passed. In January 1858 the Government began to arrange with Russell, Majors, and Waddell to
transport approximately sixteen million pounds of freight, most
of it destined for Utah. To fulfill this assignment the firm was
compelled to acquire 40,000 oxen and 1,000 mules, and to hire
more than 4,000 teamsters; altogether the Government ordered
the contractors to send to the Territory at least 100 trains, each
composed of twenty-six wagons.[12]

During the spring men poured into Jefferson Barracks and Fort
Leavenworth from Fort Columbus, Newport Barracks, New York,
and many other posts. The streets of Leavenworth swarmed with
teamsters and troops. Piles of provisions intended for the army assumed mountainous proportions: food, clothing, two tons of medi-
cine, half a ton of percussion caps, weapons, and all the other supplies requisite for a great campaign. The fort nearby became congested with officers and enlisted men who had been ordered to
Camp Scott. In March one detachment of some 330 men left Fort
Leavenworth to join Hoffman on the Plains. On May 7 the first
organized column set out, followed during the rest of the month
and early June by the next five units. On June 15 Harney himself
left to join his command.[13] There was no evidence here of intent
on the part of the Administration to settle the Mormon War
amicably, on terms pleasing to the Saints. Furthermore, the messages that traveled back and forth between senior officers were all
couched in terms of war, not peace. On April 2, 1858, Winfield
Scott advised Johnston concerning the best strategy to "force
the passes to Salt Lake." [14] A little later Harney wrote that there

would be 3,000 men and a great quantity of supplies at Camp Scott; "Whatever military operations may be necessary can be commenced with vigor and tolerable efficiency." [15]

If Buchanan had wished desperately to end the Mormon War in 1858, certainly he would have seized upon any excuse to announce the restoration of peace. He did not follow this policy. Early in June Kane arrived in Washington and described his efforts to settle the crisis; later Governor Cumming's communications reached the Capital, bringing word that the Saints had received him peacefully. Still the Administration refused to give full credence to these reports. For two weeks the cabinet discussed the matter, studied statements, and quizzed Kane closely before it concluded that hostilities were apparently over. At last, on June 28, the War Department recalled General Harney. The next day Scott reassigned most of the reinforcements originally sent to join the expedition, cautiously observing that the Government was doing so "on the supposition, which, at this distance seems probable, that the Mormons no longer intend to oppose an armed resistance to the entrance of the United States troops into the Valley of Salt Lake." Even so, the Administration was careful not to act too hastily. In his order Scott strengthened Johnston's command by attaching to it another regiment of infantry, thus making the army potent enough to mount an offensive against Indians or Mormons.[16]

It is difficult to judge the influence of newspaper opinion as a cause of peace. In this instance, as in the case of the other supposedly moderating factors, some writers believe that Buchanan abandoned his determination to bring the Mormons to obedience by force because the press, once favorable to such a course, became increasingly hostile to it after the army entered winter quarters.[17] Although it is true that in 1858 the country's editors were not so unanimous in their denunciation of the Saints as they had been in the previous year, they showed no unified attitude toward the war. In fact, study of editorial opinion indicates that if Buchanan had consulted the American newspapers in the hope of devising a happy resolution of his troubles with the Mormons, he must have been dismayed by the resulting cacophony. Certainly there was no deafening, unanimous condemnation of his action compelling him to re-examine and alter his policy.

It is to be observed, then, that the Saints' resistance to the army, a public opinion divided on the merits of the campaign, and the other considerations reportedly working to soften the President's Mormon policy did not materially influence Buchanan. Yet it remains true that during the winter he began to ponder the desirability of convincing the Mormons that they were not obliged to fight the United States in order to preserve their lives and their religious freedom. Although he did not go so far as to authorize Kane and the peace commissioners to negotiate with the Church, he now permitted these men to examine with the Mormons the issues existing between them and the Government. Perhaps this change, slight as it was, came from a realization that, having failed to investigate the situation in Utah before he sent an army to correct it, he should now remedy this omission, lest he be charged with having needlessly precipitated a civil war. Perhaps, too, his difficulties in Kansas influenced Buchanan to seek a solution to this other diverting problem. Of more importance, however, were certain developments in Congress.

Despite their later assurances to the contrary, the members of Buchanan's Administration had obviously underestimated both the cost of an expedition against Utah and the number of troops necessary to stifle any resistance offered by the Mormons. Thus during the winter, when his army was huddled along Black's Fork instead of parading in triumphal possession of the Territory, the President found himself required to ask Congress for assistance, first to end the financial embarrassment into which the Government was plunged by the Utah War and the Panic of 1857, and second to bring the army to a strength adequate to meet any opposition from the Saints. When both the Senate and the House of Representatives delayed action on these requests for several months, Buchanan saw the desirability of seeking a peaceful end to his difficulties.[18]

The President's appeal for four regiments met with a cold reception in Congress. In the Senate, Jefferson Davis completely altered the Administration's proposal, but the measure still fell under criticism from pacifists, Free Soilers who opposed the President's policy in Kansas, and the Southerners who feared the result of this precedent if the Republicans should win control of the Government's military establishment in later years. In their deliberations the senators remained as hostile toward the Mormons as they had been earlier in the decade, but with these other considerations in mind they rejected the Administration's request for additional regiments. The President's appeal for a deficiency appropriation of $6,700,000 to discharge the unanticipated expenses of the campaign also received unsympathetic treatment.[19] It was the same story in the House. Sentiment among the representatives was so decidedly antagonistic to the Mormons that the Administration might well have expected prompt approval of its two requests.[20] Yet there, too, the Utah problem became involved in the more serious controversy over slavery. On April 9, after considerable discussion, Congress at last approved a bill to authorize the enlistment of two regiments of volunteers, but it was not until May 4 that it passed the deficiency appropriations so urgently needed. These actions came too late. During the first week of April, or possibly even earlier, the President and his advisors had decided to investigate whether the Mormons desired peace with the United States.

While sentiment in Washington was veering away from the view that extermination or at least forceful punishment of the Mormons was wise, the military and civilian personnel at Camp Scott lost none of its bitterness toward the Saints. As they hunkered down over their smoky fires or stumped on tingling feet through their patrol duty, the officers and enlisted men were not often given to amiable thoughts about Brigham Young's people. Many of the soldiers expected a military engagement as soon as warm weather permitted them to march. Their commanding officer shared this feeling.[21] A sentence in one of Johnston's reports revealed his intentions most clearly. He would continue toward Salt Lake City, he advised his superiors, as soon as possible, without regard to the Mormons; "if they desire to join issue, I believe it is for the interest of the government that they should have the opportunity." [22]

The civil officers in the camp had an equally bilious attitude toward the Mormons. Even Alfred Cumming and Jacob Forney, who later became defenders of the Church, to the manifest irritation of unreconstructed Gentiles, were as belligerent as Eckels when they thought of the Saints. After the Governor had issued his moderate proclamation to the people of Utah on November 26, there was considerable anxiety among the military over the firmness of his anti-Mormonism.[23] The alarm was unfounded in these early months. When he wrote to the Assistant Secretary of State in late January, Cumming commented upon the excellent condition of the troops as though he expected war as soon as the snows had melted. With his wife he shared the camp's conviction concerning the Mormons' defiance of the nation.[24]

The new Governor's initial hostility toward the people of Utah undoubtedly drew strength from Garland Hurt. In December the Indian agent, whose recent flight from the Territory had temporarily interrupted his feud with the Saints, wrote Cumming that the Church's leaders had instilled in their people a "heartfelt hatred for the people of the United States." [25] The Governor considered Hurt's interpretations worthy of careful consideration, for, he told Cass, "Mr. Hurt is a man of character whose statements in matters of fact are entitled to confidence." [26] At this time the new superintendent of Indian affairs, Jacob Forney, also displayed none of his later disposition to treat the Saints as victims of persecution rather than as debauched rebels.[27] Into this sizable depot of anti-Mormonism galloped young Thomas Leiper Kane, exhausted by his long trip from the East Coast to Black's Fork by way of California and Salt Lake City, but as ready as ever to defend the interests of the Church of Jesus Christ of Latter-day Saints.

Kane had performed many valuable services for the Mormons during the decade. President Fillmore himself admitted to Kane that in his selection of the first governor of Utah "I relied upon you for the moral character and standing of Mr. Young," although Kane was a Democrat and not well known to the President.[28] During the next years the Mormon leaders turned to him for help in their periodic troubles with the Government. For his part the young humanitarian gave the Mormons advice, worked for them in the Capital, and made his home a haven for their missionaries. Willard Richards expressed the affection which bound his people and Kane one to another when he wrote to introduce a missionary traveling to England: "It is esteemed one of the greatest honors and blessings that we can confer upon our friends going abroad, to receive an introduction to Colonel Kane, of Independence Hall;

whose name and memory are embalmed in the hearts of thousands, whom tho' many have not seen, they love for his works' sake." [29]

When 1857 brought the relations between the Saints and the nation to the breaking point, the spokesmen of the Church once more called upon Kane for assistance. Early in that year Brigham Young, anticipating an explosion of Gentile hostility because of the labors of Drummond and other former officers, asked Kane to seek statehood for Utah or, if that should prove impossible, to urge the appointment of Mormons to vacant territorial positions.[30] Kane soon discovered that the new Administration was in no mood to heed such suggestions. Unable to dissuade the President either from removing Young or from sending an army to support his new appointees, he fretted through the summer and fall, powerless to protect his friends from the blow that seemed certain to strike them. But when the expedition failed to reach Salt Lake Valley in 1857, he saw an opportunity to help by mediating between them and their opponents.

During his conversations with the President and his cabinet in the winter Kane failed to win modification of the Government's policy. He could not induce them to call off the campaign against Utah, nor did he receive authority to negotiate a settlement of the war. Instead Buchanan, in reply to his urgent appeal for some communication before he left for Utah, wrote only to say that Kane was pursuing this mission on his personal initiative alone. But this message was enough, for it gave Kane quasi-official permission to depart for Salt Lake City. Another presidential letter of the same date announced: "As you have been impelled by your own sense of duty to visit Utah, and having informed me that nothing can divert you from this purpose, it affords me pleasure to commend you to the favorable regard of all officers of the United States whom you might meet in the course of your travels." [31] Kane was to find that the introduction did little to thaw the iciness of General Johnston and his impatient command.

Apparently wishing first to investigate conditions in Utah and to apprize himself of the Mormons' plans before meeting with the civil and military officers at Camp Scott, Kane went by sea to California and hurried on to Salt Lake City by way of Cajon Pass and the western route, traveling under the pseudonym of Dr.

Osborne. By early March he had reached the Territory safely and
had entered into secret conferences with the members of the
Hierarchy. The nature of these talks is not known. Certainly one
Church historian's account, drawn from the jealously guarded
"History of Brigham Young," was not accurate: "Dr. Osborne
had pleaded with him [Young], in his own name, to stay the hand
of the brethren against the army, for they are in our power." [32]
It is more plausible to presume that the Mormon leaders and
Thomas Kane, worried lest the arrival of warm weather bring an
irresistible attack by Johnston, sought an arrangement that would
protect the Saints from another encounter with armed and angry
Gentiles. Kane could only hope for a truce, giving the Mormons
time to evacuate the Territory, for he wrote his father: "The day
may be, and probably is past to make peace, but not to save our
poor fellows." [33]

On the evening of March 12 Kane reached Camp Scott, too
exhausted to dismount from his horse, or even to speak. After a
lengthy sleep he was ready the next day to pursue the purpose of
his long journey—that is, to convince the civil and military officers
that there was no need to attack the Mormons. Admittedly his
task was difficult. Camp Scott was a military post commanded by
a stiff-necked and humorless individual who wished all men to
observe protocol. Accordingly it behooved Kane to treat the
General with courtesy, to flatter his pride and fulfill his demands
for deference. This was doubly necessary, for if the young ally
of the Mormons was to arrange for the army's peaceful entrance
into the Salt Lake Valley, he had to persuade Johnston, shocked
by the Saints' apparent treason and irritated at his own embarrassing position, to forego his intention to exterminate Young's
followers.

Kane faced still other problems of diplomacy. Another important personage at Scott was Governor Alfred Cumming, also
jealous of his prerogatives and inordinately concerned about the
status of his reputation in the East. Already fretting over his
subordinate position in the camp, a civil officer whose powers
were negligible in a military garrison, Cumming was a difficult
man to discuss sensitive matters with. Thus in his role as peacemaker Kane had to steer skillfully through currents of envy,

ambition, and war-mongering. His capabilities were not adequate to this assignment.

As soon as he had recovered from his trip, he set about his task. With some understanding of the ways of an army camp he paid his first visit to General Johnston, not to Cumming. But he mishandled the interview, riding his horse so close to the entrance of Johnston's tent that one officer expected him to ride on inside. Then, remaining in his saddle, Kane ordered his servant to inform Johnston of his presence. When the newly breveted General came to the entrance, thus obstructed by Kane's horse, he could find no way to squeeze by. Instead he was forced to crouch, thrust his head through an unoccluded portion, and finally, with his cheek pressed against the horse, peer at the newcomer and ask who he was. Kane gave his name, said that he carried important dispatches, and requested permission to see Cumming. Although Johnston approved the request, he and the other officers present were not pleased by this first meeting with Kane, whose breathless, excited manner of speaking implied that he considered himself bent upon a mission of great moment.[34]

A few soldiers in Camp Scott were familiar with Kane's former defense of the Saints, and soon the rumor circulated that he was a Mormon spy. Some of the men in Gove's company even wanted to do him harm. This result was inevitable, given Kane's singular conduct. By spending most of his first two days closeted in deep and secret conversation with the governor he invited such suspicions. His failure to take the military into his confidence, to urge upon these angry men the arguments in behalf of peace which quickly convinced Cumming, caused both officers and enlisted men to embrace their anti-Mormon sentiments the more eagerly. If relations between Utah and the nation were to be improved, it was going to be necessary to convert the army, as well as Cumming. Kane failed to accomplish, or even to attempt, this conversion.[35]

When he finally approached Johnston, Kane experienced unyielding hostility and cold rebuff. In earlier conferences with Brigham Young he had formulated a plan for reducing the army's enmity toward the Mormons, or at least of placing the expedition in the Church's debt. The scheme was so naive as to be fantastic. Kane was to carry with him to Scott the Church's offer of enough meat and flour to keep the troops from starvation. It was the present of salt again, but on a larger scale. The fact that Johnston had curtly rejected the earlier gift and was known to detest the Saints did not deter Kane. Accordingly when he arrived in Scott he sent to the commanding general Young's offer of fifteen to twenty thousand pounds of flour and 200 head of cattle belonging to Gerrish, a Salt Lake City merchant. The note's unfortunate wording infuriated Johnston. Unwilling to pass up this opportunity to taunt the army, Young attributed his action to a report that "the troops are very destitute of provisions," a phrase so pleasing to him that he used it again in a letter to Cumming. The Mormon leader also indirectly accused Johnston of holding Gerrish prisoner in the camp.[36]

Johnston was not amused. With more vainglory than accuracy he denied that his men lacked provisions. He then proceeded to explain his attitude toward the Mormons in words that should have discouraged further communication on this matter: "Whatever might be the need of the Army under my command for food, we would neither ask, nor receive from President Young and his confederates any supplies while they continue to be enemies of the Government." Gerrish, he said, had already left the camp for the States; he had at all times been free to go anywhere except "to Salt Lake City or some position occupied by an armed body of Mormons opposed to the Government, all intercourse with the enemy being prohibited by the 56th and 57th Articles of War." He warned, in words bearing ominous implications for the future: "Having the question of peace or war under his control President Young would, should he choose the latter, be responsible for all the consequences." [37] Johnston could not have rejected the offer of food more emphatically had he thrown it in Kane's face, yet the self-appointed messenger of peace persisted in hoping that the general might be persuaded to change his mind. Accordingly he again wrote Johnston, warning that "it must greatly prejudice the public interest to refuse Mr. Young's proposal in such a manner at the present time." There is no record of a second answer from Johnston.[38]

Kane had other problems than urging upon a straight-laced army officer the acceptance of an impossible proposal. On his journey to Camp Scott he had been accompanied by a small party of Mormons. These men remained in the vicinity of Black's Fork in order to serve as messengers between Kane and Salt Lake City; Kane especially wished them to be available to inform Young that Johnston would welcome the gift of meat and flour. It was reasonable to expect that clashes would occur, and in fact skirmishes did take place. When Kane protested to Johnston in writing that these Mormons were part of his escort and of vital importance to him, he again received a curt reply.[39]

This little episode was characteristic of the inefficacy of efforts to end the Mormon War, and it revealed a cause for the continuation of friction between civil and military officers during and after 1858. Kane and Johnston were men of education and some maturity. Neither desired to see the conflict between Utah and the nation degenerate into a needless civil war. Yet when minor irritants or major complications arose to jeopardize the establishment of peace in the Territory, neither sought the other out to talk frankly. Except in a few instances, all communication between Kane and Johnston was conducted by written message. Separated geographically by only a few hundred yards, the two men might as well have tried to settle their differences by hallooing across the Uinta Mountains.

From the first day Kane's relations with Johnston's command became a nightmare of misunderstanding. After his arrival in camp the general had assigned a sergeant to accompany Kane to Cumming's quarters, where he was to protect his possessions and then conduct him, when he was ready, to Johnston's headquarters for an official call. Cumming, ever quick to take offense at any fancied affront, considered the soldier Johnston's spy and announced that Kane was an agent accredited to him, an erroneous statement. On another occasion a more serious incident almost resulted in a duel between Kane and Johnston, the former becoming so aggrieved that he rejected Cumming's pleas to ignore the matter and began to put his affairs in order.

Comic altercations followed one upon another until, in a nearly tragic episode, Kane was almost killed. On March 17 he had left camp for a conference with his Mormon escort several miles away and did not return until nightfall. Stormy weather had reduced visibility and, fearing that a patrol might shoot him, he hit upon the curious expedient of firing his gun four times as a signal of his approach. Gove's men turned out rapidly on the logical assumption that an attack was in progress, patrols scoured the vicinity, and finally one soldier, stumbling upon Kane, shot at him from two paces but unaccountably missed.[40]

On March 19, after a week of fumbling overtures, frustrations, and hairbreadth escapes, Kane was disposed to abandon his mission as hopeless.[41] But his discouragement at the seeming lack of progress in the quest of peace was not entirely justified. Although his relations with the army had produced nothing but animosity, his many conversations with Cumming had begun to bear fruit.

The Governor had not yet come to think of the Mormons as a guiltless, persecuted people, but by the end of March he had accepted the Administration's view that consultation with the Saints should be tried before military force was used against them. In all probability it was Kane who persuaded him to visit Utah before the army could march, lest a bloody engagement make any peaceful settlement impossible. Whatever the source of his thinking, the Governor suddenly informed Johnston on April 3 of his intention to set out for Salt Lake City within two days. This decision, however, did not come from a revolutionary change of heart. The letters of his wife show that Cumming left Camp Scott with little intention to negotiate with the Saints, but rather to assert the authority of the federal government.[42]

When Cumming made up his mind to hurry ahead of the army, he was not aware that the Saints had resolved to leave the Territory, or at least make a pretense of leaving it. Already they had prepared for the evacuation of all settlements north of Provo. One Mormon historian has said of this episode: "The brilliantly conceived and executed maneuvers attending every stage of the offensive-defensive program of President-Governor Young during the Utah War reached their culminating climax in the spectacular heroism of the 'exodus.' "[43] This movement of people was to become a significant chapter in Mormon history.

It had long been Brigham Young's fixed belief (as shown above, Chapter 6) that in the regions south or southwest of the Mormons' principal settlements there were, hidden in the barren deserts, areas sufficiently fertile to support a great multitude of people, perhaps as many as 500,000. These verdant but inaccessible places, he felt, would provide excellent retreats if Gentiles should drive his Saints from the Salt Lake Basin. Although in the mid-1850's Bishop David Evans had uncovered no such oases despite a thorough search, Young refused to discard his dream. When during the war the Church, losing its confident expectation of victory, turned from bold resistance to flight, its leaders decided on March 18 "to go into the desert and not war with the people [of the United States], but let them destroy themselves." [44] Once more Young expressed his faith in the existence of the southern valleys; once more he sent out explorers to discover them. Two parties under George W. Bean and William H. Dame, the former containing more than 100 men, dutifully scoured the desolate reaches west of Parowan for these nonexistent sanctuaries. Although Bean left forty-five men to establish a farm in one place, neither detachment found valleys capable of supporting 500,000 people, or even a fraction of that number. The failure of these missions, however, did not stop the "exodus," for when the men finally returned, Bean in April and Dame in June, the great "Move South" already was under way.[45]

The Mormons' decision to leave their homes was not irrevocable, but was contingent upon the actions of Johnston's soldiers. The strategy called for the evacuation of all settlements north of Provo, with only a few sturdy men remaining in each village and town. In Provo the Church would wait to discover the army's disposition. If by word or deed the troops should reveal the fanatical hatred of the Missouri and Illinois mobs once they had reached the Valley, then demolition of all buildings would be ordered.[46] Yet Young hoped that such desperate measures would not be necessary, for he did not order the immediate destruction of the Mormons' homes, and he had the foundations of the Temple concealed rather than razed. Furthermore, he was cool to one proposal to remove his people from the United States. In May 1858 two agents of a Colonel Kinney, who owned, or pretended to own, a vast portion of the Mosquito Coast in Central America, visited Utah with the proposition that the Church buy these holdings, some thirty million acres, for ten cents an acre. Young rejected the offer with the remark: "We are just where we want to be, and where we intend to stay." [47]

The exodus, then, was conceived as a means of preventing any contact between the Mormons and the army until the Hierarchy had studied the intentions of the civil and military officers. It was also designed to win sympathy for the Church in the States, by creating a picture there of the Mormons as an oppressed people once more driven from their homes by armed mobs. With this in mind Young arranged to publish the *Deseret News* in Fillmore, and later in Parowan, from which towns the editions of the paper could be regularly sent to California and then on to the East Coast.[48]

Once having decided to leave their homes, the Mormons set about the task with characteristic vigor. Church officials packed their records for removal to Provo, the *Deseret News* press was sent to Fillmore, and the grain in the tithing house was distributed among the villages in the southern part of the Territory.[49] On April 1, while Cumming was making his way across the snowy Wasatch Mountains, Brigham Young, George A. Smith, Heber Kimball, and Daniel Wells left Salt Lake City on the dusty road to Provo, their possessions piled high in fifteen wagons. Soon the inhabitants of the town and of the other villages to the north had gathered their belongings together, boarded up the windows of their houses, and followed their leaders. Plagued by scarcity of forage, by rains and at times by snow, with their women and children unprotected in open carts, the Saints stoically pressed on. Some authorities have set the number involved in this hegira at 30,000; one enthusiastic diarist returning from a mission to Hawaii said that the flight from Nauvoo looked like "a small rivulet by the side of a mighty river when compared with the seventy-five thousand men and women and children that we now met in one continuous line of travel." [50]

While most of his constituency was thus in the process of evacuating part of the Territory, Governor Cumming, after difficulties with Indians and the severe weather, had met a well-mounted party of Mormons under Porter Rockwell and in its company was passing through Echo Canyon and down into the Salt Lake Basin. At one town he was given a hearty reception, during which the local band serenaded him with the "Star-Spangled Banner" and other patriotic tunes. [51] In response to this apparent cordiality the new Governor made a few impromptu remarks on the sacredness of individual rights. But in spite of the surface appearance of good will, the Mormons looked upon Cumming as only another Gentile come to destroy their religious and political freedom. It was well for his peace of mind as he entered Salt Lake City that he was ignorant of George A. Smith's comment: "[The] City Corporation, Mayor, Aldermen, and some councilors went out to meet the animal, styled Gov. Cumming." It was also well that he had not heard Kane advise Brigham Young that having "caught the fish, now you can cook it as you have a mind to." [52]

For two days after his arrival in the Mormon capital Cumming and the Church leaders, who had come from Provo to meet the new executive, discussed the problems before them. At first their rambling conversations concerned inconsequential topics, but on April 14 the interview turned to more vital matters. Although Young complained with some heat about the recent interruption of the postal services, he devoted more time to the accusation that the army had made the Indians, once peacefully inclined, murderous and insolent by offers of rewards for dead Mormons. According to Smith, after this conference had ended Young "said that he was fully satisfied by the talk with Cumming that he desired the destruction of the Saints." [53] In the light of Cumming's subsequent actions, this conclusion was completely inaccurate. Having decided to work for a peaceful *modus operandi* with the Mormons, the new governor had quickly shed his earlier dislike for them and his more recent misgivings about his safety at their hands. Now he was willing to make concessions for the sake of peace. He accepted Young's charge concerning the army's relations with the Indians as worthy of serious consideration, and he praised Young as a good man and an excellent leader.[54]

Cumming's eagerness to reach an understanding at almost any cost is revealed in his remarkable letter to General Johnston of April 15, three days after his arrival in Salt Lake City. "I have been everywhere recognized as the governor," he declared, "and am gratified in being able to state to you that . . . I have been universally greeted with such respectful attentions as are due to the representative of the executive authority of the United States in the Territory." Since Cumming had met only a handful of the Mormon leaders, the rest remaining two days' ride away in Provo, the basis of this assertion is difficult to discover. The grievances advanced by Young in the previous day's interview assuredly provide little justification for the assumption that the Mormons were peacefully disposed. These matters did not bother Cumming. Although he had not taken an audit of the public property and records, including those of Judge Stiles' ill-starred court, he wrote that everything was in order. At the end of his message he indicated his acceptance of one of the Mormons' accusations: "With feelings of profound regret I have learned that Agent Hurt is charged with having incited to acts of hostility the Indians in the Uinta valley. I hope that Agent Hurt will be able to vindicate himself from the charges." [55]

Cumming had decided to establish peace between Utah and the nation by the simple expedient of unilaterally announcing the end of the war, only to discover that the Mormons' belligerent attitude endangered this Cheshire-cat policy. In a long private conversation Wells and Kimball told him there could be no peace so long as the army remained in or near the Territory of Utah. It was an ominous declaration, since the new Governor was powerless to control Johnston's movements.[56] At a public meeting in the Tabernacle on April 25 Cumming received more distressing evidence of the Saints' uncooperative sentiments. After he had demanded of the Mormons "an unconditional submission on their part to the dictates of the law," at the same time assuring them of his and the army's pacific intentions, he asked for comments from the audience. The result was reminiscent of Brocchus' experience seven years earlier. The Church Historian recorded Gilbert Clemens' reply: " 'Shall we have hirelings foisted upon us by the point of the bayonet, (One loud "No").' " Cumming's observation that he had no bayonet, not even a penknife, passed unheeded for "the congregation became greatly excited, and joined the speakers in their intemperate remarks." From the Governor's point of view the only pleasant part of the conference was Young's expression of hope for the settlement of all disputes.[57]

Cumming did not permit these rebuffs to discourage him. After a belated inspection of the territorial records he informed Lewis Cass that everything was in a state of "perfect preservation." [58] Since Stiles, Drummond, and others had advanced the Mormons' destruction of federal documents as reason enough for intervention in Utah, and the public in the States had become greatly concerned for the safety of these papers, Cumming obviously felt that he had made a case for his portrayal of the Mormons as law-abiding citizens. Further discovery convinced him of the falseness of another charge against the Saints. In Gentile minds the Church stood convicted of having imposed a cruel tyranny upon the people of Utah. In fact, one of the loudest arguments in favor of the expedition held that many Mormons, oppressed but unable to flee, would rush to the army as soon as it was near enough to provide protection. When on April 24 Cumming publicly offered assistance to all who "considered themselves unlawfully restrained of their liberties," only fifty-six men, thirty-three women, and seventy-one children responded, and most of the adults told Cumming that they "had no complaint against anyone" but only had found Utah economically unrewarding.[59]

One problem still vexing the Governor was the Mormons' evacuation of northern Utah. It was his intention to remove all obstructions to peace, to answer all charges against the Church, before the army was able to resume its march toward Echo Canyon and on into Salt Lake Valley. If the Saints continued to abandon their homes, he could not maintain that the situation in the Territory was serene. He could not even be governor if there was no one to govern. Cumming's appeals to Young to halt the exodus were unsuccessful, for the latter expressed his intention to leave Utah and stay away as long as his Church was threatened by an army.[60] In desperation, therefore, Cumming visited Provo and the Saints' other temporary homes, hoping to bring the people back by a direct appeal.

When he arrived at the teeming campground on Provo Bottoms, called "Shanghai" by some, the Governor was pained by "scenes of great trial and suffering." On the public square in Provo the Church had erected buildings for Young and the other members of the Hierarchy, but the majority of the Saints who had left their homes were forced to construct whatever cover they could on the treeless expanse west of town. The families with wagons used them as rudimentary houses. Others, less fortunately equipped, made tents of cloth, built board or log huts, and fabricated shelters out of willow branches and twigs. Some could only burrow holes into the ground. In this fashion several thousand Mormons lived in squalor for two months, awaiting instructions to march on or return home.[61]

Mormons of that day and later have insisted that despite the misery and sacrifice—even the loss of life—accompanying the exodus the people yielded cheerfully to their Church's wishes. This is inaccurate. Many left their homes not in dutiful reply to Brigham Young's mandate but because the Hierarchy compelled them to do so. When in September 1857 Young had spoken of a possible flight from Utah, he had advised all who were unprepared for such an eventuality to leave the Territory, "for when the time comes to burn and lay waste our improvements, if any man undertakes to shield his, he will be sheared down." Having decided that the interests of the Church did indeed demand flight, or at least the semblance of it, Young carried out his warning. One Mormon historian has written: "Though many of his group did not recognize the social significance of the move, and procrastinated in their departure, Brigham Young pressed the movement remorselessly and threatened condign punishment on those who did not comply with the order." [62] Once settled on Provo Bottoms a number of Saints became discontented and talked of going back, a development that led Young to deliver several sermons on the necessity of doing the Lord's will.[63]

In spite of the discomfort and occasional grumbling involved in the Move South, Cumming received little attention when early in May he urged the Mormons to retrace their steps. For their part the Church leaders had few qualms about abandoning the homes and property they had labored ten years to erect. George Smith wrote of his new $12,000 house: "I think my buildings will make a good fire, should Johnston advance on a sudden." [64] Similarly most of their followers embarked upon this new undertaking with as much vigor as they had exhibited in their trek to Utah, their creation of Y. X. Carrying Company, and their other services to the Church. When on March 21 Young called for 500 volunteers to prepare a New Zion, John McAllister requested permission to go, and became so persistent after being refused that the First Presidency asked him, he said, "to be patient and pursue the even tenor of my ways." His behavior was typical of the spirit of other Mormons.[65] Cumming's appeal accordingly fell upon deaf ears; the people chose to remain in their huts and wickiups until their rulers released them.

Although he failed to bring the Saints back to their homes, Cumming made progress in his single-handed effort to establish peace. The Mormons' initial hostility toward him began to thaw by the end of the first week in May. Now Young could see that the new Governor, for all his unfortunate physical appearance, was not planning either to interfere officiously in the affairs of his Church or to treat his followers as rebels against the Government. When he wrote to Mormons traveling toward Utah, Young warned them at all costs to avoid capture by Johnston's soldiers, but he added: "We intend to provide you, if possible, with passports from Gov. Cumming, who at present is with us and really seems disposed to take hold of the thread of justice." To Cumming, Young wrote that his "highly commendable efforts in behalf of law, order, and the extension of civil and religious rights, are cheerfully and promptly sustained by the people as well as by myself." By this time the Governor had divested himself of his old anti-Mormon feelings and had acquired a fondness for some of the Church's leaders, if not for their theology.[66]

Yet two statements in Young's flattering letter to Cumming showed that the task of ending the war was not completed. In his communication the Mormon leader warned: "the nearer approach of the United States troops will at once greatly complicate and jeopardize the loyal efforts of yourself and your numerous friends, at least until a candid investigation has preceded their further movement towards our settlements." [67] Cumming knew that the army at that moment was impatiently awaiting the opening of the roads and the arrival of supplies, already near at hand, before resuming its march toward Salt Lake City. He therefore resolved to pay a hurried visit to Camp Scott, hoping to convince Johnston that the situation in Utah did not require the immediate presence of the military.

Another passage in Young's letter contained assertions even more inimical to the establishment of cordial relations between Gentile and Mormon in the Territory. "I cannot be responsible," the Lion of the Lord growled, "for the safety of certain Governmental appointees, such as Dr. Garland Hurt, H. F. Morrell, C. L. Craig, and, perhaps, others which your better judgment will probably dictate, should they venture to come into our settlements." This attitude had been the principal cause of the war in the first place —namely, the assumption that the Mormons need not obey and would not tolerate federal officers of whom for any reason they did not approve. Now, after all the events of the campaign, after the mediative efforts of Kane and Cumming, Young could still say, with words echoing his remarks to Brocchus in 1851, that "in a country where the people are so justly esteemed sovereign, all rulers must realize that their influence and real security are and rightly should be, based upon their own correct official and private conduct, which of itself insures the protection and respect of all good men."

While Cumming was devoting his talents to the cause of peace, a sizable portion of the civil and military personnel in Camp Scott was not at all pleased with his activities. Everywhere there was the cold suspicion that he had sold out the interest of his country by truckling to the Mormons. Many in the camp felt that, "over-confident in his own genius," he had thoughtlessly given up the right policy of bludgeoning the Saints into obedience in favor of an attempt to convert Brigham Young by persuasion. The thought that Cumming might bring the war to an end tormented the frost-bitten and hungry troops, who desired no "compromise with those who destroyed the food for which we are now suffering." [68]

In Camp Scott there were two champions of the Governor and of his labors. His wife was sorely wounded by the "backbiting and defaming" but could do little to combat this vilification.[69] Jacob Forney, the semiliterate Indian superintendent, was of more service. Like Cumming, Forney during the winter months had emerged from the cocoon of his anti-Mormonism into the sunlight of Brigham Young's smile. Whether from sincere conviction or from the realization that it was politically expedient to embrace the peace policy, supported as it was by the Administration as well as by Cumming, the superintendent traveled about the camp, try-ing to defend the Governor and his actions from all criticism. Aware that some were bombarding Buchanan's cabinet with at-tacks upon the executive and his moderate course, he laboriously scrawled five messages to Attorney General Black. If the crisis with Utah should end without war, he wrote, Cumming should receive all the credit, for "The Govenor [sic] has had no aid, either by Advise [sic] or otherwise from any other Civil officer—but am sorry to say the reverse." Later he complained: "I am in a very bad humor at some of our Civil Government officers. It does seem to me that it is there [sic] full determination to precipitate matters to a fatal issue." [70]

Among the civilians, as Forney soon discovered, Delana R. Eckels was the most resolute anti-Mormon. Toward the end of May the superintendent complained to Black: "Why Judge Eckels is thus striving to bring war upon us, after what the Govenor [sic] has accomplished is certainly strange." [71] That Eckels wished a bloody collision between the army and the Mormons is questionable; probably, like Johnston, he considered the Church traitorous, meriting punishment rather than forgiveness. At any rate, the long months of hibernation in his crude quarters had not lessened his spleen. He emphatically disapproved of Cumming's decision to visit Salt Lake City in advance of the army. While the Governor was striving to settle the difficulties in Utah, Eckels was, as Forney feared, writing Cass that there was no reliable evidence of the Mormons' loyalty and that Cumming was virtually a prisoner of Brigham Young. In another letter to the Secretary of State he described his recent discoveries concerning the tyranny of Young, the Church's murder of apostates, and the "fearful oath" extracted at the endowment ritual. He also tried to make his court an instrument to nullify Cumming's efforts at peace. [72]

When he returned to Camp Scott on May 16, Cumming faced not only the stony antagonism of civil and military personnel but also the necessity of conducting some delicate negotiations with General Johnston. The Mormons had demanded of Cumming that he stop the expedition from marching into the Salt Lake Basin. Although he realized the impossibility of this request, he apparently hoped to still the Saints' fears of an early attack from the army by persuading Johnston to keep his forces in winter quarters until all arrangements with Brigham Young had been completed. This task was a difficult one, for the general was slow to accept Cumming's subsequent assurances that the war was over. [73]

During May, Cumming made little headway in bringing Johnston around to his point of view. The distant relationship between the two men made any agreement most difficult. Although he had arrived at Black's Fork on May 16 with pressing matters to discuss, Cumming did not contact Johnston until his fifth day in camp, impelling Johnston, with some justification, to complain of his ignorance concerning developments in Utah. When Cumming did communicate with the general, whose headquarters were not far from the Governor's accommodations, he used letters rather than personal interviews. At last, on May 21, the governor wrote: "After a careful investigation I am gratified in being able to inform you that I believe there is at present no organized armed force of its inhabitants in any part of this Territory, with the exception of a small party subject to my orders in or near Echo Canyon." Johnston replied to this note with a terse expression of satisfaction, but on the same day he advised his superiors: "My present impression is, if there shall be need to do it, that it will be quite practicable to turn the passes." The grim general still thought in terms of war, Cumming's optimistic assertions notwithstanding. To Hoffman, who was to bring supplies from Laramie, Johnston wrote of Cumming's statement concerning the Mormons' militia; he warned the colonel, however, "not on this account to relax the vigilance which should be exercised in any enemy's country to secure your trains and herds." [74]

While Cumming was urging upon the Mormons a dutiful attitude toward the Government and its representatives and upon Johnston the abandonment of his ruthless spirit, he was unaware that the Administration in Washington had decided early in April to send a commission to Utah for the purpose of bringing the embarrassing war to an end, if possible. When he learned of this development the Governor was vastly displeased. Although at the same time he had received a dispatch from Cass praising him and expressing the President's "entire confidence" in him, he knew that the credit for settling the troublesome Utah question would now be garnered by others.[75] Yet in truth Cumming did need help in restoring peace to the Territory: the spokesmen of the Church still displayed a defiant attitude, and bloody imprecations were often heard in the tents along Black's Fork.

During a debate in the Senate over a request from the citizens of Salt Lake City for statehood, Stephen A. Douglas spoke of the two members of Buchanan's peace commission as "men of distinction and national reputation." [76] His remarks were accurate. Departing from its practice of appointing indifferently qualified and at times unworthy individuals to positions in Utah, the Government had at last chosen men of good qualifications for the delicate roles of peacemakers. Lazarus W. Powell, the commissioner who spoke most often during the conferences with the Saints, had served as governor of Kentucky and had been recently elected to the Senate from that state. Ben McCulloch, the more quiet of the two, had acquitted himself well in the Texas Revolution and the Mexican War.[77] Fortunately for the success of their mission, neither man was greatly motivated by a desire to win political advantage through a pro-Mormon or anti-Mormon stand.

Since the commission was sent to Utah under the supervision of the War Department, it became Floyd's duty to draft its orders. In his instructions of April 12 the Secretary ordered Powell and McCulloch to take with them the President's proclamation, issued a few days earlier, which censored the Mormons for their "spirit of insubordination" and urged them to accept the federal officers and the nation's laws in order to earn "a free pardon for the seditions and treasons heretofore by them committed." [78] With this document the commissioners were to hurry to Utah, for "it is hoped you will reach the forces commanded by General Johnston, before hostilities shall have been actually commenced." Although Floyd thus stressed the Government's desire to avoid war, he also reminded Powell and McCulloch that they were not to negotiate a settlement or a compromise with the Saints. "It is the great object of the President to bring these misguided people to their senses, to convert them into good citizens and to spare the effusion of human blood." This goal the commissioners were to reach not by the curtailment of federal authority over the Territory but by convincing the Mormons that no one would interfere with their religion. The Administration, Floyd warned, was not prepared to pay any price for peace: "It is the duty and determination of the federal government to see that the officials appointed and sent out by the President shall be received and installed, and due obedience be yielded to the laws and to their official acts." In conclusion the Secretary suggested that Powell and McCulloch might obtain help in their work from Kane, despite that gentleman's status as a private citizen.[79]

Conscious of the Administration's anxiety lest they fail to reach Utah in time to prevent a clash between the Mormons and Johnston's command, Powell and McCulloch hastened to Fort Leavenworth and on across the Plains, until on May 29 they reached the headquarters of the army on Black's Fork. The soldiers at first greeted them sullenly. To these embittered men the President's proclamation had appeared an astonishing capitulation, a disgraceful appeasement of traitors. They took the arrival of the commissioners as further evidence of the Administration's intention to arrange dishonorable terms with the Mormons. But their spirits soon rose, for reports from the conference tents indicated that Powell and McCulloch, far from being instructed to negotiate with the Church, would use firmness in all dealings with Brigham Young's followers. Noticing the Governor's distressed attitude, Gove and his friends correctly read this sign as evidence of Cumming's displeasure over the abandonment of his conciliatory policy.[80]

After they had listened to the comments and advice of Johnston and Cumming, the commissioners sent Floyd a letter expressing opinions strongly antithetical to those held by Cumming. "From information received from Mormons and others recently from the City of Salt Lake," they cautioned, "we fear that the leaders of the Mormon people have not given the Governor correct information as to the condition of affairs in the valley." Concerning the thorny matter of the Church's opposition to the entrance of the soldiers into the Basin, a point on which Cumming agreed with Young, Powell and McCulloch acidly wrote: "We would respectfully suggest that the presence of the army here, and the additional force that has been ordered here, will be the chief inducement that will cause this deluded people to submit quietly and peacefully to the civil authorities (in the event they should do so)." [81]

On June 2 the peace commissioners set out for Salt Lake City, followed a day later by the anxious Governor Alfred Cumming, his wife, and the faithful Jacob Forney. The treatment accorded these individuals upon their arrival in the city reveals the course which the Mormons had determined to follow. The President's proclamation having cleared them of treason, they now wanted to make the most favorable arrangement possible concerning the disposition of the army and the policy toward polygamy.

It became obvious that Young and his colleagues were expecting to obtain a satisfactory settlement by flattering Cumming's considerable pride and alienating his sympathies from those of Powell and McCulloch. Hence they greeted Cumming and his wife with great cordiality and gave them use of a house furnished with a piano, chairs, china, and other articles gathered from the deserted homes in the community. As a man of friendly disposition, Forney also received comfortable accommodations. On the other hand, the peace commissioners had to content themselves for two weeks with a wagon as a residence, until the Church provided them with one unfurnished room. When Eckels finally arrived in Salt Lake City, he slept on the ground.[82]

The mood of the Mormon dignitaries was mixed during their discussions with Powell and McCulloch. They were aware that further resistance to the army was impossible; and they were reluctant to leave their Valley, which, while it may not have "blossomed like a rose," as they liked to declare, did show the fruitful results of their labor during the past decade. These considerations, however, did not make them meek supplicants for the President's mercy. During these critical days Wilford Woodruff wrote in his "Journal" a passage reminiscent of the Saints' initial confidence in the first weeks of the war: "Now he [Buchanan] wants peace, because he is in the wrong, and has met with strong resistance from a high-minded people in these mountains, which he did not expect. We are willing to give him peace upon any terms that are honorable." [83] Although Young and his fellows did not openly show such haughty intransigence in their conferences with the Government's representatives, they refused to behave like spokesmen for a hopelessly beaten people.

The first meeting between the commissioners and the Mormon notables, with Cumming and Forney as interested spectators, was too largely attended to permit a settlement of delicate problems involving the freedom of a church and the honor of a nation. It could serve only as a forum for exploratory talks and introductory statements of opinion. Powell announced at once that he and McCulloch were not empowered to make a treaty with the Saints but could only remind them of their duties and inform them of the President's views. The Government's intentions, he declared, included the establishment of law and order in the Territory; the insistence upon obedience to the constitution, statutes, and officers; and the protection of the Mormons' constitutional rights. He warned that the army would enter the Valley whenever Buchanan ordered but advised that it would not injure the inhabitants. He concluded with an appeal to the people to accept the President's pardon. When their turn to speak came, the Mormons ignored the commissioner's plea to avoid discussion of the past in favor of preparation for the future; rather, they dwelt with bitterness upon their early misfortunes in the Territory, poured animadversions upon Buchanan, and even referred to the days of Missouri and Nauvoo. So far as the President's proclamation was concerned, they rejected its application to themselves, since they had committed no offense demanding a pardon.[84]

This somewhat stormy meeting inspired little hope for an immediate resolution of the Utah problem. During the evening, however, more progress was made in private conferences limited to the two commissioners on the one side and Young, Kimball, Wells, and Smith on the other. Relieved of the necessity of posturing before an audience, the men ultimately reached the question whether Johnston's army should march through or around Salt Lake City, having at last settled the more important issue, whether the Mormons would oppose the soldiers' entrance into the valley.[85]

After this night's work the meetings of the following day, if not a love feast, in reality marked the end of the war. Although they disguised their capitulation behind a flood of face-saving rhetoric, the Saints accepted the Administration's demands. George A. Smith, the Church's spokesman on this difficult occasion, delivered a skillful address which, while accusing Buchanan of including forty-two false charges in his proclamation and bewailing other injustices heaped upon his people, announced that he would accept the pardon in order to save the lives of innocent men. Although he affirmed the Mormons' ability to stop Johnston's army on the battlefield, he said that the Saints would permit the United States soldiers to enter the Valley as proof of their peaceful intentions and the falseness of the charges against them.[86]

Later in the day, in a rambling address to a delegation of Mormons from Provo, Brigham Young announced the termination of hostilities, using much the same justifications that had occurred to Smith. He insisted that the Mormons had always dutifully obeyed the Constitution; he challenged the accuracy of the charges contained in the President's proclamation; and he boasted of the Mormons' ability to defeat any force sent against them. Yet in between these sturdy assertions the Lion of the Lord also announced his acceptance of the pardon and even, surprisingly, suggested that Albert Sidney Johnston was probably a fine man.[87]

Having thus received the Mormons' complex act of submission, Powell informed a public assembly in the afternoon of June 12 that all difficulties between Utah and the United States had been happily settled. With McCulloch he returned to his cramped quarters, where the two men wrote hurriedly to Floyd that peace had been established in the Valley of Salt Lake. To Johnston they communicated the same news, but they appended requests that he protect the Mormons' property and try to soothe the Saints' apprehensions by a formal statement of intentions. Two days later Governor Cumming, whom the commissioners had ignored in their meetings with the Mormons and whose name did not appear in their dispatches to Floyd, made his own formal proclamation of the war's end. At the same time General Johnston expressed his gratification at the cessation of the hostilities in a message "To the people of Utah" from his camp on the Bear River. As might have been expected, in composing this message the self-righteous officer could not avoid reminding the Mormons of their previous misdeeds, but he nevertheless included the necessary guarantees of freedom from molestation at the hands of his soldiers. He also advised the Saints that "they will find the army (always faithful to the obligation of duty) as ready now to assist and protect as it was to oppose them while it was believed they were resisting the laws of their government." The assurance probably evoked little enthusiasm in the Valley of the Great Salt Lake.[88]

In this fashion the peace commissioners and the Church reached a tentative agreement which, if it did not remove the major causes of friction between Mormon and Gentile in Utah, at least provided for the peaceful entrance of the army into the Territory. But a misunderstanding immediately threatened even this modest accomplishment. When they left Camp Scott, Powell and McCulloch, as well as Cumming, had understood Johnston to promise to stay his advance until he had their assurance that such a move was desirable. For his part, the general did not consider this agreement binding. Believing that the supplies necessary for his march would not reach him until June 20, he had, he thought, merely set that day as the approximate time of his departure from winter quarters. When Hoffman and Marcy reached him earlier than he had expected, he at once made preparations to set out for the Valley. Young learned of the army's activities on June 11, the day of his first conversations with Powell and McCulloch, and he asked them whether the report was true. In accordance with their interpretation of Johnston's statement, they assured Young that the army would not move until it had heard from them. Thus when the report of the army's departure from Camp Scott was later confirmed—when, that is, it was noted that Johnston's proclamation of June 14 had been written at a camp on Bear River many miles west of Black's Fork—Young became greatly irritated and charged everyone, the army as well as the civil officers, with a breach of faith.[89]

The importance of this episode did not lie in its effect upon the commissioners' talks with the Mormon leaders, for the latter, whether outraged or not, had no alternative but to accept the President's terms as communicated to them by Powell and McCulloch. Young could not rise in his wrath and stalk from the conference room, for he would then be committed either to a disastrous resistance of Johnston's army or to a continuance of the exodus beyond Provo and into the remote regions to the south, an act of desperation only to be used in great extremity. The army's sudden move therefore did not fatally disrupt the talks. It did, however, have a significant effect upon the relations between Cumming and Johnston, already soured during the winter months. When Cumming learned of the army's departure from Camp Scott, he wrote the general two most caustic letters accusing him of bad faith and demanding an explanation for his behavior.[90] Upon these two men would rest much of the responsibility for maintaining peace in Utah during the months that lay ahead. That their feelings one toward the other now bordered upon hatred threatened to create situations as difficult as those existing before the spring of 1857.

In another way the army's sudden move toward Echo Canyon jeopardized the unsteady peace in Utah: it dramatically revealed

Johnston's basic disagreement with Cumming over the proper course of conduct to pursue toward the Mormons. The Governor wished to have done with the animosities, the grievances, the hysteria of the past decade. With Buchanan he must have realized that the Mormon problem could not be settled by a demand for penance and a pound of flesh from the Saints. Instead, having reminded the people of their previous misdeeds, he wanted to assure them that all was forgiven and to urge them firmly yet sympathetically to give no offense in the years to come. To Cumming such a strategy demanded tactful consideration for the Mormons' feelings, open admission of their innocent sufferings throughout their history, and acceptance of their more heated speeches as merely face-saving devices. Johnston was not so pacifically inclined. To his mind the Mormons had capped a decade of insubordination by resistance to the army of the United States. If after these antics the Government should show an undue concern for the Mormons' sensibilities, it would only encourage this strange people to further seditious acts. He agreed with Cumming and Buchanan that the Mormons should be reminded of their previous misdeeds, but he wished them to know that these sins, if forgiven, were not forgotten and that future error would receive instant punishment.[91]

After their understanding with the Church leaders on the most pressing issues, the commissioners faced the necessity of convincing the followers that they were no longer at war with the United States. The task was hard, for the Saints, whose resentment toward the country, army, and Government the Church had carefully fostered throughout the past year, could not easily shed this emotion. In somewhat cloudy fashion the editor of the *Deseret News* declared: "We tender our thanks to President Buchanan for pardoning acts committed in holding the wrist to a hand grasping a weapon to destroy our lives, and that too for no breach of law on our part, for we emphatically affirm that all allegations of our disobedience to the Constitution and laws of the United States are untrue." [92] In clearer and franker words Charles Walker observed: "Ex Gov. Powell he said all things were peaceably settled etc, and we might return to our homes and a lot more of such like gas, but he lied in his heart and he knew it." [93]

Despite this chilly reaction on the part of some Mormons, the commissioners made considerable headway in persuading the people at Provo, Lehi, and other towns that the war was over. McCulloch, who apparently felt that the Mormons could find true peace only in emigration to another land, usually remained silent in these public meetings, but Powell was more persuasive. In particular, his skillful and fluent speech in Provo won the favor of his audience. After announcing the end of all difficulties between Utah and the Government, urging the Saints to consider the army a defender and Johnston "a brave and honorable officer," and praising the people for their industrious nature, he ended with an adroit reference to one of the Church's most cherished memories: "If this day the nation should be so unfortunate as to become involved in war and the Government should call on the people to fly to arms to maintain our Republican unity and glory, I hope there would be more than one Mormon Battalion to rally to battle for our common country. (Cheers.)" [94]

Although they had reason to congratulate themselves on accomplishing the aims of their mission, the commissioners decided to delay their return to Washington until they and the Mormons had drafted a satisfactory report of their conversations and until the army had peacefully entered the Valley. The former task took a surprising amount of time, some three weeks, in fact; for the spokesmen of the Church, apparently hesitating to put on paper the concessions they had made orally, seemed eager to foster the impression that they had negotiated a truce instead of having accepted the Government's stipulations.

At last, on July 3, the commissioners and the Mormon leaders agreed upon a summary of the meetings held on June 11 and 12. It was a tactful compromise containing Powell's warning that the President demanded obedience from the Mormons to the laws and the Constitution, that he was prepared to elicit such obedience by force if necessary, and that he insisted upon his authority to send the army anywhere in the nation. Yielding to the Saints' desires, it also by implication censured Johnston for moving his force too early, recorded the commissioners' refusal to investigate the murders of Gunnison and Babbitt and the other crimes charged against the sect, and noted the Mormons' acceptance of the presidential pardon only for a very few specified acts occurring in the past campaign. Yet the final sentence emphasized the fact that the Mormons had, after all, accepted the principal demands of the

Government: "it was agreed that the officers, civil and military, of the United States should peaceably and without resistance enter the Territory of Utah, and discharge, unmolested, *all their official duties.*" The wily Brigham Young, however, prepared for a later repudiation of this document if developments should make the action necessary. In his notation at the end of the report he certified that it was accurate "as far as I can recollect at present." [95]

In spite of the confident expressions in their report to Floyd, Powell and McCulloch were by no means convinced that everything was harmonious in Utah. Their private communication of July 3 to the Secretary contained sharper criticism of the Mormons than they felt advisable to include in their official statement. During the exodus, the two men declared, the sect's leaders had compelled men to leave their homes under the threat of military eviction if they should refuse. Pressing a charge heard often in the past, the commissioners condemned the Church's religious and political tyranny over its members. They ended the letter with the suggestion that the army be retained in Utah to ensure the Mormons' obedience.[96]

A prerequisite to the establishment of any real peace in the Territory was the entrance of the army and its creation of a military camp without incident. On June 13 Johnston started his command on the road to the Mormons' capital. Across Muddy Creek and Bear River the men tramped, then down Echo Canyon, its ramparts now deserted, and at last, on June 26, into the Valley of the Great Salt Lake, their objective for almost a year. Before the column reached Salt Lake City, Johnston issued orders to his regimental and corps commanders requiring them to prevent anyone from leaving the ranks on the march; at the same time he instructed quartermasters and commissary officers to keep their herds from trespassing on private property. Having taken these precautions to avoid damaging the fragile peace, Johnston sent his forces through the city. From his hiding place Robert T. Burton saw the first men arrive at ten o'clock in the morning and watched until the rearguard had passed through the empty streets at five-thirty in the afternoon. The Church Historian noted that the army marched "in the strictest order and discipline" and that Philip St. George Cooke removed his cap as he rode through the city "as a token of his respect for the Mormon Battalion," which he had commanded more than a decade ago. There was one bright moment in this grim day. When Fitz-John Porter came to Brigham Young's houses, he rode up to the bandmaster and whispered a request to him, whereupon the band broke out with "One-Eyed Riley," an obscene ballad that was popular in that era.[97]

Although its reception was not so festive as Phelps might have wished, the army had at least performed one difficult task; it had entered the Salt Lake Valley without a collision with the Saints. But Johnston could not yet congratulate himself upon the successful accomplishment of his mission. In order to prevent his men from disturbing the semideserted city, he had ordered the column to cross the little Jordan River west of the settlement and had posted a guard on the bridge to prohibit any soldier's return. He was nevertheless aware that this place would serve only as a temporary camp, since the forage along the modest stream could not support the animals of his expedition for more than a few weeks. He also knew that the Mormons, assembled in a congested throng near Provo, might soon come back to their homes.

At the end of June, Johnston, Marcy, and other officers rode out from the army's bivouac eighteen miles west of Salt Lake City to study the surrounding countryside and discover a suitable area for a permanent military post. After inspecting the western edge of the Oquirrh range and then its eastern base, they finally concluded that Cedar Valley offered the best resources and the most strategic location of any site available. This spot, however, was only a few miles west of Lake Utah, on whose shore the Mormons were now camped in a congested swarm. Realizing that any movement into their area might alarm these people, Johnston decided to hold his men on the flats near the Jordan River until the Saints had gone back to their homes. For a week he waited, and then on July 7, his forage at last exhausted, he ordered his command to march south. In this way the army met the returning Mormons on the Provo Road.[98]

Although Brigham Young never disclosed his reasons for ordering his followers home, his motivation is clearly discernible. Initially he had commanded the Saints to leave their northern settlements lest the army attack them in angry remembrance of past frustrations. Once he learned from the army's behavior that Johnston's soldiers were under rigid discipline, the major cause of the

Move South vanished. He was also aware that his people, plagued by bad water, flies, dirt, and lack of food, would not remain forever in their makeshift huts; one trusted Mormon, in fact, had informed Young on July 1 of his plan to return to Ogden as soon as possible. It must therefore have seemed wise to Young to announce the official end of the exodus before his people began to abandon it of their own accord.[99]

Mormon historians would add to the factors behind the termination of the exodus the accomplishment of one of the operation's primary goals, namely the winning of sympathy for the Church among many Gentiles.[100] The truth, however, is that although some editors did praise the Mormons' heroism in this arduous undertaking, others held to their condemnation of the Saints' fanaticism, religious beliefs, and social practices, even though they admitted elements of devotion and sincerity.[101] One must also observe that despite whatever favor the Move South may have evoked, anti-Mormonism remained a feature of Gentiles' thinking for many decades after 1860.

However the exodus may be regarded, the Church now sent its people back to their houses and their crops. Thus the Saints, plodding on foot or bouncing in their wagons through the swirling dust of the road to Salt Lake City, finally encountered Johnston's army, that instrument of Satan's scheme to destroy the faithful in these latter days. Unsure of the proper route to Cedar Valley, the army had marched back and forth between the Wasatch and Oquirrh ranges, until it became entangled with the almost endless line of returning Mormons. No explosion followed, however. The soldiers looked with scorn upon the ragged poverty of the people, and the latter made little effort to conceal their resentment at this new "persecution," but neither made a threatening gesture. On one occasion, when an enlisted man laughed at a Mormon's discomfiture caused by the overturning of a wagon, his superior officer ordered him to help right the vehicle. The incident showed that Cumming's fears of a clash between soldier and civilian at their first meeting was baseless. But it was not a reliable omen of continued peace in Utah, now that the active phase of the Mormon War was over.[102]

9. But No Peace

WITH PARTIAL ACCURACY and obvious asperity the
editor of the New York *Times* on June 17, 1858, offered his conclusions on the Mormon War:

> the whole story of the war is crowded by as much ignorance,
> stupidity and dishonesty, as any Government ever managed
> to get into the annals of a single year. An army was sent to
> chastise rebels, before it was clearly ascertained whether or
> not there were any rebels to chastise. It was sent forward in
> the Fall, just when it ought to have reached its destination.
> . . . After it had undergone six months of suffering, and
> was fully prepared to force the strongest natural position in
> the world, Commissioners were sent in search of the rebel foe,
> and it was then discovered there was no foe at all. Governor
> Cumming ought to have gone to Salt Lake City in Autumn.
> He goes there in the Spring, and is received with all the
> honors. . . . The commander of the forces writes . . . that
> Cumming is deceived, and that the Mormons are still hostile.
> The public is in suspense, and knows not which of two such
> authorities to believe, when the news comes that there were
> no more Mormons left, either to fight us, or to obey us, as they
> are abandoning our territory *en masse*, rather than submit to
> our rule. "We have made a desert, and we call it peace." [1]

Although this summary of the episode had the support of many
facts, the conclusion that the problem of Mormon-Gentile relations in Utah had been settled by the exodus was wholly inaccurate. Instead of fleeing to a New Zion in the southwestern
United States, Mexico, or some other remote haven, the Saints
returned to their homes in the Salt Lake Basin. Furthermore, they
came back in no mood to seek peace in their Territory through

compromise, understanding, and charity. The most vital question —whether in Utah the ultimate authority was the federal government or the Mormon Church—also remained unanswered. True, the presence in the governor's office of a Gentile sympathetic to the Saints promised to reduce tension. But Buchanan had appointed to most of the other important civil posts men who were as ready as W. W. Drummond had been to use their power against the people. Thus the situation in Utah bore many resemblances to the one prevailing before the war, except for the addition of a new and complicating factor: a large military garrison.

Upon their arrival in Cedar Valley on July 8 the officers and men of the expedition established a military post which they appropriately called Camp Floyd, in honor of the War Department's foremost Mormon-hater. The little valley was strategically located, for it was of approximately equal distance from the Territory's largest towns, Salt Lake City and Provo. It had the further advantage, in this semidesert climate, of a modest creek. Its cramped dimensions created a real problem, however. Only five miles in length, it did not provide the space needed to accommodate an army which, with the arrival of reinforcements, had grown to formidable proportions. When the troops entered the Basin on June 26, they numbered more than 2,400 officers and men. The departure of Colonel Loring's detachment, Bee's volunteers, and other units, and the arrival of several fresh regiments changed this figure during the next months, but throughout 1858 and 1859 there were at least 2,400 soldiers in the Territory; often the number rose above 3,000.[2] Although some of this force was detailed to garrison Fort Bridger and establish temporary posts in southern valleys, most of the men remained in Camp Floyd, where they cursed the dust, the boredom, and the Mormons.

During the first weeks at this camp the soldiers found much to keep them busy, for they had the tasks of raising adobe houses, constructing an aquaduct and a reservoir to exploit the meager water resources of the Valley, and erecting workshops, storehouses, stables, and other necessary buildings. Yet the monotonous routine of the cantonment, seven hours away from the nearest towns, soon began to erode the morale of the troops. The camp itself offered few opportunities for relaxation: no more, in fact, than a "Military Dramatic Association" (with female leads imported from

Salt Lake City) and a school for enlisted men. In a desperate search for diversion a few officers evolved a speculative scheme to found Brown City, named after the Postmaster General and designed as the Gentile capital of the Territory. When they had the opportunity, the enlisted men crept out of Camp Floyd by night to nearby "Frogtown," where a few shanty saloons dispensed an alcoholic drink that tasted vile but at least did not blind.[3]

None of these official or extracurricular diversions dulled the misery for long. Because of his meteorological interests Capt. John Phelps enjoyed observing the desert whirlwinds, but others in the camp only noticed that the ground turned to powder under their feet until it rose into the hot air and choked them. Horace Greeley, visiting Utah on his grand tour of the West, saw the clouds of dust from Floyd while he was still eight miles away. Smarting under these conditions, one visitor called the post "a hot purgatorial spot where winter was long and rigorous, summer hot and uncomfortable, a place where alkaline water curdled soap, and dust storms proved almost unendurable." According to Captain Tracy, "life in this camp gives one the feeling of convicts in prison for life clamoring to be let out and hung by way of relief." [4] Such unhappiness ultimately bred problems of discipline. The courts-martial for a period of four months handled a number of matters, including eight cases of drunkenness, eight desertions, five men absent without leave, and four cases of disrespect, including the attempt by a private to shoot his sergeant. Even Tracy was convicted of insubordinate behavior toward Colonel Alexander, and Sibley was court-martialed as the result of a heated argument with Cooke.[5]

Morbid discontent inevitably found expression in rumors that members of the Administration had forgotten the expedition or, more probably, were using it for their own financial gain.[6] But for the most part both officers and enlisted men turned their wrath upon the Mormons, enemies during the campaign and enemies still. Denied a chance to fight, cooped up in a camp ill-designed for the comfort of its inhabitants, they waited for the day when they would have a chance to meet the Saints in open battle.[7] General Johnston had as little confidence in the permanence of peace. He had selected Cedar Valley, he informed Scott, because it was "a commanding position, and the force, if called for, can

5. A typical Mormon community of the period: Ephraim, Utah

be promptly applied either in the direction of Salt Lake City or Provo." [8]

In Utah Johnston continued the practice, so noticeable in Camp Scott, of restricting his communication with Cumming to short and at times caustic notes. The correspondence between the general and the Governor seemed more a contest to score points than an effort to promote understanding between the most powerful secular officials in the Territory. There was even less communication between Johnston and the Hierarchy of the Church. Although Alexander, Cooke, Marcy, and a number of subordinate officers paid social calls on Brigham Young, who received them hospitably,[9] there is no evidence that Johnston ever ventured near the Lion House in Salt Lake City during his stay in the Territory. With an extraordinary lack of consideration, furthermore, he never advised the Saints, either informally or officially, of the army's movements in order to calm their fears of an attack upon them from Camp Floyd.[10]

Since the army and its officers were antagonistic to their interests, even to their existence, the Mormons turned to Alfred Cumming as their advocate and defender. To win his friendship, Young flattered his pride, provided for his physical comfort, and on a few occasions included him in the Church's restricted picnics. It would be erroneous, however, to conclude that these actions sprang solely from a design to woo a man in a position of authority: the Mormons had in fact come to accept him as a fair-minded gentleman who would protect rather than injure them.[11] This appraisal of Cumming was correct. Believing that permanent peace must rest upon acceptance of the Church as the dominant element in Utah, the Governor urged the Administration to follow a policy designed to placate its leaders.[12] In contrast to Johnston, he sought conferences with Young, Mayor A. O. Smoot of Salt Lake City, and other Mormon dignitaries, apparently hoping to foster concord between church and state through direct conversation.[13]

Embittered anti-Mormons condemned the Governor for having become an open apologist for the Church, a man blindly, even brazenly, sheltering a disloyal people.[14] This angry criticism was unjust. With his wife he found the Saints "generally ignorant, fanatical, superstitious, and possessing a profound disdain for the religious belief of the rest of the world." His first annual message,

furthermore, read like a stern parental lecture. In it he reminded
the Mormons that he had demanded of them an "unconditional
submission to the laws," and he concluded with the advice: "It
therefore behooves you to avoid even the resemblance of disloyalty, for in your present condition it is not sufficient that you
manifest a proper sense of that duty which you owe to the government but public opinion must be satisfied of your loyalty." [15]

Alfred Cumming, then, was not a tool of Brigham Young, as the
enemies of the Church insisted. Yet he did see the only road to
stable relations between Utah and the country. Unlike the Mormon-baiters, he accepted the fact of the Church's predominance
in the Valley, and he rejected all tactics aimed at destroying its
status. With this position as a starting point he did not listen to
those who would wring from the Saints a trembling acceptance of
every statute and official. Perhaps he knew what Garland Hurt had
once remarked and then had forgotten, that a sect may thrive upon
persecution. At any rate he used his office to give the Mormons
fair play, possibly going beyond moderation to leniency in order
to assuage the bitterness rankling in their minds.

Early in November 1858 a stranger stopped at Ephraim Hanks'
house near Salt Lake City to ask accommodations for the night.
The newcomer, Hanks observed, looked like an ox driver; he was
coarsely dressed and possessed of only one eye. The next morning
he set out on foot but later obtained a perch on a wagon-load of
wood. In this fashion John Cradlebaugh, associate justice of the
territorial supreme court, arrived in Utah. The Mormons were at
first pleased with the man, for his initial behavior marked him as
one not overly impressed with his own importance. He further
endeared himself to the Church representatives who first met him
by commenting critically on Eckels' prejudices. Yet in the years
immediately following the war no Gentile caused Brigham Young
more trouble than did this tall, lean, middle-aged lawyer from
Ohio; and the work of his court in Provo threatened to reopen
conflict between Mormons and Gentiles. As Hanks noted, Cradlebaugh "has but one eye and that is a very good one"; through it
he studied conditions in Utah and found them most unsatisfactory.[16]

The Saints already had ample reason to know that they could
expect little sympathy from another federal judge: Delana R.

Eckels had displayed at Camp Scott a fixed hostility toward the
Church, and once safely in the Valley he became a champion of
the anti-Mormon faction there. He was, moreover, a dangerous
enemy, for he enjoyed an acquaintance with Lewis Cass. Until his
departure on a leave of absence in 1858, he unceasingly informed
the Government, by means of letters and affidavits, of the deplorable situation in the Territory: of the Mormons' implication
in the Mountain Meadows Massacre, the Danite threats to life and
property, the priesthood's disloyalty to the United States. One of
these memorials summarized the judge's most cherished convictions, that "the Mormon people resident here are in Secret, if not
open rebellion . . . and that they are firm in their determination
to resist *even to a bloody issue,* the due execution of laws." [17] In
recognition of Eckels as a formidable adversary the Church hurled
many of its strongest anathemas at him and accorded him a
prominent place in its demonology, approaching that of Brocchus
and Drummond, Johnston and Cradlebaugh. He was described as
a corrupt judge, an undemocratic federal official, a panderer, "the
meanest man the administration could find." [18]

The third member of the territorial supreme court, Charles E.
Sinclair, did not plague the Mormons in a manner comparable to
the cyclopean Cradlebaugh and the malevolent Eckels. A "particular friend" of John B. Floyd, Sinclair was a *rara avis* in Utah
—a political appointee who had some qualification for his post
and whose judgment was not completely clouded by unreasoning
bias. In his handling of the suit for the disbarment of Ferguson,
who had intimidated Stiles, and in other cases before him, he
showed that he did not share Cumming's solicitude for the Mormons' feelings; and for their part, the Saints caused minor irritations to disturb the operation of his court. They also resorted to
their usual tactic when confronted with an intractable person:
that is, repetitious charges that he was "much addicted to drink-
ing" and on occasion became "beastly drunk," in fact helpless in
the gutters of Salt Lake City. But on other occasions the Church
expressed its appreciation that Sinclair had not brought the full
weight of his office to bear against it.[19]

Among the lesser officeholders only two men supported Cumming's efforts to implement the Administration's policy. The appointment of the district attorney, Alexander Wilson, was in large

part the work of that effective eastern lobbyist for the Church
Thomas L. Kane.[20] After a year's service Wilson resigned in protest
at the judges' prejudice against the Church, but the Administration sent him back to Utah, this time as an associate justice.[21]
Jacob Forney had followed Cumming's example when early in
1858 the Governor shed his anti-Mormonism. Once this exercise
had been accomplished, the superintendent of Indian affairs frequently warned his acquaintance, Jeremiah Black, that Hurt, Burr,
Eckels, and a host of other officials and civilians were using every
device, including the circulation of false reports, to provoke strife
between Utah and the nation. Forney's opposition to the bitter
enemies of the Mormons did not transform him into an agent of
the Church militant; at times he was outspokenly critical of Young
and other members of the Hierarchy, and he even showed an
inclination to arraign them for being accessories to the Mountain
Meadows Massacre. In general, however, he joined Cumming and
Wilson in advocating a policy of "conciliatory adjustment," as he
called it.[22]

In one of his letters to Black, Forney spoke of an "Ultra party,"
composed of men who wanted no quick settlement of the Utah
question.[23] This group, according to the superintendent's account,
had as its leaders Cradlebaugh and Eckels, with the young in-
ebriate Charles Sinclair playing a lesser role. Behind these men,
but active in the campaign, were Peter K. Dotson, H. F. Morrell,
and Garland Hurt. Dotson, the United States marshal, later expressed his feelings in a letter of resignation to Buchanan: "the
policy of your Administration has been fatal to federal supremacy
in Utah, and can only tend to build up, consolidate, and perpetu-
ate the political and ecclesiastical power of Brigham Young and
his successors." [24] Because of his position, Postmaster Morrell could
do much to embarrass the sect, by interfering with the mails passing through his office.[25] The other territorial official who held
membership in this popular front against the Mormons was
Garland Hurt, an even greater adversary of Young than before as
a result of the experiences leading to his flight from Utah.

This Ultra party had one advantage not possessed by earlier
opponents of the Saints in past contests—a newspaper founded
for the specific purpose of belaboring the Church. The publication
appeared for the first time in November 1858, under the editorship

of Kirk Anderson, recently connected with the *Missouri Republican*. But the paper was not the work of one man. It received financial backing for many months from John Hartnett, the territorial secretary whom some mistakenly considered a supporter of Cumming's policies. In order to bring out the first number Anderson had to borrow type and "hands" from the *Deseret News,* whose editor presumably regretted his generous assistance when he read the first issue. In this fashion the *Valley Tan* appeared, a four-page paper given the name applied to all commodities, but more especially to whisky, made of domestic materials in the Salt Lake Basin. Its existence was as precarious as its inception was unpromising; under five different editors it struggled with lack of money and newsprint during the first year and finally expired in early 1860.[26]

While it lasted, the paper became most offensive to the Mormons, who ignored it in their public utterances but privately castigated it as a "scurrilous sheet." Under various owners it accused the Church leaders of disloyalty to the country, condemned the practice of polygamy, printed complete transcripts of Cradlebaugh's investigations, charged the Danites with murder, and generally tried to make a case for the establishment of martial law in the Territory. Kirk Anderson expressed the hope of the *Valley Tan* when he predicted a "day of judgment" when "Congress will deal out stern justice and cut out the 'loathsome ulcer.' " [27] Many Gentiles agreed with this view. It was clear that the peace arranged by Powell and McCulloch, with the help of the fussy governor, was in reality an armed truce, for it left two hostile factions wrestling with each other for control of the Territory.

For all their fear of persecution by the army and the civilian officers, the Saints enjoyed a period of tranquillity in the early months following the end of the war. Although their political affairs now fell under the authority of a Gentile, they faced no serious controversies with Governor Cumming. The conduct of Utah's Indian affairs, once a constant source of irritation, now went more serenely under Jacob Forney. Surprisingly enough, even the Mormons' relations with the soldiers during this period were unmarked by serious incidents.[28] Much of this unexpected and short-lived peace arose from Johnston's sincere efforts to pre-

vent his troops from damaging the property and the rights of
Utah's citizens. Before he would approve the discharge of any
soldier in his command, he insisted that the man show evidence
of assured employment in Utah or else of definite plans to leave
the Territory, lest he become an idler in Salt Lake City. At other
times he issued orders designed to prevent friction between his
men and the Mormons.[29]

During this curious truce the relations between soldiers and
Saints occasionally became cordial; several enlisted men even spent
a week in the Mormons' homes, where they were most hospitably
entertained. But it was impossible for the situation to continue;
the hatreds of the past were too deep. The military discipline of
the camp, tight as it was, could not prevent some soldiers from
reaching Salt Lake City, where they at times disturbed the peace.
Members of Johnston's command, in turn, found excuse for their
actions in the behavior of the Saints, which was unlike the conduct expected of repentant rebels.[30]

The uneasy truce between Mormon and Gentile was finally
broken at the end of 1858. It was not the army that brought about
a renewal of strife, for the rigid fairness of General Johnston kept
it under control; rather it was the federal judges, filled as they
were with dislike for the Church. Beginning with the first session
of Charles Sinclair's court a number of factors combined to make
both the magistrates and the Mormon leaders antagonistic to each
other. Like other judges before and after him, Sinclair was exas-
perated to find that his juries, drawn as they were from the pre-
dominantly Mormon population of the community, would not return judgments against Church members; nor would witnesses
testify against their brothers in faith. His work, moreover, was
obstructed by the fact that until January 1859 the Utah legislature
made no provision for paying expenses of his court when it investigated breaches of territorial laws. On the other hand, the
Saints took umbrage at the Judge's efforts to pack his juries with
ill-favored transients and to hale Brigham Young into court on
several absurd charges.[31]

Some of the cases which were tried before Sinclair were of
minor importance. A man named F. E. McNeil, whose subsequent murder effectively silenced his complaint against the
Church, sued Young, Wells, and other prominent persons for false

imprisonment and requested $25,000 as balm for his outraged feelings. Without the approval of the proper officials in Washington, Surveyor Burr sued Young for trespass, charging that on Young's orders men had rifled his office and stolen many valuable instruments. Thomas S. Williams, the lawyer who had lost his library in the privy fire, asked for $5,000 damages. On the suggestion of John Cradlebaugh and the prompting of an anonymous letter printed in the *Valley Tan*, Sinclair also charged his grand jury with the investigation of a more sensational case, the killing of a mute by a policeman. In clumsy fashion Kirk Anderson tried to charge this death to the Danites and the "blood atonement" doctrine supposedly held by the Church. Although the Mormons never explained why "Dummy" was buried without public notice of his death having been given, the grand jury accepted the policeman's plea of self-defense.[32]

In this early term of Sinclair's court two efforts were made to dredge up past disputes, perhaps in a sincere desire to punish criminal behavior or perhaps, as the Mormons believed, to precipitate another conflict. In November 1858 Burr instituted proceedings to disbar James Ferguson on the grounds that he had slandered Judge George P. Stiles and had ultimately driven him from his bench. For a reason never made clear Sinclair desired the testimony of Young in this hearing. The Saints feared another Carthage; so when Young entered the courtroom he walked in with Kimball, Wells, Pratt, Smith, Taylor, Woodruff, and Richards clustered around him, their pistols and knives ready for service. Lest this assemblage of venerable churchmen fail to provide sufficient protection, the Church had distributed three hundred well-armed brethren about the room. There was no assault upon the person of the Lion of the Lord, however, and in due time the jury found Ferguson not guilty of the charges.[33]

The other equally futile attempt to arraign the Mormons for serious misconduct concerned the question whether the Saints had committed treason by their acts in the recent campaign. In his charge to the grand jury Sinclair advised an investigation of the matter, adding that he would not take notice of the President's pardon. Alexander Wilson refused, however, to introduce any bills of indictment.[34]

Before he finally returned to the States in the summer of 1859,

Sinclair struck one last blow at the Church, this time on the issue of the probate courts' jurisdiction. Throughout the decade Gentile magistrates had become increasingly irritated at the authority these courts had arrogated to themselves. Although the Mormons argued that the frequent absences of the federal judges had made such a course mandatory if Utah was to have any judicial system, their opponents believed the development to have been merely another device of the Church to gain domination over all the internal affairs of the Territory. In June 1859 the old problem arose again, when the probate court of the County of Salt Lake, presided over by Elias Smith, editor of the *Deseret News,* instructed its grand jury to investigate "all breaches of the penal laws of the Territory" committed within the county. The jurors soon indicted one Deloss Gibson for murder, and the accused was ultimately convicted of the crime. This action, an apparent encroachment on the powers of the federal courts, brought from Sinclair a sharp decision reversing the conviction upon the ground that no probate court had jurisdiction in criminal cases.[35] Once again Sinclair, as other less bibulous judges in the past, was beaten in the struggle. Almost a year later Governor Cumming informed Cass that the probate court in Salt Lake City had tried a number of felons and had sentenced many of them.[36]

While Sinclair was seeking without success to bring home some indictment against the Mormons' leaders and to reduce their pretensions in the judicial branch of the territorial government, John Cradlebaugh was using the powers of his court against the Church with so much enthusiasm that for a time he rivaled Drummond as the sect's Latter-day devil. The nature of his investigations angered the Saints greatly, for he set out to learn the facts of certain murders recently committed within his district, particularly the Parrish-Potter affair. But the Church was more distressed when Cradlebaugh called a large detachment of troops from Camp Floyd to Provo, for this act produced the situation Young had sought to avoid—the throwing of armed and hostile soldiers into close association with his people.

On March 6, 1859, Cradlebaugh informed Johnston that within two days he would open his district court in Provo. Since there was, he added, no prison in the town adequate to contain the individuals held for trial, he asked the general to furnish him with a

military detachment to guard these men. The request gave Johnston one more occasion to express his distaste for the Church's
"despotic ecclesiastical law" in Utah and to denounce the existence
in the Territory of "an undertow that sweeps away every principle
of liberty and the basis of our code of morals." Yet when he sent
Capt. Henry Heth and a detachment of infantry from the Tenth
Regiment to Provo, he ordered Heth to refuse any call for his
services other than for the specific task of securing the prisoners.[37]

With this assistance at hand Cradlebaugh set his judicial course
by instructing his grand jury to investigate a number of atrocities.
The Parrish-Potter murders had been called to his attention when
General Johnston sent him a letter from Mrs. Parrish requesting
punishment of the culprits. Cradlebaugh therefore placed this
affair high on his list of unpunished crimes, which also included
the Mountain Meadows Massacre and several less-familiar assassi-
nations of Gentiles alleged to have taken place recently in the Territory. Concerning the presence of the troops from Camp Floyd,
Cradlebaugh advised the citizens of the town to have no fear for
their safety, since the soldiers had as their only duties the guarding
of prisoners and the maintenance of peace.[38]

For want of a courthouse Judge Cradlebaugh opened his district
court in Provo Seminary. Directly adjacent to this building was a
corral, and in this space Henry Heth's command camped. Within
a short time after the arrival of the troops the townsfolk had
reached a state of excitement bordering upon hysteria. To the
Saints, who could remember the mobbings in Missouri and the
last days of Nauvoo, these soldiers were a flock of stormy petrels
heralding a full onslaught by the army. Moreover, they were convinced that Cradlebaugh would use this force to round up and
execute Mayor B. K. Bullock and other dignitaries without regard
to evidence of their implication in any crime. Accordingly they
sent memorials to Cradlebaugh to complain bitterly of the "military despotism" as well as to remonstrate against certain unpleasant incidents caused by the presence of troops. One passage in
Bullock's protest was noteworthy for its revelation of the tendency
to bravado so characteristic of Brigham Young and his followers
during this period. Although the Mayor denounced Heth's men
for having trampled the rights of helpless people, he also declared
that he had been compelled "to prevent indignant citizens from

doing violence to the soldiers." Like Young, when he based his decision not to oppose the expedition upon the high-minded desire to spare the lives of innocent people, Bullock maintained that in reality his people could destroy Heth's command at any time.[39]

In this battle of words Cradlebaugh and the army had some ammunition of their own. Johnston had received a petition from a group of citizens in Springville asking protection from the Church's "despotic ecclesiastical law." [40] A number of men had sent another memorial to Cradlebaugh praising the conduct of the soldiers in Provo and requesting that they not be recalled, since "we have been frequently menaced here, as elsewhere, by citizens of this district, with threats and acts of intimidation." [41] From Captain Heth came an explanation of his movements. He had intended, he wrote, to camp outside Provo, but when he discovered that the city limits extended several miles in every direction from the center of town, he had felt compelled to place his men near the seminary in order to be of service to the court.[42]

The situation worsened on March 18, when Marshal Dotson arrested several men, including Mayor Bullock, for implication in the Parrish-Potter murders, and Cradlebaugh issued warrants for the arrest of others. Provo immediately became a powder keg. Excited Mormons poured into the city to protect their leaders from round-up, imprisonment, and execution, and the city marshal warned Heth that he was adding 200 new policemen to his force. With inflamed public opinion centered upon Heth as the unwanted jailor, Colonel Smith, now commandant of Camp Floyd, and General Johnston decided to send additional forces to discourage any Mormons disposed to fight. Accordingly Brevet Major Gabriel R. Paul of the Seventh Regiment set off for Provo with eight companies of infantry and one company each of cavalry and artillery, under orders to camp outside the town and attack no body of civilians "except in sheer self-defense." [43]

It did not soothe the Mormons' anxiety to learn that Paul's command intended merely to prevent turbulent persons from inciting more responsible citizens against elements of the United States army; the fact remained that more than 800 soldiers were now camped in and around their city. Their determination to force the withdrawal of the troops gained strength from the arrival of the governor, who had come in answer to their appeals, irked that Johnston, as usual, had not informed him of this movement of troops. After a thorough examination of the tense situation in Provo, Cumming requested Johnston to remove both Heth and Paul from Provo.[44] Already strained for a long period of time, in this latest crisis the relations between the General and the Governor now broke down completely. In refusing Cumming's request for the removal of the soldiers, Johnston bluntly told Cumming: "I am under no obligation whatever to conform to your suggestions with regard to the military disposition of the troops in this department, except only when it may be expedient to employ them in their civil capacity as a posse." [45] A critical moment had been reached in the relations between Gentiles and Mormons in Utah.

In Salt Lake City a rumor spread to the effect that with the dispatch of troops to Provo, Johnston had also sent the Fifth Infantry toward the Saints' capital, for reasons unknown but in these emotional days easily imagined. No such action had in fact been ordered, but in the absence of any communication, official or unofficial, between the Church and the army officers, unfounded reports gained easy credence. Accordingly Lt. Gen. Daniel Wells, commandant of the Mormon militia, ordered his subordinates to alert their units and prepare "immediately but quietly" to repulse an assault. In the several wards of the city men were notified by night-time messengers "to have their arms and ammunition in readiness." [46] When word reached them at this moment that an army sergeant, Ralph Pike, had struck down and almost killed a young Mormon named Spencer, the people became even more certain of the army's malevolent intentions (see page 224).

Only in the heated days of 1857 had the possibility of an engagement between the Saints and the army been greater. In Salt Lake City the Mormons were melodramatically arming to the teeth for a desperate defense of their homes and their leaders. To the south Major Paul was camped near Provo with a large number of troops, as if poised for a dash into the town. Heth's detachment, whose bivouac near the makeshift courthouse had brought on the crisis, had become the object of the Mormons' bitterest condemnation. When some of his sentries were stoned on March 26, Heth, his nerves taut because of his unpromising military position, bluntly advised Mayor Bullock: "Should this be repeated, I will regret the consequences that may ensue." [47] In the courtroom Cradlebaugh,

having angrily dismissed his grand jury as incompetent, still conducted his unpopular investigation of the Parrish-Potter incident,
now aided by Judge Charles Sinclair.

The pacifically disposed Governor Cumming was tossed about
in this maelstrom. Although his failure to secure the removal of
the troops from Provo had proved his utter lack of control over
the movements of Johnston's soldiers, the Mormons still expected
some action from him to save them from persecution. Memorials
bearing hundreds of names demanded that he order the troops
away from Provo, and at midnight one evening Young decided to
visit Cumming in order to "tell him that if he was not prepared
to vindicate the duties of his office . . . the people were prepared
for the emergency and would not tamely submit to a repetition
of the Carthage Massacre." [48] For the harassed Governor there was
little to be done. He could complain to Lewis Cass about Johnston's behavior and request some authority over the arrangement
of the troops. Otherwise he could only issue a proclamation which
was in reality a public announcement of his frustration and an
admission of his helplessness in this crisis.[49] George Smith even
believed that Cumming might suffer the indignity of arrest by his
opponents, but he asserted that "the Governor has a few thousand
friends in this community, who would dislike to see the venerable
old hero in irons." [50]

Cumming's proclamation and his popularity in the community
did not deter Cradlebaugh from his self-appointed task of expos-
ing Mormon iniquity. Although he no longer had a jury to assist
him, he issued many bench warrants for the arrest of men whom
he believed to have been implicated in various crimes, and he
sent Marshal Dotson with a detachment of Dragoons to serve these
writs. Dotson diligently scoured Provo and nearby Springville for
the individuals named by Cradlebaugh, only to discover that
Bishop Aaron Johnson and every other Mormon man had fled to
the mountains.[51] To the Saints these were dark days indeed, with a
judge acting as "accusor, prosecutor, witness, and juror at the
same time" and detachments of soldiers haring about the countryside in search of their leaders. Once more, as in the grim weeks of
the past winter, Brigham Young began to talk of flight.[52]

For all the ominous rumblings, the emergency soon passed. At
the moment when Young was speaking of another exodus word

reached him that Cradlebaugh had adjourned his court, the Mormons' refusal to testify and their flight having thwarted his efforts. The closing of the court on April 2 left Captain Heth and his men in the unfavorable position of holding five prisoners in the middle of an excited populace who might try to free them by force. He therefore requested help from Paul. The latter quickly marched his command into Provo, joined his unit with Heth's, and the troops proceeded without opposition to Camp Floyd, where they were greeted as conquering heroes.[53] The Provo crisis was over.

Although discouraged by his failure to indict any prominent Mormon, Cradlebaugh pressed on with his examination of criminal activity. If he could not convict the assassins involved in the Parrish-Potter affair, he might have better luck with an investigation of a case not so easily concealed—the Mountain Meadows Massacre. This awful deed he considered "so much of a Church matter . . . that much property was taken to the Tithing Office and there sold out." On this visit to southern Utah, notwithstanding the services of 200 soldiers, Cradlebaugh failed to ferret out the criminals. He issued thirty-nine warrants for the arrest of men supposedly involved in the atrocity, and ten more for another murder, but the saddlesore Dotson once again failed to serve any of them. Utah's mountains were filled with Mormon bishops and other members of the Church, temporary fugitives from the judge and his posses, and the jails remained empty.[54] At last Cradlebaugh abandoned his efforts to bring the Saints to justice and moved to Carson Valley in the western part of Utah. When this region became part of Nevada Territory, he served as its first delegate to Congress and in this capacity had the opportunity to denounce the Church of Jesus Christ of Latter-day Saints on the floor of the House of Representatives.[55]

One question raised by Cradlebaugh's activities remained unanswered when the judge adjourned his court in early April and set out for Mountain Meadows. For the sake of peace in Utah the Government had to decide which territorial official could make a requisition upon the army for a *posse comitatus*. At Provo, Cradlebaugh had made such an application and Johnston had honored it, yet Cumming insisted that of the civil officers only he was vested with this power. More basic was another question: did the Administration wish to continue the policy of moderation displayed by its appointment of a peace commission and by the President's pardon, or did it wish now to deal more sternly with the Church? Cumming, who had faithfully carried out Buchanan's pacific intentions so far as he understood them, was confronted by the hostile actions of Johnston, Cradlebaugh, and Sinclair, who represented the unremitting animosity of John B. Floyd. The President must decide which of these two antithetical policies should have his blessing.

The members of Buchanan's Administration had not spoken with a single voice in discussing affairs in Utah after mid-1958. When informing Congress in June that there was no longer need for the two regiments of volunteers recently authorized, the President said optimistically: "there is reason to believe that our difficulty with the Territory of Utah has terminated, and the reign of the Constitution and the law has been restored." His second message of December 6, 1858, also expressed his belief that all was well in Mormondom.[56] In like vein Secretary of State Cass informed Cumming that his actions in Utah had Buchanan's approval.[57] Secretary of War Floyd was violently opposed to this lenience. He was far less sanguine of the Saints' peaceful disposition than were Cumming, Buchanan, and the rest, as his annual report of 1858 so clearly revealed. His proposal for the creation of peace was a military one: the maintenance of a large body of troops in Utah.[58]

Confronted with these decisions, President Buchanan met with Cass, Black, and Floyd to study all information available on the Utah question. The result was a series of instructions to the territorial and military officials which supported the governor unconditionally. On May 6, 1859, Floyd wrote Johnston of the change in the latter's instructions: "Peace now being restored to the Territory, the judicial administration of the laws will require no help from the army under your command . . . You will therefore only order the troops under your command to assist as a *posse comitatus* in the execution of the laws, upon the written application of the governor of the Territory, and not otherwise." [59] Cradlebaugh and Sinclair received the frankest repudiation of their actions. Attorney General Black informed them that only the district attorney could act as public prosecutor and only the marshal was entrusted with the duty of keeping prisoners. With some sarcasm he told the two men: "It did not seem either right or necessary to *instruct* you that these were to be the limits of your interference with the public affairs of the Territory." The justices were also reminded that "many willing candidates" sought the positions which they now filled. Arriving at last at the principal point under consideration, Black ruled that the governor was the only officer possessing the authority to requisition troops, a decision which did not agree with the original instructions given to Harney.[60]

It should be noted that neither the President nor his Cabinet was prepared to buy peace in Utah through abject appeasement of the Mormons. Black instructed Alexander Wilson to show the people that "nothing short of obedience to the laws will be tolerated" and he urged him to conduct a vigorous investigation of the Mountain Meadows Massacre, a "most atrocious" crime, in order to uncover the perpetrators, whether Indians or white men.[61] When a little later Cumming complained of an uncooperative and uncivil reply from Johnston to his request for help in punishing some marauding Indians, Cass curtly dismissed his grievance.[62] The Government, nevertheless, had effectively rejected the bellicose policy urged by Floyd and his partisans in Utah.

When they received Jeremiah Black's caustic admonitions, Cradlebaugh and Sinclair launched a futile campaign to vindicate themselves.[63] General Johnston, on the other hand, accepted Floyd's orders, although they went in opposition to his wishes for a more severe treatment of the Mormons. As evidence of his submission to the Administration's wishes he asked Marshal Dotson to take into custody the prisoners held by the army after Cradlebaugh had closed his court; at the same time he informed the judge that henceforth only the governor by written request could call out the army, except under the most urgent conditions. In May, when a deputy marshal requested a detachment of forty men to help serve a warrant for arrest upon a bishop, the general refused to approve the application.[64]

The Mormons were at first unaware that the Administration was prepared to support them in their struggle against the interference of zealous Gentile officials. Their fears did not subside after Cradlebaugh left Provo. Instead the circulation of many rumors kept them in a state of acute unrest: volunteers from Mis-

souri and Arkansas were marching upon the people of Iron
County to kill them; several companies of men had left Camp
Floyd to arrest their dignitaries; Johnston had told Cumming to
take care of the Saints or his army would do the job. By April 24
Brigham Young and Daniel Wells, convinced that the troops were
about to descend upon Salt Lake City, hurried to Cumming's
office for a lengthy conference.[65]

Although they began once again to pack up their documents
and records, Young and his colleagues had no serious intention
this time of embarking upon another Move South, or even the
pretense of one. In an interview with Cumming, Young admitted
that his followers would have to stay in Salt Lake Valley, since
they had no other place to go.[66] But this situation did not compel
them to accept meekly whatever punishment the army intended
for them; instead they took steps to protect themselves. From the
Spanish Fork Indian farm Garland Hurt wrote Johnston that at
least 100 armed men had left the nearby settlement, presumably
for Salt Lake City, and at the same time he warned Dotson of the
presence of other armed Mormons in the mountains. David A.
Burr, son of the controversial surveyor, wrote of the mobilization
of "minute men" in the settlements north of the capital and announced that four sentinels were posted high in the hills southeast
of Salt Lake City, watching the road from Camp Floyd, ready to
touch off a woodpile as a signal of alarm when a movement of the
army should be detected. From another source word reached Johnston that 400 Mormons had assembled in the mountains near
Goshen for some mysterious purpose. Anti-Mormons in the army
and in the civil offices of the Territory were also aware that many
Saints—Tracy thought at least a thousand—who had fled from
Cradlebaugh had never returned to their homes but were still
hiding out in inaccessible regions.[67]

As this new crisis increased in intensity, the harassed Governor
finally felt obliged to take cognizance of the tumult in his Territory. Accordingly on May 9 Cumming issued a proclamation declaring unlawful any assemblage of armed men.[68] His words failed
to ease the ugly situation, for the Mormons had no intention of
submitting to an invasion of their city by the military. They
straggled back to their homes, and an uneasy peace returned to
the Valley only when the Church learned that Johnston in fact

had never entertained the idea of sending his men into the Mormons' capital.

When he wrote Cass to summarize this most recent imbroglio,[69] Cumming stated the case one-sidedly, placing the entire blame for the troubles since 1858 upon the army and the anti-Mormon civil officials. Still, his analysis was partly true, for permanent peace in Utah was indeed impossible so long as a large garrison remained encamped near major settlements. Another incident proved the validity of Cumming's declaration. In March 1859, as mentioned, during the intense excitement over Cradlebaugh's activities in Provo, an army sergeant assaulted a young Mormon. Although on the surface the episode seemed minor, it soon threatened to destroy the peace in Utah.

Since Cedar Valley failed to provide enough forage for the expedition's large stock of animals, Johnston had been obliged to send some of his herds to graze in Rush, Tintic, and Skull valleys near by. Technically these areas were public lands, for the Mormons had neither settled them nor otherwise obtained legal title there. But in this dry country, where one might almost count the blades of grass on the range land, the people had come to depend upon the open ranges for grazing. Throughout the early fall of 1858 they complained to Johnston that their rights in these valleys were being ignored and their cattle damaged for want of forage.[70] Even Governor Cumming joined in this chorus of remonstrance; he advised Johnston that certain Mormons claimed the use of Rush Valley by right of three-year occupation. Among these Church members was Daniel Spencer, a man who, as first president of the Salt Lake Stake, had achieved a position of dignity and honor in the Church. Johnston's answer to this letter, as to all other communications from Cumming, was ill-natured. Reminding the governor that the United States still owned the land in Utah, the question of title never having been settled, he announced that the army could take possession of any section it needed. He did, however, modify his policy to the extent of informing Spencer that he could pasture his stock in the northern end of Rush Valley.[71]

Until the first of March 1859 this compromise worked with some success, although the elderly Spencer charged that the soldiers had killed some of his cattle and had damaged his modest buildings in the Valley. But on March 1 the army requested

Spencer to remove his cattle from the valley. This action did not bring an immediate protest from the Saints or from their advocate in the governor's office, but before the month was out a disturbance occurred that caused the Mormons again to look to their weapons.[72]

Like so many scrimmages during this period, the facts of the attack upon Howard Spencer by Sergeant Ralph Pike were buried under the emotional charges of the Church and the angry replies of the army, each party offering an account at variance with the other's. To the Mormons the outline of the episode was clear. Howard Spencer, a nephew of the man who owned the controversial herds, had visited Rush Valley to inspect his uncle's animals and property. While he was engaged on this peaceful mission, a detachment of troops ordered him away, and when the young man refused to leave a soldier struck him down with his rifle, fracturing his skull.[73] The army's version, as might have been expected, placed the entire blame for the affair upon Spencer, asserting that Pike had acted in self-defense. It also introduced a complicating factor not mentioned in the Mormons' account, the statement that in his part of Rush Valley, Spencer had permitted the maintenance of a tavern, which had become a nuisance to the army. Reduced to its important elements, the army's charge was that Howard Spencer had appeared near this building in an intoxicated condition, had dared any two or more men to evict him, had seized a pitchfork with which to spear Pike, and had been prevented from inflicting physical harm only by a blow upon the head.[74]

Whatever the cause, the results were unfortunate. The Mormons, alarmed at the army's exercises in Provo, had already begun to mobilize their militia. Pike's encounter with Spencer greatly increased their excitement, for it reminded them that they had no legal title to their land and property, a situation easily exploited by soldiers who were not kindly disposed toward them. In a somber mood the Church Historian wrote: "Unless the Lord wards off the blow, it looks as though we were to have war and bloodshed, for our enemies are determined on our overthrow." [75] The breakdown of relations between Cumming and Johnston prevented them from serving as mediators between the army and the Church. The Governor accepted the Mormons' version of the event and demanded prompt investigation. Johnston's reply, in addition to rejecting all accusations against his men, contained sarcastic statements indirectly accusing the Governor of having become highly prejudiced in favor of the Church.[76]

The incident did not end with this exchange of acid communications. Four and a half months after the initial tragedy another occurrence aggravated the already sensitive situation almost beyond remedy. On August 6 Alexander Wilson informed Johnston that a grand jury had indicted Sergeant Pike for assault with intent to kill and that a warrant for his arrest had been issued. In due time Pike went up to Salt Lake City from Camp Floyd for trial. One afternoon, when he was walking to his hotel during a recess of the court, he was fatally wounded by Howard Spencer. The soldiers who witnessed the shooting were outraged not only by the cold-blooded nature of the attack but also by the fact that Spencer made his escape through a mob of Mormons who, having gathered on the scene as though by prearrangement, closed in around the fleeing Spencer and made pursuit impossible.[77] The confused comment on the shooting by the editor of the *Deseret News*, in some ways reminiscent of Gentile approval of Parley Pratt's murder two years earlier, revealed the highly emotional state of the Mormons at this time: "We do not approve of the act, but if it shall finally be made to appear, that young Spencer was the murderer, there are many no doubt, who will justify the deed, and laud the bravery of a lad, who thus avenged the wrong that had been committed upon him without provocation." [78]

The murder of the unlucky Sergeant Pike increased passions among both his comrades and the Saints. The few troops who were in Salt Lake City at the time of the assassination were badly outnumbered, and far from being in a position to seek revenge could only hope to escape destruction. "The excitement in this city is intense, and a riot may commence soon," Porter informed Johnston while Dr. Garland Hurt was laboring in vain to save Pike's life.[79] At Camp Floyd, Johnston decided after a hasty study of the situation that he dared not send troops to the city, lest the Mormons take the movement as an attack upon themselves and wipe out Porter's command.[80] After a war of nerves lasting for several days, the troops finally left Salt Lake City without having come to blows with the Saints.

Those in Camp Floyd were not willing to let the matter die so easily. One night a week later several men from Gove's company, in which Pike had been a sergeant, conducted a raid upon the nearby Mormon settlement of Cedar Fort, a small, unprosperous village, and inflicted some damage upon the property and stock of the residents. It is possible that their anger would have impelled them to more serious acts of vengeance had not their commanding officer called the attack "dastardly" and revoked all passes until the commotion had subsided.[81]

One prominent anti-Mormon had taken no part in the alarums following Governor Cumming's proclamation of peace in June 1858. Delana R. Eckels had returned to the States soon after the arrival of the army in the Valley and had been absent during the subsequent crises. In the summer of 1859, when most of the other Gentile officers had left Utah, he returned and opened his court in Nephi, a town south of Provo. Convinced that the Saints had been implicated in countless enormities, including the Mountain Meadows Massacre, he tried to bring some of these alleged criminals to speedy justice. Within less than two weeks he was forced to adjourn his court for lack of funds to meet costs, and except for one conviction he had no trophy of his war with the Church. Frustrated at every turn, he could only collect affidavits implicating Orson Hyde in the Parrish murders, charging the Mormons with robbery of immigrants, and accusing the Church of purchasing many cannons, rifles, and other implements of war.[82]

Eckels' single conviction was of minor importance. In July 1859 Marshal Peter Dotson had raided a Church tithing office hard by Brigham Young's residence and there had found evidence that a counterfeiter had been at work printing drafts upon the United States treasurer at St. Louis. Dotson seized the evidence, accidentally removing at the same time the plates of the Deseret Currency Association, and arrested twenty-six-year-old David McKenzie as the engraver. Two other men, one a well-known gambler, involved with McKenzie in the conspiracy were apparently left unpunished, but from Judge Eckels the Mormon drew a fine of fifty dollars and a sentence of two years' imprisonment. Thus after diligent efforts to bring the Saints' leaders to trial for treason, after prolonged attacks upon polygamy, and energetic tilting with the Church, Associate Justice Eckels had at last put a Mormon in jail.

Even so, he soon joined Cumming and Bernhisel in urging Buchanan to remit McKenzie's sentence.[83]

The McKenzie case seemed a fitting conclusion to the Mormon War, a farcical performance terminating a comic campaign. Jesse Gove wrote as his summary of the war: "Wounded, none; killed, none; fooled, everybody." But his disappointment at being deprived of a chance to shoot Mormons had made him incapable of forming a realistic evaluation of this chapter in the relations between the Latter-day Saints and the United States. In reality the great expenditure of money and energy on both sides had produced some good. As one of its objectives, probably its primary one, Buchanan's Administration had set out to vindicate the authority of the Government over a far-away territory. Although it had not satisfied the demands of the "Ultra party" of which Jacob Forney spoke, it had in the face of a defiant sect peacefully placed a Gentile in the governor's office and posted a sizable military garrison within the Territory. These accomplishments made an attack upon a United States district court less likely in 1860 than it had been in Stiles' day. For their part, the Mormons had also derived a few benefits from the proceedings, especially the winning of some respect in the States. Whereas angry Gentiles had once spoken facilely of hanging Brigham Young and scattering every harem to the winds, now they had more regard for the Saints' military power and some admiration for their courage, if not for their doctrine.

10. Afterward

AFTER the emotions aroused over the shooting of Pike had died down, the people in Utah, whether Gentile or Mormon, began to lose some of the hysteria that had helped to keep the Territory turbulent since the army had first marched through Salt Lake City. Yet it would be a long time before the Valley would become peaceful. Anti-Mormons still felt that the Church was trying to exercise political and judicial power for insidious, perhaps treasonable, purposes; the Saints truculently awaited another wave of persecution. The presence of the army, as Cumming had predicted, made agreement between Mormons and Gentiles almost impossible. Polygamy also impeded an adjustment between the two factions, as well as between the Territory and the nation.

To old Lewis Cass the situation at the end of 1859 seemed almost as threatening as it had been when Buchanan assumed office many months earlier, for he had in his hands letters from Cradlebaugh and Eckels reminiscent of Drummond's effusions. Cradlebaugh, his investigation of Mormon iniquity in Provo and points south having been blocked, wrote that many horrible crimes, including the Mountain Meadows Massacre, had been perpetrated by "men holding high civil office and Church officers," yet the perversion of the jury system had prevented punishment of the villains.[1] In more detail, and with an inaccuracy similar to Drummond's, Eckels also arraigned the Saints on many charges. In his district alone, he emphasized, there had been 160 murders committed, as well as innumerable lesser crimes, in most of which high ecclesiastical personages had been involved.[2]

There were many people in Washington, their prejudices undiminished after 1857, who were prepared to believe the charges of Cradlebaugh, Eckels, and anyone else who might pose as an authority. Two Senate resolutions of March 1860, one asking for information on the Mountain Meadows Massacre and similar murders in Utah, the other inquiring into the territorial judges' correspondence with the Cabinet, showed that considerable curiosity, perhaps even doubt, existed on the question whether the Saints were acting peacefully. With similar suspicion the House of Representatives also requested the President to transmit all communications of civil and military officers in Utah that might show what happened after October 1857.[3]

In the Administration several officials believed the President's moderate policy toward the Mormons misguided. The Commissioner of Indian Affairs, A. B. Greenwood, wrote a bitter report in the fall of 1859 in which, after reference to the "atrocious and dreadful" Mountain Meadows Massacre, he urged retention of the army in Utah in order to control "the population of the Territory, who contemn and disregard our laws, and are, therefore, practically in a state of rebellion." [4] The Honorable John B. Floyd was still convinced of the Mormons' seditious nature; parts of his annual report of 1859 might well have been taken from the pages of his report two years earlier, so little had his ideas changed. But morosely aware that he would not see his aggressive policies carried out, he wrote peevishly: "There is, in the present attitude of affairs, scarcely any necessity for the presence of troops in Utah, and they will be otherwise disposed of in the coming season."

Unshaken by these contrary winds, Buchanan's Administration pursued its determination to establish peace in Utah through conciliation rather than the use of force. When he received Eckels' denunciation of the Mormons, Cass asked Cumming to investigate the charges, although he knew that the Governor would not consider them sympathetically. In the same reply, written in December 1859, Cass also proved that he was not greatly disturbed by Eckels' ululations, for he announced: "It is deemed very desirable to reduce the large number of United States troops now in Utah, if it can be done consistently with the tranquillity and general interest of the Territory." [5] Jeremiah Black later displayed an even more moderate approach, bordering upon cordiality. When he wrote to Brigham Young, in itself a remarkable act, he announced the appointment of new and impartial judges, spoke of their selection for their "moral as well as intellectual qualities," and added as though addressing the ruling power in Utah: "That is what you need in order to give peace and security and safety to your rights of person, property, and reputation." [6] Buchanan's Cabinet had moved far from the verdict of its deliberations on the Mormon question in the spring of 1857.

During 1860 and 1861 the gradual reduction of the military garrison at Camp Floyd promised to remove one of the greatest obstacles to territorial peace. The Mormons derived no great benefit when Gen. Albert Sidney Johnston left Camp Scott in March 1860, for his successor, Lt. Col. Charles F. Smith, shared his views that the Church was involved in many acts of violence, specifically the robbery and murder of emigrants.[7] But within a few months Colonel Philip St. George Cooke assumed this position, and as a result the Saints had a more congenial person as commander of the troops in their midst. During this period the force was cut to approximately 700 men, a size no longer inimical to the Church's existence. Moreover, the troops who remained became so badly divided among themselves over the issue of secession that they had little time to meditate upon the behavior and religious doctrines of the Latter-day Saints. The loyal Maria Gove, who had joined her husband in Utah, wrote of "spirited and almost quarrelsome discussions with Virginians and those who glory with the South in their rebellion." Although Cooke changed the name of the post to Camp Crittenden to show his disapproval of John B. Floyd's Southern sympathies, some officers accused him of disloyal tendencies. Harassed by this internal strife, the garrison held on in Utah until mid-1861, when the last soldiers left.[8]

The freedom of the Saints from a military garrison was short-lived, however, for in 1862 another force of men arrived in the Valley, this time from the West Coast. After the outbreak of the Civil War the Mormons revealed no defect of patriotism that might have justified military occupation of their country to enforce their allegiance to the Union. Although in ideology their leaders favored the South's position concerning the right of a state to prevent federal interference with a peculiar domestic institution, whether slavery or polygamy, many of them had spent their early lives in the North. They were more inclined to call down a plague on both houses than to favor one side; some saw in the war a long-overdue punishment of all Gentiles for their mistreatment of the faithful.[9] Nevertheless the Government ordered a large de-

tachment of men to Utah ostensibly to keep open the postal and
telegraphic communications between the East and West but possibly also to ensure the Mormons' loyalty.

The return of the army brought new tension between soldiers
and Saints. The senior officer, Col. Patrick Edward Connor, openly
expressed his suspicions of the Church by establishing Fort Douglas on the high ground above Salt Lake City, from which position,
he informed the adjutant general's office in San Francisco, he
could command the Mormons' settlement and check their treason.
Like Johnston he preferred to destroy the sect's power in Utah
rather than seek out means of living in peace with it; accordingly
he wished to fill the Territory with a flood of Gentiles "sufficient
by peaceful means and through the ballot box to overwhelm the
Mormons by mere force of numbers." Because Connor followed
Johnston's example of establishing no communication with the
Church, misunderstandings once again arose. In 1863, as in 1859,
the Mormons became excited by a rumor that the troops were
mobilizing to seize Brigham Young, and more than a thousand
men poured into the streets around their leader's house to protect
him.[10]

Although the danger of an armed clash between the Territory
and the nation had passed, Utah's political history during the next
several decades was almost as riotous as in the preceding ten years.
The Mormon War, productive as it had been of some good, had
solved few of the basic problems that had created trouble in the
past. Many minor annoyances remained—Indian matters, land
titles, the probate courts' jurisdiction, poor political appointees.
They were, in turn, only symptomatic of the primary cause of dispute, the Mormons' angry insistence on the right to manage their
own affairs, which to them included most of the temporal as well
as religious business of the Territory, and their opponents' antithetical desire to reduce the Church's authority. Repugnance of
the Saints' practice of polygamy remained unabated. Shifting currents in the political tides of the nation might wash different men
into the Territory's secular offices, but the changes failed to bring
a diminution of hostility.

In May 1861 Alfred Cumming, Buchanan's most fortunate appointment despite his slowness of wit and pomposity, left for his
native state of Georgia, where he tried without success to wring

from the Northern government certain moneys owed him.[11] Of
the important civil officers appointed at the close of the war he
was the last to leave Utah, for Eckels and Sinclair had returned
to the East before him and Cradlebaugh was starting a new career
in Carson Valley. In the selection of Cumming's successor Lincoln's Administration repeated an error that had played a part in
producing the Mormon War, for the choice fell to one John W.
Dawson, a man of loose morals whom the Republican chieftains
of Fort Wayne had nominated in order to rid themselves of an
objectionable person. He immediately antagonized the Mormons
by vetoing their petitions for statehood. When he also made im-
proper advances to his housekeeper, a member of the Church, the
Saints drove him from the Territory.

For several months after the arrival of another governor in July
1863 the Mormons believed that they had, for the first time since
Cumming's departure, a sympathetic individual in this important
position. But Stephen S. Harding, like John F. Kinney before him,
was merely concealing his real opinions from the Saints. To the
Secretary of State, William Seward, he wrote in August that the
Church ruled the Territory "with an absolutism scarcely to be
credited," that its leaders were not loyal to the Union, that murders had gone unpunished, and that the peace of Utah demanded
the stationing of troops there.[12] In his annual message Harding
made his feelings known to the people, for in that document he
criticized them for lack of patriotism and for the practice of
polygamy. When two federal judges, Charles B. Waite and
Thomas J. Drake, also petitioned Congress for laws to break the
Church's control over the territorial judicial system, the Mormons
became incensed and in March 1863 held a mass protest meeting
in their Tabernacle. After hearing many denunciatory speeches,
the angry convocation sent a committee, including John Taylor,
to wait upon the officials. In this way they learned that Drake
was not so timorous as the runaway officials had been twelve years
earlier, for he told the delegation: "Go back to Brigham Young,
your master—the embodiment of sin and shame and disgust—
and tell him that I neither fear him, nor love him, nor hate him—
that I utterly despise him. Tell him, whose tools and tricksters
you are, that I did not come here by his permission, and that I
will not go away at his desire or by his directions." [13]

The men who became Utah's governors and judges later in the 1860's performed their duties in a manner more pleasing to the Church, and so there came at last a brief period of tranquil relationship between church and state rare in the Territory's early history.[14] But the harmony between Utah and the United States turned sour when the national revulsion against polygamy again reached fever pitch, and Congress stood ready to curb this practice by law. Thus, when the question of the Mormons' supposed rebelliousness—their schemes to stir up the Indians, subvert the courts, and take other steps toward independence—had finally been relegated to an unimportant place in Gentile thinking, the matter of their morals caused indignation to rise against them.

In 1862 Congress had passed the Morrill Act, providing for fines and imprisonment for the practice of polygamy in the territories, but the statute was not enforced. Public opinion, however, continued to hold in detestation the Mormons' doctrine of plural marriage, and in 1875 Attorney General Edward Pierrepont spoke for a host of Gentiles when he branded it "a social system corrupting and degrading, abhorrent to the principles of the Christian religion, and never yet permitted by any Christian nation." [15] The Edmunds Act of 1882 was a far more serious thrust at polygamy, for it included in its punishments disfranchisement and the loss of the right to hold political office, as well as fine and imprisonment. Rudger Clawson, the first Mormon to be tried under this act, was convicted in 1884. When the Supreme Court upheld the verdict the following year, the Saints became fair game. Soon many of them had lost the privileges of citizenship and others had gone into hiding. An informal exodus to Mexico and other havens began.

Worse was to come. The Edmunds-Tucker Act of 1887 threatened the very existence of the denomination, for by its terms the Corporation of the Church of Jesus Christ of Latter-day Saints was dissolved and all its property made liable to confiscation, under one pretext or another.[16]

So long as John Taylor was president of the Church, nothing could be done to moderate the Church's stand on polygamy, for the old man adamantly insisted that plural marriage was a doctrine of divine origin, not a human innovation, and could not lightly be deleted from the creed. But after his death, the sentiment of

the Mormons was more and more to insist upon some solution
of the problem before the Church should be destroyed. Some men
had even begun to obey the federal laws concerning plural marriage, in defiance of ecclesiastical admonition. With 200 of his
brethren in jail and many more "on the underground," Wilford
Woodruff, a sturdy pillar of the faith for almost sixty years, realized that his people could never find a place in monogamous
American society if they continued their pluralistic matrimonial
practices. Accordingly as president of the Church he issued in
1890 a manifesto advising Mormons that polygamy was not, after
all, an essential doctrine, and a general conference of the denomination soon upheld his ruling. In 1896 Utah at last attained statehood.

The removal of this stumbling block to reconcilation between
Mormon and Gentile did not at once end the animosities and
suspicions on both sides. Gentiles had too long thought of the
Church as a collection of traitors and reprobates to seek an understanding of this native American religious movement. In 1911
Cosmopolitan Magazine carried a series of articles which, the editor explained, was intended to inform the people of the country
"what Mormonism really means; how it has already cinched its
slimy grips upon the politics and business of a dozen states," and
so forth. On the following pages, each bearing a picture of a large,
open-mouthed rattlesnake, there were stern admonitions to the
American people: "Mormonism is growing and spreading and
creeping over the face of the people like ivy on a wall"; "Every
Mormon from his cradle days is taught to look upon this nation
as the arch-enemy." [17] And so, a half century after the end of the
Mormon War, the restless spirits of the foolish Brocchus, the debauched Drummond, the vindictive Eckels, the sincere Hurt, the
egocentric Young, the crude Kimball, and the dignified Wells
still divided Mormon from Gentile in the United States.

Bibliographical Essay

CONCEIVING their Church as the only true one, destined to spread until all kingdoms and principalities had embraced its tenets, the leaders of Mormonism have believed that every action and conversation, every letter sent or received, even vivid dreams, are of vital importance and should be set down. Thus their official records are extensive. For the same reason the Mormons have been enthusiastic diarists. Many of their journals and other accounts are available either in their original form or in copies preserved at various depositories. Many people not members of the Church, the "Gentiles," have found the Latter-day Saints interesting enough to motivate publication of observations, conclusions, criticisms, and, more rarely, praise.

Unfortunately much of this output is of little value. The biases of non-Mormon authors have been discussed in the text. For their part, the Saints had no reason to be critical of a religious movement they considered sponsored by God, and their writings, both of yesterday and of today, are less than objective. One Mormon has summed up the prevailing attitude among his fellow authors: "And it becomes patent to anyone who undertakes to chronicle the events of even an epoch of our history, that there is an undercurrent of heroism, faith, and even devotion, governing and directing the energies of our people which requires the subtle power of inspiration to appreciate and the gifted pen of one, who sees with 'the eye of faith' to depict" (*Contributor, 3,* 1882).

The following essay on authorities does not list all the works on the Mormon War and its origins but only the sources that were useful to my investigation of the subject.

Manuscripts

The best collection of materials about the Mormons exists, of course, in the archives of the Church of Jesus Christ of Latter-day Saints in Salt Lake City. Here are to be found, in addition to an excellent library of books on the Church's history, such items as the records of many wards, minute books, and letter books. There are two sources of primary importance, however. The first and best is the "Manuscript History of Brigham Young," in which are copied all the important documents, conversations, and other significant happenings of each day. It is regrettable that the volumes are not open to the Gentile scholar, or even to most Mormon historians; the custodian of the portals, A. Will Lund, is adamant in his refusal to let all but the most faithful dip into this record. I am grateful that the other source, the "Journal History," was made available to me. Like the "Manuscript History" it contains copies of documents and letters, conversations held among members of the Hierarchy, and other matters. For the early years of the 1850's it was not helpful for it is limited principally to excerpts from the *Deseret News;* thereafter it included more significant items and even has portions of the "Manuscript History."

The Bancroft Library at the University of California is another great repository of materials. Here are unpublished memoirs of many men and women, both ordinary people and those high in the councils of the Church. Here also is the anonymous "Early Records of Utah," which apparently is composed of passages from the "Manuscript History." A brief catalogue of the library has been printed by S. George Ellsworth in "A Guide to the Manuscripts in the Bancroft Library Relating to the History of Utah," *Utah Historical Quarterly, 22,* 1954.

The Yale Collection of Western Americana at Yale University has a large and growing mass of materials—newspapers, diaries, rare books, unpublished letters, and the like—which cannot be found elsewhere. The curator of this library, Archibald Hanna, is most generous in offering his assistance to the student.

There are many typed copies of diaries and memoirs at Brigham Young University. Although some are valueless because of their brevity or illiteracy or for other reasons, several were of help in the preparation of this monograph. The "Autobiography and

Diary of James Pace" contains the experiences of an officer of the
Nauvoo Legion. The "History and Journal of Jesse W. Crosby,"
in reality memoirs rather than a journal, has a few details by
another member of the Mormons' army. A teamster who traveled
with the expedition wrote down his recollections in the "Diary
of William Wallace Hammond." The "Diary of George Laub"
runs to three volumes, but only Volume 2 pertains to this subject.
Although the "Diary of John D. T. McAllister" is very concise,
it is a good source of information by a man who served in the
militia. There are some details in the "Biography of George
Orrin Pitkin." For all its eight volumes, the "Diary of Hosea
Stout" is of little help, since most of its pages concern Stout's legal
activities. Wayne Stout, *Hosea Stout, Utah's Pioneer Statesman*
(Salt Lake City, privately printed, 1953), publishes selections from
the diaries, but it is a crude job, unimportant to one who does
not see with the eyes of faith. The "Diary of Charles L. Walker"
covers the period of the war in Volumes 1–3, but Walker was
young at the time and only semiliterate.

The library at Brigham Young University has copies of other
manuscripts, three of which should be mentioned: "Records of
Orders, Returns and Courts-Martial of the Second Brigade, First
Division, Nauvoo Legion"; "Record of the Provo Military Dis-
trict Command, 1857–1858"; and "A List of Donations toward
Fitting Out Soldiers for the Army of Israel, First Ward, Odgen
City, Weber County, 1st. Feby., 1858."

The Utah Historical Society has copies of some significant
Mormon diaries, in particular the "Biographical Sketch of the
Life of Peter Wilson Conover." The society also has an unpublished study of the Nauvoo Legion by Colonel Hamilton Gardner.

Several other collections of unpublished materials proved valuable. The Papers of Jeremiah S. Black are located in the Manuscripts Division of the Library of Congress; these include a number of letters from Forney and other persons. Although the John
Wolcott Phelps Diaries in the New York Public Library are
voluminous, they are somewhat disappointing as a source of information. Phelps wrote at length of whirlwinds and other natural
phenomena but said little about his fellow officers and the progress of the campaign. The Alfred Cumming Papers at Duke Uni-

versity contain more than 700 items, some of which are on microfilm in the Utah Historical Society. The Adjutant General's Office, Utah National Guard, Salt Lake City, has muster rolls of the
Nauvoo Legion as well as occasional letters of interest.

Public documents. The National Archives, Washington, D.C.,
contain many papers concerning both the military and the political
affairs of early Utah. In the Department of State section there are
the Territorial Papers, Applications and Recommendations for
Office, Miscellaneous Letters, and Domestic Letters, all of which
provide essential facts. In the Department of the Interior section
the Papers of the Indian Division and of the General Land Office
are useful. The Appointment Files of the Department of Justice
have nothing about officers who preceded Kinney, but the later
materials are helpful. The Attorney General's Records, 1789–1870,
include a "Synopsis of Letters Relative to Affairs in Utah Territory." The records of the War Department are indispensable, for
in them are Letters Received, Letters Sent, Orders and Circulars,
Field Returns, and other excellent sources.

The Utah Department of State, Salt Lake City, has in its archives several boxes of manuscripts dealing with the 1850's. Of
particular interest are the "Executive Record, Book 'B,' 1852–
1871," "Executive Proceedings, 1850 to 1854, and Elections and
Commissions," and "Acts and Resolutions of the Legislative Assembly of the Territory of Utah."

The Executive Documents, Miscellaneous Documents, and Reports of both Houses of the United States Congress were vital to
an understanding of this problem, as the footnotes in the text
have indicated. One of these collections is of especial importance
and so deserves mention here again: 35th Congress, 1st Session,
House of Representatives Executive Document 71.

Newspapers

The *Deseret News,* owned by the Church and operated by its
agents, is a most valuable source, for in addition to facts concerning events in Utah it published sermons of members of the Hierarchy, biographies of many of the Church's leaders, editorials, and
other matters of historical interest. Wendell J. Ashton, *Voice in*

the West; Biography of a Pioneer Newspaper (New York, Duell, Sloan, and Pearce, 1950) unfortunately has little useful information about the *Deseret News,* but its sketches of the men who were connected with it are interesting. The *Valley Tan,* the anti-Mormon organ founded by Gentiles after the arrival of Johnston's army, was short-lived and so biased that its reliability is always suspect, yet on some subjects it offers a good antidote to the Church's broadsides.

A number of newspapers published in other parts of the country provide fact as well as evidence of Gentile opinion toward the Mormons. The Washington *Union* was close to the Buchanan Administration and at times spoke for it. The St. Louis *Republican's* articles were considered so important that they were often quoted in the *Union* and the *National Intelligencer.* The New York *Tribune* was one of the few journals in the East that pursued a sympathetic editorial policy toward the Saints during the war. It had two correspondents with Johnston's forces whose dispatches are useful if their anti-Mormon bias is kept in mind. The San Francisco *Evening Bulletin,* always hostile toward the Church, has a number of interesting articles in the last half of 1857. The St. Louis *Leader,* the Crescent City (Iowa) *Oracle,* and the *Daily Alta California* are also good reflectors of the feeling toward the Mormons during the period. The *Annals of Cleveland 1818–1935* (W.P.A., 1937) has abstracts and at times direct quotations from the *Daily True Democrat* and the *Leader.* The text of speeches from the floor of Congress are printed in the *Congressional Globe.*

Early Published Sources

Many of the sermons by leaders of the Church are recorded in *Journal of Discourses, by Brigham Young, His Two Counsellors, and the Twelve Apostles,* a multivolume series published in Liverpool, England. One significant defense of the Latter-day Saints is Thomas L. Kane's *The Mormons. A Discourse Delivered before the Historical Society of Pennsylvania, March 26, 1850,* Philadelphia, 1850. Jedediah M. Grant's plea for understanding of his people appeared in *The Truth for the Mormons; Three Letters to the New York Herald, from J. M. Grant, of Utah.*

Brandebury, Brocchus, and Harris presented their story in *The Spiritual Wife Doctrine of the Mormons Proved from the Report of the Judges of the Utah Territory to the President of the United States, Given Entire from the New York Herald, of January the 10th., 1852*. One of the Runaways explained his position in *Letter of Judge Brocchus, of Alabama, to the Public, upon the Difficulties in the Territory of Utah*, Washington, Lemuel Towers, 1852. A bitter attack upon the Mormons by one of their consistent enemies was made in *Utah and the Mormons. Speech of the Hon. John Cradlebaugh, of Nevada, on the Admission of Utah as a State*, 1863. Franklin D. Richards, *Latter-day Saints in Utah* (Liverpool, privately printed, 1852), is a collection of three documents answering charges against the Mormons. In a rambling fashion *A Series of Instructions and Remarks by President Brigham Young at a Special Council, Tabernacle, March 21, 1858* announced the Church's plans for the "exodus." The testimony and affidavits in *A Brief Statement of the Claims of Majors and Russell; Also the Evidence upon Which It Rests*, in the Yale Collection offers information on part of the march to Fort Bridger and the raids of Lot Smith.

Published Memoirs, Letters, and Biographies

The recollections of certain visitors to Utah who were not connected with the war contain general comment and background information. John W. Gunnison, *The Mormons, or Latter-day Saints in the Valley of the Great Salt Lake* (Philadelphia, Lippincott, Grambo, 1852), is the work of an army officer who was not sympathetic toward the Saints but who tried with much success to be objective. Horace Greeley, *An Overland Journey from New York to San Francisco in the Summer of 1859* (New York, Saxton, Barker, 1860), sets forth the brief observations of this colorful personality upon the political situation in Utah after the end of the war. *A Journey to Great-Salt-Lake City, by Jules Remy and Julius Brenchley* (London, W. Jeffs, 1861), is of less value.

Some of the federal officers and their ladies who were in the Territory before the start of the war confided their thoughts to the nation. Sarah Hollister Harris, *An Unwritten Chapter of Salt*

Lake, 1851–1901 (New York, privately printed, 1901) has a great deal of information. Mrs. Harris, however, was apparently writing from memory long after the incidents which she was describing had passed, and a number of mistakes appear in her account. Benjamin G. Ferris, *Utah and the Mormons* (New York, Harpers, 1854), has very little about his experiences in Utah and a great deal about the evils of Mormonism. Mrs. B. G. Ferris, *The Mormons at Home, with Some Incidents of Travel from Missouri to California, 1852–1853* (New York, Dix and Edwards, 1856), is composed of letters which Mrs. Ferris edited for publication. Her hostility toward the Church comes through undimmed in these communications. Most of the letters had already been published in "Life among the Mormons," *Putnam's Monthly Magazine, 6* (1855).

The recollections of many persons more directly connected with the war than those just noted have also been published. The best of these by far is Otis G. Hammond, ed., *The Utah Expedition, 1857–1858. Letters of Capt. Jesse A. Gove,* New Hampshire Historical Society Collections, 12 (Concord, New Hampshire Historical Society, 1928), which includes a great many facts concerning the march of the army from Leavenworth to Salt Lake City. The second part of the book, composed primarily of articles written by Gove to the New York *Herald,* is of less value than the first. Theodore F. Rodenbough, *From Everglade to Cañon with the Second Dragoons* (New York, Van Nostrand, 1875), is made up of accounts written by men who had served with the Dragoons, each prefaced by the compiler's introduction. Philip St. George Cooke's memoirs add little fact not found more easily elsewhere, but the lengthy selections from the diary of trumpeter William Drown vividly describe the march to Utah and the experiences of the soldiers during winter quarters. Several interesting stories appear in Henry S. Hamilton, *Reminiscences of a Veteran* (Concord, Republican Press Association, 1897), but their reliability is doubtful, since they were written long after the events. Randolph B. Marcy, *Thirty Years of Army Life on the Border* (New York, Harpers, 1866), has something about Fort Bridger and Salt Lake City. George P. Hammond, ed., *Campaigns in the West, 1856–1861. The Journal and Letters of Colonel John Van Deusen Du Bois* (Tucson, Arizona Pioneers Historical Society, 1949), gives

an account of Marcy's return trip from New Mexico to Fort
Bridger but is light on other aspects of the war. Ralph P. Bieber,
ed., Olga Bandel and Richard Jente, translators, *Frontier Life
in the Army, 1854–1861, by Eugene Bandel* (Glendale, Arthur H.
Clark, 1932) tells of the supply train sent to relieve Johnston
in 1858. One Mormon's narrative, James S. Brown, *Life of a Pioneer, Being an Autobiography* (Salt Lake City, George Q. Cannon and Sons, 1900) has a little information on the Church's defensive campaign. Oscar O. Winther, ed., *The Private Papers of
Thomas Leiper Kane, A Friend of the Mormons* (San Francisco,
Gelber-Lilienthal, 1937), is short, with nothing that bears directly
on the period.

Some useful memoirs have appeared in periodicals. A teamster
for Russell, Majors, and Waddell has left an entertaining de-
scription of his journey to Utah; it appears in William Clark, "A
Trip across the Plains in 1857," *The Iowa Journal of History and
Politics, 20, 1922.* "The Journal of Captain Albert Tracy," *Utah
Historical Quarterly, 13* (1945), was edited first by Herbert S.
Auerback and, after his death, by J. Cecil Alter from the original
in the New York Public Library. Since the diary began in March
1858, it can be used only for the period after the end of the war.
It is difficult reading but of much value. There is almost nothing
in "From the Journal of John Pulsipher. Part II. 'The Utah
War,'" *The Western Humanities Review, 3,* 1949. Hamilton
Gardner, "A Territorial Militiaman in the Utah War; Journal of
Newton Tuttle," *Utah Historical Quarterly, 22* (1954), is the tale
of a soldier who ran about a good deal without notable accomplishment. A. R. Mortensen, ed., "The Governor's Lady. A Letter from
Camp Scott, 1857," *Utah Historical Quarterly, 22* (1954), has some
information about that aspect of the war.

A scholarly study of Brigham Young is badly needed, and until
one appears, this giant of the American past will only be dimly
visible to us, a star of the second magnitude in the Western sky.
Such a work cannot be done, of course, without free access to the
materials in the Church's archives, and there seems at present
little possibility that they will be made available. The Church appears to be content with Preston Nibley's *Brigham Young, the
Man and His Work* (Salt Lake City, Deseret News Press, 1936),
a fulsome biography lacking footnotes, bibliography, or any

other evidence of competent scholarship. Clarissa Young Spencer and Mabel Hunter, *One Who Was Valiant* (Caldwell, Idaho, Caxton, 1940), has no redeeming feature. Edward W. Tullidge wrote *Life of Brigham Young, or, Utah and Her Founders* (New York, privately printed, 1876), after he had left the Church, but it is a worthless panegyric. M. R. Werner, *Brigham Young* (New York, Harcourt, Brace, 1925), is the only critical biography of Young in existence. The author was unsympathetic toward Mormonism and hostile to Young, but he did give a fair appraisal of Young's accomplishments and of his virtues. Many minor details in the book are inaccurate and the chapters are too short, but the main weakness lies in the fact that the author used the *Journal of Discourses* as his chief source. Milton R. Hunter, *Brigham Young the Colonizer* (Independence, Zion's Printing and Publishing Company, 1945), has a little information on San Bernardino.

The other important figures in the denomination have fared biographically as badly as the Lion of the Lord. There is considerable material scattered throughout Bryant S. Hinckley, *Daniel Hanmer Wells and Events of His Time* (Salt Lake City, Deseret News Press, 1942), but the book, like so many works by devout Mormons, lacks scholarly apparatus. B. H. Roberts, *The Life of John Taylor* (Salt Lake City, George Q. Cannon and Sons, 1892), is useful up to 1856. There is little in Matthias F. Cowley, *Wilford Woodruff. History of His Life and Labors, as Recorded in His Daily Journals,* Salt Lake City, Deseret News Press, 1909. Franklin L. West, *Life of Franklin D. Richards* (Salt Lake City, Deseret News Press, 1924), is a eulogistic account by a devoted grandson. T. E. Lyon, "Orson Pratt, Pioneer and Proselyter," *Utah Historical Quarterly, 24* (1956), has some facts objectively presented. Orson F. Whitney, *Life of Heber C. Kimball* (1888), is valueless to the serious student. The biographical sketches in three other volumes are equally weak: Matthias F. Cowley, *Prophets and Patriarchs of the Church of Jesus Christ of Latter-day Saints,* Chattanooga, Ben E. Rich, 1902; Mabel Harmer, *The Story of the Mormon Pioneers,* Salt Lake City, Deseret News Press, 1943; and Wendell J. Ashton, *Theirs Is the Kingdom,* Springville, Utah, Art City Publishing Company, 1945. For brief studies of the leaders in the early history of the Church, as well as for thoughtful analyses of Mormonism, one should use Fawn M.

Brodie, *No Man Knows My History. The Life of Joseph Smith, the Mormon Prophet,* New York, Knopf, 1946. Two Masters' theses provided almost no biographical information: "Dr John Milton Bernhisel, Utah's First Delegate to Congress" (University of Utah, 1947), by Robert H. Sylvester, and "Almon Whiting Babbitt, Mormon Emissary" (University of Utah, 1953), by Jay D. Ridd.

Biographies of non-Mormons who played a part in the war are a little better than those of their adversaries. W. Eugene Hollon, *Beyond the Cross Timbers. The Travels of Randolph B. Marcy, 1812–1887* (Norman, University of Oklahoma Press, 1955), has an excellent, well-documented account of Marcy's winter journey to New Mexico. The best parts of William Preston Johnston, *The Life of Albert Sidney Johnston* (New York, Appleton, 1878), are the letters written by Johnston and the reports of Fitz-John Porter. Otis E. Young, *The West of Philip St. George Cooke, 1809–1895* (Glendale, Arthur H. Clark, 1955), relies mainly on official reports and Rodenbough's book. Some details concerning Bridger's troubles with the Mormons and later with the Government are found in J. Cecil Alter, *James Bridger; Trapper, Frontiersman, Scout and Guide* (Salt Lake City, Shepard Book Company, 1925). Cecil H. C. Howard, *Life and Public Services of Gen. John Wolcott Phelps* (Brattleboro, Vermont, Housh and Co., 1887), has too little about the war to be of much service. Albert L. Zobell, Jr., "Thomas L. Kane, Ambassador to the Mormons," *Utah Humanities Review, 1* (1947), uses only secondary materials, except for a few letters the sources of which are not given.

Studies of the Mormon War

No adequate investigation of the Mormon War exists; the two books written about it are both inferior. E. Cecil McGavin, *U.S. Soldiers Invade Utah* (Boston, Meador Publishing Co., 1937) relies upon pitifully few sources, and the author, who favored the Church, made no effort to be objective. Cornelius Conway, *The Utah Expedition, Containing a General Account of the Mormon Campaign . . . by a Wagon Master* (Cincinnati, Safety Fund Reporter, 1858), is full of stories of the Mormons' villainy; it reads better as fiction than as fact.

Magazine articles, while of greater merit than the books, are also disappointing. In the *Atlantic Monthly, 3* (1859), there are three articles under the title "The Utah Expedition; Its Causes and Consequences," which were probably the work of a correspondent for the New York *Times.* In these articles, particularly in the first two, there are many details not found in any other place. But the author was openly anti-Mormon and he failed to give the sources of his information. Furthermore, he seems to have been writing to prove a thesis—that popular sovereignty could not work in other territories, since it had failed in Utah. "The Echo Canyon War," *Contributor, 3* (1882) and *4* (1883)— a series of articles, one of them the narrative of Lot Smith—gives much detail but again without documentation. John Cleveland Robinson, "The Utah Expedition," *Magazine of American History* (1884), is faulty in its analysis of the causes of the war but does have some facts concerning the expedition. Paul Bailey, "Holy Smoke, A Dissertation on the Utah War," *The Westerners' Brand Book, 1948* (Los Angeles, 1949), is superficial.

There are several Masters' theses on the war, but again none is satisfactory. "The Utah War" (University of Utah, 1947), by Everett L. Cooley, is a competent job based upon thorough research, but unfortunately it tends to follow Leland Creer's partisan defense of the Church. "The Mormon War: A Study in Territorial Rebellion" (George Washington University, 1938), by M. Hamlin Cannon, is very anti-Mormon, but it makes a laudable effort to interpret the facts; its bibliography of sources available in Washington, D.C., is useful. "A Study of the Alleged Mormon Rebellion" (Brigham Young University, 1931), by Lorna B. Allen, is based upon very few sources and has many errors.

General Accounts and Monographic Studies

Several general histories of Utah provide a starting point for further research. Hubert Howe Bancroft, *History of Utah* (San Francisco, the History Company, 1889), draws upon many manuscripts, the elusive "Manuscript History of Brigham Young," federal and state records, and other excellent sources. It is critical of some aspects of Mormonism but not blind to the industry and accomplishments of the Saints in Utah. Although the early sections of Andrew Love Neff, *History of Utah, 1847 to 1869*

(Salt Lake City, Deseret News Press, 1940), edited and annotated
by Leland H. Creer, make an effort at unbiased reporting, all ob-
jectivity disappears in the later passages, the description of the
Mormon War being completely one-sided. The book, nevertheless, is a veritable encyclopedia of names, dates, and events. Leland
Hargrave Creer, *Utah and the Nation* (Seattle, University of Washington, 1929), contains many quotations from a wide selection of
sources and a satisfactory bibliography; otherwise it offers no new
interpretations and depends heavily upon B. H. Roberts (below).
The American Guide Series, *Utah. A Guide to the State, Compiled
by Workers of the Writers' Program of the Works Projects Administration for the State of Utah* (New York, Hastings House,
1941), has a good bibliography as well as a concise survey of the
state's history. Edmund T. Olson, *Utah. A Romance in Pioneer
Days* (Salt Lake City, privately printed, 1931), is well written, but
the author had no interest in dates, footnotes, and similar matters.
Maurine Whipple, *This Is the Place: Utah* (New York, Knopf,
1945), tries to explain the Mormons to Gentiles and to reveal the
greatness of their Church.

There are two studies of the earliest days of Utah. Although
Thomas C. Romney, *The Story of Deseret* (Independence, Zion's
Printing and Publishing Co., 1949), is very pro-Mormon, it makes
wide use of unpublished materials and gives an excellent picture
of the Church's organization. Dale L. Morgan, "The State of
Deseret," *Utah Historical Records Survey* (Salt Lake City, 1940),
is also of value for this period.

So far as local histories are concerned, Edward W. Tullidge,
History of Salt Lake City (Salt Lake City, Star Printing Co., 1886),
is a huge work with many interesting quotations, but it lacks footnotes and bibliography. American Guide Series, *Provo, Pioneer
Mormon City* (Portland, Binfords and Mort, 1942), and Hamilton
Gardner, *History of Lehi* (Salt Lake City, Deseret News Press,
1913), are so brief as to be of minor importance.

Most histories of the Mormon Church fall into two categories,
those which praise and those which condemn; only a few are objective enough to be of merit. Volumes 3 and 4 by B. H. Roberts,
*A Comprehensive History of the Church of Jesus Christ of Latter-
day Saints, Century I* (6 vols. Salt Lake City, Deseret News Press,
1930), are in reality a long essay defending the Mormon point

of view, yet it does contain much information and has many quotations from the "Manuscript History of Brigham Young." One ambitious work by an apostate, T. B. H. Stenhouse, *The Rocky Mountain Saints: A Full and Complete History of the Mormons* (London, Ward, Lock, and Tyler, 1874), has a considerable amount of material, but the prejudice of the author necessitates caution. Andrew Jenson, *Encyclopedic History of the Church of Jesus Christ of Latter-day Saints* (Salt Lake City, Deseret News Publishing Company, 1941), is limited to developments in the wards and stakes (divisions of the Church); the earlier work, Andrew Jenson, *Church Chronology. A Record of Important Events* (Salt Lake City, Deseret News Press, 1899), is a good reference book. William Alexander Linn, *The Story of the Mormons* (New York, Macmillan, 1902), is long, dull, and frankly anti-Mormon, composed only from published sources. Yet it was one of the first serious works by a critic of the Church that avoided unsubstantiated statements and personal reminiscences of Mormon-baiters. John Henry Evans, *One Hundred Years of Mormonism* (Salt Lake City, Deseret Sunday School Union, 1905), is a thin production, though pronounced satisfactory by the Hierarchy of the Church. The best study is Thomas F. O'Dea, *The Mormons* (Chicago, Chicago University Press, 1957), a scholarly analysis of the origins of the sect, the forces shaping its doctrines, the history of the Church as a denomination, and other topics.

Several essays which deal with specific phases of Church history deserve mention. Therald Jensen, *Mormon Theory of Church and State* (Chicago, Chicago University Press, 1940), offers some facts of interest. Ephraim E. Ericksen, *The Psychological and Ethical Aspects of Mormon Group Life* (Chicago, Chicago University Press, 1922), a provocative study, suggests that Mormonism has passed through three phases in its development. Juanita Brooks, *The Mountain Meadows Massacre* (Stanford, Stanford University Press, 1950), deserves high praise, for it is an excellent investigation of a subject about which much trash has been written. It draws upon many published and unpublished materials; it also contains a very helpful bibliography. Its analysis of the emotional state of the Saints in the late 1850's goes far to explain some of their actions and attitudes during the Mormon War. Kimball Young, *Isn't One Wife Enough?* (New York, Holt, 1954),

---

is a thorough study of all aspects of polygamy by a learned sociologist. Austin and Alta Fife, *Saints of Sage and Saddle. Folklore among the Mormons* (Bloomington, Indiana University Press, 1956), is a satisfactory work on that topic.

A number of specific investigations of other phases of the Mormon War are available. "Administrative History of the Nauvoo Legion in Utah" (Brigham Young University, 1954), by Ralph Hausen, is a Master's thesis that makes good use of a number of sources. Raymond W. Settle and Mary Lund Settle, *Empire on Wheels* (Stanford, Stanford University Press, 1949), is a good account of Russell, Majors, and Waddell. Dale L. Morgan, "The Administration of Indian Affairs in Utah, 1851–1858," *Pacific Historical Review, 17* (1948), is complete, detailed, impartial, and of far greater value than Alban W. Hoopes, *Indian Affairs and Their Administration, with Special Reference to the Far West, 1849–1860,* Philadelphia, University of Pennsylvania Press, 1932. Leonard J. Arrington, "Mormon Finance and the Utah War," *Utah Historical Quarterly, 20* (1952), is of considerable use, although most of the information is taken from the "Journal History." W. N. Davis, "Western Justice. The Court at Fort Bridger, Utah Territory," *Utah Historical Quarterly, 23* (1955), is primarily concerned with the period after 1858. Franklin D. Daines, "Separatism in Utah, 1847–1870," *Annual Report of the American Historical Association* (1917), is too brief. The footnotes in Averam B. Bender, *The March of Empire. Frontier Defense in the Southwest, 1848–1860* (Lawrence, University of Kansas, 1952), are useful. For developments in the colony of San Bernardino see George W. Beattie and Helen Pruitt Beattie, *Heritage of the Valley. San Bernardino's First Century,* Pasadeno, San Pasqual Press, 1939; Paul Bailey, *Sam Brannan and the California Mormons,* Los Angeles, Westernlore Press, 1943; and William Glover, *The Mormons in California,* Los Angeles, Glen Dawson, 1954.

Anti-Mormon Literature

Anti-Mormon literature is as vast and empty as interstellar space and has no place in a bibliography of this type. Nevertheless, several works have been published that are helpful to the historian, either because they reveal the minds of the authors or because, if used with great caution, they give some information not found elsewhere. The most important of these titles are John Hyde, *Mormonism: Its Leaders and Designs*, New York, W. P. Fetridge, 1857; Samuel Hawthornthwaite, *Adventures among the Mormons, as an Elder during Eight Years*, Manchester, England, privately printed, 1857; Nelson Winch Green, *Fifteen Years among the Mormons, Being the Narrative of Mrs. Mary Ettie V. Smith*, New York, H. Dayton, 1857; *The Mormons. The Dream and the Reality . . . Edited by a Clergyman*, London, 1857; Mrs. C. V. Waite, *The Mormon Prophet and His Harem*, Chicago, J. S. Goodman, 1867; J. H. Beadle, *Life in Utah; or, the Mysteries and Crimes of Mormonism*, Philadelphia, National Publishing Company, 1870; J. H. Beadle, *Brigham's Destroying Angel, Being the Life, Confession, and Startling Disclosures of the Notorious Bill Hickman*, New York, George Crofutt, 1872; Mrs. T. B. H. Stenhouse, *"Tell It All"; The Story of a Life's Experience in Mormonism*, Hartford, 1875; Frank J. Cannon and George L. Knapp, *Brigham Young and His Mormon Empire*, New York, Revell, 1913; Charles Kelley and Hoffman Birney, *Holy Murder. The Story of Porter Rockwell*, New York, Milton, Balch and Company, 1934.

Abbreviations

"Early Records of Utah"   Manuscript, Bancroft Library, University of California.

Hammond, *Utah Expedition*   Otis G. Hammond, ed., *The Utah Expedition, 1857–1858. Letters of Capt. Jesse A. Gove*, New Hampshire Historical Society Collections, 12, Concord, 1928.

JH   "Journal History," manuscript, archives of the Latter-day Saints, Salt Lake City.

NA   National Archives.

OIA   Office of Indian Affairs, National Archives.

Phelps, Diary   John Wolcott Phelps, "Diary," manuscript, New York Public Library.

RG   Record Group.

"Utah Expedition"   35th Cong., 1st Sess., House Exec. Doc. 71.

Notes

1. Beginnings

1. Andrew L. Neff, *History of Utah, 1847 to 1869* (Salt Lake City, Deseret News Press, 1940), p. 108. Thomas C. Romney, *The Story of Deseret* (Independence, Zion's Printing and Publishing Co., 1948), p. 61.

2. Neff, pp. 114 ff. John H. Evans, *One Hundred Years of Mormonism. A History of the Church of Jesus Christ of Latter-day Saints from 1805 to 1905* (Salt Lake City, Deseret Sunday School Union, 1909), p. 485. Andrew Jenson, *Encyclopedic History of the Church of Jesus Christ of Latter-day Saints* (Salt Lake City, Deseret News Press, 1941), p. 181.

3. Neff, pp. 114 ff.

4. Jay D. Ridd, "Almon Whiting Babbitt, Mormon Emissary" (M.A. thesis, University of Utah, 1953), pp. 58–59. Evans, *One Hundred Years of Mormonism,* p. 487. Hubert H. Bancroft, *History of Utah* (San Francisco, the History Co., 1889), pp. 451–55.

5. *DAB.* Wendell J. Ashton, *Theirs Is the Kingdom* (Springville, Utah, Art City Publishing Co., 1945), pp. 208 ff. Oscar O. Winther, ed., *The Private Papers of Thomas Leiper Kane, a Friend of the Mormons* (San Francisco, Gelber-Lilienthal, 1937), pp. vi, 1, 21–22. Bernard De Voto, *The Year of Decision* (Boston, Little, Brown, 1943), p. 242. "Journal History," Church Archives, Salt Lake City (hereafter cited as JH), July 11, Sept. 24, 1850. Kane to Black, Dec. 21, 1857, in Jeremiah Black MSS, Library of Congress. Kane to Marcy, April 30, 1847; Medill to Kane, Jan. 1848: Kane MSS, Library of Congress. "Notes for an Address on the Mormons Introducing Elders Benson and Little" and "Report to the Commissioner of Indian Affairs on the Status of the Mormons": Yale Collection of Western Americana.

6. Leland H. Creer, *Utah and the Nation* (Seattle, University of Washington, 1929), p. 77. William A. Linn, *The Story of the Mormons*

(New York, Macmillan, 1902), p. 431. Romney, *Story of Deseret,* p. 96. *Congressional Globe,* Dec. 31, 1849. JH, March 21, 1850.

7. JH, March 21, April 4, Aug. 9, 1850. *Cong. Globe,* July 8, 18, Sept. 7, 1850.

8. For the debates in Congress concerning the creation of the Territory of Utah see *Cong. Globe,* Dec. 27, 1849, Jan. 22, 1850. See also JH, March 5, 27, 1850.

9. JH, July 4, 1851.

10. Howard Stansbury, *Exploration and Survey of the Valley of the Great Salt Lake of Utah* (Philadelphia, Lippincott, Grambo, 1852), p. 147.

11. Some say 40,000 in the late 1850's; others, 60,000 or more: Neff, *History of Utah,* p. 165; Ephraim E. Ericksen, *The Psychological and Ethical Aspects of Mormon Group Life* (Chicago, University of Chicago Press, 1922), p. 44. The census of 1860 set the foreign segment at 12,000, but Ericksen states that between 1849 and 1858 at least 22,000 Mormon immigrants arrived. It would seem safe to say that approximately a third of the Mormons during the years under consideration were of foreign origin.

12. M. R. Werner, *Brigham Young* (New York, Harcourt, Brace, 1925), pp. 271–72. Bancroft, *History of Utah,* pp. 414–15, 449. *Annals of Cleveland, 1818–1935* (WPA, 1935), *43,* 516. *National Intelligencer,* May 8, 1857. New York *Times,* June 27, 1857. *Missouri Republican,* April 29, 1858. 34th Cong., 1st Sess., Sen. Exec. Doc. 1, Vol. 2, Pt. II.

13. Neff, *History of Utah,* p. 530. See also Thomas F. O'Dea, *The Mormons* (Chicago, University of Chicago Press, 1957), pp. 91 ff.

14. Washington *Union,* June 24, 1857.

15. Bancroft, *History of Utah,* p. 485. Dale L. Morgan, "The Administration of Indian Affairs in Utah, 1851–1858," *Pacific Historical Review, 17,* (1948), 395.

16. *Deseret News,* June 16, 1854.

17. For typical remarks of this nature see Neff, *History of Utah,* p. 468; *Deseret News,* March 30, Sept. 7, 14, 1854, July 1, 1857, Feb. 3, 1858.

18. Creer, *Utah and the Nation,* p. 92. Bancroft, *History of Utah,* p. 367. Therald Jensen, *Mormon Theory of Church and State,*

(Chicago, University of Chicago Press, 1940), p. 2. Dale L. Morgan, "The State of Deseret," *Utah Historical Records Survey* (Salt Lake City, Utah Historical Society, 1940), *8*, 69. "Brigham Young," *DAB*.

19. *Deseret News,* Nov. 18, 1857.

20. Jensen, *Mormon Theory,* p. 1. *Deseret News,* Aug. 17, Sept. 14, 1854, Sept. 12, 1855, June 17, Aug. 19, 1857.

21. *Acts and Resolutions Passed by the Second Annual Assembly of the Territory of Utah* (1853). Morgan, "State of Deseret," p. 69. *Journal of Discourses, by Brigham Young, His Two Counsellors, and the Twelve Apostles* (Liverpool, 1857), *4*, 259 ff. *Deseret News,* Feb. 13, 1855, July 15, 1857.

22. "Executive Proceedings 1850 to 1854, and Elections and Commissions" (MS, Utah Historical Society), pp. 14, 88. JH, July 26, Aug. 10, 1852. "Diary of Hosea Stout" (MS, Brigham Young University), *7*, 309.

23. Creer, *Utah and the Nation,* p. 59. Neff, *History of Utah,* pp. 186, 189. *Deseret News,* Aug. 10, 1850, Sept. 21, 1854.

24. Neff, *History of Utah,* pp. 194-95.

25. *Deseret News,* March 12, 1856.

26. T. B. H. Stenhouse, *The Rocky Mountain Saints: A Full and Complete History* . . . (Salt Lake City, Shepard Book Co. 1904), pp. 282-83. Nels Anderson, *Desert Saints. The Mormon Frontier in Utah* (Chicago, University of Chicago Press, 1942), p. 93.

27. *Acts and Resolutions of the Legislature Assembly of the Territory of Utah,* 1st Sess. (1851-52). Kinney to Cushing, March 1, 1855, in Appointment Papers, Department of Justice, National Archives (NA), Washington, D.C. *Valley Tan* (newspaper), Feb. 8, 1859.

28. Wayne Stout, *Hosea Stout, Utah's Pioneer Statesman* (Salt Lake City, privately printed, 1953), p. 192. Werner, *Brigham Young,* pp. 258, 265. Neff, *History of Utah,* p. 227. Linn, *Story of the Mormons,* p. 117. *Deseret News,* Jan. 12, 1854, April 14, Nov. 28, 1858. JH, March 8, 1857.

29. Allan Nevins, *The Emergence of Lincoln* (2 vols. New York, Scribner's, 1950), *1*, 315. Werner, *Brigham Young,* p. 258. For examples of Young's speech see *Deseret News,* Dec. 10, 1856, March 25, April 15, 22, Aug. 5, 1857.

30. Wilson to Black, Nov. 26, 1858, in Attorney General's Records, 1789–1870, NA. New York *Evening Mirror*, Feb. 20, 1855.

31. *Deseret News*, April 2, 1853.

32. For example, see Neff, *History of Utah*, p. 498; *Deseret News*, Aug. 1, 1855.

33. *Deseret News*, July 18, 1855.

2. Early Troubles

1. *Deseret News*, June 29, 1850.

2. Ray to Cumming, Nov. 20, 1858, in Cumming MSS, Duke University. J. H. Beadle, *Life in Utah, or, the Mysteries and Crimes of Mormonism* (Philadelphia, National Publishing Co., 1870), p. 166. Linn, *Story of the Mormons*, p. 440. Daniel W. Jones, *Forty Years among the Indians* (Salt Lake City, Juvenile Instructor's Office, 1890), pp. 32 ff. Waldemar Westergaard, "Diary of Dr. Thomas Flint," *Annual Publications, Historical Society of Southern California, 12* (1921–23), 100. JH, Feb. 28, Nov. 29, 1851. New York *Tribune*, Aug. 2, 1858.

3. Stansbury, *Exploration and Survey* (above, p. 252; n. 10), pp. 123, 146. John W. Gunnison, *The Mormons, or Latter-day Saints in the Valley of the Great Salt Lake* (Philadelphia, Lippincott, Grambo, 1852), pp. 64–65. *Deseret News*, July 6, 1850.

4. Sarah H. Harris, *An Unwritten Chapter of Salt Lake, 1851–1901* (New York, 1901), pp. 7–8, 30–33. *The Truth for the Mormons; Three Letters to the New York Herald, from Jedediah M. Grant of Utah* (pamphlet reprint), pp. 5–6. JH, May 16, 1851.

5. Neff, *History of Utah*, p. 176. Grant, *Truth for the Mormons*, p. 6.

6. B. H. Roberts, *A Comprehensive History of the Church of Jesus Christ of Latter-day Saints, Century I* (6 vols. Salt Lake City, Deseret News Press, 1930), *3*, 517. *Cong. Globe*, Jan. 9, 1852.

7. Harris, *An Unwritten Chapter*, pp. 36–37, 39–40, 43.

8. Creer, *Utah and the Nation*, pp. 94–95. Grant, *Truth for the Mormons*, p. 8. Neff, *History of Utah*, pp. 170–71, 173–74. JH, Sept. 15, 1851. *Masonic Address Delivered by Perry E. Brocchus at Santa Fe, New Mexico, December 27, 1854,* St. Louis, Benjamin Charles, 1855. E. M. Bailey to Black, Dec. 13, 1857, A. [Orten?] to Black,

Dec. 13, 1859: in Jeremiah Black MSS, Library of Congress. JH, Sept. 15, 1851.

9. American Guide Series, *Utah. A Guide to the State* (New York, Hastings House, 1941), pp. 64–65. JH, July 23, 1851.

10. Neff, *History of Utah*, pp. 171–72. Harris, *An Unwritten Chapter*, p. 34. Lorna B. Allen, "A Study of the Alleged Mormon Rebellion" (M.A. thesis, Brigham Young University, 1931), pp. 56–57. *Cong. Globe*, Jan. 9, 1852. 82d Cong., 1st Sess. Sen. Exec. Doc. 12, pp. 1 ff.

11. For details concerning the Brocchus affair see "Early Records of Utah" (MS in the Bancroft Library, University of California; microfilm copy available in the Church archives, Salt Lake City). See also Creer, *Utah and the Nation*, p. 96; *Cong. Globe*, Jan. 9, 1852.

12. Young to Brocchus, Sept. 19, 1851, in JH, Sept. 19, 1851. Brocchus to Young, Sept. 19, 1851, in *Deseret News*, Oct. 16, 1852.

13. Young to Brocchus, Sept. 30, 1851, in JH, Sept. 30, 1851. Young's purpose in writing this letter is indicated in Bernhisel to Young, May 8, 1852, ibid., May 8, 1852.

14. "Executive Proceedings . . . and Commissions" (above p. 253, n. 22), p. 16; *Cong. Globe*, Jan. 9, 1852. Judge Zerubbabel Snow, the only important federal officer to remain in Utah at this time, later ruled upon the validity of the election and upon Young's official actions in connection with it. He declared that in his opinion the entire procedure had been somewhat irregular but nevertheless had been conducted in accordance with the law. See *Deseret News*, Nov. 29, 1851; Neff, *History of Utah*, p. 192.

15. *Cong. Globe*, Jan. 9, 1852.

16. "Executive Proceedings . . . and Commissions," pp. 25–26. Bancroft, *History of Utah*, p. 457. Harris, *An Unwritten Chapter*, p. 59. JH, Sept. 24, 1851.

17. JH, Sept. 29, 1851.

18. New York *Tribune*, Jan. 26, 1852.

19. *Letter of Judge Brocchus, of Alabama, to the Public, upon the Difficulties in the Territory of Utah* (Washington, D.C., Lemuel Towers, 1852), p. 27.

20. *Cong. Globe*, Jan. 9, 1852.

21. *Deseret News,* April 9, 1856. JH, May 27, 1852. Bernhisel did not always receive the unqualified approval of the Church's Hierarchy, and in 1863 he was abruptly retired to political and social obscurity. For information concerning Bernhisel see Robert H. Sylvester, "Dr. John Milton Bernhisel, Utah's First Delegate to Congress," M.A. thesis, University of Utah, 1947; David M. Bernhisel, "Dr. John Milton Bernhisel," *Utah Genealogical and Historical Magazine,* 3 (1912), 173–77.

22. W. W. Phelps to Kane, June 25, 1852, Yale Collection. JH, May 13, 1852.

23. Bernhisel to Kane, July 17, 1852, Yale Collection. JH, July 17, 1852.

24. Neff, *History of Utah,* p. 175. *Cong. Globe,* Dec. 15, 1851, Jan. 24, May 20, 1852. JH, March 25, 1852.

25. *Cong. Globe,* May 20, 1852.

26. Ibid., Jan. 9, 20, 1852. *Letter of Judge Brocchus,* pp. 4 ff. "Executive Proceedings . . . and Commissions," p. 46. Whittlesey to Stuart, Feb. 27, 1852, in Attorney General's Records, NA. Harris, *An Unwritten Chapter,* p. 82. JH, March 25, 1852.

27. *Cong. Globe,* Jan. 6, 9, 13, 14, 1852. JH, March 25, May 8, 1852. Territorial Papers, Utah Territory, State Department Archives, National Archives. *Letters of Judge Brocchus,* p. 16. Neff, *History of Utah,* p. 176.

28. *Annals of Cleveland,* 35, 473–74. New York *Tribune,* Jan. 6, 26, 1852. *Deseret News,* Dec. 27, 1851.

29. *Missouri Republican,* Nov. 3, 6, 21, 1851, Jan. 20, 1852. JH, Jan. 31, 1852.

30. JH, Dec. 12, 1851, Feb. 20, 29, 1852. Gunnison, *The Mormons,* p. 155.

31. *Letter of Judge Brocchus,* p. 16.

32. Dale L. Morgan's "Administration of Indian Affairs" (above, p. 252, n. 15) is an exhaustive study of this subject.

33. Ibid., pp. 389, 395.

34. Young to Holeman, Aug. 11, 1851, in Office of Indian Affairs (OIA), Utah Superintendency, NA.

35. Holeman to Lea, Sept. 21, Nov. 28, Dec. 28, 1851, Feb. 29, March 29, April 29, Nov. 3, 1852, March 5, 1853; Young to Lea, May 28, Sept. 29, 1852: OIA, NA. Morgan, "Administration of Indian Affairs," pp. 385, 390–93.

36. Bedell to Manypenny, Sept. 30, 1853; Young to Manypenny, March 31, April 29, 1854; Manypenny to McClelland, April 10, 1854: OIA, NA.

37. *Acts and Resolutions of the Legislative Assembly of the Territory of Utah,* 2d Sess. (1852–53), pp. 17, 34. Hockaday to Manypenny, June 17, 1854; Mix to McClelland, Sept. 15, 1854; Fleming to Manypenny, Aug. 15, 1854: in "The Utah Expedition," 35th Cong., 1st Sess., House Exec. Doc. 71 (hereafter cited as "Utah Expedition"), pp. 166–69. Fleming to Mix, Aug. 15, 1854; Mix to McClelland, Sept. 15, 1854: OIA, NA.

38. J. H. Beadle, *Brigham's Destroying Angel* (New York, George Crofutt, 1872), p. 118. Randolph B. Marcy, *Thirty Years of Army Life on the Border* (New York, Harper's, 1866), p. 401. Otis G. Hammond, ed., *The Utah Expedition, 1857–1858. Letters of Capt. Jesse A. Gove,* New Hampshire Historical Society Collections, *12* (Concord, N.H., 1928), 220–21. J. Cecil Alter, *James Bridger: Trapper, Frontiersman, Scout, and Guide* (Salt Lake City, Shepard Book Co., 1925), pp. 244 ff. Andrew Jenson, "History of Fort Bridger and Fort Supply," *Utah Genealogical and Historical Magazine, 4* (1913), 32. New York *Herald,* Nov. 15, 1857. JH, Aug. 31, 1855, Oct. 18, 1858.

39. "Records of the States of the United States of America, Collected and Edited under the Direction of William Sumner Jenkins," Library of Congress Photoduplication Service, 1949.

40. There is disagreement among authorities on Utah's history concerning the spelling of Justice Reed's name. I have adopted the spelling most frequently used.

41. Neff, *History of Utah,* p. 178. *Deseret News,* July 9, 1853, July 4, 1855, March 12, 1856. "Early Records of Utah," p. 71.

42. Edward W. Tullidge, *History of Salt Lake City* (Salt Lake City, Star Printing Co., 1886), p. 96. Stenhouse, *Rocky Mountain Saints,* pp. 279–80. *Deseret News,* July 4, 1855, May 12, 1858.

43. Benjamin G. Ferris, *Utah and the Mormons* (New York, Harper's, 1854), pp. vii, viii, 171 ff. JH, Oct. 29, 1852, Feb. 27, 1853. New York *Times,* May 23, 1857.

44. "Life among the Mormons," *Putnam's Monthly Magazine, 6* (1855), 102 ff.

45. *Cong. Globe,* Jan. 27, 1852, May 4, 10, July 24, 1854, Feb. 19, 1855. JH, Jan. 3, 1853.

46. 34th Cong., 1st and 2d Sess., Sen. Exec. Doc. 1, Vol. 2, Pt. II. Linn, *Story of the Mormons,* p. 467.

47. Averam B. Bender, *The March of Empire. Frontier Defense in the Southwest, 1848–1860* (Lawrence, University of Kansas Press, 1952), p. 176. Nolle Mumey, *J. W. Gunnison,* Denver, Artcraft Press, 1955. Anderson, *Desert Saints,* p. 130. Josiah F. Gibbs, "Gunnison Massacre," *Utah Historical Quarterly, 1* (1928), 67–75. Report of Brigham Young, Nov. 30, 1853, OIA, NA.

48. Drummond to Mrs. John Gunnison, April 27, 1857, in Office of Indian Affairs, NA. *Deseret News,* March 30, 1854.

49. Steptoe to McClelland, April 5, 1855; Steptoe to Manypenny, April 5, 1855: OIA, NA. See also Joseph Holeman to Steptoe, March 28, 1855, Appointment Papers, Department of Justice, NA.

50. Kinney to Caleb Cushing, April 1, 1855, Appointment Papers, Department of Justice, NA.

51. 34th Cong., 1st and 2d Sess., Sen. Exec. Doc. 1, Vol. 2, Pt. II, pp. 157 ff.

52. Neff, *History of Utah,* pp. 180, 183. American Guide Series, *Utah. A Guide to the State,* p. 67. Bernhisel to Pierce, Aug. 8, 1854; Memorial of Utah Legislature to Pierce, Dec. 21, 1854: Applications and Recommendations for Office, 1853–61, Department of State, NA.

53. JH, Dec. 30, 1854.

54. Petition to Pierce, Dec. 30, 1854, Applications and Recommendations for Office, 1853–61, Department of State, NA.

55. Neff, *History of Utah,* pp. 183–84. JH, May 29, 1855. Steptoe to McClelland, April 5, 1855; Steptoe to Manypenny, April 5, 1855: OIA, NA. Steptoe, Hurt, and Kinney to Pierce, April 1, 1855; Kinney, Steptoe, and Hurt to Pierce, April 1, 1855: Appointments and Recommendations, NA.

56. *Deseret News,* Aug. 1, Sept. 19, 1855. The blackmail version of this episode, which states that Young compromised Steptoe with two Mormon women in order to force his endorsement of the petition to

Pierce and the colonel's departure from Utah, lacks substantiation. See Anderson, *Desert Saints*, pp. 147–48. Mrs. C. V. Waite, *The Mormon Prophet and His Harem* (Chicago, J. S. Goodman, 1867), pp. 27–28. Jerry MacMullen, *Paddle-wheel Days* (Stanford, Stanford University Press, 1944), p. 171. See also the cryptic remarks in Sidney Webster to Jesse Gove, n.d., and Webster to Gove, Feb. 26, 1859: Gove MSS, New Hampshire Historical Society Collections, Concord, N.H.

57. 34th Cong., 1st and 2d Sess., Sen. Exec. Doc. 1, Vol. 2, Pt. II, p. 157. Roberts, *Comprehensive History* (see above, p. 254, n. 6), *4*, 260–61. Jules Remy, *A Journey to Great-Salt-Lake City* (2 vols. London, W. Jeffs, 1861), *1*, 478–79. *Deseret News*, Aug. 1, 1855. JH, Oct. 18, 22, 27, Nov. 18, Dec. 27, 1854.

3. The Shadows Lengthen

1. Thomas Hendricks to McClelland, Oct. 17, 1856, enclosing a letter from Burr, Sept. 30, 1855, Letters to the Surveyor General, Utah, General Land Office, Department of the Interior, NA.

2. Craig to Burr, Aug. 1, 1855; Burr to Hendricks, Sept. 20, 1856; Hurt to Young, Oct. 31, 1856: "Utah Expedition," pp. 116–17. Annual Report of Burr, Sept. 30, 1856, 34th Cong., 3d Sess., Sen. Exec. Doc. 5, Vol. 2.

3. Burr to Hendricks, Aug. 30, 1856, Feb. 5, March 28, June 11, 1857, in "Utah Expedition," pp. 118 ff.

4. Landon to Burr, Sept. 18, 1857; Burr to Hendricks, Oct. 19, 1857: "Utah Expedition," pp. 121–23. William Bell to Burr, March 1, 1858, Letters Received, General Land Office, NA. Baltimore *Sun,* June 8, 1857. New York *Times,* Dec. 15, 1857. *National Intelligencer,* Oct. 2, 1857. New York *Tribune,* Jan. 18, 1858.

5. Letter from Charles W. Moeller, June 26, 1857, OIA, NA. Burr to Hendricks, June 24, Aug. 1, 1857; Hockaday, Dotson, and Burr to Hendricks, Aug. 1, 1857; Charles Moeller affidavit, July 9, 1858: Letters Received, General Land Office, NA. Hendricks to Burr, May 21, July 12, July 29, 1857; Hendricks to Jacob Thompson, Feb. 11, 1859: Letters to the Surveyor General, NA. New York *Herald,* June 27, July 27, 30, 1857. *Missouri Republican,* Aug. 27, 1858.

6. Letter from J. M. Elliott, Dec. 20, 1856, OIA, NA. New York *Tribune,* Aug. 9, 1858.

7. *Deseret News,* Feb. 13, Aug. 29, 1855; Hurt to McClelland, Feb. 7, 1855; Manypenny to Hurt, June 20, 1855; Hurt to Young, n.d.; Hurt to Young, Sept., Nov. 29, 1856: OIA, NA. Alban W. Hoopes, *Indian Affairs and Their Administration, with Special Reference to the Far West, 1849–1860* (Philadelphia, University of Pennsylvania Press, 1932), p. 149. Later this policy pursued by Burr and Young was praised highly; see Morgan, "Administration of Indian Affairs," pp. 408–9; *Annals of Cleveland, 43,* 517.

8. Johnson to Wells, Aug. 18, 1857, Adjutant General's Office, Utah National Guard, Salt Lake City.

9. Young to Denver, Oct. 7, 1857, OIA, NA.

10. Young to Hurt, Sept. 26, 1857, in "Early Records of Utah," pp. 15–16. Young's offer of help was farcical, for he and the local officials of the Church, far from wanting to facilitate Hurt's departure, actually intended to arrest him. Young wrote the letter in question only after he had learned of Hurt's flight, in order to provide himself with ammunition in case the agent should later claim to have been persecuted by the Church. He had used the same artifice during his squabble with Brocchus. See Morgan, "Administration of Indian Affairs," pp. 405–6.

11. "Early Records of Utah," p. 18. Johnson to Wells, Oct. 1857, in Adjutant General's Office, Utah National Guard.

12. Hurt to Johnson, Oct. 21, 1857, in "Utah Expedition," pp. 205–8. Johnson to Wells, Oct., 1857, Adjutant General's Office, Utah National Guard.

13. Hurt to Cumming, Dec. 17, 1857, Territorial Papers, Utah Territory, State Department, NA.

14. Hurt to Manypenny, May 2, 1855, Aug. 30, 1856, OIA, NA. See also Hurt to J. M. Elliott, Oct. 1, 1856, ibid.

15. Charles E. Mix to McClelland, July 10, 1855; Mix to Thompson, Aug. 13, 1855: 35th Cong., 1st Sess., Sen. Exec. Doc. 11, Vol. 2, Pt. II, pp. 594–96. Mix to Thompson, Aug. 15, 1855; Manypenny to Hurt, Nov. 14, 1855; Hurt to Manypenny, March 2, 1856, Nov. 20, 1856; Hurt to Denver, July 2, 1857: OIA, NA. Report of Manypenny, Nov. 27, 1856, 34th Cong., 3d Sess., Sen. Exec. Doc. 5, Vol. 2. Morgan, "Administration of Indian Affairs," pp. 394, 398, 400.

16. Hurt to Manypenny, May 2, 1855, OIA, NA.

17. "Early Records of Utah," p. 21; *Deseret News*, May 30, Sept. 12, 1855, July 16, 1856. JH, June 2, 1856. Roberts, *Comprehensive History*, 4, 208. Neff, *History of Utah*, pp. 328 ff.

18. Beadle, *Brigham's Destroying Angel*, pp. 113-17. Neff, *History of Utah*, p. 331. JH, March 1, 1857.

19. JH, Aug. 29, 1857. See also Neff, *History of Utah*, pp. 328-32; Tullidge, *Salt Lake City*, pp. 150 ff.; *Deseret News*, Feb. 6, 1856, April 1, 1857.

20. *Deseret News*, Aug. 5, 1857.

21. JH, May 22, 1857.

22. Memo from Elisha Whittlesey, Oct. 21, 1856; draft of letter to Heywood, July 12, 1856: Attorney General's Records, 1789-1870, NA. Hooper to James Guthrie, Jan. 7, 1857; Whittlesey to Cass, March 21, 1857: Territorial Papers, NA. Secretary of the Treasury to William Medill, May 21, 1857, Utah Department of State Archives. Edward W. Tullidge, *Life of Brigham Young* (New York, 1876), supplement, pp. 25 ff. "Hon. W. H. Hooper," *Tullidge's Quarterly Magazine*, 2 (1883), 662-64.

23. Young to Kane, Jan. 7, 1857, Yale Collection.

24. More recently the term has been applied to apostates.

25. Andrew Hopkins to Black, April 26, 1856, Black MSS. Waite, *The Mormon Prophet and His Harem*, p. 38. Bancroft, *History of Utah*, p. 489. Linn, *Story of the Mormons*, pp. 467, 469.

26. JH, June 21, 1858. Kinney to Cushing, March 1, 1855; Kinney, Drummond, Bell, Burr, and Hurt to Cushing, n.d.; Kinney to Black, n.d.: Appointment Papers, Department of Justice, NA.

27. *Millennial Star*, May 23, 1857.

28. W. I. Appleby to John Taylor, April 25, 1857, Black MSS.

29. JH, Jan. 18, 20, May 25, 1865, May 29, 1875, Jan. 29, 1881, July 10, 1885.

30. See, for example, San Joaquin *Republican*, June 18, 1857; Neff, *History of Utah*, p. 447. It is perhaps worthy of note that Joseph Smith, to advance the interests of his Church, once embraced Dr. John Cook Bennett, whose odious character was in many ways similar to that of Drummond; see Fawn M. Brodie, *No Man Knows My History. The*

Life of Joseph Smith, the Mormon Prophet (New York, Knopf, 1946), pp. 266 ff.

31. Remy, *Journey to Great-Salt-Lake City, 1,* 468–69. "Diary of Hosea Stout," 7, 245. Young to Kane, Jan. 31, 1857, Yale Collection. G. A. Smith to Taylor, April 14, 16, 1857, Black MSS. *Deseret News,* May 20, 1857, Jan. 27, 1858. JH, Jan. 31, 1857.

32. Kinney to Cushing, n.d., Appointment Papers, Department of Justice, NA.

33. Linn, *Story of the Mormons,* p. 469.

34. Roberts, *Comprehensive History, 4,* 202. Tullidge, *Salt Lake City,* pp. 142–43. "Records of the Proceedings of the Supreme Court," Jan. 1856–March 1857, Territorial Papers, NA. "Diary of Hosea Stout," 6, 194. American Guide Series, *Utah. A Guide to the State,* p. 69. Bancroft, *History of Utah,* p. 490.

35. Kinney, Drummond, Bell, Burr, and Hurt to Cushing, n.d., Appointment Papers, Department of Justice, NA. Drummond, Hurt, and Burr to Pierce, March 1, 1856; Drummond to Whittlesey, April 1, 1856: Attorney General's Records, 1789–1870, NA.

36. "Utah Expedition," pp. 212–14. Tullidge, *Salt Lake City,* pp. 131–32. For rebuttals to Drummond's charges see Tullidge, pp. 135–36; Curtis E. Bolton to Black, June 26, 1857, in "Utah Expedition," pp. 214–15; and JH, April 15, 1857.

37. Roberts, *Comprehensive History, 4,* 199. Bancroft, *History of Utah,* p. 488.

38. Stenhouse, *Rocky Mountain Saints,* p. 282. Bancroft, *History of Utah,* pp. 486–89.

39. Bancroft, *History of Utah,* pp. 486–89. Roberts, *Comprehensive History, 4,* 198 n., 199 n. Stenhouse, *Rocky Mountain Saints,* p. 283 n.

40. Hurt to Cumming, Dec. 17, 1859, Territorial Papers, NA. "Diary of Hosea Stout," 7, 279. For a sketch of Williams see Dale L. Morgan, *The Great Salt Lake* (New York, Bobbs-Merrill, 1947), pp. 263–66.

41. Forney to Black, June 12, 1858, Black MSS. JH, April 19, 1858.

42. New York *Times,* Aug. 13, 1858. New York *Tribune,* Aug. 2, 1858. *Valley Tan,* Nov. 19, 1858.

43. Letters and affidavits in "Early Records of Utah." Letter from John Hartnett, Oct. 22, 1858, Utah Department of State Archives.

Bolton to Black, June 26, 1857, in "Utah Expedition," pp. 214–15.
Cumming to Cass, Oct. 22, 1858, Territorial Papers, NA.

44. The importance of the episode in Buchanan's decision to send
the army to Utah is seen by the fact that when he at last pardoned the
Mormons in 1858 the President listed as one of their flagrant offenses
the destruction or theft of Stiles' records. See John Bassett Moore, *The
Works of James Buchanan* (12 vols. Philadelphia, Lippincott, 1910),
10, 202 ff.

45. New York *Times*, April 21, May 26, June 9, 25, Aug. 24, 1857.
National Intelligencer, April 20, 1857. *United States Magazine, 4*,
June 1857. *Valley Tan*, Nov. 19, 1858.

46. New York *Herald*, Aug. 1, 1857. New York *Times*, Sept. 12,
1857. JH, May 30, June 13, 1857. New York *Tribune*, June 10, 1857.

47. New York *Tribune*, April 13, 1857. *National Intelligencer*, April
14, 1857. New York *Times*, April 14, 21, June 8, July 2, 1857. *Harper's
Magazine, 15* (Oct. 1857), 116.

48. New York *Times*, March 30, May 11, June 3, June 8, 1857. Washington *Union*, April 8, June 9, 1857. *National Intelligencer*, June 6,
1857.

49. (San Francisco) *Daily Alta California*, May 17, 1857.

50. Young to Kane, Jan. 31, June 27, 1857, Yale Collection. See also
addresses in *Journal of Discourses* (above, p. 253, n. 21), *4*, 259, 347, and
5, 5, 10. *Deseret News*, July 8, 15, 29, 1857.

4. Causes of the War

1. "Utah Expedition," pp. 1–2.

2. The Washington *Union*, the Administration's organ, made only
minor references to the Mormon problem until June 9, 1857.

3. Kane to Black, March 21, 1857, in Black MSS. New York *Times*,
April 25, 1857.

4. Memo, Scott to Floyd, May 26, 1857, Department of War, *Correspondence of the Secretary of War*, 1857. Scott's circular, May 28,
1857, in "Utah Expedition," pp. 4–5. General Orders No. 8, in *The
Utah War—General Orders for Troop Movements—1856–1858*, Pam-
phlets, Yale Collection.

5. Like many anti-Mormons in these years, Magraw possessed an unenviable character. After the mail contract had been taken from him, he became superintendent of a crew constructing a federal road across the Plains, and while serving in that capacity he was guilty of shady practices, if not outright theft of government property. See F. W. Lander to Black, Sept. 7, 1857, Frederick W. Lander MSS, Library of Congress; E. G. Rehrer to Black, Sept. 7, 1857, Black MSS; John Wolcott Phelps Diary, MSS, New York Public Library (cited as Phelps, Diary), Vol. 16, entry dated Sept. 3, 1857.

6. "Utah Expedition," pp. 2-3. In further proof, the newspapers shortly after that date began to refer to the expedition as definitely arranged. See, for example, New York *Times*, May 21, 1857; Baltimore *Sun*, May 21, 1857.

7. See Buchanan's first sentence in his section dealing with Utah and the theocratic system of government there: Moore, *Buchanan, 10,* 152.

8. Hendricks to Burr, July 13, 29, 1857, Letters to the Surveyor General, NA. Eugene B. Burr to Black, May 2, 1857, Black MSS.

9. Mix to Thompson, Feb. 22, 1858, OIA, NA.

10. It is true that Denver, not Mix, was Commissioner of Indian Affairs in 1857. But Mix had served for some time in that office and thus would have been familiar with these dispatches if Denver had worked with them. Furthermore, Thompson, if he had known of the letters, would have directed Mix to them.

11. Tullidge, *History of Salt Lake City,* p. 152. "Utah Expedition," p. 192. See above, p. 207, n. 37.

12. Kinney to Pierce, Oct. 1, 1854, Appointments and Recommendations, NA. Kinney to Cushing, March 1, April 1, 1855; Kinney, Drummond, and others to Cushing, n.d.; Kinney to Cushing, n.d.; Kinney to Black n.d.; Kinney to Black, March 20, 1857: Appointment Papers, Department of Justice, NA.

13. New York *Tribune,* May 18, June 11, 1857. Drummond to Black, April 18, 1857; Stiles to Black, May 15, 1859: Black MSS.

14. Lay to Harney, June 29, 1857, in "Utah Expedition," pp. 7-9. Cass to Cumming, July 30, 1857, Utah Affairs, Territorial Papers, Utah Territory, Vol. 1, NA. Black to "Gentlemen," Sept. 25, 1857, Black MSS. Moore, *Buchanan, 10,* 152, 202 ff. 35th Cong., 1st Sess., House Exec. Doc. 2, Vol. 2, Pt. II, pp. 6-9. Washington *Union,* April 25, June 10, 1857. New York *Herald,* June 25, 1857.

15. May 9, 1858.

16. New York *Herald*, June 5, 1857.

17. Hurt to Elliott, Oct. 1, 1856, OIA, NA. Drummond to Black, April 18, 1857, Black MSS. New York *Times*, June 9, 1857. New York *Tribune*, May 18, 1857. San Francisco *Evening Bulletin*, May 21, 1857. *Daily Alta California*, April 23, 1857. New York *Herald*, May 17, 1857. San Joaquin *Republican*, July 15, 1857. *National Intelligencer*, July 13, 1857. Baltimore *Sun*, June 7, 1857. *Annals of Cleveland, 40*, 364.

18. Moore, *Buchanan, 10*, 6–9. Yet it must also be noted that the War Department advised Harney, who was at first put in command of the expedition, to "anticipate resistance, general, organized, and formidable," from the Mormons: see Lay to Harney, June 29, 1857, in "Utah Expedition," pp. 7–9. See also Washington *Union*, April 8, 1858.

19. 35th Cong., 2d Sess., House Exec. Doc. 2, Vol. 2, Pt. II, p. 165.

20. Lay to Harney, June 29, 1857, in "Utah Expedition," pp. 7–9.

21. See the description of Van Vliet's mission, below, pp. 106–7. Even if the Church had been prepared to share the Valley's food with the army, because of recent crop failures there would have been pitifully few supplies available.

22. JH, April 15, 1857.

23. St. Louis *Intelligencer*, Nov. 23, 1857. New York *Evening Post*, June 17, 1858. *Deseret News*, Aug. 4, 1858.

24. George W. Fuller, *A History of the Pacific Northwest* (New York, Knopf, 1946), p. 172.

25. E. Cecil McGavin, *U. S. Soldiers Invade Utah* (Boston, Meador Publishing Co., 1937), p. 53. Jones, *Forty Years among the Indians*, p. 128.

26. Stenhouse, *Rocky Mountain Saints*, p. 346 n. John Cleveland Robinson, "The Utah Expedition," *Magazine of American History* (1884), p. 340. Mabel Harmer, *The Story of the Mormon Pioneers* (Salt Lake City, Deseret News Press, 1943), p. 262. Lurton D. Ingersoll, *A History of the War Department of the United States* (Washington, Francis B. Mohun, 1879), pp. 326–27.

27. "Vaux," "The Echo Canyon War," *Contributor, 3* (1882), 51.

28. George T. Curtis, *Life of James Buchanan* (New York, Harper's, 1883), pp. 411 ff.; A. Howard Meneely, *The War Department* (New York, Columbia University Press, 1928), pp. 42–43. "John B. Floyd," *DAB*. 36th Cong., 2d Sess., House Report No. 85, Vol. 2. It is possible that Senator James Mason of Virginia entertained the idea of distributing federal arms to Southern states in preparation for secession as early as 1856: see Meneely, *War Department,* p. 28.

29. Robert M. Hughes, "A Vindication of John B. Floyd," *William and Mary Quarterly,* 5 (1925), 280–81.

30. *Annals of Cleveland, 40,* 578. Crescent City (Iowa) *Oracle,* June 25, 1858. *Deseret News,* July 29, 1857, Oct. 6, 13, 1858. *National Intelligencer,* April 6, 1858.

31. Roberts, *Comprehensive History, 4,* 402. McGavin, *U. S. Soldiers Invade Utah,* pp. 48–49. Stenhouse, *Rocky Mountain Saints,* p. 381.

32. *Memoirs of Lieut.-General Scott, LL.D. Written by Himself* (2 vols. New York, Sheldon, 1864), *2,* 604. See also Marcus J. Wright, *General Scott* (New York, Appleton, 1894), p. 294.

33. Roy F. Nichols, *The Disruption of American Democracy* (New York, Macmillan, 1948), p. 179.

34. St. Louis *Democrat,* Aug. 24, 1858, quoted in *Deseret News,* Oct. 20, 1858. See also *Annals of Cleveland, 40,* 579, *41,* 560; "The Utah War: Its Causes and Consequences," *Atlantic Monthly, 3* (April 1859), 478.

35. *Memoirs of Lieut.-General Scott, 2,* 604.

36. *A Brief Statement of the Claims of Majors and Russell; Also the Evidence upon Which It Rests* (n.d., Yale Collection), p. 2. Raymond W. Settle and Mary L. Settle, *Empire on Wheels* (Stanford, Stanford University Press, 1949), p. 17. For a copy of the contract see 35th Cong., 1st Sess., Sen. Exec. Doc. 31, Vol. 7.

37. 36th Cong., 2d Sess., House Report No. 78. J. S. Black and James O. Broadhead, *Letter to the Secretary of War upon the Legal Liability of the Government to Meet Certain Acceptances of the Late Secretary Floyd* (Washington, Scammell, 1862), pp. 4–5. *Court of Claims, United States,* Jan. 1866. Thomas W. Peirce v. the United States, p. 37. *The Acceptances of the War Department, Given in Favor of Russell, Majors, and Waddell. Statement of Ex-Secretary*

Floyd (Washington, Lemuel Towers, 1861), pp. 4–5, 8. Curtis, *Buchanan*, pp. 407 ff. Robert M. Hughes, "Floyd's Resignation from Buchanan's Cabinet," *Tyler's Quarterly Historic and Genealogical Magazine, 5* (Oct. 1923), 1–3. "John B. Floyd," *DAB.* "Jacob Thompson," *DAB.*

38. Philip G. Auchampaugh, *Robert Tyler, Southern Rights Champion* (Duluth, Himan Stein, 1934), p. 180.

39. George F. Milton, *The Eve of Conflict. Stephen A. Douglas and the Needless War* (New York, 1934), p. 178. *Speech of the Hon. Abraham Lincoln, in Reply to Judge Douglas, Delivered in Representatives' Hall, Springfield, Illinois, June 26, 1857* (pamphlet, Rare Book Room, Library of Congress). Washington *Union,* May 15, 1857, Jan. 20, 23, April 24, 1858.

40. "Memorial and Resolutions to the President of the United States Concerning Certain Officers of the Territory of Utah," Appointments and Recommendations, NA.

41. Phelps, Diary, *15,* entry of June 15, 1857. M. Hamlin Cannon, "The Mormon War: A Study in Territorial Rebellion" (M.A. thesis, George Washington University, 1938), p. 12. *Deseret News,* March 16, 1854, Nov. 28, 1855.

42. Stenhouse, *Rocky Mountain Saints,* pp. 286–88. See also JH, Aug. 15, 1857. Kimball Young, *Isn't One Wife Enough?* (New York, Holt, 1954), p. 292, maintains that such aggressive condemnation of their enemies might have been caused by the Mormons' feelings of guilt over their practice of polygamy.

43. G. A. Smith to Kane, Jan. 14, 1859; Taylor to Cannon, Jan. 12, 1859: Yale Collection. JH, Jan. 1, 1859.

44. I. McGee Van Dusen and Maria Van Dusen, *Startling Disclosures of the Great Mormon Conspiracy* (New York, 1849), p. 5; Nelson W. Green, *Fifteen Years among the Mormons* (New York, H. Dayton, 1857), p. v.

45. (New Orleans) *Louisiana Courier,* March 27, 1858. New York *Times,* July 3, 1857. New York *Tribune,* Jan. 6, 1857.

46. Quoted in Roberts, *Comprehensive History, 4,* 408.

47. (San Francisco) *Evening Bulletin,* Aug. 28, 1857. New York *Times,* April 21, 1857.

48. Cornelius Conway, *The Utah Expedition, Containing a General Account of the Mormon Campaign* (Cincinnati, Safety Fund Reporter Office, 1858), p. 3.

49. Grant, *Truth for the Mormons*, p. 6.

50. *Daily Alta California*, May 11, 1858.

51. For instance, O. S. Belisle, *The Prophets: or, Mormonism Unveiled* (Philadelphia, William Smith, 1855), which reveals that the author had at best a rudimentary knowledge of his subject.

52. Mrs. B. G. Ferris, *The Mormons at Home*, New York, Dix and Edwards, 1856.

53. New York *Herald*, May 22, 1857.

54. *Mormonism Unvailed* [sic], Eber D. Howe, 1834.

55. New York *Tribune*, May 28, 1857. (Leavenworth) *Kansas Weekly Herald*, Dec. 20, 1856, Aug. 22, 1857. New York *Tribune*, May 22, Sept. 10, 1857. *Jefferson* (City) *Examiner*, Aug. 15, 1857. Baltimore *Sun*, Aug. 22, 1857. *Daily Alta California*, April 11, 17, 1857.

56. *National Intelligencer*, July 31, 1857. St. Louis *Leader*, Aug. 8, 1857.

57. New York *Times*, April 21, 1857. *Daily Alta California*, May 21, 1857. *National Intelligencer*, April 20, 29, 1857.

58. *Isn't One Wife Enough?*—a thorough study of all aspects of polygamy.

59. John Hyde, *Mormonism: Its Leaders and Designs* (New York, Fetridge, 1857), pp. 34, 151. New York *Tribune*, Feb. 13, 1857. New York *Times*, April 22, July 18, 1857. New York *Herald*, May 24, 1857.

60. New York *Times*, March 30, 1857. *National Intelligencer*, April 20, 1857. *Daily Alta California*, June 18, 1857.

61. Maria Ward, *Female Life among the Mormons*, New York, J. C. Derby, 1855; Austin N. Ward, *Male Life among the Mormons*, (New York, J. C. Derby, 1859).

62. Green, *Fifteen Years among the Mormons*, p. 50.

63. San Joaquin *Republican*, May 22, 1857.

64. *Cong. Globe,* Jan. 22, May 20, 1852, May 4, 5, 10, 14, 1854, Dec. 21, 1857.

65. Hyde, *Mormonism,* p. 51. See also New York *Times,* April 16, 1857.

66. Hurt to Manypenny, May 2, 1855, in "Utah Expedition," pp. 176 ff. New York *Times,* April 21, 22, June 23, 1857. *Daily Alta California,* Dec. 10, 1858. *Deseret News,* March 16, 1854.

67. Neff, *History of Utah,* p. 100. Charles Ellis, *Utah, 1847–1870* (Salt Lake City, 1891), p. 4. Creer, *Utah and the Nation,* pp. 46, 64. Roberts, *Comprehensive History, 3,* 414.

68. Romney, *Story of Deseret,* p. 100.

69. Law passed Jan. 21, 1858, in *Acts and Resolutions of the Legislative Assembly of the Territory of Utah,* 7th Sess. (1857–58). Leonard J. Arrington, "Mormon Finance and the Utah War," *Utah Historical Quarterly,* 20 (1952), 233.

70. Hamilton Gardner, *History of Lehi, Including a Biographical Section* (Salt Lake City, Deseret News Press, 1913), p. 124. Jensen, *Mormon Theory,* pp. 4–5. Roberts, *Comprehensive History, 3,* 493–97. *Deseret News,* July 13, 1854. JH, July 4, 1857.

71. "Remarks" by Young, in *Deseret News,* Nov. 18, 1857. This statement repeated what Young had said on July 8, 1855: see *Deseret News,* Aug. 1, 1855. For similar expressions of loyalty see speech by Wells, July 24, 1857, in Bryant S. Hinckley, *David Hanmer Wells and Events of His Time* (Salt Lake City, Deseret News Press, 1942), p. 143; "Discourse" by Young of Feb. 18, 1855, in *Deseret News,* March 1, 1855; Bernhisel to editor of *United States,* Nov. 12, 1852, in *Deseret News,* May 3, 1853; *Journal of Discourses, 4,* 347; JH, April 30, 1852.

72. March 30, 1857.

73. *Annals of Cleveland, 38,* 78.

74. April 21, 1857.

75. San Joaquin *Republican,* June 16, 1857. *National Intelligencer,* April 20, 1857. New York *Times,* April 21, 1857. *United States Magazine, 4,* June 1857. Neff, *History of Utah,* p. 369, cautiously puts the Indian population of the Territory during this decade at about 12,000.

76. *Daily Alta California,* Oct. 18, 1857. *National Intelligencer,* Nov. 21, 1857.

77. New York *Herald,* April 11, 1857. New York *Times,* April 16, June 11, 23, 1857. New York *Tribune,* May 21, 1857. *Daily Alta California,* July 15, 1857. Washington *Union,* Jan. 20, 1858. See also Green, *Fifteen Years among the Mormons,* p. 162. There is no doubt that the Mormon Church founded the Danites in the 1830's as a defensive arm. Whether the organization functioned in Utah, and, if so, what it did there, are questions which cannot be satisfactorily answered now. See Linn, *Story of the Mormons,* pp. 189 ff.; Bancroft, *Utah,* p. 124; Brodie, *No Man Knows My History,* pp. 213–16; Green, *Fifteen Years among the Mormons,* p. 162; New York *Herald,* April 11, 1857; New York *Times,* April 16, June 11, 23, 1857; New York *Tribune,* May 21, 1857; *Daily Alta California,* July 15, 1857.

78. Juanita Brooks, *The Mountain Meadows Massacre* (Stanford, Stanford University Press, 1950), is an excellent investigation of this tragedy. An extensive literature dealing with the massacre exists, but it must be read with an eye to bias. See *History of the Mountain Meadows Massacre,* San Francisco, Pacific Art Co., 1877; Charles Penrose, *The Mountain Meadows Massacre,* Salt Lake City, 1884; John W. Clampitt, *Echoes from the Rocky Mountains,* Belford, Clarke, 1888; Josiah F. Gibbs, *The Mountain Meadows Massacre,* Salt Lake City, 1910; Hoffman Birney, *Zealots of Zion,* Philadelphia, Pennsylvania Publishing Co., 1931; Robert G. Cleland and Juanita Brooks, eds., *A Mountain Chronicle, The Diaries of John D. Lee, 1848–1876,* 2 vols. San Marino, Huntington Library, 1955.

79. Stenhouse, *Rocky Mountain Saints,* pp. 462 ff. Beadle, *Life in Utah,* p. 178. "Journal of Captain Albert Tracy," *Utah Historical Quarterly, 13* (1945), 43 n. John Cradlebaugh, *Utah and the Mormons. Speech of the Hon. John Cradlebaugh, of Nevada, on the Admission of Utah as a State* (pamphlet, 1863), appendix. *Valley Tan,* April 5, 12, Aug. 24, 1859.

80. *National Intelligencer,* May 20, 1857. Baltimore *Sun,* May 21, 1857. Washington *Union,* June 9, 1857. New York *Tribune,* Feb. 13, March 23, May 18, 21, 1857. New York *Times,* April 21, July 2, 1857.

81. See missionaries' reports as recorded in JH, Jan. 22, Feb. 27, March 2, April 13, Aug. 12, 15, 18, 1855, Jan. 23, June 20, July 9, 15, 1857.

82. Frank Esshom, *Pioneers and Prominent Men of Utah,* Salt

Lake City, Utah Pioneers Book Publishing Co., 1913. Romney, *Story of Deseret*, p. 140. But also note comments in Brodie, *No Man Knows My History*, pp. 202-3.

83. Werner, *Brigham Young*, p. 406. (Van Buren) *Arkansas Intelligencer*, May 15, 22, 1857. San Francisco *Evening Bulletin*, July 1, 1857.

84. *Daily Alta California*, July 9, 1857. New York *Times*, many references during the first two weeks of June 1857. *Arkansas Intelligencer*, May 16, 1857. Chicago *Weekly Ledger*, June 13, 1857, copied in JH, May 13, 1857.

85. *Arkansas Intelligencer*, May 15, 1857.

86. *Evening Bulletin*, July 18, 1857. See also *Arkansas Intelligencer*, May 22, 1857.

87. New York *Times*, March 30, April 21, 23, May 11, 13, June 4, 23, 1857, Jan. 28, 1858. Baltimore *Sun*, May 19, 29, 1857. *National Intelligencer*, April 20, 21, 1857. *Daily Alta California*, May 21, June 8, 1857. *Arkansas Intelligencer*, May 22, 1857. New York *Herald*, June 11, 1857. *Annals of Cleveland, 40*, 359. *United States Magazine, 4*, June 1857. New York *Tribune*, June 10, July 25, 1857. Crescent City *Oracle*, July 31, 1857.

88. Edmund T. Olson, *Utah: A Romance in Pioneer Days* (Salt Lake City, privately printed, 1931), p. 334. Roberts, *Comprehensive History, 3*, 508-9.

89. *Deseret News*, July 27, 1850, Aug. 7, 1852, Jan. 12, 1854, April 16, Nov. 19, 1856. See also JH, Jan. 10, Feb. 22, March 15, 1857.

90. Neff, *History of Utah*, p. 414.

91. "Diary of John D. T. McAllister" (typescript, Brigham Young University), pp. 101, 103, 106, 117.

92. "Discourse" by Kimball, in *Deseret News*, Dec. 5, 1855. See also "Discourses" by Young of April 6, June 17, 1855, in *Deseret News*, April 25, July 18, 1855; "Remarks" by G. A. Smith of Aug. 5, 1855, in *Deseret News*, Aug. 22, 1855; "Sermon" by Orson Hyde, n.d., in *Deseret News*, March 18, 1857.

93. M. R. Werner, "Brigham Young," *Ladies' Home Journal, 42* (June 1925), 36. Linn, *Story of the Mormons*, p. 441. Werner, *Brigham Young* (above, p. 252, n. 12), pp. 398 ff.

94. "Address" of July 13, 1855, in *Deseret News*, Oct. 24, 1855.
See also "Discourse" by Young of Oct. 8, 1855, in *Deseret News*,
Nov. 28, 1855; "Remarks" by Grant of March 2, 1856, in *Deseret
News*, March 12, 1856.

95. *Deseret News*, Sept. 24, Oct. 1, 8, 22, 29, Nov. 5, 12, 1856.

96. Bancroft, *History of Utah*, p. 540. Linn, *Story of the Mormons*,
p. 445. Neff, *History of Utah*, pp. 549–53. *Millennial Star*, Feb. 14,
1857. St. Louis *Leader*, March 7, 1857.

97. "Remarks" of March 2, 1856, in *Deseret News*, March 12,
1856. For similar statements see Grant's speech in *Deseret News*, Nov.
12, 1856; "Remarks" by Young of Nov. 2, 1856, in *Deseret News*,
Nov. 12, 1856.

98. "Discourses" by Young of Sept. 21, 1856, Feb. 8, 1857, in
Deseret News, Oct. 1, 1856, Feb. 18, 1857; "Remarks" by Grant of
Sept. 21, 1856, in *Deseret News*, Oct. 1, 1856. Note also that the
addresses of the Hierarchy were at times edited before they were
published: *Deseret News*, Aug. 12, 1857, quoted in Cannon, "The
Mormon War" (above, n. 41), p. 18.

99. Brooks, *Mountain Meadows Massacre*, pp. 292 ff.

100. March 2, 1856, in *Deseret News*, March 12, 1856.

101. Brooks, *Mountain Meadows Massacre*, p. 8. Neff, *History
of Utah*, p. 552. Stenhouse, *Rocky Mountain Saints*, pp. 292 ff.

5. An Unheroic Anabasis

1. U. S. Department of War, *Correspondence of the Secretary of
War*, 1857. See the President's later comment on Scott's position, in
Mr. Buchanan's Administration on the Eve of the Rebellion (New
York, Appleton, 1865), p. 239.

2. Hammond, *Utah Expedition*, p. 7.

3. Nichols, *Disruption of American Democracy*, p. 101. Washington
Union, April 25, 1857. New York *Times*, April 28, May 21, 22, June
6, 9, 22, 27, 1857. New York *Herald*, May 3, 8, June 6, 1857.
Baltimore *Sun*, May 21, 1857. Phelps, Diary, *15*, entry dated July
5, 1857. Cass to Cumming, July 13, 1857, Domestic Letters, Records
of the Department of State, NA.

4. A. B. Norris to Black, Aug. 7, 1857, Black MSS. Washington *Union*, July 8, 1857. New York *Times*, June 20, 1857. As in the case of Associate Justice Reed, there is disagreement over the spelling of Eckels' name. Neff and a number of authorities have given it as "Eckles." I have used the other form, since it appears more frequently in the writings of the time; furthermore, the Judge himself seems to have used it when he signed legal papers: see *Deseret News*, Oct. 19, 1859.

5. O'Neill to Black, Aug. 19, 1857; O'Neill to Black, n.d.; W. H. Witte to Black, Aug. 27, 1857; O'Neill to Black, n.d.; David Lynch to O'Neill, Sept. 10, 1857; Lynch to Black, Dec. 1, 1857; O'Neill to Black, Feb. 8, 1858: Black MSS.

6. William Stokes to Black, April 17, 1857; John Dawson to Black, May 2, 1857; Forney to Black, Aug. 17, 28, 30, 1857, March 9, 1858; James Myers to Black, Sept. 1, 1858: Black MSS.

7. Cass' instructions to Cumming, July 30, 1857, in "Utah Affairs," Territorial Papers, Utah Territory, Vol. 1, NA.

8. Lay to Harney, June 29, 1857, in "Utah Expedition," pp. 7–9.

9. General Orders, Nos. 8, 12, in *The Utah War—General Orders* (above, p. 263, n. 4). McDowell to Harney, June 29, 1857, in "Utah Expedition," p. 5. Phelps, Diary, *15*, entry dated June 23, 1857.

10. Pleasanton to Smith, Aug. 18, 1857, Letters Sent, Department of Utah, Vol. 1, NA. New York *Herald*, Aug. 27, 1857.

11. Robinson, "The Utah Expedition" (above, p. 265, n. 26), p. 336. William A. Ganoe, *The History of the United States Army* (New York, Appleton-Century, 1942), p. 240.

12. McDowell to Harney, June 29, 1857; McDowell to Crossman, June 29, 1857: "Utah Expedition," pp. 5–6. General Order No. 12, June 30, 1857, in *The Utah War—General Orders*. New York *Times*, July 8, 1857.

13. *National Intelligencer*, June 26, 1857.

14. Phelps, Diary, *15*, entry dated June 27, 1857. Hammond, *Utah Expedition*, p. 6. Francis B. Heitman, *Historical Register and Dictionary of the United States Army* (Washington, 1903), p. 156. Bancroft, *History of Utah*, p. 514.

15. General Order No. 5, July 19, 1857, Records of the War Department, RG 94, Records of the Adjutant General's Office, NA.

Robinson, "The Utah Expedition," p. 336. Phelps, Diary, *15*, entries dated July 10, 18, 1857. One newspaper reported that one-third of the Fifth Infantry had deserted and the result was "all but total annihilation of an entire regiment": New York *Times*, Sept. 2, 1857.

16. Harney to A.A.G., July 18, 1857, Letters Sent, Department of Utah, Vol. 1. NA.

17. *Mr. Buchanan's Administration*, p. 234. For another version of Harney's recall see William P. Johnston, *The Life of Albert Sidney Johnston* (New York, Appleton, 1878), p. 210.

18. McDowell to Johnston, Aug. 28, 1857, in "Utah Expedition," p. 13; General Order No. 12, Aug. 29, 1857, in *The Utah War— General Orders*.

19. General Order No. 8, Sept. 11, 1857, in Records of the War Department, RG 94, NA.

20. General Order No. 3, Jan. 7, 1858, ibid. Phelps, Diary, *15*, entry dated July 26, 1857, and *17*, entry dated Oct. 8, 1857. Hammond, *Utah Expedition*, pp. 18–19. Alexander to Cooper, Aug. 10, 1857, in "Utah Expedition," pp. 18–19.

21. W. Eugene Hollon, *Beyond the Cross Timbers. The Travels of Randolph B. Marcy, 1812–1887* (Norman, University of Oklahoma Press, 1955), p. 209. Conway, *The Utah Expedition*, p. 6. St. Louis *Leader*, Oct. 17, 1857. Phelps, Diary, *15*, entry dated Aug. 7, 1857. Theodore F. Rodenbough, *From Everglade to Cañon with the Second Dragoons* (New York, Van Nostrand, 1875), p. 209.

22. Phelps, Diary, *15*, entry dated Aug. 17, 1857. Hammond, *Utah Expedition*, p. 45. New York *Tribune*, Sept. 10, 1857. Alexander to Cooper, Sept. 3, 1857, in "Utah Expedition," pp. 19–20.

23. Alexander to Cooper, Sept. 3, 1857, in "Utah Expedition," pp. 19–20.

24. Hammond, *Utah Expedition*, pp. 13, 56, 58–59, 62, 64–65.

25. Alexander to Phelps, Sept. 22, 1857; Maynadier to Phelps, Sept. 25, 1857: John W. Phelps MSS, Yale Collection.

26. Cooper to Harney, July 21, 1857, in "Utah Expedition," p. 11. Van Vliet to Dickerson, July 27, 1857, Letters Sent, Department of Utah, Vol. 1, NA. Harney to Van Vliet, July 28, 1857; Pleasanton to Van Vliet, Aug. 16, 1857: 35th Cong., 1st Sess., House Exec. Doc. 2, Vol. 2, Pt. II.

27. Van Vliet to Young, Sept. 10, 1857; Young to Van Vliet, Sept. 11, 1857: 35th Cong., 1st Sess., House Exec. Doc. 2, Vol. 2, Pt. II, pp. 35–36. "Diary of John D. T. McAllister," p. 123. JH, Sept. 9, 1857. *Journal of Discourses, 5,* 227. "Early Records of Utah," p. 19. *Deseret News,* Sept. 16, 1857.

28. Van Vliet to Pleasanton, Sept. 16, 1857, in "Utah Expedition," pp. 25–26. Van Vliet to Floyd, Nov. 20, 1857, 35th Cong., 1st Sess., House Exec. Doc. 2, Vol. 2, Pt. II, p. 37. Brooks, *Mountain Meadows Massacre,* p. 103. "Early Records of Utah," pp. 11–12.

29. Hammond, *Utah Expedition,* p. 59.

30. Ibid., pp. 59–67. Phelps, Diary, *15,* entries dated July 21–Sept. 29, 1857.

31. Proclamation dated Sept. 15, 1857, in "Utah Expedition," pp. 34–35.

32. Young, "To the officer commanding the forces invading Utah Territory," Sept. 29, 1857, ibid., p. 33.

33. Alexander to Young, Oct. 12, 1857, ibid., pp. 83–85.

34. Young to Alexander, Oct. 14, 1857, ibid., pp. 48–50.

35. Young to Alexander, Oct. 16, 1857, ibid., pp. 50–54.

36. Alexander to Young, Oct. 18, 1857, Oct. 19, 1857; Taylor to Marcy, Oct. 21, 1857; Young to Alexander, Oct. 28, 1857; Alexander to Young, Nov. 1, 1857: ibid., pp. 54–62, 85.

37. Maynadier to "Colonel," Oct. 2, 1857, ibid., p. 79. See also Hammond, *Utah Expedition,* pp. 70–71.

38. Linn, *Story of the Mormons,* p. 490. Settle and Settle, *Empire on Wheels,* pp. 19–20. Johnston, *Life of Johnston,* p. 211. Hammond, *Utah Expedition,* p. 74. "The Utah Expedition," *Atlantic Monthly, 3* (March 1859), p. 372. New York *Tribune,* Jan. 18, 1858.

39. *A Brief Statement of the Claims of Majors and Russell,* pp. 2, 4, 6–8, 10, 19–24. William Clark, "A Trip across the Plains in 1857," *Iowa Journal of History and Politics, 20* (1922), 191–93.

40. *A Brief Statement of the Claims of Majors and Russell,* pp. 5, 12–14, 18. Conway, *The Utah Expedition,* p. 11. Clark, "A Trip across the Plains," pp. 191–93.

41. Alexander to Cooper, Oct. 9, 1857, in "Utah Expedition," pp. 30–32.

42. McDowell to Harney, July 30, 1857; Johnston to McDowell, Oct. 13, 1857: "Utah Expedition," pp. 12, 29–30. Special Order No. 20, Aug. 13, 1857, Records of the War Department, RG 94, NA. Johnston to A.A.G., Sept. 11, 1857, Letters Sent, Department of Utah, Vol. 1, NA.

43. Johnston to A.A.G., Sept. 11, 1857; Johnston to McDowell, Sept. 16, 1857: "Utah Expedition," pp. 21–22.

44. Johnston to McDowell, Sept. 24, 29, Oct. 13, 15, 1857, in "Utah Expedition," pp. 22–24, 29–30. Porter to Magraw, Oct. 16, 1857, Letters Sent, Department of Utah, Vol. 1, NA. 35th Cong., 1st Sess., Sen. Exec. Doc. 1, pp. 73–74.

45. Alexander to "Officers of the U. S. Army," Oct. 8, 1857; Alexander to Cooper, Oct. 9, 1857; Johnston to McDowell, Oct. 13, 1857: "Utah Expedition," pp. 29–32, 38–40. Phelps, Diary, *17*, entry dated Oct. 6, 1857. Hammond, *Utah Expedition,* p. 71.

46. Alexander to "Officers of the U. S. Army," Oct. 8, 1857; Alexander to Cooper, Oct. 9, 1857: "Utah Expedition," pp. 30–32, 38–40.

47. Phelps, Diary, *17*, entry dated Oct. 7, 1857. Hammond, *Utah Expedition,* pp. 71–72, 75–76.

48. Wells to Taylor, Oct. 4, 1857; Alexander "to any officer of the United States army, en route to Utah, or Governor Cumming," Oct. 14, 1857: "Utah Expedition," pp. 38, 56–57. Hammond, *Utah Expedition,* pp. 77–78. Henry S. Hamilton, *Reminiscences of a Veteran* (Concord, New Hampshire, Republican Press, 1897), pp. 82–83. JH, June 7, 1858.

49. Alexander to "Colonel," Oct. 18, 1857; Alexander to Porter, Oct. 22, 1857; Alexander to A.A.G., Nov. 17, 1857: "Utah Expedition," pp. 66–68, 80–81. Hammond, *Utah Expedition,* pp. 79–80. Phelps, Diary, *17*, entry dated Oct. 17, 1857.

50. Porter to Cooke, Oct. 18, 1857, Letters Sent, Department of Utah, Vol. 1, NA. Johnston to McDowell, Oct. 18, 1857; Porter to Alexander, Oct. 24, 1857: "Utah Expedition," pp. 35–37, 67.

51. Alexander to "Colonel," Oct. 18, 1857, in "Utah Expedition," pp. 66–67.

52. Johnston to McDowell, Oct. 18, 1857, ibid., p. 35.

53. General Order No. 10, Nov. 5, 1857, Records of the War Department, RG 94, NA.

54. Johnston, *Life of Johnston*, pp. 213–15. "Diary of William Wallace Hammond," (MS, Brigham Young University), p. 13. *Frontier Life in the Army, 1854–1861, by Eugene Bandel*, Ralph P. Bieber, ed. Olga Bandel and Richard Jente, trans. (Glendale, Cal., Arthur H. Clark, 1932), p. 218. Hammond, *Utah Expedition*, pp. 90–94. Phelps, Diary, *17*, entries dated Sept. 30–Nov. 17, 1857. *National Intelligencer*, March 26, 1858.

55. Settle and Settle, *Empire on Wheels*, pp. 19–25. *A Brief Statement of the Claims of Majors and Russell*, pp. 5, 15–17. A. R. Mortensen, ed., "The Governor's Lady," *Utah Historical Quarterly*, 22 (1954), 168.

56. H. F. Clarke to Porter, Nov. 4, 1857; Johnston to McDowell, Nov. 5, 1857; Porter to Hoffman, Nov. 13, 1857; John H. Dickerson to Porter, Nov. 24, 1857: "Utah Expedition," pp. 46–47, 62–63, 73, 101–2. Special Order No. 42, Nov. 7, 1857, Records of the War Department, RG 94, NA. Phelps, Diary, *17*, entries dated Nov. 13–25, 1857.

57. Porter to Cooke, Sept. 11, 1857; Johnston to Cumming, Sept. 16, 1857: Letters Sent, Department of Utah, Vol. 1, NA. Johnston to McDowell, Sept. 16, 1857; Cooke to A.A.G., Nov. 21, 1857: "Utah Expedition," pp. 21–22, 92.

58. Cooke to A.A.G., Oct. 12, 1857, Nov. 21, 1857: ibid., pp. 82–83, 92–94. General Order No. 18, March 22, 1858, Records of the War Department, RG 94, NA. Elizabeth Cumming to Anne Smith, Oct. 25, 1857, Cumming MSS. Forney to Black, March 9, 1858, Black MSS. Mortensen, "The Governor's Lady," pp. 169 ff. New York *Tribune*, Jan. 18, 1858. Tullidge, *Salt Lake City*, pp. 194–95. Linn, *Story of the Mormons*, p. 492. Rodenbough, *From Everglade to Cañon*, pp. 208 ff. Otis E. Young, *The West of Philip St. George Cooke, 1809–1895* (Glendale, Cal., Arthur H. Clark, 1955), pp. 294 ff.

6. The Mormons Organize

1. Young, "To the officer commanding the forces now invading Utah Territory," Sept. 29, 1857, in "Utah Expedition," p. 33.

2. Young to Cumming, July 1, 1858, MS, Utah Historical Society. For other examples see "Memorial," Jan. 6, 1858, and "Remarks" by Young of July 5, 1857, in *Deseret News*, Jan. 13, 1858, and July

13, 1857, respectively. Governor's Message, Dec. 15, 1857, in "Utah Expedition," p. 33.

3. JH, Sept. 18, 1857. "Early Records of Utah," p. 40.

4. "Early Records of Utah," p. 10. Bieber, *Frontier Life in the Army,* passim. Baltimore *Sun,* April 21, 1857. *Missouri Republican,* May 13, 1858. New York *Times,* Sept., 2, 1857.

5. Phelps, Diary, *16,* entry dated Aug. 24, 1857.

6. *Deseret News,* Jan. 27, 1858. New York *Times,* June 17, 1858.

7. Marcy to Taylor, Oct. 13, 1857, in *Deseret News,* Jan. 13, 1858. L. U. Reavis, *The Life and Military Services of Gen. William Selby Harney* (St. Louis, Bryan, Brand and Co., 1878), pp. 276–79. Phelps, Diary, *15,* entry dated June 10, 1857. Smith to A.A.G., Oct. 13, 1857, in "Utah Expedition," p. 44. Hammond, *Utah Expedition,* pp. 58–59, 75–76.

8. 35th Cong., 2d Sess., House Exec. Doc. 2, Vol. 2, Pt. II, pp. 46–47. "Diary of William Wallace Hammond," pp. 10–11. Clark, "A Trip across the Plains," pp. 163–72. New York *Tribune,* Aug. 3, 1857. New York *Times,* Oct. 28, 1857.

9. Jan. 6, 1858, in 35th Cong., 1st Sess., House Misc. Doc. 100, Vol. 3, pp. 1 ff.

10. Roberts, *Comprehensive History, 4,* 376. "Discourses" by Woodruff of Sept. 27, 1857, by Kimball of Sept. 27, 1857, by C. C. Rich of Oct. 7, 1857, by Amasa Lyman of Oct. 7, 1857, in *Journal of Discourses, 5,* 267, 299, 319, 322.

11. Wells to Pace, Aug. 1, 1857, in "Records of Provo Military District Command, 1857–1858," MS, Brigham Young University. Young to Mormons in Honolulu, Sept. 4, 1857, in Neff, *History of Utah,* p. 468. Richards to Kane, Sept. 16, 1857, Yale Collection. Brooks, *Mountain Meadows Massacre,* pp. 17–18, 21.

12. See Young's statement to Smith that he had not ordered the trains burned, in JH, Oct. 4, 1859. See also Ferguson to Young, Jan. 7, 1858, Utah Historical Society; JH, Sept. 29, Oct. 25, 1857. *Deseret News,* May 12, 1858. Wells to Lot Smith, Oct. 14, 1857, in Neff, *History of Utah,* p. 577. Matthias F. Cowley, *Wilford Woodruff* (Salt Lake City, Deseret News, 1909), p. 387.

13. "Discourse" by Young of July 8, 1855, in *Deseret News,* Aug. 1, 1855.

14. Young to Dame, Sept. 14, 1857, in Brooks, *Mountain Meadows Massacre,* p. 99 n. Wells issued similar orders to the Nauvoo Legion.

15. Kane to Judge Kane, Feb. 4, 1858, Yale Collection. Hammond, *Utah Expedition,* pp. 68–69. Brooks, *Mountain Meadows Massacre,* p. 24. "Early Records of Utah," pp. 9, 11, 16, 37, 39–40. JH, Aug. 26, Sept. 4, 28, 30, Oct. 14, 1857. *Deseret News,* Aug. 5, Sept. 23, Oct. 28, 1857.

16. Ferguson to Young, Jan. 7, 1858, Utah Historical Society.

17. Blair to Houston, Jan. 28, 1858, in Crescent City *Oracle,* March 26, 1858. JH, Dec. 2, 1857, April 5, May 10, 1858.

18. "Diary of George Laub, 1814–1880" (MS, Brigham Young University), 2, 6. Cowley, *Wilford Woodruff,* p. 396. JH, Jan. 19, May 18, 1858. Ferguson to Young, Jan. 7, 1858, Utah Historical Society.

19. JH, March 18, 1858.

20. *A Series of Instructions and Remarks by President Brigham Young at a Special Council, March 21, 1858* (pamphlet).

21. "Instructions" by Young of March 28, 1858, in *Deseret News,* April 14, 1858. See also JH, March 21, 1858.

22. "Remarks" by Young of Oct. 25, 1857, by Taylor of July 26, 1857; "Discourse" by Kimball of Aug. 2, 1857, by Taylor of Dec. 6, 1857: *Deseret News,* Aug. 5, 19, Nov. 18, Dec. 16, 1857, respectively. For similar speeches by Hyde, Taylor, Kimball, and Young see ibid., Aug. 26, Sept. 2, 9, 23, 1857.

23. Cowley, *Wilford Woodruff,* p. 391. "Remarks" by Kimball of July 26, 1857, in *Deseret News,* Aug. 12, 1857.

24. "Remarks" by Young of Sept. 13, 1857, in "Early Records of Utah," 5, 342. "Remarks" by Kimball of July 26, Nov. 8, 1857, in *Deseret News,* Nov. 11, Aug. 12, Nov. 18, 1857, respectively. Brooks, *Mountain Meadows Massacre,* p. 16.

25. "Diary of Charles L. Walker, 1833–1904" (MS, Brigham Young University), *1,* 16.

26. "Remarks" by Young of Nov. 15, 1857, in *Deseret News,* Nov. 25, 1857. "Diary of Charles L. Walker," *1,* 33. See also "From the Journal of John Pulsipher. Part II. The Utah War," *Western*

Humanities Review, 3 (Jan. 1949), 51; *Deseret News,* Nov. 18, Dec. 16, 1857, Jan. 13, 1858.

27. "Discourses" by Young of Oct. 4, 18, 1857, in *Deseret News,* Oct. 14, 23, 1857; JH, Oct. 1, 1857.

28. "Utah Expedition," pp. 34–35. Brooks, *Mountain Meadows Massacre,* p. 122.

29. Clark, "A Trip across the Plains," p. 207. Beadle, *Brigham's Destroying Angel,* pp. 122 ff. Hamilton Gardner, "A Territorial Militiaman in the Utah War," *Utah Historical Quarterly,* 22 (Oct. 1954), 311 n. New York *Tribune,* March 1, Aug. 9, 1858. New York *Times,* Aug. 3, 1858.

30. *Missouri Republican,* April 17, 1858. See also *Deseret News,* May 12, 1858.

31. Roberts, *Comprehensive History, 4,* 242, 245. Stenhouse, *Rocky Mountain Saints,* p. 353 and n. M. R. Hunter, *Brigham Young, the Colonizer* (Independence, Mo., Zion's Publishing Co., 1945), p. 79. *Daily Alta California,* March 14, 1858.

32. George W. Beattie and Helen Pruitt Beattie, *Heritage of the Valley. San Bernardino's First Century* (Pasadena, San Pasqual Press, 1939), pp. 171, 287, 294–97. Paul Bailey, *Sam Brannan and the California Mormons* (Los Angeles, Westernlore Press, 1943), pp. 164 ff. Neff, *History of Utah,* p. 219. The dissentions that had shaken the colony may also have persuaded Young to recall the faithful there: see Stout, *Hosea Stout* (above, p. 253, n. 28), p. 203.

33. Beattie and Beattie, *Heritage of the Valley,* pp. 288–90. Alton B. Poulsen, "The Mormon Outpost of San Bernardino, California" (M.A. thesis, University of Utah, 1947), p. 100. "Biographical Sketch of the Life of Peter Wilson Conover," MS, Utah Historical Society. McGavin, *U.S. Soldiers Invade Utah,* p. 102. JH, Oct. 26, 1857.

34. Arrington, "Mormon Finance and the Utah War," pp. 220, 223 n. JH, Oct. 10, 1857.

35. Ferguson to Young, Jan. 7, 1858, Utah Historical Society.

36. Leonard J. Arrington, "Coin and Currency in Early Utah," *Utah Historical Quarterly,* 20 (1952), 56–65. Phelps to Kane, June 25, 1852, Yale Collection.

37. Arrington, "Mormon Finance and the Utah War," pp. 219 ff. *Atlantic Monthly, 3* (April 1859), 480. "Diary of Charles L. Walker," *1*, 18, 46. Sheridan L. McGarry, *Mormon Money* (Salt Lake City, n.d.), p. 22. *Deseret News,* Sept. 1, 1858. JH, May 1, 10, 20, 1858.

38. Report from David McKenzie, Jan. 1858; Ward to Hunter, Jan. 5, 1858; Hasker to Young, Jan. 15, 1858; Johnson to Pace, Aug. 14, 1857: Adjutant General's Office, Utah National Guard, Salt Lake City. Arrington, "Mormon Finance and the Utah War," p. 211 n. "Diaries of Thomas Sirls Terry" (MS, Brigham Young University), p. 69. "Records of Provo Military District Command," pp. 13, 30. Stout, *Hosea Stout* (above, p. 253, n. 28), pp. 222-23.

39. Pace to Wells, Sept. 18, 1857, in "Records of Provo Military District Command," p. 23. Johnson to Fullmer, Nov. 10, 1857, Adjutant General's Office, Utah National Guard.

40. JH, Nov. 10, 11, 12, 1857, May 17, 1858. Clark, "A Trip across the Plains," p. 200. "Diary of John D. T. McAllister," pp. 124, 129. "Report of the Condition of the Tooele Division," Oct. 12, 1857, Adjutant General's Office, Utah National Guard.

41. James S. Brown, *Life of a Pioneer* (Salt Lake City, George Q. Cannon and Sons, 1900), p. 390. Wells to Pace, Aug. 13, 1857, in "Records of Provo Military District Command," p. 8. Richards to "Sir," in "Records of Orders, Returns, and Courts-Martial of 2nd. Brigade, 1st. Division, Nauvoo Legion," MS, Brigham Young University. Johnson to Packard, Oct. 14, 1857, Adjutant General's Office, Utah National Guard. JH, April 6, 1857, July 25, 1858.

42. See muster rolls, Adjutant General's Office, Utah National Guard.

43. Ferguson to Young, Jan. 7, 1858, Utah Historical Society.

44. "Biographical Sketch of the Life of Peter Wilson Conover," MS, Utah Historical Society. Snow to Wells, Aug. 17, 1857, Adjutant General's Office, Utah National Guard. Johnson to Wells, Aug. 18, 1857; Pace to Ferguson, Sept. 8, 1857; Blackburn to Pace, Sept. 2, 1857: "Records of Provo Military District Command."

45. *National Intelligencer,* May 8, 1857.

46. Brooks, *Mountain Meadows Massacre,* p. 102. Linn, *Story of the Mormons,* pp. 496-97. New York *Times,* May 19, 1858.

47. JH, March 21, May 19, 1857. *Deseret News,* May 12, 1858.

48. Ferguson to Young, Jan. 7, 1858, Utah Historical Society.

49. Governor's Message, Dec. 11, 1855, Dec. 15, 1857, in "Records of the States of the United States of America" (above, p. 257, n. 39). *Acts and Resolutions of the Legislative Assembly of the Territory of Utah,* 2d Sess. (1852–53), p. 65. Pace to Snow, Jan. 11, 1857, in "Records of Provo Military District Command." Brooks, *Mountain Meadows Massacre,* p. 17. JH, May 21, 1857, Feb. 17, 1858. Young to Kane, Jan. 31, 1857, Yale Collection. Neff, *History of Utah,* pp. 301–310. *Deseret News,* May 12, 1858. For details concerning the Las Vegas project see *Nevada State Historical Society Publications, 5,* 1925.

50. J. C. Alter, ed., "The State of Deseret," *Utah Historical Quarterly, 8* (1940), 77–78. Hinckley, *Wells* (above, p. 269, n. 71), p. 117. JH, Jan. 17, Feb. 1, 1857.

51. *Deseret News,* April 1, 15, 1857. Johnson to Thurber, April 17, 1857, Adjutant General's Office, Utah National Guard.

52. Letter from Wells, Aug. 1, 1857; orders from Pace, Aug. 4, 1857; Wells to Pace, Aug. 13, 1857; Pace to Follett, Aug. 17, 1857; Young to Pace, Oct. 8, 1857: "Records of Provo Military District Command." General Order No. 3, Aug. 13, 1857, in Gardner, "A Territorial Militiaman," p. 302 n. Johnson to Pace, Aug. 14, 1857; Johnson to Spafford, Oct. 30, 1857; Johnson to Fullmer, Oct. 9, 1857: Adjutant General's Office, Utah National Guard. Richards to "Sir," Sept. 30, 1857; Richards to Pettigrew, Sept. 30, 1857: "Records of 2nd. Brigade, 1st. Division." JH, Sept. 30, Oct. 12, 1857.

53. Brown, *Life of a Pioneer,* pp. 379–83, 385–90.

54. Werner, *Brigham Young,* pp. 435–36. Linn, *Story of the Mormons,* p. 541.

55. Ferguson to Young, Jan. 7, 1858, Utah Historical Society. "Vaux," "The Echo Canyon War," *Contributor, 3* (1882), 117 ff.

56. "Diary of Hosea Stout," 7, 316 ff. "The History and Journal of Jesse Crosby, 1820–1869" (MS, Brigham Young University), pp. 92–93. Stenhouse, *Rocky Mountain Saints,* pp. 362–63.

57. See for instance Stout, *Hosea Stout,* p. 217.

58. "Diary of Hosea Stout," 7, 321. *Contributor, 3* (1882), 270. Neff, *History of Utah,* p. 492. JH, June 23, 1858.

59. Hammond, *Utah Expedition,* pp. 176, 334–37. "Journal of Captain Albert Tracy," (above, p. 270, n. 78), p. 23. See also London *Times,* Sept. 1, 1858.

60. Gardner, *History of Lehi,* pp. 83 ff. Franklin L. West, *Life of Franklin D. Richards* (Salt Lake City, Deseret News Press, 1924), p. 145. *Contributor, 3* (1882), 270 ff. "Diary of Hosea Stout," 7, 316 ff. Neff, *History of Utah,* p. 479. Richards to Harmon, Sept. 28, 1857, in "Records of 2nd. Brigade, 1st. Division." JH, Sept. 25, 28, 29, Oct. 8, 25, 1857.

61. Hinckley, *Wells,* pp. 100–1. JH, Sept. 29, Oct. 14, 1857.

62. Neff, *History of Utah,* p. 475. JH, Oct. 14, 25, 1857.

63. Richards to Harmon, Sept. 25, 1857; Richards to Bennion, Sept. 27, 1857: "Records of 2nd. Brigade, 1st. Division." Neff, *History of Utah,* 478.

64. "Diary of John D. T. McAllister," p. 124.

65. Wells to Taylor, Oct. 4, 1857, in "Utah Expedition," pp. 56–57.

66. JH, Nov. 16, 1857.

67. Ibid., Nov. 16, 1857, June 7, 1858.

68. Tullidge, *History of Salt Lake City,* p. 173. *Contributor 3* (1882), 270–74, and *4* (1883), 27.

69. Gardner, "A Territorial Militiaman," pp. 299 ff. Neff, *History of Utah,* p. 477. *Contributor, 3* (1882), 49.

70. Gardner, "A Territorial Militiaman," pp. 299 ff. Roberts, *Comprehensive History, 4,* 288. *Contributor, 3* (1882), 49. JH, Oct. 25, 1857.

71. JH, Oct. 20, 24, Dec. 2, 5, 1857.

72. Ibid., Oct. 14, 1857.

73. Ibid., Oct. 21, 1857.

74. Neff, *History of Utah,* p. 479. "Early Records of Utah," p. 54.

75. Burton to Collister, Nov. 25, 1857; General Orders, Nov. 30, 1857; Ferguson to Young, Jan. 7, 1858: Utah Historical Society. Gardner, *History of Lehi,* pp. 83 ff. "From the Journal of John Pulsipher," p. 49. West, *Life of Richards,* p. 145. Hinckley, *Wells,* p. 107. Tullidge, *History of Salt Lake City,* p. 197. JH, Dec. 1, 1857.

7. Winter Quarters

1. Bridger to Butler, Oct. 22, 1873, 50th Cong., 2d Sess., Sen. Exec. Doc. 86, p. 13.

2. Ibid., pp. 2–4. See also Alter, *James Bridger* (above, p. 257, n. 38), pp. 315 ff.

3. Dickerson to Porter, Nov. 22, 1857; Johnston to McDowell, Nov. 30, 1857: "Utah Expedition," pp. 77, 100. Cooke to A.A.G., Dec. 31, 1857, in 35th Cong., 2d Sess., House Exec. Doc. 2, Vol. 2, Pt. II, p. 37. Field Report, Nov. 27, 1857, Records of the War Department, RG 94, NA. Bieber, *Frontier Life in the Army*, pp. 216–18. Bancroft, *History of Utah*, pp. 520–22. Robinson, "The Utah Expedition," p. 337.

4. Field Returns, Nov. 27, Dec. 25, 1857, Jan. 31, 1858, Records of the War Department, RG 94, NA. Circular from Porter, Nov. 19, 1857; Johnston to McDowell, Nov. 30, 1857, in "Utah Expedition," pp. 77, 90. "Diary of William Wallace Hammond" (MS, Brigham Young University), pp. 13–14. Clark, "A Trip across the Plains," pp. 195–223.

5. "Utah Expedition," pp. 106–7. "Journal of Captain Albert Tracy," p. 1. Porter to Bee, March 5, 1858, Records of the War Department, Department of Utah, Letters Sent, 1857–61, NA.

6. Clarke to Porter, Nov. 28, 1857; Johnston to McDowell, Nov. 30, Dec. 13, 1857: "Utah Expedition," pp. 77, 104, 108. General Orders, Nos. 16, 19, 54, Records of the War Department, RG 94, NA. Clark to A.A.G., May 19, 1858, Letters Received, Headquarters of the Army, 1858, NA. New York *Tribune*, Jan. 18, 1858. Rodenbough, *From Everglade to Cañon*, pp. 219–20, 228.

7. Hammond, *Utah Expedition*, p. 125.

8. Rodenbough, *From Everglade to Cañon*, p. 192.

9. Stenhouse, *Rocky Mountain Saints*, p. 377. Mrs. Cumming to Anne Smith, Dec. 13, 1857, Utah Historical Society. Young to Johnston, Nov. 26, 1857, "Utah Expedition," p. 110. Hamilton, *Reminiscences of a Veteran* (above, p. 276, n. 48), p. 93.

10. "Journal of Captain Albert Tracy," p. 1.

11. *Missouri Republican*, March 15, 1858. New York *Tribune*, Jan. 18, 1858. Rodenbough, *From Everglade to Cañon*, p. 218.

12. Hammond, *Utah Expedition*, p. 162. Rodenbough, *From Everglade to Cañon*, p. 220. New York *Tribune*, Jan. 18, June 10, 1858.

13. Porter to Hoffman, Nov. 30, 1857, Records of the War Department, Department of Utah, Letters Sent, 1857-61, NA.

14. Lynde to A.A.G., Dec. 2, 1857, 35th Cong., 2d Sess., House Exec. Doc. 2, Vol. 2, Pt. II, p. 36.

15. Porter to Lynde, Jan. 4, 1858, ibid., pp. 37-38. Johnston to McDowell, Dec. 13, 1857; Johnston to A.A.G., Jan. 4, 1858; Johnston to McDowell, Feb. 5, 1858: Records of the War Department, Department of Utah, NA. Bieber, *Frontier Life in the Army*, pp. 49 ff.

16. Porter to Hawes, March 10, 1858, Records of the War Department, Department of Utah, NA.

17. McDowell to Cooper, March 1, 1858; Johnston to McDowell, June 4, 1858; Hoffman to A.A.G., June 10, 1858: 35th Cong., 2d Sess., House Exec. Doc. 2, Vol. 2, Pt. II, pp. 39, 107, 177. Porter to Hoffman, April 27, 1858; Porter to Hoffman, May 15, 1858; Porter to "Officer of the 2d. Dragoons," May 20, 1858: Records of the Army, Department of Utah, NA. Bieber, *Frontier Life in the Army*, pp. 49-54.

18. Field Returns, Nov. 22, 1857, Records of the War Department, RG 94, NA.

19. See Hollon, *Beyond the Cross Timbers* (above, p. 274, n. 21).

20. For details of this venture see the excellent study by LeRoy R. Hafen, "A Winter Rescue March across the Rockies," *Colorado Magazine, 4*, 1927. See also Porter to Marcy, Nov. 26, 1857, in "Utah Expedition," p. 103. Marcy to Porter, June 12, 1858; Marcy to Cooper, Jan. 2, 1858; Marcy to McDowell, Jan. 23, 1858: 35th Cong., 2d Sess., House Exec. Doc. 2, Vol. 2, Pt. II, pp. 187-94. Hollon, *Beyond the Cross Timbers*, pp. 215 ff.

21. 35th Cong., 2d Sess., House Exec. Doc. 2, Vol. 2, Pt. II, pp. 33-34, 38, 41-42, 108-9, 182, 187-94. New York *Tribune*, March 1, 1858.

22. Lay to Marcy, May 29, 1858, in 35th Cong., 2d Sess., House Exec. Doc. 2, Vol. 2, Pt. II, pp. 106-7. Hollon, *Beyond the Cross Timbers*, pp. 227 ff.

23. Johnston, *Life of Johnston*, p. 218. Hamilton, *Reminiscences of a Veteran*, p. 92. Rodenbough, *From Everglade to Cañon*, pp. 223,

305–6. Phelps, Diary, *20,* entry dated May 31, 1858. General Order No. 20, April 24, 1858, Records of the War Department, RG 94, NA. New York *Tribune,* March 1, 23, 1858. *Missouri Republican,* March 15, 1858. *Atlantic Monthly, 3* (March 1859), 374–75.

24. Young, *Cooke* (above, p. 277, n. 58), pp. 303, 331. Rodenbough, *From Everglade to Cañon,* pp. 192, 227.

25. Porter to McClellan, Feb. 28, 1858, George B. McClellan MSS, Library of Congress. Hamilton, *Reminiscences of a Veteran,* p. 94. Rodenbough, *From Everglade to Cañon,* pp. 221–22, 308. Robinson, "The Utah Expedition," p. 338. Phelps, Diary, *18,* entries dated Jan. 15, 16, 1858, *19,* entries dated April 1, 2, 1858, *20,* entry dated June 11, 1858. New York *Times,* March 5, June 17, 1858. *Atlantic Monthly, 3* (March 1859), 374.

26. Quoted in records of courts-martial, Records of the War Department, RG 94, NA. Porter to Reno, Jan. 16, 1858, Records of the War Department, Department of Utah, NA. *Missouri Republican,* May 15, 1858.

27. Porter to Cooke, Nov. 26, 1857, in "Utah Expedition," pp. 103–4.

28. Porter to Marcy, Jan. 11, 1858; Porter to Hoffman, May 22, 1858: Records of the Army, Department of Utah, NA.

29. Porter to Phelps, Dec. 4, 1857, ibid. Porter to Bee, Jan. 12, 1858; Porter to Sibley, March 2, 1858; Porter to Cooke, March 2, 1858; Porter to Bee, March 3, 1858: 35th Cong., 2d Sess., House Exec. Doc. 2, Vol. 2, Pt. II, pp. 43, 59–61. *Atlantic Monthly, 3* (April 1859), 479. Hammond, *Utah Expedition,* pp. 113, 115. General Order No. 1, Jan. 5, 1858, Fitz-John MSS, Library of Congress. Phelps, Diary, *18,* entry dated Jan. 9, 1858, *19,* entry dated March 16, 1858. New York *Tribune,* March 23, 1858.

30. Roberts, *Comprehensive History 4,* 265–66. JH, March 23, April 5, 13, June 8, 1858.

31. Young to Commissioner of Indian Affairs, April 5, 1858, OIA, NA.

32. Magraw and Bridger to Porter, April 28, 1858, 35th Cong., 2d Sess., House Exec. Doc. 2, Vol. 2, Pt. II, pp. 82–84.

33. Forney to Cumming, April 21, 1858, ibid., p. 78. See also Hammond, *Utah Expedition,* p. 66; New York *Tribune,* March 1, 1858.

34. Porter to Forney, March 3, 1858, April 26, 1858: Records of the War Department, Department of Utah, NA.

35. Porter to Dickerson, Dec. 4, 1857, ibid. Johnston to McDowell, April 17, 1858; Ficklin to Porter, April 21, 1858; deposition of Craven Jackson, April 21, 1858; deposition of John W. Powell, April 21, 1858: 35th Cong., 2d Sess., House Exec. Doc. 2, Vol. 2, Pt. II, pp. 68, 79–81. Neff, *History of Utah*, p. 235.

36. Eckels to Dotson, April 21, 1858, Territorial Papers, NA.

37. Dotson to Eckels, April 27, 1858; Eckels to Cass, April 29, 1858: ibid. Hammond, *Utah Expedition*, pp. 155, 245–46. "Journal of Captain Albert Tracy," p. 9.

38. Tullidge, *Salt Lake City*, p. 239. Roberts, *Comprehensive History, 4*, 366. Hooper to Cumming, April 13, 15, 1858, 35th Cong., 2d Sess., House Exec. Doc. 2, Vol. 2, Pt. II, pp. 74–76. New York *Times*, June 12, 1858. New York *Tribune*, Aug. 9, 1858. *Atlantic Monthly, 3* (April 1859), 479.

39. Johnston to Cumming, April 21, 1858; Hurt to Cumming, April 21, 1858: 35th Cong., 2d Sess., House Exec. Doc. 2, Vol. 2, Pt. II, pp. 77–78. Hurt to Mix, Sept. 8, 1860 (with many enclosures), OIA, NA.

40. Johnston, *Life of Johnston*, p. 235. Clark, "A Trip across the Plains," pp. 195 ff. New York *Tribune*, Jan. 18, 1858. *National Intelligencer*, March 18, 1858.

41. Twiss to Cumming, Sept. 15, 1857; Denver to Thompson, Nov. 7, 1857; Twiss to Denver, Nov. 7, 1857; Denver to John Haverty, Nov. 11, 1857; Denver to J. C. Collins, Nov. 24, 1857: "Utah Expedition," pp. 188, 193 ff.

42. 35th Cong., 1st Sess., Sen. Exec. Doc. 11, Vol. 2, p. 298.

43. "Report of a Party of Observation," Utah Historical Society.

44. *Mountain Meadows Massacre,* p. 22.

45. Wells to Pace, Aug. 13, 1857, in "Records of Provo Military District Command." See also Johnson to Pace, Aug. 14, 1857, ibid. Joseph C. Ives, *Report upon the Colorado River of the West* (Washington, Government Printing Office, 1861), pp. 88–89. Clark, "A Trip across the Plains," p. 207. JH, Nov. 26, 1857.

46. Porter to Sibley, April 15, 1858, Records of the Army, Department of Utah, NA. Phelps, Diary, *17*, entry dated Nov. 12, 1857. *Mis-*

souri Republican, Feb. 12, 1858. Rodenbough, *From Everglade to Cañon,* p. 215. New York *Tribune,* Jan. 18, 1858. Elizabeth Cumming to Anne Smith, Dec. 13, 1857, Cumming MSS.

47. "Utah Expedition," pp. 77–79. "Executive Record, Book 'B,' 1852–1871," p. 82. JH, Nov. 28, 1857.

48. "Alfred Cumming," *DAB.* "Journal of Captain Albert Tracy," p. 84. Hammond, *Utah Expedition,* p. 187. Hoopes, *Indian Affairs* (above, p. 263, n. 7), p. 33. Nevins, *The Emergence of Lincoln* (above, p. 253, n. 29), *1,* 319. New York *Tribune,* June 26, 1857. *Daily Alta California,* June 25, 1857. *Valley Tan,* March 1, 1859.

49. JH, April 13, 1858.

50. "Utah Expedition," pp. 75–76.

51. Cumming to Young, Nov. 21, 1857, ibid., p. 76.

52. Cumming to Cass, Nov. 28, Dec. 13, 1857, Jan. 5, 1858, in "Utah Affairs," Territorial Papers, Utah Territory, Vol. 1, NA.

53. See several memorials dated early 1857, Appointments and Recommendations, NA. Eckels to Thompson, March 25, 1857, ibid.

54. Bright and Fitch to Buchanan, March 14, 1857, ibid. Eckels to Black, June 10, 1858, Appointment Papers, Department of Justice, NA. (Leavenworth City) *Kansas Weekly Herald,* Aug. 8, 1857.

55. "Utah Expedition," pp. 55–56, 68. Eckels to Black, Appointment Papers, Department of Justice, NA. New York *Tribune,* Dec. 28, 1857, Jan. 18, 1858.

8. End of Hostilities

1. Tullidge, *Salt Lake City,* p. 175. Roberts, *Comprehensive History, 4,* 411. Neff, *History of Utah,* pp. 481, 490–91.

2. 35th Cong., 1st Sess., House Exec. Doc. 2, Vol. 2, Pt. II.

3. Ibid.

4. Moore, *Buchanan* (above, p. 263, n. 44), *10,* 152.

5. Ibid., pp. 202 ff., 242 ff.

6. 35th Cong., 2d Sess., House Exec. Doc. 2, Vol. 2, Pt. II.

7. See Neff, *History of Utah,* p. 490.

8. Buchanan to Kane, Dec. 31, 1857, in Moore, *Buchanan, 10,* 167. In his second annual message the President again stressed the fact that Kane had acted "from motives of pure benevolence and without any official character or pecuniary compensation."

9. Floyd to Powell and McCulloch, April 12, 1858, 35th Cong., 2d Sess., House Exec. Doc. 2, Vol. 2, Pt. II. Cass to Cumming, April 7, 1858, Cumming MSS.

10. Lay to Johnston, Jan. 23, Feb. 4, 1858, "Utah Expedition," pp. 15-16. Quite possibly the Government had given some thought to a movement against Utah from the West even earlier than the winter of 1858, for in the previous year it had ordered Lt. Joseph Ives to take a party of men and a small steamship up the Colorado River. See MacMullen, *Paddle-wheel Days* (above, p. 259, n. 56), pp. 101-2; Frederick S. Dellenbaugh, *The Romance of the Colorado River* (New York, Putnam, 1909), pp. 154 ff.; Pearson H. Corbett, *Jacob Hamblin, the Peacemaker* (Salt Lake City, Deseret Book Company, 1952), pp. 135, 507; Ives, *Report upon the Colorado River,* p. 82; *Deseret News,* Jan. 27, July 21, 1858; *Daily Alta California,* May 12, 1858.

11. General Orders, No. 1, Jan. 8, 1858, No. 4, Jan. 16, 1858, in *The Utah War—General Orders.*

12. General Order No. 8, April 15, 1858, ibid. General Order No. 3, May 17, 1858, Records of the War Department, RG 94, NA. *National Intelligencer,* April 2, 1858. Alexander Majors, *Seventy Years on the Frontier* (Chicago, Rand, McNally, 1893), p. 143. New York *Tribune,* April 14, 1858.

13. Special Order No. 4, May 7, 1858, Records of the War Department, RG 94, NA. Harney to A.A.G., June 15, 1858, Records of the War Department, Department of Utah, NA. *National Intelligencer,* March 26, 1858. *Missouri Republican,* May 10, 1858. *Annals of Cleveland, 1819-1935, 40,* 579.

14. McDowell to Johnston, April 2, 1858, 35th Cong., 2d Sess., House Exec. Doc. 2, Vol. 2, Pt. II, p. 67.

15. Harney to Army Headquarters, May 27, 1858, ibid., pp. 105-6.

16. Cass to Cumming, June 29, 1858, Cumming MSS. Harney to A.A.G., July 8, 1858, Records of the War Department, Department of Utah, NA. General Order No. 17, June 29, 1858, in *The Utah War—*

General Orders. New York *Times,* June 16, 1858. New York *Tribune,* June 22, 1858. Washington *Union,* July 15, 1858.

17. Roberts, *Comprehensive History, 4,* 411. Neff, *History of Utah,* p. 481.

18. See Nichols, *Disruption of American Democracy,* pp. 177–78, for an excellent discussion of events in Congress that influenced the actions of the Administration.

19. *Cong. Globe,* Jan. 28, March 24, April 14, 1858. Roberts, *Comprehensive History, 4,* 374–75. Nichols, *Disruption of American Democracy,* pp. 101–2. Moore, *Buchanan, 10,* 220. *National Intelligencer,* March 19, April 23, 1858.

20. *Cong. Globe,* Dec. 21, 23, 1857, Jan. 27, March 11, 16, May 13, 1858. See also Washington *Union,* April 8, 1858; Stephens to Cass, Jan. 25, 1858, Miscellaneous Letters, Department of State, Foreign Affairs Section, NA.

21. Hammond, *Utah Expedition,* pp. 103, 133. Porter to Lynde, Jan. 4, 1858, 35th Cong., 2d Sess., House Exec. Doc. 2, Vol. 2, Pt. II, pp. 37–38. Porter to McClellan, Feb. 28, 1858, George B. McClellan MSS, Library of Congress.

22. Johnston to McDowell, Jan. 20, 1858, 35th Cong., 2d Sess., House Exec. Doc. 2, Vol. 2, Pt. II, p. 44.

23. New York *Tribune,* Jan. 18, 1858.

24. Cumming to Appleton, Jan. 24, 1858, Territorial Papers, Utah Territory, State Department Archives, NA. Elizabeth Cumming to Anne Smith, April 5, 1858, Utah Historical Society.

25. Hurt to Cumming, Dec. 17, 1857, in Morgan, "Administration of Indian Affairs" (above, p. 252, n. 15), p. 394.

26. Cumming to Cass, Jan. 30, 1858, Territorial Papers, NA.

27. Forney to Black, March 9, 1858, Black MSS.

28. JH, July 4, 1851.

29. Richards to Kane, Aug. 31, 1851, March 4, 1852, Yale Collection. JH, Sept. 24, 1850.

30. Young to Kane, Jan. 7, 31, June 27, 1857, Yale Collection. JH, June 29, 1857.

31. Buchanan to Kane, Dec. 31, 1857, in Moore, *Buchanan, 10,* 167.

32. Roberts, *Comprehensive History, 4,* 347, also p. 345; see also JH, Aug. 15, 1858.

33. Kane to Judge Kane, Feb. 4, 1858, Yale Collection. New York *Tribune,* June 19, 1855.

34. Phelps, Diary, *19,* entries dated March 3, 14, 1858.

35. Ibid., same entries. Hammond, *Utah Expedition,* pp. 134, 208. New York *Tribune,* May 24, 1858. W. J. Ghent, "Kane," *DAB.* See also Stenhouse, *Rocky Mountain Saints,* p. 383.

36. Young to Kane, March 9, 1858; Young to Cumming, April 16, 1858, 35th Cong., 2d Sess., House Exec. Doc. 2, Vol. 2, Pt. II, pp. 87–88, 91.

37. Johnston to Kane, March 15, 1858, ibid., p. 88.

38. Kane to Johnston, March 16, 1858, Porter MSS, Library of Congress.

39. Kane to Johnston, March 14, 15, 1858; Johnston to Kane, March 15, 1858: 35th Cong., 2d Sess., House Exec. Doc. 2, Vol. 2, Pt. II, pp. 89–90.

40. Grover to Porter, March 16, 1858, Cumming MSS. Porter to Johnston, March 17, 1858; Johnston to Cumming, March 17, 1858: Records of the War Department, Department of Utah, NA. Kane to Cumming, March 16, 1858, Cumming MSS. Stenhouse, *Rocky Mountain Saints,* p. 383. Hammond, *Utah Expedition,* p. 134. Hamilton, *Reminiscences of a Veteran,* p. 98. Johnston, *Life of Johnston,* p. 224. New York *Tribune,* May 24, 1858.

41. Kane to Cumming, March 19, 1858, Cumming MSS.

42. Elizabeth Cumming to Anne Smith, April 5, 22, 1858, Utah Historical Society.

43. Neff, *History of Utah,* p. 494.

44. JH, March 18, 1858.

45. Roberts, *Comprehensive History, 4,* 361 ff. JH, April 7, 25, June 7, 1858.

46. Brooks, *Mountain Meadows Massacre,* p. 113. JH, May 24, June 18, 1858.

47. Roberts, *Comprehensive History*, *4*, 361-63. JH, Feb. 25, May 24, 25, 30, 1858, April 16, 1859. New York *Times*, May 28, Aug. 23, 1858.

48. "Early Records of Utah," p. 9.

49. Ibid., p. 5. Creer, *Utah and the Nation* (above, p. 251, n. 6), p. 135. D. C. Johnson, *A Brief History of Springville, Utah* (Springville, William F. Gibson, 1900), p. 49.

50. Arrington, "Mormon Finance and the Utah War," p. 227. "The Move South," *Heart Throbs of the West*, *20* (1949), 255. JH, May 11, 1858.

51. Roberts, *Comprehensive History*, *4*, 381. Elizabeth Cumming to Anne Smith, April 22, 1858, Utah Historical Society.

52. Roberts, *Comprehensive History*, *4*, 396-97. "Diary of John D. T. McAllister," p. 134. JH, April 12, 13, 1858.

53. JH, April 14, 1858. See also Roberts, *Comprehensive History*, *4*, 383.

54. Linn, *Story of the Mormons*, p. 507. Hooper to Cumming, April 13, 15, 1858, 35th Cong., 2d Sess., House Exec. Doc. 2, Vol. 2, Pt. II, pp. 92-97.

55. Cumming to Cass, May 2, 1858, 35th Cong., 2d Sess., House Exec. Doc. 2, Vol. 2, Pt. II, pp. 92-97.

56. JH, April 20, 1858.

57. Cumming to Cass, May 2, 1858, 35th Cong., 1st Sess., House Exec. Doc. 138, Vol. 13, p. 5. JH, April 25, 1858. See also "Diary of Charles Walker, 1833-1904" (MS, Brigham Young University), *1*, 36. Stout, *Hosea Stout*, p. 228.

58. Cumming to Cass, May 2, 1858, 35th Cong., 1st Sess., House Exec. Doc. 138, Vol. 13, p. 4.

59. Cumming to Cass, May 2, 1858, ibid., p. 4. "Notes of Some Persons Who Left This City in May, 1858," Cumming MSS.

60. JH, April 30, 1858.

61. Bancroft, *History of Utah*, p. 535. Hammond, *Utah Expedition*, p. 351. "Biography of George Orrin Pitkin, 1837-1910" (MS, Brigham Young University), pp. 11-12. JH, June 10, 1858. Cumming to Cass,

May 11, 1858, 35th Cong., 2d Sess., House Exec. Doc. 2, Vol. 2, Pt. II, p. 99. New York *Times,* July 30, 1858.

62. Neff, *History of Utah,* p. 498.

63. *Deseret News,* July 28, 1858. *Journal of Discourses,* 7, 58.

64. JH, April 5, 1858.

65. "Diary of John D. T. McAllister," p. 234. "From the Journal of John Pulsipher" (above, p. 279, n. 26), p. 50. Jones, *Forty Years among the Indians,* pp. 126–27. JH, Feb. 25, May 10, June 23, 1858.

66. JH, May 8, 1858. Young to Cumming, May 8, 1858; Elizabeth Cumming to Anne Smith, May 28, 1858: Utah Historical Society.

67. Young to Cumming, May 8, 1858, Cumming MSS.

68. Hammond, *Utah Expedition,* pp. 174, 227. Phelps, Diary, *20,* entry dated June 8, 1858. Bieber, *Frontier Life in the Army,* p. 222. New York *Times,* June 24, 1858.

69. Elizabeth Cumming to Cumming, April 21, 1858; Elizabeth Cumming to Anne Smith, April 22, 31, 1858: Utah Historical Society.

70. Forney to Black, April 18, May 1, 6, 26, 1858, Black MSS.

71. Forney to Black, May 26, 1858, ibid.

72. Eckels to Cass, April 23, 1858, Miscellaneous Letters, Department of State, Foreign Affairs Section, NA. Phelps, Diary, *20,* entry dated April 21, 1858. Forney to Black, May 1, 1858, Black MSS. Elizabeth Cumming to Anne Smith, May 28, 1858, Utah Historical Society. Hammond, *Utah Expedition,* pp. 264, 281.

73. Johnston to Cumming, April 21, 1858; Johnston to McDowell, April 22, May 7, 1858: 35th Cong., 2d Sess., House Exec. Doc. 2, Vol. 2, Pt. II, pp. 71, 97–98. New York *Tribune,* June 17, 1858.

74. Johnston to McDowell, May 21, 1858; Cumming to Johnston, May 21, 1858; Johnston to Cumming May 21, 1858; Porter to Hoffman, May 21, 1858: 35th Cong., 2d Sess., House Exec. Doc. 2, Vol. 2, Pt. II, pp. 98 ff. Johnston to McDowell, May 21, 1858, Records of the War Department, Department of Utah, NA.

75. Cass to Cumming, April 7, 1858, Cumming MSS.

76. *Cong. Globe,* April 14, 1858.

77. Linn, *Story of the Mormons*, p. 511. Johnston, *Life of Johnston*, p. 228. New York *Times*, June 30, 1858.

78. Moore, *Buchanan, 10, 202.*

79. Floyd to Powell and McCulloch, April 12, 1858, 35th Cong., 2d Sess., House Exec. Doc. 2, Vol. 2, Pt. II, pp. 160 ff.

80. Powell and McCulloch to Floyd, April 25, May 3, 1858, ibid., p. 163. Hammond, *Utah Expedition*, p. 170. New York *Times*, June 30, 1858. New York *Tribune*, July 8, 1858.

81. Powell and McCulloch to Floyd, June 1, 1858, 35th Cong., 2d Sess., House Exec. Doc. 2, Vol. 2, Pt. II, p. 165.

82. Elizabeth Cumming to Sarah Cumming, June 17, 1858, Cumming MSS. New York *Times*, Aug. 9, 1858.

83. Tullidge, *Salt Lake City*, p. 214.

84. Powell and McCulloch to Floyd, June 26, 1858, 35th Cong., 2d Sess., House Exec. Doc. 2, Vol. 2, Pt. II, pp. 168–72. Roberts, *Comprehensive History*, 4, 422–24; JH, June 10, 11, 1858.

85. Powell and McCulloch to Floyd, June 26, 1858, 35th Cong., 2d Sess., House Exec. Doc. 2, Vol. 2, Pt. II, pp. 168–72. JH, June 11, 1858.

86. Roberts, *Comprehensive History*, 4, 428. JH, June 12, 1858.

87. JH, June 12, 1858.

88. Powell and McCulloch to Floyd, June 12, 1858; Powell and McCulloch to Johnston, June 12, 1858; proclamation dated June 14, 1858: 35th Cong., 2d Sess., House Exec. Doc. 2, Vol. 2, Pt. II, pp. 119–21, 167–68. Proclamation dated June 14, 1858, in "Executive Record, Book 'B,' 1852–1871," Utah Historical Society. *Deseret News*, June 23, 1858.

89. Johnston to Cumming, June 19, 1858, ibid., pp. 116–17. Powell and McCulloch to Cumming, June 18, 1858, Cumming MSS. Cumming to Cass, June 18, 1858, Territorial Papers, NA. Young to Kane, Aug. 6, 1858, Yale Collection. JH, June 9, 1858.

90. Cumming to Johnston, June 15, 17, 1858, 35th Cong., 2d Sess., House Exec. Doc. 2, Vol. 2, Pt. II.

91. Johnston to McDowell, June 20, 1858, ibid., p. 44.

92. *Deseret News*, June 23, 1858.

93. "Diary of Charles L. Walker, 1833–1904," *1*, 42.

94. *Deseret News*, July 14, 1858. For McCulloch's attitude see "Early Records of Utah," p. 50; JH, Oct. 2, 1858.

95. Powell and McCulloch to Floyd, Aug. 24, 1858, 35th Cong., 2d Sess., House Exec. Doc. 2, Vol. 2, Pt. II, p. 175.

96. Powell and McCulloch to Floyd, July 3, 1858, ibid., p. 172.

97. General Order No. 32, June 25, 1858, Records of the War Department, RG 94, NA. "Journal of Captain Albert Tracy," p. 27. Young, *Cooke*, p. 309.

98. Porter to Floyd, Feb. 10, 1859, Attorney General's Records, 1789–1870, NA. "Journal of Captain Albert Tracy," p. 29.

99. Roberts, *Comprehensive History*, *4*, 447–48. *Tullidge's Histories, Containing the History of All the Northern, Eastern, and Western Counties of Utah* (Salt Lake City, Juvenile Instructor, 1889), *2*, 31–32. JH, June 13, 1858.

100. Tullidge, *Salt Lake City*, p. 220. Neff, *History of Utah*, p. 494. See also Werner, "Brigham Young" (above, p. 271, n. 93), p. 69. Werner, *Brigham Young*, p. 395.

101. Neff, *History of Utah*, p. 499. *Annals of Cleveland, 1818–1935, 40*, 580. New York *Times*, June 14, 17, 1858. *Deseret News*, July 28, Sept. 8, 1858. London *Times*, Sept. 9, 1858.

102. "Journal of Captain Albert Tracy," pp. 29–30. JH, July 6, 1858. *Emerson's Magazine*, 7 (Sept. 1858), 322. New York *Times*, Aug. 13, 1858.

9. But No Peace

1. New York *Times*, June 17, 1858. See also Hammond, *Utah Expedition*, p. 351.

2. The size of the garrison is revealed in communications in RG 98, United States Army Commands, Department of Utah; RG 94, Office of the Adjutant General, Expedition Returns S–Z; Records of the War Department, Department of Utah: all in NA.

3. Robinson, "The Utah Expedition," p. 399. Neff, *History of Utah*, p. 514. Johnston to McDowell, summer 1858, Records of the War Department, Department of Utah, National Archives. Porter to Johnston,

Feb. 10, 1859, Attorney General's Records, 1789-1870, NA. New York *Tribune,* Dec. 16, 1858.

4. Neff, *History of Utah,* pp. 514-15. Rodenbough, *From Everglade to Cañon,* p. 192. Johnston to McDowell, July 22, 1858, 35th Cong., 2d Sess., House Exec. Doc. 2, Vol. 2, Pt. II, p. 124. Phelps, Diary, *22a,* entries for March, April, 1859, and *25,* entry dated Aug. 20, 1859. New York *Times,* Oct. 4, 1858.

5. Records of the War Department, RG 94, NA. Phelps, Diary, *22,* entries for Feb.–May 1859. *Missouri Republican,* Aug. 27, 1858. Young, *Cooke,* p. 310.

6. Phelps, Diary, *23,* entries dated June 16, 17, 1858. Robinson, "The Utah Expedition," p. 339.

7. Gove to Rolfe, May 1, 1861, Gove MS, New Hampshire Historical Society. Montgomery to Greenwood, Aug. 17, 1859, OIA, NA. Hammond, *Utah Expedition,* pp. 176, 279. "Journal of Captain Albert Tracy," pp. 32, 45-46. Brooks, *Mountain Meadows Massacre,* p. 133. Phelps, Diary, *22a,* entry dated March 28, 1859, and *23,* entry dated June 4, 1859.

8. Johnston to McDowell, July 8, 1858, 35th Cong., 2d Sess., House Exec. Doc. 2, Vol. 2, Pt. II, pp. 122-23. Porter to Johnston, Feb. 10, 1859, Attorney General's Records, 1789-1870, NA.

9. JH, Aug. 8, 9, 12, 1858.

10. Ibid., May 20, 1859.

11. Roberts, *Comprehensive History, 4,* 454-55. Resolutions of the Legislature dated Jan. 21, in *Acts and Resolutions of the Legislative Assembly of the Territory of Utah,* 8th Session (1858-59). Young to Cumming, June 19, 23, Cumming MSS. *Deseret News,* June 23, 1858. JH, Aug. 26, 1858.

12. Cumming to Cass, July 16, Nov. 5, 1858, Territorial Papers, NA.

13. JH, Nov. 29, 1858.

14. Hammond, *Utah Expedition,* p. 379. New York *Times,* Aug. 3, 1858. *Valley Tan,* March 1, 1859.

15. Elizabeth Cumming to Anne Smith, Sept. 24, 1858, Utah Historical Society. *Deseret News,* Dec. 22, 1858.

16. JH, Nov. 4, 1858.

17. Eckels to Cass, June 4, July 9, 1858, Jan. 14, 1859, Territorial Papers, NA. Eckels to Buchanan, Aug. 17, 1859, memorial dated Aug. 17, 1859, Appointment Papers, Department of Justice, NA. Affidavit of James Lynch, July 27, 1859, OIA, NA.

18. JH, March 30, May 20, Sept. 13, 1858, Jan. 15, 1859. *Deseret News*, Aug. 3, 1859.

19. Roberts, *Comprehensive History, 4,* 456. JH, Oct. 27, Dec. 25, 1858. *Deseret News*, Sept. 14, 21, Nov. 2, 1859.

20. Kane to Young, Aug. 25, 1858, Yale Collection. See also Kane to Thompson, July 27, 1858, Kane MSS, Library of Congress.

21. Wilson to Black, Nov. 26, 1858, Attorney General's Records, 1789–1870, NA. Wilson to Black, April 8, 1859, Appointment Books, Department of Justice, NA.

22. Forney to Black, Sept. 15, Dec. 3, 1858, June 1, 1859; Forney to Mix, June 22, 1858: 36th Cong., 1st Sess., Sen. Exec. Doc. 42, p. 45. Forney to Mix, Sept. 6, 1858, 35th Cong., 2d Sess., House Exec. Doc. 2, Vol. 1, pp. 561 ff. Morgan, "Administration of Indian Affairs," pp. 406 ff.

23. Forney to Black, Sept. 15, 1858, Appointment Papers, Department of Justice, NA.

24. Dotson to Buchanan, Aug. 1, 1859, Attorney General's Records, 1789–1870, NA.

25. Phelps to Kane, Feb. 10, 1859, Yale Collection. *Deseret News*, June 8, 1859.

26. Wendell J. Ashton, *Voice of the West* (New York, Duell, Sloan, and Pearce, 1950), pp. 97, 99. JH, Sept. 7, Nov. 2, 6, 1858, April 25, 1859. *Valley Tan,* Jan. 25, May 24, 1859.

27. *Valley Tan,* March 1, 1859.

28. *Deseret News*, Oct. 13, 1858. See also Taylor to Cannon, Jan. 12, 1859, in JH, April 19, 1859.

29. General Order No. 38, July 14, 1858, Records of the War Department, RG 94, NA. Johnston to Cumming, Oct. 31, 1858, Records of the War Department, Department of Utah, NA. Porter to Sanders, Jan. 26, 1859, Records of the War Department, RG 98, NA.

30. Hamilton, *Reminiscences of a Veteran*, pp. 110–12. JH, June 27, Aug. 27, 1858, Oct. 12, 1859. Gay to Porter, Aug. 15, 1859, 36th Cong.,

1st Sess., Sen. Exec. Doc. 42, pp. 22 ff. Hammond, *Utah Expedition,* pp. 185, 187. "Journal of Captain Albert Tracy," pp. 48–50.

31. Cumming to Cass, Jan. 28, 1859, Territorial Papers, NA. *Valley Tan,* Jan. 25, March 1, 1859. Winther, *Private Papers of Kane* (above, p. 251, n. 5), p. 60. JH, Nov. 29, 1858.

32. Cradlebaugh, *Utah and the Mormons* (above, p. 270, n. 79), p. 23. Young to Eldredge, Nov. 20, 1858; Young to Cannon, Dec. 24, 1858: Yale Collection. JH, Nov. 5, 20, Dec. 17, 1858, Jan. 4, 1859. New York *Tribune,* Dec. 1, 1858. *Valley Tan,* Aug. 17, Dec. 10, 17, 1858, Jan. 4, 1859.

33. JH, Nov. 15, 30, Dec. 1, 3, 1858, Jan. 11, 1859. *Deseret News,* Dec. 1, 22, 1858.

34. JH, Nov. 29, 1858, Jan. 10, 1859. *Deseret News,* Nov. 24, Dec. 1, 1858. *Valley Tan,* Nov. 26, 1858.

35. *Deseret News,* June 15, 22, July 27, Aug. 10, Sept. 14, 1859. *Valley Tan,* Aug. 31, 1859.

36. Cumming to Cass, March 22, 1860, Territorial Papers, NA.

37. Cradlebaugh to Porter, March 6, 1859; Porter to Heth, March 9, 1859: 36th Cong., 1st Sess., Sen. Exec. Doc. 2, Vol. 2. Johnston to Thomas, March 10, 1859, Records of the War Department, RG 98, NA.

38. Porter to Cradlebaugh, Dec. 19, 1858; Porter to Elwood, Jan. 2, 1859: Records of the War Department, RG 98, NA. *Deseret News,* March 16, 1859.

39. The various petitions may be found in Territorial Papers, NA; Bullock to Cradlebaugh, March 11, 15, 1859; Cradlebaugh to Bullock, March 12, 1859, 36th Cong., 1st Sess., Sen. Exec. Doc. 2, Vol. 2, p. 142.

40. Johnston to Thomas, March 10, 1859, Records of the War Department, RG 94, NA.

41. Memorial dated March 14, 1859, 36th Cong., 1st Sess., Sen. Exec. Doc. 2, Vol. 2, p. 144.

42. Heth to Bennett, March 12, 1859; Heth to Porter, March 18, 1859: ibid., pp. 141–42.

43. Porter to Paul, March 19, 1859; Johnston to Cradlebaugh, March 19, 1859: ibid., pp. 147–49.

44. Cumming to Johnston, March 20, 1859, ibid., p. 149.

45. Johnston to Cumming, March 22, 1859, ibid., pp. 151–52. See also Johnston to Thomas, March 24, 1859, ibid., p. 139.

46. Order from Wells dated March 21, 1859, in "Records of the 2nd. Brigade, 1st. Division." "Diary of Charles L. Walker," *1*, 72–73. *Valley Tan,* March 22, 1859.

47. Heth to Bullock, March 27, 1859, Records of the War Department, Headquarters of the Army, Letters Received, NA. See also Heth to Johnston, March 27, 1859, 36th Cong., 1st Sess., Sen. Exec. Doc. 2, Vol. 2, p. 159.

48. "Memorial and Petition," March 22, 1859, Territorial Papers, NA. JH, March 22, 24, 29, 1859. *Valley Tan,* March 29, 1859.

49. Cumming to Cass, March 24, 1859; proclamation, March 27, 1859: Territorial Papers, NA.

50. JH, March 30, 1859.

51. Dotson to Johnston, March 24, 1859; Porter to Paul, March 24, 1859: 36th Cong., 1st Sess., Sen. Exec. Doc. 2, Vol. 2, pp. 155–56. Paul to A.A.G., March 31, 1859, Records of the War Department, Headquarters of the Army, Letters Received, NA. JH, March 26, 30, 1859.

52. *Deseret News,* March 30, 1859. JH, March 30, 1859.

53. Phelps, Diary, *22a,* entry dated April 5, 1859.

54. Cradlebaugh to Porter, April 6, 1859, in Records of the War Department, Headquarters of the Army, Letters Received, NA. Dotson to Cradlebaugh, June 3, 1859, in Appointment Papers, Department of Justice, NA. JH, April 27, May 4, 5, 1859. Cradlebaugh to Buchanan, June 3, 1859, in JH, June 3, 1859.

55. Stenhouse, *Rocky Mountain Saints,* p. 410. "William M. Cradlebaugh, Nevada Biography. San Francisco, 1883," Bancroft Library, University of California.

56. 35th Cong., 1st Sess., House Exec. Doc. 138, Vol. 13, p. 1. Moore, *Buchanan, 10,* 242 ff.

57. Cumming to Cass, Sept. 4, 1859, Territorial Papers, NA.

58. Annual Report of Dec. 6, 1858, 35th Cong., 2d Sess., House Exec. Doc. 2, Vol. 2, Pt. II.

59. Floyd to Johnston, May 6, 1859, 36th Cong., 1st Sess., Sen. Exec. Doc. 2, Vol. 2.

60. Black to Cradlebaugh and Sinclair, May 17, 1859, Letters Sent, Department of Justice, NA.

61. Black to Wilson, May 17, 1859, ibid.

62. Cumming to Cass, Aug. 12, 1859, Territorial Papers, NA. Cass to Cumming, Sept. 15, 1859, Domestic Letters, Department of State, NA.

63. Cradlebaugh and Sinclair to Buchanan, July 16, 1859, Appointment Papers, Department of Justice, NA.

64. See several letters between Dotson and Johnston during April and June, 1859, 36th Cong., 1st Sess., Sen. Exec. Doc. 2, Vol. 2, pp. 196–200. Porter to Ruggles, May 20, 1859, Records of the War Department, Headquarters of the Army, Letters Received, NA.

65. JH, April 18, 22, 24, 1859.

66. Ibid., April 23, 24, 1859.

67. Hurt to Johnston, May 1, 1859; Burr to Sinclair, May 5, 1859; R. Johnston to Turnbey, May 6, 1859: Records of the War Department, Headquarters of the Army, Letters Received, NA. Kay to Cumming, May 16, 1859, Territorial Papers, NA. Ruggles to Porter, May 18, 1859; Ruggles to Johnston, June 2, 1859: 36th Cong., 1st Sess., Sen. Exec. Doc. 2, Vol. 2, pp. 177–78, 185. "Journal of Captain Albert Tracy," pp. 67–68. JH, May 19, 1859.

68. Burr to Sinclair, May 5, 1859, Records of the War Department, Headquarters of the Army, Letters Received, NA. Affidavit of Joseph Logue, May 25, 1859, Utah Department of State Archives. Cumming to Ferguson, May 5, 1859; proclamation dated May 9, 1859: Utah Department of State Archives.

69. Cumming to Cass, May 19, 1859, Territorial Papers, NA.

70. Smith to Kane, Sept. 11, 1858, Yale Collection. Petition to Cumming, May 28, 1859, Cumming MSS.

71. See correspondence between the Mormons and Johnston, 36th Cong., 1st Sess., Sen. Exec. Doc. 2, Vol. 2, pp. 124 ff. Another irritant in these early months after the war was the army's refusal to pay for damages the Mormons insisted the soldiers had done to private property: see JH, July 6, 8, 1858.

72. Spencer to Johnston, Feb. 28, 1859; Cunningham to Johnston, Feb., 1859: 36th Cong., 1st Sess., Sen. Exec. Doc. 2, Vol. 2, pp. 137, 171.

73. Cowley, *Woodruff* (above, p. 278, n. 12), p. 406. Spencer to John-

ston, March 31, 1859, 36th Cong., 1st Sess., Sen. Exec. Doc. 2, Vol. 2, p. 159. JH, March 22, 1859.

74. Marshall to Smith, March 22, 1859; Marshall to Porter, March 25, 1859; Johnston to Cumming, March 26, 1859; Marshall to Johnston, April 29, 1859; Porter to Spencer, May 23, 1859: 36th Cong., 1st Sess., Sen. Exec. Doc. 2, Vol. 2, pp. 138 ff. See also "Journal of Captain Albert Tracy," pp. 72-73; Phelps, Diary, 22a, entry dated March 23, 1859.

75. JH, March 22, 1859.

76. Cumming to Johnston, March 24, 1859; Johnston to Cumming, March 26, 1859: 36th Cong., 1st Sess., Sen. Exec. Doc. 2, Vol. 2, pp. 138-39, 158.

77. Porter to Smith, Aug. 6, 1859; Porter to Johnston, Aug. 15, 1859: Porter MSS, Library of Congress.

78. *Deseret News,* Aug. 17, 1859. See also JH, Aug. 11, 1859.

79. Porter to Johnston, Aug. 11, 1859, Porter MSS.

80. Porter to Johnston, Aug. 11, 1859, 36th Cong., 1st Sess., Sen. Exec. Doc. 2, Vol. 2, p. 214.

81. Deposition of C. F. Smith, May 14, 1860, Records of the War Department, RG 98, NA. "Journal of Captain Albert Tracy," p. 73. Hamilton, *Reminiscences of a Veteran,* pp. 112-13. JH, Aug. 16, 30, 1859.

82. Eckels to Cass, Sept. 27, 1859, Territorial Papers, NA. Some of the affidavits may be seen ibid. and in OIA, NA.

83. Cradlebaugh, *Utah and the Mormons,* pp. 24-25. Stenhouse, *Rocky Mountain Saints,* pp. 410-12. McGarry, *Mormon Money* (above, p. 281, n. 37), p. 23. "Journal of Captain Albert Tracy," p. 71. Arrington, "Mormon Finance and the Utah War," p. 234. JH, July 8, 12, 13, 15, Sept. 3, 1859, March 6, 1860.

10. Afterward

1. JH, June 3, 1859.

2. Eckels to Cass, Sept. 27, 1859, Territorial Papers, NA.

3. 36th Cong., 1st Sess., Sen. Exec. Doc. 42, Vol. 2.

4. 36th Cong., 1st Sess., Sen. Exec. Doc. 2, Vol. 1.

5. Cass to Cumming, Dec. 12, 1859, Cumming MSS.

6. Black to Young, July 12, 1860, Appointment Papers, Department of Justice, NA.

7. Brewer to Phelps, March 20, 1860, Phelps MSS, Yale Collection. Smith to A.A.G., June 4, Aug. 1, 1860, Records of the War Department, RG 98, NA.

8. Maria Gove to her sister, May 1, 1861, Gove MSS, New Hampshire Historical Society. Cooke to Thomas, June 19, 1861, Records of the War Department, RG 98, NA. Rodenbough, *From Everglade to Cañon*, pp. 192–93. Young, *Cooke*, pp. 322 ff. Post returns from Camp Crittenden may be found in Records of the War Department, RG 94, NA.

9. Jensen, *Mormon Theory of Church and State* (above, p. 252, n. 18), p. 6. Neff, *History of Utah*, pp. 617, 619. But see also Linn, *Story of the Mormons*, p. 543.

10. Maurine Whipple, *This Is the Place: Utah* (New York, Knopf, 1945), p. 187. Werner, *Brigham Young*, pp. 360–61. Neff, *History of Utah*, pp. 630, 632, 637. Linn, *Story of the Mormons*, pp. 544–45, 549. Hinckley, *Wells* (above, p. 269, n. 71), pp. 179 ff.

11. Wootton to Seward, Sept. 5, 1861; Cumming to Seward, April 11, 1862: Territorial Papers, NA. Linn, *Story of the Mormons*, p. 537.

12. Harding to Seward, Aug. 30, 1862, Feb. 3, 1863, Territorial Papers, NA.

13. Bancroft, *History of Utah*, pp. 609–11. Hinckley, *Wells*, p. 177. Neff, *History of Utah*, pp. 651–52.

14. Hinckley, *Wells*, p. 181. Neff, *History of Utah*, pp. 652–55. Irish to Dole, June 29, 1865, 39th Cong., 1st Sess., House Exec. Doc. 1, pp. 317–18.

15. Homer Cummings and Carl McFarland, *Federal Justice* (New York, Macmillan, 1937), p. 253.

16. For an outline of the antipolygamy crusade see ibid., p. 253; Werner, *Brigham Young*, p. 364 ff.; Linn, *Story of the Mormons*, pp. 568, 590 ff.; O'Dea, *The Mormons*, pp. 105 ff.; Young, *Isn't One Wife Enough?* passim.

17. *Cosmopolitan Magazine*, 50 (1911), 444–45. See also Frank J. Cannon and George L. Knapp, *Brigham Young and His Mormon Empire*, New York, Revell, 1913.

Index

The Bibliographical Essay and the notes have not been indexed.

Aikens Party, 129

Alexander, Edmund, 100, 102, 104 f., 107 ff., 119, 134, 140, 143 f., 149, 154, 156, 159, 206 f.

Alona, Miguel, 155

Anderson, Kirk, 211, 213

Arapeen, Indian chief, 45

Babbitt, Almon W., 3, 7, 22 ff., 29, 43, 53, 57, 200

Baker, Jim, 155

Baltimore *Sun*, 91

Bean, George W., 183

Bear Lake, 138, 143, 162

Bear River, 113 f., 140, 145, 197 f., 201

Bear River Valley, 160

Bedell, Edward A., 36

Bee, Barnard E., 150, 205

Benson, Ezra T., 129

Benton, Thomas Hart, 10

Bernhisel, John, 7, 9 f., 13, 16, 21 f., 29, 31 f., 42, 70, 84, 169, 227

Big Blue River, 101

Big Cottonwood Canyon, 119

Big Mountain, 133

Big Sandy River, 109, 144

Black, Jeremiah S., 54, 56 ff., 64, 66 f., 97, 190 f., 210, 220 f., 229

Black's Fork, 37, 116, 118, 145 f., 148 f., 157 f., 161, 165, 168, 174, 181, 192, 194, 198

Boggs, Lilburn, 1 f., 4, 92

Book of Mormon, 33–34

Brandebury, Lemuel G., 21 f., 25 ff., 37

Bridger, Jim, 5, 35, 37, 43, 77, 112, 148, 154, 159. *See also* Fort Bridger

Brigham Young Express and Carrying Company, 52 f., 70, 131, 188

Brocchus, Perry, 13, 36 f., 39, 42, 46, 51, 56, 79, 81, 106 f., 165 f., 186, 209, 234; described, 23; Pioneers' Day speech, 24–26; one of the "Runaways," 27–29; complains to Washington, 31–32, 33

Brooks, Mrs. Juanita, 163

Brown, James S., 138, 163

Buchanan, James, 120, 123 f., 190, 195 f., 200, 220, 228, 230; orders expedition to Utah, 48, 51, 91; Administration, 51, 57, 67–69, 95, 158, 174, 227; Young expects friendship of, 61; justifies war, 62–69, 91; fumbles over getting expedition started, 95 ff.; careless in framing Utah policy, 119; Mormons claim that they forced abandonment of policy, 168; reluctant to change policy, 169–73; one reason for change, 174; appeals to Congress for funds, 174–75; Kane talks with, 177; confidence in Cumming, 192; Mormons thank, 199; poor choice of *1858* appointees, 205; urged to remit McKenzie's sentence, 227; belief that his moderate policy was misguided, 229

Bullock, B. K., 215 ff.

Burns, John F., 157

Burr, David A., 164, 210, 213, 222

Burr, David H., 45 ff., 51 ff., 60, 64 ff., 68, 75, 77, 89, 94

Burton, Robert T., 137, 139, 141 f., 145, 201

Cajon Pass, 177

Calhoun, John C., 10

California, 5 f., 40, 164

Camp Crittenden, 230

Camp Floyd, 205 ff., 214 ff., 219, 222, 225, 230

Camp Scott, 149 f., 152, 154, 156, 159, 160–67, 170, 173, 175, 178, 180, 182, 189 ff., 197, 207, 230

Camp Winfield, 111, 113 f.

Carrington, Albert, 23

Carson Valley, Utah (now Nevada), 19, 35, 67, 85, 123, 130, 135, 219, 232

Carthage, Illinois, 3, 6, 140, 213, 218

Cartter, David, 30–31, 84

Cass, Lewis, 8, 10, 63 f., 67 f., 80, 96 ff., 186, 192, 209, 214, 218, 220, 223, 228 f.

Cedar Fort, 226

Cedar Valley, 202 f., 205 f.

Chase, Salmon P., 10

Civil War, 7, 71 f., 157, 230

Clawson, Hiram B., 131

Clawson, Rudger, 233

Clarke, H. F., 150

Clay, Henry, 10

Clemens, Gilbert, 186

Cobb, Howell, 10

Cochetopa Pass, 155

Colfax, Schuyler, 84

Colorado River, 155

Congress, asks for justification of war, 62–63

Congressional Globe, pro-Mormon letter in, 10

Connor, Patrick E., 231

Conover, Peter, 130, 134

Cooke, Philip St. George, 101, 112, 116 ff., 149, 151, 156, 158, 201, 206 f., 230

Corwin, Thomas, 10

Cosmopolitan Magazine, anti-Mormon article in, 234

Cottonwood Canyon, 60

Council Bluffs, Iowa, anti-Mormon memorial from, 9

Council of the Twelve Apostles, 6, 16

Cradlebaugh, John, 77, 97, 164 f., 208 ff., 213 f., 216 ff., 223, 228, 232

Craig, C. L., 47, 77, 189

Crooked River, Battle of, 1

Cumming, Alfred, 122, 180, 194 f., 197, 203, 209, 214, 226 ff.; Hurt complains to, 50; on Stiles' paper-burning, 58; Cass' instructions to, 67, 97–98, 171; appointed governor of Utah, 96; Cooke escorts to Utah, 117; described, 164–65; berates Young, 165–66; idle all winter, 166; received well by Saints, 173; initial hostility toward Mormons, 175 f.; Kane meets, 178 f.; decides to visit Utah in March, 182; goes to Salt Lake City, 184–92; acquires fondness for Mormon leaders, 189; returns to Camp Scott, 191; relations with Johnston soured, 198–99; criticized for not going to Salt Lake City in autumn, 204; Mormons flatter, 207–8; quarrels with Johnston over use of troops, 217–18, 220, 222–23, 224; blames army for new troubles, 223; leaves for Georgia, 231–32

Cumming, Mrs. Alfred, 117, 151, 164, 194 f.

Cummings, Colonel, 141

Dallas, George M., 8

Dame, William H., 124, 183

Danites, 2, 12, 39, 46, 53, 56, 69, 78, 88, 209, 211, 213

Davis, Jefferson, 174

Dawson, John W., 232

Day, Henry R., 25, 30 f., 34 f., 65 f.

Democratic party, 72, 166

Denver, James W., 48, 88, 162

Deseret, State of, 6, 10, 35, 85

Deseret Currency Association, 86, 131 f.

Deseret News, 24, 72, 81, 92, 131, 159, 184, 199, 211, 214, 225

Devil's Gate, 117

Diaz, Porfirio, 88

Dickerson, J. H., 148

Donner Party, 5

Dotson, Peter K., 88, 117, 160, 164, 210, 216, 218 f., 221 f., 226

Douglas, Stephen A., 10, 12, 75, 88, 192

Drake, Thomas J., 232

Drummond, W. W., 13, 48, 52, 60, 70, 75, 123, 166 f., 186, 205, 209, 234; influential in bringing on war, 18; appointed federal judge to Utah, 38; described by Mormons, 54–55, 77, 214; Mormons outraged by behavior, 55–56; his celebrated summary of Mormon wrongdoing, 56–57, 58, 60, 64, 69, 169; writes vitriolic letters to the press, 59; uses influence in Washington, 66;

claims Mormons dissatisfied with
Young, 68; careless with facts in charges
against Mormons, 79, 228

Eads, William, 166
Echo Canyon, 113, 124, 133, 138, 139–40,
141 f., 146 f., 151, 184, 187, 192, 198, 201
Eckels, Delana R., 97, 157, 160, 163 ff.,
175, 234; living quarters at Camp Scott,
164; anti-Mormon attitude in letters
to Cass, 191, 208–9, 228 f; sleeps on
ground on arrival in Salt Lake City,
195; Mormons try to discredit, 209; a
leader of the Ultra party, 210; unsuccessful attempt to indict Mormon
criminals, 226; return to East, 232
Eckelsville, 150, 163 f
Edmunds Act (1882), 233
Edmunds-Tucker Act (1887), 233
Evans, David, 183
Evans, Henry, 157
Exodus. See "Move South"

Fancher Party, 40
Far West, Missouri, 2, 120
Ferguson, James, 58, 125, 131, 134 f., 137,
141, 209, 213
Ferris, Benjamin G., 39, 45, 53, 79
Ferris, Mrs. Benjamin G., 39–40, 82
Ficklin, B. F., 110, 159 f.
Fifth Infantry, 99, 101, 107, 109, 111, 113,
122, 150, 217
Fillmore, Millard, 10 f., 21 f., 27, 29 ff.,
37–38, 61, 90, 176
Fillmore, Utah, 32, 41, 46, 184
First Cavalry, 171
Florida, 73, 99
Floyd, John B., 67, 70 ff., 95, 98, 123, 156,
169 f., 172, 193, 197, 201, 209, 220, 225,
229 f.
Foote, H. S., 10
Forney, Jacob, 58, 97, 117, 159, 161, 163 f.,
175 f., 190 f., 194, 210 f., 227
Forts: Bridger, 5, 27, 37, 43, 50, 62, 67,
72, 85, 105, 107, 109, 115, 117, 125,
139, 141 f., 145 ff., 149, 154, 205, see
also Bridger, Jim; Columbus, 172;
Douglas, 231; Hall, 144; Kearney, 102,
104, 106, 112, 117; Laramie, 35, 101 f.,
104, 112, 117, 120, 152 f., 158; Leavenworth, 63, 66, 96, 99 ff., 104 ff., 111 f.,

114, 116, 119, 121, 125, 149, 151, 153,
168, 172, 194; Massachusetts, 155; Supply, 37, 105, 125, 141 f.; Union, 154 ff.
Fourth Artillery, 99
Free Soil party, 7, 174

Gaines Mill, Battle of (Civil War), 157
Gerrish (Salt Lake merchant), 180
Gettysburg, Battle of, 7
Gibson, Deloss, 214
Giddings, Joshua, 31
Gladdenites, 19, 76
Gove, Capt. Jesse, 100, 102, 104 f., 107,
115 f., 121, 140, 149, 151 f., 158, 164,
179, 182, 226 f.
Gove, Maria (Mrs. Jesse), 230
Grant, Jedediah M., 17, 30, 43, 79, 81,
92 ff., 128
Great Salt Lake, 4 f., 8
Greeley, Horace, 8, 32, 206
Green River, 35 ff., 40, 105, 107, 109 f.,
144, 154 f., 159
Greenwood, A. B., 229
Gunnison, John W., 21, 32, 40 f., 44, 46,
53, 57, 60, 87, 200
Gunnison River, 155

Hamblin, Jacob, 163
Hamlin, Hannibal, 30
Ham's Fork (Green River), 107, 109, 111,
113, 115 f., 119, 140, 142 f., 145, 159
Hancock, Charles B., 49
Hanks, Ephraim, 208
Harding, Stephen S., 232
Harney, William S., 63, 67, 95, 98 ff.,
104 ff., 112, 121, 133, 141, 172 ff.
Harrington, Leonard, 16
Harris, Broughton D., 22, 24, 26 ff., 31,
35, 37, 39
Harris, Mrs. Broughton D., 22 ff., 39
Hartnett, John, 77, 117, 164, 211
Haun, Jacob, 1
Haun's mill, Massacre of, 1
Hendricks, Thomas A., 64 f.
Henry's Fork, 150
Heth, Henry, 215 ff., 219
Heywood, Joseph L., 43, 53
Hickman, William, 3, 52, 129
"History of Brigham Young" (Church
manuscript), 161, 178
Hockaday, J. M., 164

Hoffman, William, 152 ff., 158, 172, 192, 198

Holeman, Jacob, 30 f., 34 ff., 41, 45, 47, 51, 65 f., 87

Hollman, Joseph, 43

Hooper, William H., 53, 161

Hurlbut, Philastus, 80

Hurt, Garland, 38, 52 ff., 56, 58 f., 66, 68, 70, 94, 164, 189, 210, 222, 225, 234; Indian agent, 42; advises removal of Babbitt, 43; charges Mormons stirred up Indians, 45–46, 50–51, 65, 87; well-liked by Indians, 47; competence, 47; progress with Indians, 48; forced to flee Utah, 48–50; composes list of Mormon offenses, 50; declares Mormons thrive on persecution, 51, 208; believed Mormons tried to kill him, 77; in Camp Scott, 160–61; Mormons fear his influence with Utes, 161; writes Cumming that Mormons hate U.S., 176; Cumming believes Indians incited by, 186

Hyde, John, 80, 84

Hyde, Orson, 19, 32, 37, 130, 137, 226

Illinois, Mormon troubles in, 3 f., 9, 11, 15, 24, 76, 120, 127, 136, 183

Indians, 45, 87 f., 159–63, 185, 221, 231; Mormon relations with, 28, 33–37, 41–42, 45, 47–51, 65–66, 87–89, 161–63, 170, 233; massacre of Gunnison, 41, of Babbitt, 53; Arapahoes, 162; Bannocks, 160; Blackfeet, 148; Brulé Sioux, 104; Cheyennes, 163; Nez Percé, 160; Omahas, 8; Seminoles, 99; Shoshones, 162; Sioux, 163; Snakes, 37, 160; Utes, 161; Weber Utes, 160. See also Forney, Holeman, Hurt, Mountain Meadows Massacre, Parrish-Potter murders, Salmon River Massacre

Ingalls, Rufus, 42

Ingersoll, Robert, 54

Iowa, 5, 136

Jefferson Barracks, 99, 172

Johnson, Aaron, 48 f., 132 f., 134, 138, 218

Johnson, Benjamin F., 16

Johnston, Albert Sidney, 117, 171 ff., 177, 185, 209, 220 ff., 231; dedicated opponent of Mormons, 98, 115, 215; appointed to command army, 101; journeys across Plains to join army, 112–13; establishes contact, 114; to die in Civil War, 116; orders Alexander to return, 143; orders march to Fort Bridger, 145; Mormons excited over advance of, 146; in winter quarters, 149, 151, 153–54, 156, 158, 160 f.; resolves to continue to Salt Lake City, 175; meets Kane, 179; communicates with Kane only by letter, 181; hostile to Cumming, 191 ff., 199, 207, 217, 222; Young compliments, 197; peace message to Mormons from, 197 f.; censured for moving forces too early, 200; arrives in Salt Lake City, 201; marches to Cedar Valley, 202–3; tries to prevent damage to Mormon property, 211–12; assists Cradlebaugh, 214–17; leaves Camp Scott, 230

Jordan River, 202

"Journal History" (of the Church), 165, 195

Kane, Elisha Kent, 7

Kane, John K., 7

Kane, Thomas Leiper, 7, 8–9, 11, 30, 53, 61, 96, 158, 169 ff., 173 f., 176 ff., 185, 190, 193, 210

Kansas, 73, 88

Kansas Weekly Herald, 166

Kerr, John, 84

Kimball, Heber Chase, 6, 14 ff., 23, 32, 43, 81, 92, 122, 126 ff., 133, 137, 149, 184, 186, 196, 213, 234

Kimball, Hiram, 51 f., 64

Kinney, Colonel, 183

Kinney, John F., 41 ff., 54 ff., 66, 77, 232

Kirtland, Ohio, 2

Kirtland Safety Society Bank, 2

Know Nothing party, 77

Landon, C. G., 46 f.

Laramie, Wyoming, 192

Lawrence, Kansas, 101

Lea, Luke, 36

Leavenworth City, 122

Lee, John D., 3

Lehi, Utah, 200

Limhi, Mormon colony at, 35, 160

Lincoln, Abraham, 75, 232

Little, Jesse A., 8
Little Blue River, 101
Livingstone and Kincead Company, 131, 135, 150
Loring, W. W., 156, 205
Louisiana Courier, 78
Lynde, Isaac, 152 f.
Lyon, Caleb, 84

Magraw, W. M. F., 51 f., 63 f., 79, 112, 159
Majors, Alexander, 144
Manypenny, George, 36
Marcy, Randolph B., 112, 114, 121, 144, 154 ff., 158, 198, 202, 207
Marcy, William, 8
Margetson, Frederick, 80
MacAllister, John, 92, 141 f., 188
McClelland, Robert, 41, 157
McCulloch, Ben, 96, 171, 193 ff., 197 f., 200 f., 211
McKenzie, David, 131, 226 f.
McLean, Hector, 89 f.
McLean, Mrs. Hector, 89 f.
McLean, Mrs. John, 10
McNeil, F. E., 129, 212
Mexican War, 5, 7, 100, 164, 193
Mexico, 9, 13, 70 f., 88, 148, 204, 233
Millennial Star, 54 f.
Millson, John, 84
Mississippi River, 8, 136; Mormons cross (*1846*), 4
Missouri, Mormon troubles in, 1, 4, 9, 11, 15, 24, 34, 76, 88, 120, 127, 164, 183, 196, 215, 222
Missouri Republican, 32, 120, 211
Missouri River, 100, 159
Mix, Charles E., 65 f., 161
Mogo, Charles, 46 f.
Mormon (periodical), 129
Mormon Battalion, 5, 24, 127, 131, 200 f.
Mormon War (*1857-58*)
    CAUSES, 62–94; condemnatory dispatches and verbal reports from federal officers, 63–67; decision to send army, 67; charges of Administration bungling, 68–70; role of partisan controversy, 70–71; Floyd's role, 71–72; charges of fraud, 73–74; as diversion from slavery issue, 74–75; Administration conviction of Mormon rebelliousness, 76–76; mistreatment of federal

officers, 76–77; part played by public opinion, 77–91; polygamy as factor, 81–84; conspiracy charge, 84–87; dealings with Indians, 87–88; Danites and Mountain Meadows, 88–89; Parrish murder, 89; Pratt affair, 89–90; hostility of Mormons as factor, 91–94; religious revival, 92–94.

    THE FEDERAL TROOPS, 95–167; delay in starting, 95–101; composition of troops, 99–101; departure of army, 101; morale, 102, 104–5, 156–57; Fort Kearney, 102; route of march, 103; Van Vliet's report, 105–7; Young-Alexander correspondence, 107–9; exposed position, 109; supplies destroyed, 109–10, 116, 144; Russell, Majors, and Waddell charge negligence, 110–11; Camp Winfield, 111; Johnston takes command, 112; Alexander advances up Ham's Fork, 113; winter strikes, 114, 117–18; Johnston orders return to Camp Winfield, 114; winter at Fort Bridger, 116, Cooke's march, 116–18; types of soldiers, 120–21; hostile attitude of officers, 121; winter quarters, 148–67; clothing, 150; food, 150–54; mounts, 154–55; Marcy's expedition to Fort Union, 154–56; conduct and misconduct of soldiers, 156–57; Johnston's vigilance, 158–59; Indian relations, 159–63; civilian officials in camp, 163–67.

    THE MORMONS, 119–47; destroy supplies, 109–10, 116, 144; mobilization, 119, 136, 146–47; fear of soldiers, 120–21, of drivers and wagon masters, 121–22; of new federal officers, 122; strategy, 123–29, 168; morale, 125; propaganda, 126–29; martial law, 129; recall of missionaries and colonists, 129–30; finance, 130–32; food, clothing, and arms, 132–35; organization of army, 136–37; deployment, 137–38; raiders, 138–39; Echo Canyon fortified, 139–41, 146; policy of avoiding direct contact, 141–42; mounted patrols, 142, 144–45; Taylor's capture, 142–43.

    END OF HOSTILITIES, 168–203; Mormon version of reasons for peace, 168–69; actual reasons, 169–74; bellicose attitude of soldiers, 175–76; Kane's mis-

Mormon War (continued)
    sion to Johnston, 176–82; the Mormons'
    "Move South," 182–84, 188, 202–5;
    Cumming goes to Salt Lake City, 184–
    90; anti-Mormons in Camp Scott, 190,
    191–92; Cumming tries for peace, 191–
    92; War Department peace commission,
    192–201; official end of the war, 196–
    97; the Mormons' attitude, 198–99; the
    army in Salt Lake City, 201–2; estab-
    lishment of Camp Floyd, 205; life in
    camp, 205–6; morale, 206. See also
    Mormons.
Mormons: at Far West, Mo., 1 f.; Haun's
    mill massacre, Mo., 1; Danites, 2; at
    Kirtland, Ohio, 2; at Nauvoo, Ill.,
    2–3; leaders murdered at Carthage,
    Ill., 3; removal to Utah, 5; the Mor-
    mon Battalion, 5; leaders, and hier-
    archical organization, 6; State of
    Deseret, 6; lobbyists, 7–9, 10, 30; Ter-
    ritory of Utah, 9 f.; attacked in Con-
    gress, 9–10; first federal officers, 11;
    causes of early difficulties with federal
    government, 11–12, 13–14, 18; reasons
    for public disapproval, 12, 14–15, 19,
    59–61, 77–91 (see also Polygamy); theo-
    cratic government, 15–16; the courts,
    17–18; Brigham Young's influence, 18–
    20; early troubles in 1850's, 21 ff.; first
    federal appointees, 21–23; disagree-
    ments between them and Mormons,
    23 ff.; Brocchus' Pioneers' Day speech,
    24–26; pressure on Harris, 26–27; the
    "Runaways," 27–29; controversy of
    Runaways decided in favor of Mor-
    mons, 32; theology and dogma, 33–34;
    the Indian question, 33–37 (see also
    Indians); trouble with Bridger, 37, 148–
    49; period of calm (1852–55), 37–40;
    Steptoe and Gunnison, 40–44; Mormon
    dislike of federal troops, 44; difficulties
    with Burr, 45–47, with Hurt, 48–51;
    the mail contract, 51–53; more trouble
    with federal officers, 53–59; and Drum-
    mond, 54–57; and Stiles, 57–59; causes
    of war, 62–94 (see also Mormon War);
    policy of blackening opponents' char-
    acter, 76–77; newspaper condemnation,
    90–91; motivation for unruly conduct,
    91–92; religious revival (1856), 92–94;

choice of new governor, 96–97; the new
    federal officers, and their orders, 97–
    99; the Mormons woo Cumming, 207–8;
    the new federal officers, 208–10; the
    Ultra party, 210–11; the Valley Tan,
    211; federal judges vs. Mormons,
    212–21; troops in Provo, 216–19;
    alarums and excursions, 221–27; attack
    upon Spencer, 224; Pike murdered,
    225; wind of opinion in Washington,
    228–29; garrison troops reduced, then
    increased, 230; Mormon relations to
    1896, 230–34; public antipathy in 1911,
    234. See also Danites, Indians, Mormon
    War, Polygamy, Young
Morrell, H. F., 164, 189, 210
Morrill Act (1862), 233
Morris, Joseph, 139
Morrisites, 139
Mountain Meadows Massacre, 40, 50, 88,
    94, 138, 140, 163, 209 f., 215, 219, 221,
    226, 228 f.
"Move South," 126, 132, 182–84, 187–89,
    202–3, 222
Muddy Creek (present-day Wyoming),
    201
Munroe, James, 29

Nauvoo, Illinois, 2 f., 8 f., 32, 44, 52, 57,
    85, 91, 120, 126, 136, 184, 196, 215
Nauvoo Expositor, 3 f., 57, 80
Nauvoo Legion, 3, 123, 132, 136 ff., 146 f.
Nelson, James, 133
Nephi, Utah, 226
New York City, 83
New York Herald, 28, 63, 80
New York Times, 39, 78, 86 f., 90 f., 120 f.,
    204
New York Tribune, 32, 152, 161
Newport Barracks, 172

Ogden, Utah, 203
Ohio, Mormon troubles in, 4
O'Neill, John C., 97
Oquirrh Mountains, 202 f.
Organic Act, of Utah, 119
Osborne, Dr. (pseudonym of Thomas L.
    Kane), 177–78
Overland Trail, 35

Pace, William, 16, 132 f., 138, 163
Palmyra, New York, Smith's golden
    plates found near, 33

Panic of *1857*, 174
Parowan, Utah, 183 f.
Parrish, William, 88 f.
Parrish, Mrs. William, 215
Parrish-Potter murders, 76, 88–89, 214 ff., 218 f., 226
Paul, Gabriel R., 216 f., 219
Peteetneet, Indian chief, 48 f.
Phelps, John W., 99 ff., 105, 107, 109, 111 f., 115, 120 f., 202, 206
Pierce, Franklin, 38, 42 ff., 56, 64
Pierrepont, Edward, 233
Pike, Ralph, 217, 224 f., 228
Pike's Peak, 156
Pioneers' Day, 91, 119; in *1851*, 24; in *1857*, 60
Platte River, 5, 101 f., 104
Poland Act (*1874*), 18
Polk Administration, 5
Polygamy, Gentile attitude toward, 3, 9, 12, 39–40, 68, 81–84, 90, 228, 233–34
Porter, Fitz-John, 156 f., 162, 202, 225
Potter (murdered with Parrish), 89
Powell, Lazarus W., 171, 193 ff., 197 ff., 211
Pratt, Orson, 19, 81, 129
Pratt, Parley Parker, 89 f., 135, 137, 213, 225
The Prophets: or, Mormonism Unveiled, 83
Provo, Utah, 182 ff., 187 f., 196, 198, 200, 202, 205, 207 f., 214 ff., 224, 226, 228

Quorum. *See* Council of the Twelve Apostles

Reed, Lazarus, 38 f.
Reno, Jesse, 99, 107, 109, 111 f.
Rich, Charles C., 137
Richards, Franklin D., 93, 140, 142
Richards, S. W., 123
Richards, Willard, 6, 28, 32, 42, 176, 213
Richardson, William A., 31
Rigdon, Sidney, 4
Rockwell, Porter, 3, 48, 52, 116, 141 f., 144, 184
Rose, Stephen B., 34
"Runaways" (Brocchus, Harris, and Brandebury), 27–29, 31–32, 33, 38, 40, 44, 70
Rupe, James, 166
Rush Valley, Utah, 44, 159, 223 f.

Rusk, Thomas J., 10
Russell, Majors, and Waddell, 73 f., 109 f., 116, 121, 134, 149 f., 167, 172
Russell, William, 74

Salmon River, 35
Salmon River Lamanite Mission. *See* Limhi
Salmon River Massacre, 161
Salt Lake Basin, 7, 13, 35, 62, 72, 80, 85, 91, 183 f., 191, 211
Salt Lake City, 8, 19, 35 f., 40, 49, 60, 62 f., 69, 77, 80, 83, 89 f., 105 f., 113, 115, 117, 138, 140, 142, 147, 170, 175, 177, 181, 184 f., 191, 201 f., 204, 217, 222
Salt Lake Valley, 5 f., 10 f., 21, 34, 37, 109, 123, 131, 135, 168, 172, 177 f., 187, 201 f., 222
San Bernardino Valley, California, 19, 35, 68, 85, 130, 134, 137
San Joaquin *Republican*, 83
Scott, Winfield, 73, 95, 115, 118, 149, 156, 172
Second Artillery, 172
Second Dragoons, 99, 100–1, 112, 116, 172
Seventh Infantry, 171, 216
Sevier River, 41
Seward, William, 10, 232
Shaver, Leonidas, 38 f., 53, 57
Sheen, Isaac, 80
Sibley, Henry H., 163, 206
Simonds, Ben, 160, 162
Simpson, Lewis, 144, 166
Sinclair, Charles E., 58, 77, 97, 164, 209 f., 212 ff., 218, 220, 232
Sixth Infantry, 102, 171
Skull Valley, 223
Smith, 21
Smith, 84
Smith, Charles F., 111 ff., 121, 216, 230
Smith, Elias, 214
Smith, George A., 137 f., 141, 149, 165, 184 f., 188, 196, 213, 218
Smith, Hyrum, 3, 92
Smith, Jedediah, 149
Smith, Joseph, 1 ff., 9, 12, 14, 57, 78, 80 f., 92, 126, 136, 159
Smith, Lot, 109 f., 125, 137, 141, 143 f., 150, 154, 159, 167, 169
Smith, Persifor F., 120, 172
Smith, Sardius, 1

Smith, Truman, 10
Smith, W. D., 111 f.
Smith, William, 9, 12, 80
Smoot, A. O., 207
Snow, Warren, 134, 145
Snow, Zerubbabel, 22, 38
Sonora, Mexico, 70
Sons of Dan. See Danites
South Pass (of the Continental Divide),
    5, 50, 97, 101, 105, 112, 139
Spanish Fork, 48 ff., 222
Spencer, Daniel, 223 f.
Spencer, Howard, 217, 224 f.
Springville, Utah, 216, 218
Stansbury, Howard, 21
State of Deseret. See Deseret, State of
Stephens, Alexander, 31
Steptoe, Edward Jenner, 40 ff., 66, 92
Stiles, George P., 3, 43, 57, 59 f., 66, 75,
    77, 88, 90, 94, 137, 167, 186, 209, 213,
    227
Stout, Hosea, 3, 16
Stowell, William, 143, 166 f.
Sweetwater River, 112

Taos, New Mexico, 154 f.
Taylor, John, 106, 137, 141, 213, 232 f.
Taylor, John, 142 f., 166 f.
Taylor, Robert, 75
Taylor, Zachary, 10, 24, 28
Tenth Infantry, 99, 101 f., 104, 107, 109,
    111, 113, 121, 150, 215
Texas Revolution, 193
Thompson, Jacob, 64 ff., 74, 157, 162
Tintic Valley, Utah, 223
Tooele Valley, Utah, 159
Tracy, Albert, 151, 164, 206, 222
Trollope, Frances, 12
Troskolawsski, Joseph, 46, 54
Twiss, Thomas S., 52, 66, 162

Uinta Mountains, Utah, 154, 161, 181
Uinta Valley, 161, 186
Ultra party, 210-11, 227
Underwood, Warner, 9
Utah, Territory of, 10, 14, 34 f., 62 f., 234

Valley Tan, 211, 213
Van Vliet, Stewart, 69, 105 ff., 110, 113,
    129, 141

Vasquez, Louis, 37
Vaughn, John R., 29

Waite, Carlos A., 109 ff.
Waite, Charles B., 232
Walbridge, Hiram, 84
Walker, Charles, 199
Walker, Robert J., 101, 116
Warsaw, Illinois, 3
Wasatch Mountains, 116, 184, 203
Washakie, Indian chief, 162
Washington Union, 67 f., 75
Webster, Daniel, 10, 32 f.
Wells, Daniel H., 4, 24, 37, 48, 82, 114,
    123, 126, 131 ff., 137 ff., 141, 143 ff.,
    148, 167, 184, 186, 196, 212 f., 217, 222,
    234
Wentworth, John, 9
Western Standard, 129
Whipple, Edson, 16
Whittlesey, Elisha, 31
Williams, Bill, 149
Williams, Thomas S., 58, 213
Wilmot, David, 10
Wilson, Alexander, 209 f., 213, 221, 225
Wilson, John, 21
Wilson, William W., 46 f.
Wild River Mountains, 112-13, 114
Wood, Fernando, 83
Woodruff, Wilford, 82, 127, 137, 195,
    213, 234

Y. X. Carrying Company. See Brigham
    Young Express and Carrying Company
Young, Brigham, 13, 32, 37, 42, 45 f., 50,
    53, 63, 65, 68, 75, 78 f., 81 f., 84 ff., 94,
    96, 106 ff., 113, 115, 178 f., 185 f., 198,
    227, 229, 231 f., 234; escaped dragnet
    in Missouri, 2; capable leader, 5; Gov-
    ernor of Utah, 6; Babbitt in disfavor
    with, 7; Fillmore liked, 11; urges
    obedience, 16; authority of, 18; in-
    fluence, 18; described, 19-20; early
    charity toward Gentiles, 21; welcomes
    Harris, 22; baited by Mrs. Harris, 23;
    conducts census, 24; believes Zachary
    Taylor in hell, 24; answers Brocchus'
    Pioneers' Day speech, 25-26; epistles
    to Brocchus, 26; tries to coerce Harris,
    26-27; advises Government on choice
    of federal officers, 28; Runaways'

charges against, 28–29; confidence in
God, 30; Treasury refuses to honor
drafts of, 31; superintendent of Indian affairs, 34; praises Holeman, 35;
Holeman critical of, 36; Hurt an opponent of, 38; considers Ferris cooperative, 39; gubernatorial reappoint-
ment asked, 43; retains governorship,
44; charged with extorting false testimony from Burr, 47; agrees with Hurt
on Indian question, 48; denies intention to harm Hurt, 48–49; creates
mail-carrying company, 52–53; accused
of despotism, 56; refuses to aid Stiles,
58; hopes for Buchanan's friendship,
60–61; expert handling of Van Vliet,
106; views army as mob, 119–20; sermons reveal secessionist spirit, 128;

orders Wells to rest, 145; Bridger
charges robbery by, 148; writes Washington on Indian trouble, 159; charged
with inciting Indians, 162, 170;
charged with plotting separation from
U.S., 169–70; asks Kane to seek statehood, 177; offers Johnston supplies,
180; lauded by Mormons for leadership, 182; expresses intention to leave
Utah, 187; woos Cumming, 189, 207;
refuses to behave like defeated leader,
195; announces termination of hostilities, 196–97; signs memorandum on
peace meetings, 201; haled into court,
212–13; talks of second flight, 218; ad-
mits Mormons must remain in Valley. *See also* Mormon War, Mormons

Young, Kimball, 82